Song of Praise for a Flower

One Woman's Journey through China's Tumultuous Twentieth Century

By Fengxian Chu / 朱鳳仙

With Charlene Chu

Chu, Fengxian
Song of Praise for a Flower

For My Beloved Husband and Children

Table of Contents

Foreword

I moved to Beijing from the United States in 2006 for the purpose of writing a book, but not this one. I had gone to China to learn more about my father and his family for a book about my parents. During my research, I auspiciously discovered this memoir written by my cousin Fengxian (Fŭng-syěn). The manuscript was so exceptional and moving that I decided to place my original project on hold and focus on giving a voice to Fengxian's story.

That my cousin and I were able to meet at all is remarkable. I arrived in China with no names or addresses of any living relatives. The only piece of information I possessed was an inchoate instruction from my father a decade earlier about how to locate the farm that he grew up on: "Go to Fengmen (Fŭng-mŭn) Railway Station in Huaguo (Hwŏ-gwŏ) village, Hunan, and ask for the Chu residence."

My father was born in the early 1900s during the Qing (Chĭng) dynasty, when China's population was a third of what it is today. Knowing how China's population has grown, how scores of formerly small villages have mushroomed into large cities, and how clusters of communities containing hundreds of people with the same surname are common, I thought it would be impossible to just show up at a train station, inquire about an old house, and find it. So I bought several detailed maps and pored over them. I eventually located a town named Huaguo and a train station called Fengmen. With those starting points, I flew to Hunan, hired a driver named Mr. Kong (Kōng), and told him about my search. Kong was eager to help.

The two of us set out on a quest that spanned several days over multiple visits. During this time, we traversed a large part of the province in his old, maroon sedan. We encountered rivers with no bridges to cross them, bridges with locked steel gates and no attendant, and dozens of miles of rocky, unpaved dirt paths. In many places the roads were unmarked, and it wasn't uncommon to find ourselves completely lost in the middle of nowhere.

During our search, we met several Chu families, some of whom had members who had immigrated to the U.S. However, none of their names matched my list of family members. We were directed to other villages called Huaguo and other villages with a large number of families surnamed Chu. At one point, we were informed about a Huaguo village in eastern Hunan that sounded promising. When we arrived at the local Communist Party headquarters — which is where Kong insisted that each new search start to avoid trouble with the authorities — we were informed that Huaguo was the village's new name, and that nearly every village in Hunan had been relabeled after the Communist Party took control of the country in 1949.

"You are searching for a place that hasn't existed for decades. I doubt you're ever going to find it," the official told us.

Our spirits sank. On the way back to the hotel that evening, Kong's car broke down on a dirt road in a remote area. We waited for hours in the pitch dark for roadside assistance. Fortunately, the mechanics were willing to work overnight to have the car in working condition for the next day.

Early the next morning, Kong and I met in the hotel lobby. By then, all of my ideas about how to locate the farm had been exhausted. Our last option was to try what my father had instructed me to do from the outset. I told him that the plan for that day was to go to Fengmen Station and ask for the Chu residence.

We identified a town where we thought the train station was located and headed straight to the Communist Party headquarters. Both of us were hopeful that it would lead to something promising, but the authorities there also knew nothing. When we asked if the previous name of the village had been Huaguo, no one in the office recognized that name.

"Ms. Chu, your father would be very proud of how hard you've tried to find his hometown," Kong said, trying to comfort me. "But we are looking for a place that only exists in history — not in reality. It's an impossible task."

"Let's try one last thing before you take me back to the airport," I said. "I saw some old people sitting outside a shop when we drove through this town. Let's go back and talk to them. We keep talking to people in their 40s and 50s when we should be talking to people in their 70s and 80s."

I approached the old couple and explained my predicament. I asked if the village had been called Huaguo many years ago.

"Yes, Huaguo!" the man said and chuckled. "I had completely forgotten about that!"

I handed him my list of family member names. He recognized one of them and gave us directions to where he thought the house was located.

The dirt path the man told us to take skirted a pond and became narrower and narrower the farther we got from town. Eventually, Kong was forced to stop driving. A thorny bush blocked his door, so he asked me to open mine to see how much room we had. The front passenger tire was teetering on the edge of a small cliff. If we drove any farther, the car would topple six feet into the pond.

We decided to return to town but, because the path was so narrow, we couldn't turn the car around. Instead, we treacherously inched our way back in reverse. In town, Kong found two boys with motorcycles who were willing to take each of us to the house for a fee. After a bumpy 15-minute ride through quaint, lush rice paddies, we arrived at a simple two-story concrete home on a small hill overlooking some paddies. A man in his mid-40s came out to greet us.

"Sorry to bother you, sir," I said. "I am searching for some long-lost relatives. My father grew up in Hunan and emigrated to the U.S. many years ago. Do you recognize this man?" I handed him a picture of my father from the 1920s.

We caught the man off-guard. He stared intently at the picture for about 20 seconds, raised his eyes, then pondered for a few more seconds.

"Chu Jusheng (Jü-shǔng)," he blurted out. "I think his name is Chu Jusheng. He emigrated to the U.S. and married an American woman. He has a daughter named Xialian (Syǒ-lē-ěn)."

I was stunned. I expected that if we ever found the right family, someone would recognize my father's name, but I never anticipated anyone to know my Chinese name. "I am Xialian," I replied, barely able to get the words out. Tears welled up in both our eyes. Even Kong became choked up.

"My name is Ping. Wait here!" he said excitedly. He returned a few minutes later with a letter my father had written to his family 25 years earlier. I couldn't believe it. I had found my father's farm. I should have followed his simple instructions from the start.

Ping rushed outside to notify other family members who were working in the fields, while Kong and I read my father's letter. Soon the house was packed, and I was bombarded with questions about my father and mother and life in America. The women quickly prepared a celebratory meal. As the guest of honor, I was given the best pickings on the table: a large bowl of pig fat.

"Pig fat!" I said and smiled, not wanting to be rude. "What a treat!"

I made as large a dent in the bowl as I could. The men joined me at the dining table, while the women sat along the edges of the room, eagerly listening to our conversation but remaining dutifully silent, despite our shared gender.

I visited the farm numerous times after that. On one trip, Ping gave me the address and phone number of my cousin Fengxian, who lived in Shenzhen, a large city located across the border from Hong Kong. As the oldest living member in our family, I was eager to meet her. No one on the farm was over 65, so they could tell me little about my father and his generation.

I arrived on Fengxian's doorstep excited and overflowing with questions. Our eyes filled with tears the moment we saw each other, and we embraced. At a petite four-foot, seven-inches tall, the top of Fengxian's head barely reached my chin. She had cropped salt-and-pepper hair and a wide, oval face with delicate, almond-sized eyes, a broad nose, and round, protruding cheekbones. I was struck most by her hands, which were identical to my father's, albeit smaller, with lines and curves in nearly all the same places.

We spoke about our family all afternoon. Fengxian was patient and open as I bombarded her with questions, but, because I didn't speak her dialect, she could convey only so much through conversation. During one visit over a year later, she offered to let me read this memoir to give me a more detailed picture of the early part of my father's life in China. She grew up in the same colorful household as he did.

For 16 years, the manuscript had been locked in a bank vault, waiting to be passed on to Fengxian's children. The pages were humbly bound together by thin cardboard and string in four volumes. Fengxian had written it by hand in a complex mix of traditional Chinese characters and her own shorthand, which made reading agonizingly slow. After the first 60 pages, I could see that it had tremendous potential. When I offered to help Fengxian publish it overseas, I expected her to balk and refuse. Still scarred by the past, she continued to shut the door and whisper whenever politically sensitive topics came up. But when I raised the idea, she smiled widely and said she always wanted to publish the book abroad but never knew how. That began a multi-year collaboration to bring this work to print.

The version here is an English rendering of the original authored by myself. In many places, few alterations were made, and it is a direct translation of the original. In other places, substantial changes were made, either to add historical context or to make the stories more complete and stylistically familiar to a foreign audience. Some chapters were revised to incorporate material my father told me about our forefathers, as well as his own experiences with the Communist Party's re-education process. Fengxian also added details in several places that she had left out of the initial version and inserted new chapters at the end to bring the work up to the present day. At the age of 92, Fengxian's memory is exceptional, but inaccuracies cannot be ruled out, particularly with regard to information on our ancestors, which is based on very patchy and at times conflicting oral history that is too old to be verified.

The most significant changes were the insertion of information on Chinese history and politics. This material was left out of the original because the book initially was intended for Fengxian's children and grandchildren, all of whom are familiar with Chinese history, and because she herself lacked a full understanding of historical events. For decades, Fengxian and her family lived with limited access to information about the goings on around them. Even today, the Communist Party's tight control over information about controversial moments during its rule means that she still has many unanswered questions about the past.

Given my broader access to information, my version of some events has differed from Fengxian's incomplete knowledge of what occurred and why. In these instances, we have chosen to go with my interpretation, which is based on a much broader and varied set of sources, even though this is a book about her life told through her voice and perspective. This is not ideal, but such are the difficulties of wading through the flaws, inaccuracies, and misinformation contained in much of modern Chinese history.

As Fengxian states in her closing dedication, life is a drama. Yet often performers are too close to the action to perceive the full picture. Sometimes it takes an outside eye — a spectator — to piece it all together. That has been my role in this project. In different ways, this book has represented for each of us an attempt at making sense of certain aspects of our lives. For Fengxian, my ability to shed light on the political and historical forces behind some episodes in her life has helped her begin to understand why certain seemingly senseless events occurred, while at the same time giving her story a long-desired voice. For me, working on the manuscript has provided a rich depiction of the environment in which my father grew up and details of a family I never knew. Imagine embarking on a quest for information about your father only to find someone who had already documented a portion of it for posterity. For this, I am indebted to Fengxian.

The last time our fathers saw each other was in 1949. If they were alive today, they would be astonished to know that Fengxian and I had met at all, let alone that we had collaborated so closely on such a large project, given our vast cultural and language differences and 46-year age disparity. I'm sure our fathers are smiling down on us, proud to see the relationship they were unable to maintain restored by us. Both of us are honored and eternally grateful to have been their daughters.

— Charlene Chu

Preface

The seed for *Song of Praise for a Flower* was first planted in the 1980s by my husband's relatives abroad, who urged me to document our family's stories as a legacy for future generations. One long, sleepless night in 1989, I was so restless and overcome with memories that I got out of bed, took out a pen and paper, and began to record my recollections.

The project soon evolved beyond a simple documentation of my experiences. As a mother, I had always felt guilty about how much my children had suffered growing up. The book served as an opportunity not only to teach my children about their roots but also to convey the complex forces at work that led to our family's circumstances. Chinese people believe that knowing one's family history is imperative because it is the starting point of one's life. Only by knowing what went before us, and the context in which our lives began, can we begin to understand our place in this world.

I completed the manuscript in 1992. After much deliberation, I decided against sharing it with my children, who at the time were wrapped up with their own young families. I didn't know how they would react to my revealing so many intimate details. Instead, I decided I would bequeath it to them as a final surprise gift upon my death. By then, they would be older and more open to and appreciative of the content. I bound the pages and locked them in a safe deposit box at my bank, content with the knowledge that one day my children and grand-children would discover and learn from them.

The manuscript sat there untouched for 16 years until Charlene, a young cousin from America who I never dreamed I would meet, showed up on my doorstep one day seeking information about her father and our family. Touched by how eager Charlene was to learn her family history, I dug out the pages for her. The book contains little information about her father, who was my Uncle Jusheng, but the setting of his and my childhood was identical. I knew the manuscript would give her a picture of her father's youth that she could get nowhere else.

During one visit, Charlene offered to help me publish the manuscript abroad. I had always secretly dreamed of publishing the book overseas but never thought such a lofty goal was possible for an elderly, inconsequential Chinese woman like me. Yet even at this late age, life is full of new possibilities.

The stories in this book, all of which are true, detail the long, arduous path of my life. I have encountered more dreadful than sweet moments. My fate has not been good. I am not from a famous or politically well-connected family. My stories are not elaborate or filled with intrigue. I am a simple woman who spent most of her life living and working on a farm, just as the majority of Chinese people have done for millennia.

This book is not intended to be critical, flattering, or political. My only aim is to teach my children, grandchildren, and future generations the importance of being upstanding, decent people; to not abandon good for the sake of gold; to cherish their relatives and friends; and, perhaps, to learn from my experiences and mistakes.

Stories form the basis of history, and we must maintain and respect history if we are to learn from it. Today when I look back on these stories, it is difficult for me to discern at what points I was right or wrong, whether I failed or was successful, or what my true character and disposition is. Yet this is the very nature of life, which unfolds itself in a rich multitude of colors and is rarely black and white.

For much of my existence, sorrow and grief have left me crying in silence. I am eternally indebted to Charlene, the publisher, and the readers for finally giving my stories a voice. I also want to thank the people in China who helped Charlene locate her relatives. Without you, we never would have been reunited, and these stories would remain locked in darkness.

Lastly, as an old woman, my memory is fading. Most of the stories here were written decades after they occurred. Please forgive me for any inaccuracies.

— Fengxian Chu

Song of Praise for a Flower

If you wonder where my home is, please read this story,
If you wonder what my name is, mine is that of a flower, Vermilion Impatiens,
whose colorful soul has accompanied me through many years.
O, elegant Impatiens, O, beautiful Impatiens,
You reside in me, and I in you, our souls are one.

Through careful nurturing, I have helped you grow verdant and blossom,
You endure even through battering rains and wind,
Hardship, misery, and drought have never defeated you,
Always you return to being fragrant, radiant, alive.

Yes, you have withered, and I have wept, both of us have borne many woes,
But at last spring always returns with nourishing rain and a tender breeze.
Soon the flower resumes its glow, the girl becomes more lovely,
They have both survived and been reborn in glory.

The flower takes pride in blossoming after a bitter winter,
The girl finds comfort in her resilience and strength,
Both will endure forever, for when the girl passes,
Her breath will transform into a soft breeze,
protecting the Vermilion Impatiens through eternity.

— Fengxian Chu

A Note on Names

In order to present manageable names for non-Chinese readers while preserving the meaning of Chinese names, we introduce the full names for all key characters and then shorten most to one syllable. This is not common practice in China and may come across as awkward to some Chinese readers.

Pronunciation guidance is provided only for names that non-Chinese readers tend to have difficulty pronouncing and that appear multiple times. The pronunciation symbols shown denote the sounds for spoken English, not Mandarin pinyin (e.g., mā denotes a long 'a' sound, not first tone Mandarin mā). Note that in China surnames are always presented first, and women's surnames do not change after marriage.

Due to ongoing sensitivities within China about some of the subject matter in these stories, as well as a desire to preserve the anonymity of living family members, most names of people and places have been changed. For individuals with more than one name, which was common among males from older generations, only one name is provided.

After much deliberation, Fengxian courageously chose to use her real name for the book.

PART ONE

Reminiscences of Huaguo

The Xiang River

For millennia, the mighty Xiang (Syŏng) River has pulsed through the lush, rolling hills of Hunan Province in southern China. The region's famous rice paddies derive their rich, green hue from the Xiang, and it is on the banks of this river that generations of Hunanese families have flourished. In Chinese, "Xiang (湘)" is the abbreviated name for Hunan, which I think makes perfect sense because, whenever we natives think of home, often the first thing that comes to mind is this beloved river. Several decades ago, when I was a young woman, I bade farewell to the Xiang and have had the opportunity to return only twice. Yet the river continues to run through my veins as vigorously today as it did when I was just a little girl.

Nestled amid the long and winding current of the Xiang River rests the small, graceful village of my youth: Huaguo, or Flower and Fruit, in eastern Hunan Province. Huaguo embraces miles of fertile land and luxuriant forest, crisscrossed with green willows and tall bamboo. Small homes dot the hillsides. Men cultivate the fields while women weave in the courtyards, each working diligently every day. Grey-haired seniors play with lively children, bringing abundant smiles and harmony to the village.

Huaguo is surrounded by numerous hills to the north, east, and south and the Xiang River to the west. Deep within the hills are ancient caves and dozens of narrow, winding paths leading to small valleys. In this openness lie numerous small brooks, gurgling and glistening in the sun, and grass and wild flowers that emit a beautiful, delicate fragrance. Huaguo is the kind of place the soul never forgets.

At the entrance of Huaguo stands Fengmen Railway Station. Although not large, the station used to serve as a key stop for trains passing through Hunan because of its proximity to the water. Day and night, trains stopped at Fengmen Station to add water to the steam engines, bringing business and swarms of passengers to the village.

The passenger cars, platform, and waiting hall would become over-run with villagers hawking food and other goods, their cries sonorous and rhythmic. Many of the hawkers were young and as agile as monkeys, leaping across the tracks and climbing into passenger cars. Sometimes these boys would remain on the train selling goods even after it took off, jumping down fearlessly only after the train reached full speed.

Not far from Fengmen Station was a narrow street that used to form the center of town and was filled with small restaurants, stores, tea houses, gambling parlors, and the local fortune teller. The street terminated at the Xiang River, where several small ferry boats sat waiting to transport passengers across the water to the town of Fengmen, another village bustling with activity.

When I was growing up as a young girl, one of the liveliest times of year was the annual Dragon Boat Festival, when teams from Huaguo and Fengmen would compete in a race on the Xiang River. The festival, held on the fifth day of the fifth month of the lunar calendar, commemorates the famous Chinese poet Qu Yuan, who, according to legend, drowned himself in a river for his motherland in 278 B.C. To distract the fish from eating the poet's corpse, the legend says that villagers threw rice and other food into the river. In honor of Qu Yuan's patriotism, Chinese people re-enact this event every year by tossing pyramid-shaped dumplings into water.

The day of the festival, villagers from Huaguo and Fengmen would don their best clothes and flock to the river to toss dumplings and watch the race. On both sides of the river, the streets and banks would be packed with a sea of horse carts and spectators. At the crack of a drum, a dozen colorfully decorated dragon boats would charge ahead, splashing spectators with water as they sped down the river to the beat of the drum. The cheers of the villagers would mingle with the roars of the drums and reverberate through the sky, awakening the God of Heaven and Dragon King of the Ocean. After the race, colorful pennants would be handed to each member of the triumphant team, and the audience would linger for hours, basking in the joy of the moment.

The province of Hunan is said to be a land flowing with milk and honey, with picturesque scenery and a soothing climate of four distinct seasons. In spring, plants sprout, flowers blossom, and birds sing in joy. In summer, trees become lush and verdant. In autumn, ripening fruits tug at tree limbs, and red and yellow leaves fall to the ground signaling the approach of winter, when leaves wither and die, and a thin layer of white blankets the land.

Women of Hunan are known for their gentleness, courtesy, and passion. They love the young and respect the old and are virtuous wives and mothers. Hunan's women are the shining pearl of the province. It is no wonder so many ancient emperors and leaders, including Chairman Mao, came from this magical environment.

Grandeur of the House of Chu

Generations ago, during the time of China's first Opium War against the British, a wealthy man from Fujian Province on the east coast of China traveled westward in search of a safe, comfortable place to relocate his family and business away from the fighting. The journey was long and brought him across numerous rivers. The man stopped when he reached the Xiang River near Huaguo, for he had stumbled upon a place more beautiful and abundant than anything he had ever dreamed of. It was a perfect place to start anew.

The man was surnamed Chu, which means "vermilion." He chose a spot on a hill underneath the shade of a large, ancient banyan tree to build his new home, which he called "Rongshuxiali," or Rongxia (Rōng-syǒ) for short, which means "under the banyan tree." The tree consisted of two large branches twisting up from the earth. Both branches were vibrant and sturdy and reached high into the sky. The trunk was thick and the foliage dense and green, like a large umbrella.

Nestled amid the branches resided a myriad of birds that flew in and out throughout the day, singing beautiful melodies. Under the tree was a small pond filled with tall, bright red lotus flowers. During the summer, children would flock to the pond to pick the flowers and collect lotus roots and water chestnuts. The tree provided coolness in the summer and warmth in the winter, and the soothing temperatures and caressing breezes could be so intoxicating that it was often difficult to depart its shelter.

Beneath the shade of the banyan tree and above acres of sprawling, lush rice paddies, the man constructed a house out of auburn-colored bricks, green roof tiles, and engraved wood beams. The windows were painted with intricate patterns of landscapes, flowers, birds, and men and women. The home resembled a crystal palace and was surrounded by large gardens, exquisite kiosks, a platform to view the moon, and pavilions for reciting poetry and playing the flute. The house was sheltered on two sides by small hills adorned with tea and tangerine trees, which provided protection from bitter winter winds.

The most unique trait of all was the bright red door separating the grounds from the outside world. A pair of stone lions and several fearsome stone dogs sat guard in front of the door. Adorning the upper right and left corners of the door were two lanterns, each inscribed with one character: "Chu House." The light of the lanterns illuminated four large Chinese characters written in gold above the door: "Harmony Brings about Fortune." Hanging vertically on the right and left doorposts were two writings that together formed a couplet: on the right, "Blossoming Flowers Hide Heavenly Treasure of Harmony," and on the left, "Fruitful Trees Retain Earthly Auspice of Happiness." Both carry deep meaning for Chinese people and indicate that the inhabitants of the house were educated, refined, and wealthy.

The Chu family attached great importance to education and believed that learning was the noblest human pursuit. As a result, many of their descendants were college graduates, some of whom traveled overseas to further their studies or engage in business. Out of the Chu house came officials, scholars, military generals, millionaires, and lawyers, though regrettably no martial arts masters. With so much talent, the house of Chu overflowed with glory and fortune.

To signal the family's noble status, the settler hung a large black board above the door inscribed with four dazzling but peculiar characters: "Home of Foreigners (洋人之家)." At the sight of the sign, people passing by would often stop to look inside, hoping to catch sight of a foreigner whom, they had been told, were tall and rotund, with blonde hair, a white face, green eyes, and a high, pointed nose. They always went away unhappy.

Generations later, one night a local villager, who also was educated, climbed atop the door. He crossed out the golden characters and scribbled in black: "False Home of Foreigners (假洋人家)." Then he flipped the board over and wrote: "The false can never be true. You are Chinese. Why do you label your house a home of foreigners?"

At dawn the next day, one of the servants was sweeping in front of the door when he sensed something amiss. He looked up and saw that the golden inscription had been replaced by black characters. He hurried to tell his master. The master quickly instructed his eldest son to investigate. The son rushed to the door and discovered the sentences written by the man. The son felt very angry but also ashamed because he realized that what the man had written was true. Theirs was not a home of foreigners but rather of people who did business with foreigners and whose wealth and comforts came from overseas. Why did our ancestors write this?

The son appealed to his father to change the characters. The old man explained that the board had been brought from Fujian by their ancestors. Because Fujian was located on the coast, its two largest cities were treaty ports, and dealings with foreigners were common there. It could be beneficial for business to signal that one's home was welcome to foreigners. Now that someone was objecting to it, the master agreed that the sign should be changed. Later a new sign was hung with the inscription: "Home of People Traveling Abroad (出洋之家)."

This tale was passed on to each generation that lived in the Chu house as a lesson and reminder of humility and of the famous Chinese saying: "Clever people often become victims of their own cleverness (聪明反被聪明误)."

Joy Turns into Mourning

It is said that the master of the house in the tale above was my great-grandfather Yu (Yü). It was one of Yu's forefathers, whose name we have lost, who re-located his family from Fujian to Hunan and built the house under the banyan tree. Yu inherited a very successful tea export business in Hankou (Hǒn-kō), Hubei Province, just north of Hunan. Most of the tea was distributed to large cities within China, while some was shipped as far away as Russia. The business was extremely lucrative and brought the family much wealth and honor.

Yu and his wife gave birth to three sons. The third son was named Hai (Hī), which means "sea." He later became my grandfather. When Hai was a teenager, he was commissioned by his father to help with the family business in Hankou, but before departing his parents insisted that he first be married. As a son, it was critical for Hai to propagate the family lineage so assets could be properly passed down to later generations.

Yu and his wife searched for a suitable partner. Back then, this meant at a minimum that the girl had to be from an equally respected and wealthy family and had to possess exquisite, dainty "golden lilies," which is what Chinese people called bound feet. The smaller the feet, the better. Anything exceeding four inches in length would have been considered unacceptable for a family with the status of the Chus. Yu and his wife settled on a young, beautiful, petite girl from a nearby village.

A lavish wedding was held at Rongxia before Hai departed for Hankou. The two youngsters had never met and were bashful when they were introduced to one another. Both were pleased with their parents' arrangement. They quickly fell in love.

Within a year, Hai's wife gave birth to a son. They named him Jing, which means mirror. He later became my father. Hai's wife was ecstatic and relieved at accomplishing early on what was considered the preeminent duty of every woman: producing a son to carry on her husband's ancestry. Hai's wife quickly gained the respect of everyone in the Chu family. She had proven she was a worthy choice. It was 1901 — the start of a new century — and Rongxia was overflowing with joy.

In the ensuing years, Hai traveled back and forth to Hankou, where he further expanded his father's thriving tea business. As the company grew, he spent longer and longer periods away from home. By the time his wife gave birth to a second son in 1904, Hai was living almost year-round in Hankou, a booming city where successful young men could have access to anything they wished and indulge any desire. Hai's weakness was women, and it wasn't long before his wife became a distant memory.

Although her lively young sons kept her occupied around the clock, Hai's wife hated it when he was away. Despite garnering the respect of everyone at Rongxia, she was lonely and felt like an outsider in her husband's home. As with most Chinese women living in the countryside at that time, the day Hai's wife married was the day she relinquished her entire prior identity. She moved into Rongxia and became known only as Wife Number 3, or San taitai (Sǎn tī-tī, numbers 1 and 2 being the wives of Hai's older brothers). Regrettably, to this day, I still do not know my grandmother's real name or anything about her life before she married my grandfather.

Each time Hai returned to Rongxia, San taitai begged him to bring her and their sons to Hankou, but his response was always the same: "I promise I will, just not now." Hai's wife waited patiently, but that day never came. As weeks turned into months and months turned into years, she became increasingly distraught.

San taitai's one saving grace was that the Chus were wealthy enough to hire servants to do the chores that most other wives labored at day and night. But this also had one important downside: it gave her an abundance of time to wallow in loneliness and jealousy. During the day, San taitai directed her energies into looking after her sons and teaching them to be honorable young men, but at night feelings of abandonment, isolation, and anger took over. The tears flowed.

Whenever San taitai received word that Hai would be returning for a visit, she spent days picking out what to wear and thinking about what to say to win back his heart and convince him to bring her to Hankou. Each time his visits grew shorter and shorter, and his words to her more impatient and terse. She could see that he had lost all interest in her. She had become an afterthought, a nuisance.

On one of his visits, San taitai demanded that Hai tell her if he was seeing another woman. "Yes," he replied flatly, without a shred of remorse or empathy. That was the final straw. San taitai was overcome with rage — at her husband for his betrayal, at her parents for arranging the marriage, at the Chus for knowingly allowing Hai to be unfaithful. Yet none of that compared with the anger she felt toward herself for failing to keep her own husband interested in her.

The only people San taitai wasn't angry with were her two sons. Both were growing into handsome, well-behaved boys, but they were getting older and becoming more independent. She knew that soon they also would be leaving her for boarding school. A wicked depression slowly began to take hold. San taitai became increasingly withdrawn, and the lively playfulness she used to display with her sons disappeared.

When her eldest son Jing reached primary school age, he left Rongxia for boarding school. San taitai's despair began to intensify. She stopped eating and spent hours locked alone in her room, crying day and night. She was inconsolable and slowly became emaciated.

In the beginning, the Chus empathized with San taitai and reached out to comfort her. But as her depression deepened, they began to look down on her and criticize her inability to hold herself together. Family members and servants began to speak of her as a madwoman, and her mother-in-law chastised her for being an "unworthy wife and mother." Any respect San taitai had gained from giving birth to two sons vanished.

San taitai no longer had the wherewithal to attend to her younger son, who was approaching five. Yu's wife took the lonely boy under her wing. During school breaks, her eldest son would return and try to cheer up his mother. Yet even his filial piety couldn't make up for what she longed for most: Hai's love and attention.

One hot, humid summer day San taitai had a breakdown from which she never recovered. Yu's wife was turning 50, and Rongxia was preparing for a big celebration. Dozens of guests had been invited, and the family had arranged for a small Hunanese opera to be staged on the grounds in her honor. Notice was sent to Hai about the celebration, but he was consumed with living the high life in Hankou and couldn't be bothered returning.

On the day of the celebration, thundering gongs and drums announced the special day to all who could hear. Neighbors and guests slowly filled the greeting hall. The mood was festive and joyful. As the opera's female lead was entering the stage, San taitai suddenly burst into the crowd, cloaked in a long fox fur robe, her face covered in heavy makeup. Family members and servants smiled at the sight of San taitai mixing with people. Guests approached to welcome her. But it didn't take long for everyone to see that something was amiss.

San taitai stood motionless in the crowd. Her eyes, empty and disengaged, were fixed in the distance. Then, suddenly, she began to laugh, cry, and dance wildly, colliding into a number of guests. Her movements were so haphazard that the servants were unable to catch her. The guests stepped back, leaving an empty circle around her. San taitai paused and scanned the crowd. Then, with all eyes on her, she lifted her hands to her face, dug her nails into her cheeks, and clawed down her face over and over and over again, all the while shrieking and groaning.

The servants eventually seized San taitai and guided her back to her room. They tried to calm her and attend to her bloodied face and hands, but when they looked into her eyes they could see that she was no longer present. The beautiful, young girl who had brought Rongxia so much joy years earlier had turned into a gaunt, bloody, empty shell.

From that point on, San taitai no longer recognized anyone and was unaware of her surroundings. Occasionally, she would rush off the grounds and curse and beat anyone she came in contact with. She refused food and began to consume her own excrement.

At that time, mental illness was a foreign concept in China. Anyone who lost their mind was considered defective or possessed by demons, and having them around was believed to bring misfortune. The Chus had nowhere to take San taitai for help. In the end, they did what Chinese families had done for centuries to women who cheated on their husbands, brought shame to the family, or had a breakdown: they locked her in chains and shackled her to the wall in one of the small storerooms on the edge of the property. There, they left her to die.

When news of what had happened reached Hankou, Hai reacted cheerfully and smiled. He was finally rid of her. Some people, though not everyone, at Rongxia were infuriated and appalled at Hai's reaction, saying his heart was as poisonous as a bee sting. No matter how deeply a man may love a woman, that love can disappear as quickly as a bursting bubble.

Good Is Rewarded with Good and Evil with Evil

There is a saying in China about justice: "One's actions cannot escape the vast net of heaven (天网恢恢, 疏而不漏)." In the case of San taitai, although she ultimately was crushed by the cruelty and indifference that tormented her for years, her heart was pure, and in the end that goodness was rewarded with goodness. As it is for most mothers, San taitai's redemption came in the form of her two darling, lively young sons, who, despite the devastating loss of their mother and frequent absence of their father, grew into honorable, upstanding men. Both would leave a deep impression on every life they touched.

San taitai's eldest son, Jing, my father, was mild-mannered, generous, and unfailingly optimistic. He smiled often and possessed none of the arrogance of a son raised in a rich household. He treated everyone politely, no matter who they were, and was especially kind to the disabled, often giving them food, clothes, and money. Owing to his mother's attention to his education from the time he was young, my father grew into a talented intellectual. A literary master was hired to teach him poetry, literature, and a special style of essay writing that had to be mastered to pass the imperial examination during the Ming and Qing dynasties.

My father was gifted at playing the vertical and horizontal flutes, the harmonica, and the Chinese zither, or guqin (gū-chǐn), and friends and neighbors often invited him to play for them. He also was an eloquent debater and petition writer. When disputes arose in the village, plaintiffs frequently requested that my father write the complaint. He won many cases, but often refused to accept money for the work. "What I detest most in this world is injustice. This is my way of ridding it from the planet," he often said.

Of course, like all of us, Father had his faults. Similar to his own father, he had a weakness for women, which got him into trouble on numerous occasions during the early years of my parents' marriage. My father also loved having a good time, and this, combined with his warm-heartedness and ability to see the best in others, made it easy for him to make friends. However, this ability to overlook faults in others occasionally led to his mixing with the wrong sort of people, which, in turn, sometimes resulted in his engaging in behavior very uncharacteristic of his true self.

Father's younger brother had been born at the peak of tangerine season at Rongxia and was aptly named Jusheng, which literally means "born at the time of tangerines" but has a broader connotation that means "fruitful." Uncle Jusheng was humble and generous as well as extremely handsome. Many women had crushes on him. Unlike Father, Uncle Jusheng always had an air of sadness about him from the time he was very little, most likely a result of his mother's dark depression. He was still at home that fateful day his mother lost her mind. He was only five. One can imagine how he felt as he watched her fall to pieces and heard her screams as she lay shackled in the shed dying.

After San taitai's breakdown, Yu's wife looked after Uncle Jusheng. When he turned eight, he left Rongxia for boarding school. From then on, he spent very little time at home with the rest of the family. After graduating from university in Shanghai, Uncle Jusheng married a woman whose father was a high-ranking officer in Chiang Kai-shek's Nationalist Army, also known as the Kuomintang or KMT. He introduced his son-in-law to the idea of joining the military. Uncle Jusheng was accepted into the famous Whampoa Military Academy and, by the eve of China's civil war, had risen to the level of general.

Uncle Jusheng's success in the military earned him much admiration and respect, particularly from my father, who also briefly attended Whampoa but chose to drop out because of the hard labor the cadets were required to do. Uncle Jusheng had little interest in money and renounced his right of inheritance to any property he was entitled to in the Chu family. After the Communist Party took over in 1949, Uncle Jusheng, his wife, and daughter fled to Hong Kong, where many decades later they would provide much-needed assistance to my own husband and son.

In stark contrast with the righteousness of San taitai's legacy, Grandfather's cold-heartedness eventually met an equally cruel fate. In August 1931, heavy rain in the Yangtze River Delta resulted in a massive flood in Hankou. The water destroyed his prized tea business and home, and he was forced to move back to Rongxia.

When Grandfather returned, he brought with him a concubine, known as Qie (Chyě) in Chinese, who was a selfish, miserable witch. Grandfather and Qie had been together more than 10 years and had produced five children. Qie was accustomed to a luxurious life in the city and couldn't adapt herself to our slow, simple life at Rongxia. She insisted that they live elsewhere, so Grandfather rented a home across the water in Fengmen, where all of them settled down.

Qie was extremely demanding of her servants, requiring them to comb her hair, help her dress, fan her during the hot summer, and warm her clothes in the cold winter. She spent most of her days sprawled across the bed like a dead body, smoking opium and playing mahjong.

Qie gave birth to three sons and two daughters, but these children didn't possess the grace or refinement of my father and Uncle Jusheng. They were mean-hearted and poorly behaved, their minds damaged from conception by their mother's opium use. From the moment they were born, Qie insisted on hiring wet nurses to feed her children, which continued until the child was four or five. She was picky about whom she selected. Grandfather spent a lot of money on the wet nurses, who not only were paid salaries much higher than average but also were fed expensive delicacies on a daily basis. The wet nurses enjoyed high status in the family and occasionally would go on strike demanding even more compensation.

Qie paid almost no attention to raising her children, leaving that work to her servants. As a result, over time her children took on more characteristics of the staff and lost the sophistication and class of the rest of the Chu family. Herself uneducated, Qie had no interest in seeing to her children's education. Consequently, they grew to be spoiled, conceited adults.

Qie's eldest son was six years older than me and had inherited his father's strong sexual desire. He was the best looking of her children and was very popular among girls. Many girls maintained promiscuous relations with him, coveting his money. Qie's second son was extremely slow from the day he was born, while her third son was aggressive and often picked fights with other boys. Grandfather frequently had to pay the medical bills for the people he injured.

Previously, the Chu family had been distinguished and tight-knit, but that all began to change the day Qie entered the scene. Her poisonous cruelty split the Chu family into factions that remain to this day. In the end, God's justice reigned. Hai's ruthlessness toward San taitai was rewarded not only with the loss of his business in Hankou, but also, perhaps more fittingly, he would spend the rest of his days catering to and under the spell of wicked Qie.

My Family

When my father was in his late teens, his family arranged for him to be married to a young girl from the same village. The girl, who later became my mother, had a pair of four-inch golden lilies and was beautiful, virtuous, and hard-working. Mother had been raised in a traditional rural family in which girls were not taught to read or write and spent their entire youths in the confines of their homes preparing for marriage. This included going through the excruciating process of having their feet bound beginning around the age of three and learning how to embroider, sew, make shoes, and cook. Although their views of the world differed, my parents matched each other well. They gave birth to five children: two girls (I was the second), followed by three boys.

My mother was an extremely hard worker and very humble. Although the Chus employed many servants to tend to every chore, Mother worked with them side-by-side every day. Whenever we had a special meal, Mother always invited others to partake. Her kindness and graciousness toward the staff earned her much respect and praise from neighbors and friends. She was never idle and spent many hours making clothes and shoes for my siblings and me.

Because their personalities were so different, my mother was the eyesore of Qie and bore the brunt of her cruelty. However, Mother always tried her best to respond with kindness and a smile. She never quarreled with Qie for the power of managing family affairs, for she was not someone drawn to power or keeping score.

As for us girls, my father frequently spent time with my sister and me in the garden where we helped him plant, water, and fertilize the trees and flowers. Sometimes he played the guqin or flute for us in the garden. The music, accompanied by the rustling of leaves, made the most beautiful, tender melodies.

Because of his love for the guqin, my father named my elder sister after a legendary guqin player in ancient China called Boya (Bō-yǒ). My father's love of flowers inspired my name. Our family often sat in the garden at night under the moonlight enjoying the trees and flowers. My father's favorite was the Impatiens, or Fengxian in Chinese, which is what he named me. The Impatiens is a small, delicate flower that is fragrant and bright and whose branches do not spread far. My father loved this flower so much that he even wrote a poem about it:

"The flowers of the Impatiens are so exquisite
That even immortals tend to and admire them,
The fragrant, colorful buds scent the spring breeze
And even Xi Shi shies away from their beauty"
(Xi Shi was one of the renowned Four Beauties of ancient China and said to have been so beautiful that fish would forget how to swim and sink in her presence.)

This name has left an indelible mark on my life. Whenever I think of this flower, I think of my father and the beauty of the flower and its name. In China, we believe a person's name symbolizes his character and fate — dark or bright, cheerful or somber, fortunate or unfortunate. I have been given a beautiful name that I treasure deeply, all of which I owe to my father.

My mother took great pride in the three sons she bore, which earned her great respect in the Chu family. The first was Liang (Lē-ǒng), whose name means "good." Liang was born prematurely at just seven months when my mother slipped and fell one day. It was so early in the pregnancy that her body wouldn't produce enough milk to nurse him, so she and my father resorted to feeding him cow's milk. No one knew what to expect because at the time people believed only in feeding women's milk to babies, yet Liang grew to be plump and adorable. One night when my mother was pregnant and nearly due with my second brother, she had a dream of a shining star falling from the sky into her arms, then dropping to snow-laden ground. She awoke in great pain and gave birth to a boy. My father believed the dream was an auspicious sign that his second son would have a brilliant future, so he named him Yingdian, which means "to enter the book of champion scholars," or Dian (Dē-ĕn) for short. My youngest brother was named Xiangrong, which means "to thrive and prosper," or Rong (Rōng) for short. In reality, from the time he was a toddler, Rong was weak and sick and unable to play as freely and vigorously as the rest of us.

One of my happiest recollections from childhood is playing with my siblings in the outdoor patio next to the main greeting hall of Rongxia. The patio contained several ornate pots full of fragrant flowers. At the center of the patio was a deep pool of water surrounded by colorful wood rails, which served as the drainage system for the entire complex. Every room in Rongxia was equipped with a drain and pipe that fed into this pool, which, in turn, flowed into the lotus pond outside. In this way, the grounds never flooded. Water from the bathing area could be quickly whisked away, and we could brush our teeth and wash our faces in the privacy of our own rooms.

The main attraction of the pool was the dozen gold-coin turtles that lived inside the pipes to help keep them clear. My siblings and I spent hours watching the clever, cute animals as they crawled in and out of the pipes and swam around the pool. Whenever it was about to rain, the turtles stuck their heads out of the pipes, gazed up at the sky, and then quickly crawled back inside. Within minutes, it would begin to pour. We loved watching those wise weathermen.

Turtles are considered an excellent tonic for nourishing the body, so whenever our family entertained guests, the servants captured and cooked some of the turtles. On one occasion when one of my uncles was visiting, he instructed the cook to let us play with one of the turtles before it was killed. We studied the animal from head to toe. Uncle pointed out the special pattern in the animal's back. "These three parallel lines are what give the gold-coin turtle its name," he said. "These animals are very rare and expensive. When you grow up, don't be cheated by someone trying to sell you a regular turtle for the price of a gold-coin turtle." All of us fervently shook our heads and pledged never to be so stupid.

After my mother had given birth to three grandsons, Grandfather spent more time with our family at Rongxia. Often he gave pocket change to me and my siblings, which we used to buy candy in town. This attention made Qie jealous. Once, she sent a servant to our home to spy on Grandfather. The servant was instructed not to allow Grandfather to return to their house in Fengmen for several days. When he finally did return, she insisted that he choose between us and her and her children. In the end, Grandfather chose them and cut off most of his contact with us.

Qie had no concern for the destruction she wreaked on our family, yet my father took it all in stride. He continued to be amiable and always spoke to her with a smile. Gains and losses were never on my father's mind.

Stand Near Red and You Turn Red, Stand Near Black and You Turn Black

After Grandfather lost his business in Hankou, he moved back to Hunan and opened a new company headquartered in Fengmen. Grandfather was an excellent businessman, and it didn't take long for the new company to begin booming. The brand of tea produced and sold at Grandfather's shops became famous throughout the area. At its peak, the company employed hundreds of people, including tea pickers, processors, sorters, packers, porters, and retailers. Salaries were paid daily in silver and copper coins, which were transported by train every few weeks from Hankou. The trunks were accompanied by several guards armed with long, shimmering knives.

The most popular employees at the company were the young teenage girls hired to sort tea. They flaunted their beauty, youth, and virginity with colorful clothes and makeup. Their bright eyes and soft smiles were irresistibly charming to the men who worked there. All of the tea sorted by the girls had to be weighed and inspected. Sometimes, even if a girl's tea weighed only 4 kilograms, the examiner said it weighed over 5 kilograms if the girl flirted with him with winks, smiles, and whispers or allowed him to caress her hands and thighs. If the sorters were ugly or didn't like to flirt, the inspectors sometimes said the tea weighed less than it did to encourage the girls to flirt and improve their appearance. Soon cosmetics in Fengmen became hot items. Even if you were willing to pay a high price, often they were nowhere to be found. Grandfather's tea shops became pick-up joints for young men such as Qie's oldest son. Businessmen in Fengmen began calling Grandfather the "God of Fortune" for bringing so many beautiful women and so much activity to the town.

Grandfather frequently traveled to Hankou to meet with distributors and exporters. Often he stayed there for weeks at a time. Because of the proximity of the new business to our home, my father, who had had little to do with the previous company in Hankou, supervised the local stores while Grandfather was away. My father was an honorable, honest man but, as the Chinese saying goes, "stand near red and you turn red, stand near black and you turn black (近朱者赤, 近墨者黑)." It wasn't long before Father began behaving like the other men in the shops.

At the time, the prettiest woman in the shops was nicknamed Queen Tea Flower. She was Grandfather's mistress, and no man dared philander with her. Before leaving for Hankou, Grandfather repeatedly told Queen Tea Flower not to have contact with any man while he was away, as she was his exclusive treasure. She ignored his instructions.

Shortly after Grandfather left, Queen Tea Flower turned her attention to my father and seduced him. Father became obsessed with the girl. He accompanied her day and night and passed supervision of the shop to other employees. Then, one day, while the two lovers were in bed, Grandfather knocked on Queen Tea Flower's door. Father panicked and fled out the back door. He and Queen Tea Flower were able to keep their affair hidden from Grandfather for a short while, but eventually their relationship was discovered.

One afternoon Grandfather burst into Queen Tea Flower's room and discovered Father with his disheveled, half-naked mistress. He flew into a rage and slapped Queen Tea Flower across the face.

"How dare you bring such shame to yourself and me — you whore! Leave now!"

Grandfather then turned his eyes to my father. Caught red-handed, Father was at a loss for words and kept silent. "Of all the people to betray me, it is my own son!" Grandfather screamed and shook his head in disgust.

Both men stared silently at the floor while Queen Tea Flower gathered her belongings. As the girl was leaving the room, she paused, looked at Grandfather, then brazenly leapt across the room and returned the slap. It was the first time I had ever heard of a woman hitting a man. I couldn't believe her boldness.

"Both of you are bastards!" she screamed. "You have used your money and power to force me to sleep with you!" Queen Tea Flower picked up every object within reach and slammed it to the ground. She even threatened to commit suicide, after which Grandfather calmed down and tried to comfort her. He begged her not to disclose her secret affair with my father. In the end, Grandfather paid Queen Tea Flower a large sum of money to keep her mouth shut.

From then on, Grandfather regarded Father as an unfilial son. He sent Father into exile in a remote village in the mountains, where he was charged with managing the collection of raw tea leaves for the company. Father was extremely remorseful and departed quietly, leaving my mother alone with me and my siblings. Everyone in town knew why Father left, but no one dared discuss it in front of Grandfather. Nevertheless, it remained the talk of the town for weeks.

News of the incident with Queen Tea Flower spread to the mountain village before my father's arrival. A number of the villagers there plotted how they could take advantage of my father's weakness for young, beautiful women to extract money from Grandfather's company. Pretty girls swarmed Father the moment he arrived in the village. Soon he had a new companion.

The girl, a teenager, was the daughter of one of the company's main suppliers of tea leaves. Her family instructed her to seduce my father. The two quickly became inseparable and walked everywhere close together like a married couple. Any lessons Father had learned from the incident with Queen Tea Flower were quickly forgotten.

Father fell completely under the spell of this young woman and totally disregarded the business. Management of the shop was left to greedy locals. When salesmen asked Father to inspect the quality and quantity of tea they sold, he turned a deaf ear and blindly signed every contract without reading a word. After a couple of years, the shop ran out of cash and became deeply debt-ridden. With no more money to get their hands on, all of the women in the village lost interest in him. Grandfather eventually sent money to repay the debts and ordered Father to return to Rongxia.

Grandfather was so upset with the way Father had mismanaged the business in the village that he banned him from working at the main shop in Fengmen. As a result, Father had no choice but to return to a quiet life with my mother and us at Rongxia.

Fortunately, because Father was the eldest son, he had inherited money from his ancestors, which he had used to buy land in Huaguo that he rented to farmers. Back then, money was rarely used in the countryside, and farmers paid their rent in heaps of rice after each harvest. My parents set aside some rice for us and exchanged the rest for other goods. In this way, we were able to continue living a comfortable life without assistance from Grandfather. Gradually, Father abandoned his promiscuous lifestyle. He became interested in growing flowers, writing poems and song lyrics, and spent a lot of time playing the flute and teaching and joking with us kids.

A Tycoon Falls

Grandfather was an excellent businessman, but the people he entrusted to lead key parts of his company were much less reliable and experienced. Because of his long stays in Hankou, Grandfather engaged in little day-to-day oversight of the company's operations. Consequently, mismanagement and theft led to massive losses and the eventual closure of a large portion of his business. What had once been a thriving tea company in eastern Hunan dwindled to just three shops. Discouraged and regretful, Grandfather returned to Hunan full-time and managed the remaining shops himself.

From the day Qie arrived in Hunan, she insisted that Grandfather keep all of his money in cash and bank deposits. She forbade him from purchasing any land for fear that it would eventually wind up in the hands of my father or Uncle Jusheng, rather than her own sons'. As a result, unlike my father, Grandfather had no rental income to make up for the loss in revenue from his business.

Grandfather significantly reduced his expenses by closing most of the shops and cutting back on travel. However, Qie refused to adjust her lavish lifestyle despite their considerable drop in income. By then, she had become severely addicted to opium and gambling on mahjong, which burned through much of Grandfather's remaining income. In the end, Grandfather could no longer support her and their five children at the house in Fengmen, so they packed their belongings and headed to Rongxia.

The day Grandfather and Qie arrived, my siblings and I were laughing and playing in the house when we suddenly heard a loud clamor outside. We ran to the front gate to investigate. A long line of men was carrying sedan chairs on their shoulders with colorfully dressed women inside. Behind them was a long procession of servants hauling luggage. The convoy stopped outside our home. My siblings and I watched as Grandfather, Qie, and their two daughters stepped out of the sedan chairs. The women were fashionably dressed in expensive silk cheongsams, a traditional Chinese dress with short, cupped sleeves, mandarin collars, and double side-slits. Occasionally, Boya and I wore cheongsams, but on most days we wore simple skirts and tops. Grandfather also was decoratively dressed in a long, silk cloak with a tall, mandarin collar, which was common among scholars and wealthy Chinese men at that time. By contrast, Father and my brothers always wore plain pants and shirts.

After welcoming them, Father rushed inside to speak to Mother. "My father and his new family are moving back to Rongxia. Take the children to the entrance hall to greet their grandparents."

Mother grabbed our hands. "I never thought they would come back," she mumbled, shaking her head in dismay.

"From now on, we will all live together," Grandfather announced as everyone silently looked on. "We are family and should not quarrel every day. If any dispute arises, we will sit down and talk. We will take care of each other."

"Agreed," replied Father.

Grandfather reached into his pocket and took out a handful of candies, which he handed to me and my siblings. The second they touched our hands, Qie nodded at her two daughters, who were roughly the same age as Boya and me. They quickly swooped in and snatched them away.

"Those are ours," Qie snapped. "They are expensive candies, and barbarians like you aren't fit to eat them!"

Mother's eyes turned red with humiliation. She hastily led my siblings and me back to our rooms.

"Don't worry, Mother," I said. "We can eat something else. There is nothing to be angry about. They think they are rich and noble, but the truth is the contrary. We are noble and they are not."

"What kind of woman refuses to give anything of good quality to others?" Liang asked. "You and Boya may not care about not getting to eat the candy, but I do."

From that day on, Grandfather and his family lived under the same roof with us. They took over the west wing of the house, where Grandfather used to reside and which had remained empty, while we continued to reside in the east wing. Mother instructed us to draw a clear line between our family and theirs and to never cross this line. So even though we saw each other every day, we mingled as little as possible and ate every meal separately.

Compared with them, our family was poor. My parents had little cash and relied on the rental income from Father's land to put food on the table. Fortunately, my mother was a good, thrifty wife who spent little. Over time, she managed to save some silver and gold, which she kept for emergencies. Although we weren't as wealthy as Grandfather's family, our lives were comfortable. We were a happy family.

Over the years, we watched as Qie continued living her lavish, debaucherous lifestyle and squandering Grandfather's money. Not only did Grandfather have to buy the opium to feed her habit, he also had to pay hefty fines to the police who periodically cracked down on opium use and came to Rongxia searching for contraband. For a few years, Grandfather continued managing his few remaining tea shops, but eventually those were also closed as the company's profits continued to fall. Once a tycoon, famous far and wide, Grandfather's social standing plummeted.

Grandfather and his family lived off what remained of his savings, which was still sizeable and enabled them to continue to lead a well-to-do life. Periodically, he went to Hankou to visit his previous business partners. Although Grandfather no longer worked with them, he knew his savings wouldn't be enough to support Qie's opium habit indefinitely. One day he might need to borrow money from them.

Occasionally, when Grandfather returned from Hankou, he brought back new clothes for my siblings and me, but Qie quickly snatched them away. Sometimes Grandfather gave us the presents secretly, yet somehow Qie always found out and made a fuss. Eventually, Father told Grandfather not to buy us any more gifts, no matter how cheap, to maintain peace in the house.

Confined to My Boudoir

My mother was an honest, humble, hard-working woman, and to this day I admire her deeply. However, she was illiterate and maintained a narrow, feudalistic view of the world, which created a lot of conflict in our family, particularly between her and me. Mother believed wholeheartedly that women served only one purpose in life: to get married and produce sons for their husbands. But by the time I was born in the mid-1920s, such tenets of traditional Chinese society were increasingly under question.

The last dynasty to rule China, the Qing, was overthrown by popular revolt in 1911. Since that time, there had been more and more talk of modernizing Chinese society. In the countryside, this slowly manifested in greater numbers of families abandoning the old practice of foot binding, allowing girls to attend school and permitting young men and women to choose for themselves who they wanted to marry. I was excited about what these new opportunities meant for my future. I dreamed of one day graduating from college and getting a job in the city.

However, my mother would have no part of this new world. She insisted that Boya and I be raised the old-fashioned way, the exact same way that she had been raised. Our first serious conflict arose over the issue of foot binding, which, in traditional rural China, was the single most important factor determining what status of family a girl would marry into.

There were many reasons bound feet were so desirable. For starters, tiny feet were believed to bring out the beauty and elegance of a girl because the smaller the feet, the slower and more gracefully a girl had to walk, which was seductive to men. Second, bound feet prevented girls from walking or running fast or straying too far from home, which were deemed to be corrosive to a girl's virginity. Finally, a girl who successfully lived through the agony of the foot binding process — over the centuries, countless girls died from infection — had learned to surrender her own desires and interests to those of others. Such a girl would therefore more easily submit to the power of her father, husband, and son, and submissiveness was deemed to be one of the preeminent virtues to be cultivated by Chinese women.

In the countryside, foot binding was a ritual practiced predominantly by wealthy families who didn't need to rely on their daughters' labor for survival. The process typically began when a girl was between three and five years old. Using long strips of cloth, mothers tightly wrapped the feet of their daughters, forcing the toes and front of the foot to curl under the arch. Girls wore the binding 24 hours a day and were not permitted to remove it for any reason. After girls had grown accustomed to the binding — which often took months — they were forced to repeatedly walk in circles. The pain was excruciating, but walking was the only way to ensure that the feet correctly molded into their new shape. Hence, girls who stopped or refused to walk were beaten with wooden reeds or a broom.

When Boya reached the age of four, Mother bound her feet. However, Father couldn't stand seeing his daughter in so much agony, so he forced Mother to stop. Later when I turned four, Mother tried to restart the process for both my sister and me. We were terrified. Fortunately, Father empathized with us. He was a contemporary man with progressive views. He insisted that we not be put through such a painful ritual.

On one occasion while we were at this sensitive age, Father had to travel for business. Fearing that Mother might try to bind our feet in his absence, he took us to stay with Mother's family. To our dismay, when we arrived at our grandparents' home, we discovered that our aunt was in the process of binding her own five-year-old daughter's feet. Boya and I had managed to escape our own torture, but every day we had to watch our young cousin as she agonizingly walked in circles for hours in the courtyard. If she fell, stopped, or slowed her pace, our aunt smacked her legs and bum with bamboo and said, "Go faster! … Go! … Go!" No matter how loudly cousin screamed, no one ever came to help her.

When Father returned to take us back to Rongxia, Boya and I fretted the entire way home that Mother might try again to bind our feet. After seeing our cousin's anguish, we didn't know how we would be able to endure. We were very young at the time, but at some level I think we knew that, if we embarked on that path, it would be impossible to pursue the new, modern life we dreamed of. In the end, Mother succumbed to Father's wishes. Even on an issue as dear to her heart as foot-binding, she would never dream of defying her husband.

Mother instead pushed for a compromise, insisting that Boya and I at least begin learning needlework. However, Father said he believed that young girls should not be forced to labor so young. He cleared out one of the guest rooms in the east wing of the house and created a study where he taught Boya and me how to read and write. We began with *The Three-Character Classic*, a famous book that argues that man's nature at birth is good. After that, we moved on to *The Four-Character Classic for Girls*, which teaches that wise girls do not leave their boudoirs.

The idea that young girls should live a sheltered life in their parents' homes until they marry was a strongly held belief in traditional rural China. It wasn't uncommon to encounter girls who had never stepped foot outside their parents' homes until the day they wed and left. Keeping Boya and me confined to our room was a principle my mother also tried to adhere to religiously, and it became the cause of many of our later conflicts.

After a few months of Father's instruction, Boya and I progressed to reading famous poems written during the Tang dynasty, the book *Wisdom in Chinese Proverbs,* and so on. After one year, we could read and write many characters and recite numerous poems. I enjoyed learning and was diligent, but Boya often had difficulty concentrating. Father encouraged her to study harder, but sometimes he would get frustrated and criticize Boya for her inability to focus.

Whenever Father was away, Mother criticized Boya and me for wanting to learn to read and write. She believed we should focus on learning embroidery, sewing, and making shoes because if we didn't master those tasks no man would want to marry us when we grew up.

"First and foremost, girls should learn to be motherly," she said. "Poems and writing are useless to a woman once she is married. If you don't learn how to do womanly tasks, you'll be ashamed of yourselves one day. Don't blame me for not having taught you."

We could see that Mother was sincere. She truly wanted us to lead happy lives. Yet the future we dreamed of and the future she envisioned were completely different. Knowing how much it meant to her, Boya and I eventually agreed to begin learning needlework.

Because Mother kept Boya and me confined in our room, our lives were uneventful and at times painfully boring. Fortunately, Father sometimes broke the boredom by taking us out of the house to visit the center of town or the train station. Once outside, we were like joyful birds flying out of their cages. On a couple of occasions, we even rode the ferry to Fengmen. One year, Father took us to watch the dragon boat races between Huaguo and Fengmen. It was a wonderfully festive scene, and Boya and I talked about it for days after we returned. Mother was vehemently against the idea of our stepping foot outside Rongxia, but Father said it was good for us and broadened our horizons.

The first time Father took us to Fengmen Station, we sat under a tree watching the trains rumbling toward us in the distance. When one of the trains stopped at the station, Boya and I were taken aback at the numerous young girls on the train. They were carrying school bags and running around giddily.

"Mother always says there are no girls in the streets because girls aren't allowed to leave their boudoirs," I said. "But if girls can't leave their rooms, how is it that there are so many girls walking around out here? Did they sneak away?"

"Your mother has a very feudalistic mindset and doesn't like to accept change. Yet the world is changing, and human beings need to advance with it. Women should be able to do whatever men are doing. This is called gender equality. These girls have left their homes to attend school."

"Can we go to school, too?" I asked eagerly.

"Yes, when you both get older you can attend school," he said with a smile. "But right now I want to take you to see where your grandfather's old tea shop stood."

Boya and I were elated. We couldn't stop jabbering as we walked. Father grinned as he listened to us talk about what we imagined school would be like.

The building housing Grandfather's old tea shop was empty, and weeds had taken over the cracks in the walls, floors, and sidewalk. Father sighed at the sight of what had once been a bustling center of activity.

"Mr. Chu, I haven't seen you for years!" a grey-haired old man said to Father as he approached us. "Your two daughters have certainly grown. When I last saw them, they were still in their mother's arms."

The man treated us to tea at a nearby teahouse, which had become a popular place to hang out after Grandfather's shop closed. Afterward, Father took us to buy some clothes and food, and then we returned home.

The moment we entered the house, Mother pointed at Boya and me and began screaming at us. "Go to your room! Girls should not wander in the streets! You are forbidden to go outside again!"

Then she turned toward Father. "You need to be stricter with Boya and Fengxian! Girls must not be led astray. If you want to go out, then go, but don't take them with you. How can I tell them what to do and what not to do if even you don't follow the rules? As their parents, it is our responsibility to ensure that they grow into gentle young women."

From then on, Mother became even stricter with Boya and me. We were forced to spend more time learning needlework, and she forbade us from leaving our room. When we did, we were scolded and spanked. Life became very quiet and dull. Occasionally, Father sneaked into our room and led us to the study where he continued to teach us how to read and write. But as soon as Mother discovered that we had left our room, she charged toward the study and quarreled with Father. There was nothing any of us could say or do to change her views.

"No matter how many books you read," she said, "and even if one day you go to college, at some point both of you will have to marry. Then you will realize that all of this learning has done you no good. It could even become a hindrance in your marriage."

In Mother's eyes, Boya and I should have been focused on only one thing at that point: preparing for the day we would be visited by a matchmaker.

As the years passed, Father continued teaching us literature and writing while Mother instructed us in embroidery, sewing, and needlework. Eventually we outgrew the books at home. Both Boya and I were eager to learn something new, so one day, when we were alone with Father in the study, we asked him if he recalled the first time he took us to the train station.

"Yes, I remember that day," he said and smiled. He knew exactly what we were asking. "I agree that the time has come for both of you to begin studying foreign books." 'Studying foreign books' was the phrase people used back then to refer to today's modern system of education focused on reading, writing, and math, as opposed to traditional Chinese education, which centered on learning classic philosophical works.

That evening at dinner, Father announced that he planned to enroll my sister and me in primary school. Mother vehemently opposed the idea of Boya and me leaving the house every day to attend school. She feared that we would be attacked and raped by bad men, and then no one would be willing to marry us. "A girl's virginity is her most precious possession," she said.

Despite Mother's disapproval, Father stood firm. "Today is different from the past. You are illiterate, but I've never looked down on you for your ignorance. Do you want our daughters to follow in your footsteps?"

Mother was humiliated and hurt and stormed away. She knew she had no say. Yet as I watched her leaving the room, I could tell that, even though she feared what might happen to us, deep down she also dreamed of a day when women would have more voice and wouldn't be made to feel as small as she did at that moment.

Qie became jealous as soon as she heard that Boya and I would be attending school. Her own daughters were close in age to Boya and me, but they were illiterate. She insisted that Grandfather prevent us from studying and said, like Mother, that educating girls was pointless. However, Father was determined to see that we receive an education and defied the opinions of all of the adults in the house.

The next week Boya and I were enrolled in a primary school close to home that we were able to walk to every day. On our first day, we were sent to first grade, but the teacher could see how much we had learned from Father and decided that we should be placed into third grade. One-fifth of the students in our class were girls. I excelled at reading and writing. My essays always received high scores, and my classmates often admired my writing. This praise, together with the teacher's encouragement, greatly boosted my confidence in my studies.

To this day, I can still recall some of the lines of a poem we were instructed to write about spring: "Crawling worms and singing birds abound. Spring is coming! Countless flowers bloom, grasses turn bright green. What a beautiful scene!"

Father Vanishes

Father had more free time after Boya and I started school, so he went into town more often. By then, Qie's opium addiction had become fierce. She required a constant supply of the drug or her body would go into withdrawal, so Father bought raw opium for her every time he went to town.

One day Mother mentioned to Boya and me that Father was purchasing opium for Qie. "I fear that he may be becoming addicted, too," she said.

My sister and I had seen Father little in recent weeks and became worried. To find out the truth, I decided to confront Father. Just when I was entering my parents' bedroom, Qie's two daughters appeared and screamed at me.

"Your father has stolen our mother's money! Now she is beset by terrible withdrawal. She may die if she doesn't receive any opium to smoke. Tell your mother to find your father and bring us back some opium. Otherwise, we will kill you!"

"Don't accuse my father of cheating you!" I said. "He is a good man, not like you and your mother and siblings! My mother isn't home now. Go buy the opium yourselves."

One of the girls slapped me across the face. I refused to accept such abuse and humiliation, so I hit her back. The three of us fought. Boya quickly ran over to assist me. A few minutes later, Mother returned and separated us. We explained what happened. She instructed some servants to search for Father.

As Mother was chastising us for fighting, Qie emerged from her room. She was disheveled and weak, and tears, saliva, and snot were dripping down her face. Mother shook her head and handed a small amount of money to another servant. "Quickly go into town and purchase some opium."

Fortunately for Qie, Grandfather was in Hankou at the time and didn't see her in that pathetic, disgusting state. The servant soon returned with the drug. Within minutes of smoking it, Qie's nerves calmed, and her body regained its composure. After a few hours, the other servants returned.

"We searched the homes of all of Mr. Chu's friends and family, as well as all of the shops in Huaguo and Fengmen, but he was nowhere to be found. We're not even sure if he's alive."

Mother burst into tears. I immediately turned to Qie and screamed. "It's you who asked my father to purchase opium for you. Now you accuse him of stealing your money, and he his missing. This is all your fault!"

None of us slept well that night. The next day, Boya suggested that she and I go searching for Father. "Mother's feet are bound. She can't walk far. It's impossible for her to go looking for Father, even though I know she wants desperately to do so. We have no older brothers to turn to, so you and I should go instead, Fengxian."

Boya and I proposed the idea to Mother, but she refused to let us go. Even though she wanted to find Father, she feared what might happen to us if we wandered around town unescorted. "Your father is a grown man. He will return on his own. We should wait for him at home."

After several days, Father still had not come back, and there was no information about him. Around this time, Grandfather returned from Hankou. The minute he walked through the door, Qie pointed at my family and accused my Father of stealing her money. "They are out to cheat me! They hid Jing so they could steal my opium money."

Grandfather believed Qie. He walked over to my mother and cursed at her. Mother cried and denied any wrongdoing. I was furious and screamed back at him.

"Mother has done nothing wrong! There is no truth to what your concubine is saying. This is all Qie's fault for getting Father involved in buying opium for her."

Seeing that Grandfather was on their side, Qie's two daughters felt emboldened and ridiculed us. I couldn't take it and fought with them. Grandfather was outraged at the sight of us hitting each other.

"Fengxian, they are your aunts!" he yelled as he pulled us apart. "How dare you fight with them. If you act like this again, I will beat you to death!"

I was about to yell back at him when Mother intervened and ordered Boya and me to our room.

"Get out! And don't you ever talk back to me again, Fengxian," Grandfather screamed as we were leaving.

Grandfather instructed one of the servants to go to town and make a large purchase of raw opium. When the servant returned, other staff assisted him in cooking and drying the opium until it was in a consumable state.

For several days after the purchase, Qie lay motionless on her bed, smoking opium almost nonstop. Occasionally, some extended relatives would visit and smoke with her. They talked and laughed and cursed my Father as an unfilial son. I felt disgusted watching them. They couldn't care less if my Father was alive or dead. Grandfather saw me brooding one day and tried to calm me.

"Fengxian, your father took the money and is probably in a gambling den or brothel right now. He is not dead. There is no need to worry."

Because I was so young, such a thought had never occurred to me. Up to that point, I was convinced that Father had been attacked and robbed and taken somewhere. Now I had been presented with another possibility in which Father did take the money and was recklessly spending it. I didn't want to believe he could do such a thing. I was determined to find out the truth.

I spoke with Boya, and we agreed to sneak out the next day and go searching for Father. It was a Sunday, and we told Mother that we were going to attend extracurricular lessons at school. By then, she was deeply distraught and didn't suspect anything.

Boya and I went door to door inquiring about Father's whereabouts but failed to find any solid information. Some people relayed rumors they had heard about Father, but none of them had any concrete idea where he was. Many of the people were appalled to see us out in public alone. "You girls get back to your boudoir!" they shouted at us.

As we were walking on the main road through the village, we came across a middle-aged woman who was sobbing.

"What are the two of you doing out on your own?" she asked, taken aback at the sight of two young girls alone on the road.

"We're looking for our father, Chu Jing. He disappeared."

"Little girls, your father is in the next village. Follow the road behind the village. You will see a thatched hut half way up the hill. The hut is a gambling den. People also go there to smoke opium. I just left that hut myself."

"Why were you there?" I asked.

"I went there to look for my husband, who has been missing over 10 days. One of our daughters is very ill. I need money to send her to a doctor or else she could die. The two of you shouldn't go there. There is a nasty guard at the front door, who doesn't allow people like us to enter. He has two fierce dogs that will attack you if you try to force your way in. I was driven away by the dogs. My husband heard the ruckus and came outside. When he saw it was me, he beat me. When he was finished, he left me lying on the street and went back inside. Now I am returning home to my dying daughter."

My sister and I empathized with the woman's situation, but we were too young to help her. We parted ways and followed the route she told us.

Soon we came across the thatched hut she spoke of. As we approached the door, a small black dog barked and lunged at us. Boya, who was taller and stronger than me, picked up a stick of bamboo and held it tightly in her hand. The dog chased us, so we ran as fast as we could into the street. When we stopped to catch our breath, the dog also paused.

"How about we give the dog the pork-filled buns we brought with us?" Boya said. "Maybe then the dog will lose interest in us."

We tossed the buns down the street, and the dog went chasing after them. Then we returned to the hut and knocked on the door.

"What do you want?" the doorman asked.

"We're looking for our father, Chu Jing. There is an emergency at home, and Father needs to return quickly."

"Your father has already left."

"But we didn't see him on our way here," Boya said. "He must still be in this hut." She took a step forward to try to peek in.

The man pushed her back. "If you don't leave immediately, I will unleash my second dog to bite you."

We didn't know how to react, so we stood there silently for a few moments. When we didn't leave, the doorman blew a whistle, and a large yellow dog came charging at us.

"Father, your daughters are here!" I screamed. "Come out and save us. A dog is attacking us!"

No matter how loud I cried, there was no response. The dog lunged at my legs and bit into my foot. The doorman blew his whistle again, and the dog retreated. The man went inside and slammed the door shut.

Boya tore a piece of cloth off her skirt and wrapped it around my foot.

"I think we should return home and ask Mother to instruct some servants to come back and retrieve Father," she said.

We slowly limped home, saddened that we weren't able to retrieve Father and deeply disheartened at discovering that what Grandfather had said was true. It was the first time I saw my father's fallibility.

When we arrived at Rongxia, I pulled my skirt low to cover my feet, hoping to hide my injury. The minute we entered the house, Mother scolded us for lying to her and traipsing around the village indecently.

"Several adults have gone searching for your father and came up with nothing. How could the two of you possibly think you would be able to succeed when they didn't?"

"We found him," Boya said innocently. "He's playing cards in a thatched hut half way up a hill in the next village. There was a doorman guarding the door. We cried for Father to come out, but he didn't."

At hearing this, the servants praised us for being more capable than them, and Mother's anger dissipated. She ordered a maid to prepare some food for us. My foot ached terribly. I had difficulty standing on my own, so it didn't take long for Mother to discover my wound.

"Fengxian, what's wrong with your foot? Sit down and tell me what happened."

"Fengxian was bitten by a dog in front of the thatched hut," Boya said.

"Why didn't you help your sister drive away that dog? You are older than Fengxian. You have a responsibility to protect her."

"Don't blame Boya. I began to run, so the dog lunged at me first."

Mother stopped the bleeding and cleaned and bandaged the wound. Upon hearing the news that we had found Father, Qie and her daughters rushed over. They demanded that we tell them where he was, so they could retrieve their money.

"Return my money or I will kill him!" Qie shouted. She had always been a witch, but she was even worse now that the opium ruled her. She cared about nothing but that drug and was willing to do anything to get her hands on it.

Mother asked them politely to leave, but they wouldn't listen. Instead, Qie's daughters walked up to me and stomped repeatedly on my wounded foot. I screamed and cried. Mother reached out to cradle me, also crying. Eventually, Qie and her daughters left.

Word quickly spread that Boya and I had found Father in a nearby gambling den. Soon many relatives and friends came to discuss the best way to extract him from that awful place. It was decided that the next day five or six men would go.

The men headed out early in the morning. Unfortunately, by the time they arrived, the hut was already empty. They searched the vicinity but didn't find anything. Some of the men believed Father may have been kidnapped for ransom after Boya and I showed up. Others were skeptical because no instructions had been left about where to send the money. The men returned to Rongxia and conveyed the bad news.

The moment we heard that Father was no longer there, Mother, my siblings, and I were devastated. We felt helpless and didn't know what to do.

"I couldn't care less what happens to that useless, unfilial son of mine," Grandfather said and stormed away.

Mother spoke with some officials from the village government, but they were unwilling to crack down on the gangsters. For the first time since Father disappeared, we began to accept the possibility that we may never see him again. Grief began to set in. Mother was filled with sorrow, but each day she soldiered on. Over time, we resumed our routines and life continued.

With Father gone, Mother had to take over the responsibility of collecting payment from the tenants renting our land. Although she was illiterate, Mother was smart, organized, and good at mental arithmetic. Therefore, it wasn't too difficult for her to keep track of the family's receivables and payables. Even when Father was still with us, he allowed Mother to handle many of our family's affairs, including overseeing the servants. My father was fortunate to have married a woman as hard-working and virtuous as my mother.

Whole Again

With Boya and me buried in schoolwork and Mother immersed in caring for the family, time passed like lightning. Before we knew it, almost one year had passed since Father had vanished. There was still no information about his whereabouts. Nevertheless, Grandfather's concubine continued to periodically send her children to demand their money back. One day two of her nitwit sons came while Mother was away. They banged on our furniture and shouted repeatedly, "Give back our money! Give back our money!"

They grabbed my youngest brother by the hair. When he screamed in pain, Boya pushed them away and took him to our room.

"Get out!" I screamed at them. "Don't come back until my father returns. And if Father never comes back, then you'll simply never get your money!"

They raised their hands to hit me. Luckily, at that moment some of the servants stepped in to protect me, and Qie's sons left.

When Mother returned, she tried to calm Boya and me. "Be tolerant. Don't argue or fight with them. Now go get ready for dinner."

As Boya and I were turning around to go to the washroom, Father suddenly appeared before us in the hallway. He was pale, thin, and sickly-looking. His hair was long and straggly and had turned yellow. He looked and smelled awful. Yet no matter how dreadful his appearance, Father was home. We were elated and hugged each other with joy. Our family was whole again.

"What happened to you?" Mother asked him. "Where were you all this time?"

Father didn't reply but only shook his head and laughed.

Seeing him treat the situation so casually infuriated her. Mother yelled at Father nonstop for over an hour about being selfish and not giving consideration to the needs and feelings of his wife and children. I had never seen her so angry. I could tell that she wanted to hit him, but as a proper traditional wife she restrained herself.

After Mother turned quiet, Boya and I scolded Father for making us so worried. But no matter how much criticism was thrown at him, Father didn't lose his temper with us. He had been born with an even temper and, whenever he spoke, he always spoke with a smile. After a few hours, it was difficult to remain angry with him.

The truth is my father was a good man, but unfortunately he became infected with the bad behaviors and practices of hooligans. Once he began mingling with them, he lost his ability to tell right from wrong. My Father was not the only one to have fallen victim to such forces. In old Chinese society, many people engaged in gambling, smoking opium, and prostitution. These destructive practices often led to broken families and other tragedies.

After everyone calmed down, Mother ordered one of the servants to boil water for Father to take a bath. I prepared him a strong cup of tea. He bathed, changed his clothes, and then the family ate dinner together for the first time in almost a year.

When Qie heard that Father had returned, she immediately sent one of her sons to retrieve her money. By then, Father had fallen asleep on his bed exhausted. He didn't respond at all to the boy's yelling. It wasn't until Grandfather came and yanked Father out of bed that he woke up.

Grandfather grabbed Father by the shirt, pulled his face close, and looked straight into his eyes.

"Qie asked you to buy some opium, but you disappeared with the money. What have you done with it? Return it to me now!"

"I lost all the money gambling," Father said, lowering his head shamefully.

Grandfather slapped Father across the face, shoved him back on the bed, and stomped away.

Shortly after, Qie returned with her children and demanded her money back. "I will not leave this room until my money is returned!"

The commotion caught Grandfather's attention, and he stormed back. Grandfather slapped Qie's cheek.

"This is all a result of your opium smoking! You must quit. If you continue to behave like this, I will destroy all of your opium, pipes, and lamps. Then let's see if you still have so much energy to come here and shout!"

After that scolding, Qie and her children left. Finally, the storm that had been raging for the past year quieted.

Seeing Father's humiliation, Mother sat on the bed next to him and tried to comfort him. "Jing, you have the ability to start anew if you have the will. I will stick with you no matter what to maintain our happy family." Father quietly smiled but gave no reply. The next morning, he promised to turn over a new leaf and started by helping Mother with household chores.

A few days later Mother noticed that we were running low on rice, so she sent one of the servants to collect some rice from the farmers renting our land. The tenants refused to pay. "Mr. Chu signed away ownership of the fields when he was gambling," they said. "Now we have new landlords."

Mother was so upset when she heard that most of the land had been gambled away that she collapsed. Father felt ashamed and remorseful, but it was too late for him to do anything about it. Some of the land had been passed down to my father from his ancestors, while other plots had been purchased by my mother with her own hard-earned savings. She couldn't believe they were suddenly gone.

"If I wasn't illiterate, I would have been able to identify the deeds to the land and could have hidden them from your Father."

From then on, Mother began to realize the importance of education and changed her attitude toward Boya and me attending school. She set aside money for our tuition and encouraged us to study hard so we would never be cheated in the way that she was.

Mother put our family on a very tight budget. She dismissed most of the servants except a few, who had been with us for years and were like family. They stayed behind to help haul water from the well, tend to the vegetable garden, and cook. Mother also sold some of her gold jewelry to the pawn shop to help meet our monthly expenses.

During the first two weeks that Father was home, he was filled with energy every day. We thought he was elated to be back and thought nothing of it. Then one day he suddenly became very tired. He wouldn't eat, and his eyes and nose began to drip. We recognized the symptoms immediately because we had seen them so often before in Qie: Father was in withdrawal.

It was then that we realized that Father had been secretly smoking opium since he returned. He must have had it with him when he arrived. Mother, my siblings, and I confronted Father. We begged him not to smoke any more. He promised to quit, but neither he nor we were sure if he had the strength and resolve to do so.

Mother accompanied Father day and night as he went through withdrawal. She fed him candies and strong tea around the clock. During this time, my siblings and I stayed home from school. We took turns wiping the sweat from his forehead and encouraged him to keep fighting. The symptoms gradually faded. Father triumphed over the addiction. We were all proud of him.

Qie was envious when she learned that Father had kicked the habit. She knew he was in a vulnerable state and came to our house to try to lure him into smoking with her. Mother was enraged and pushed her away. "No one here wants your opium. You have poisoned him enough!"

After the drug had gotten out of his system, Father regained his mental strength. He vowed never to touch opium or gamble again. He and my mother then turned their attention to our family's ailing finances. As my siblings and I grew, we consumed more food, and soon my brothers would be reaching school age. Our expenses were rising fast, and we had little income.

In the past, Father had occasionally helped villagers who had been wronged file legal complaints. He had a very good reputation. Previously, he wrote the pleadings for free, but now that we needed money he began charging a small fee. Father also began tutoring people interested in learning to write poems and song lyrics. My Father did these things not only for money but also to make up for his previous wrongdoings. Both of my parents worked hard to support our education, and we remained a happy, tight-knit family.

Blindly Betrothed

During my last year of primary school, my head teacher was Mr. You (Yō). He was a close friend of my grandfather, and our families were also distantly related. Mr. You had an only son, who was ugly and unkempt and had an incessantly dripping nose. The boy's name was Cong (Tsōng), which means "smart" in Chinese, but in reality the boy was somewhat of an imbecile.

Mr. You was fond of me. I was a good student and decent looking. He believed I would make a perfect bride for his son. Unbeknownst to me, one day he visited my home and proposed his idea of marriage to my parents. Mr. You had money and status and lived locally. My mother had long been concerned that I wouldn't be able to find a good husband. She was overjoyed when she learned about my teacher's interest. My Father also did not oppose the engagement for fear of offending my teacher.

What about me? I was told nothing. That was the custom then. Children, particularly girls, weren't permitted to voice an opinion. Marriage was always arranged by one's parents. All that mattered to my parents was that our families be equally matched in status and wealth.

In those days, I would come home from school every day and go straight to the room I shared with Boya. Servants did the daily chores, so we spent most of our time in our room doing homework and playing. Usually on Sundays my mother allowed my sister, brothers, and me to play outside, but one Sunday morning, my mother told us we had to stay inside.

"Lots of guests will be coming to our home today. It's not appropriate for you children to mingle with the guests."

Later many people arrived. As the guests chatted happily in the courtyard, we overheard them congratulating my parents. My siblings and I were very curious, so we peeked out our window at what was going on. Mother appeared to be joyful. Father was exchanging crimson cards with someone I didn't recognize, which is a common custom at betrothals. The cards contain eight characters, indicating the year, month, day, and hour of a child's birth, and are exchanged by the families of both sides and the matchmaker at the engagement party. Neither my siblings nor I had any idea what was going on.

Mother invited the guests to take the seats of honor, while my siblings and I sat in the common seats. Firecrackers were lit, and then a banquet began. My parents toasted the guests, and the guests toasted each other. As I ate, I noticed many friends and relatives looking at me with great interest.

"Fengxian, you are smart and beautiful. You will surely have a happy life. We have heard that you can read and write. Is that true?"

Feeling embarrassed about the attention, I gave a brief reply, and then quickly returned to my room. "Today's lunch is special. What's being celebrated?" I asked Boya when we were back in our room.

She smiled and whispered that I was being betrothed, but she spoke so quietly that I didn't catch what she said. I begged Boya to repeat it, but she was afraid of being scolded by our parents. I asked her again and again. Finally, she responded with a lie, saying that we were celebrating Grandfather's birthday. I believed her. I was still quite young. My sister had not yet been engaged, and she was older than me. How was I to know it was my betrothal party?

The next day at school, my classmates were sneering at me. "Fengxian, you are shameless! Now we know why you got high grades for your writing. It's because Mr. You was showing favor to his future daughter-in-law." They shunned me. I wanted to cry but held it in.

When I returned home that afternoon, I immediately confronted my parents about the rumors at school. Mother refused to admit they were true.

"There is no such engagement. You shouldn't trust the nonsense you hear at school. Go to your room and study."

"But all of my classmates say I am engaged. I am too young. You have betrothed me to an imbecile. You are heartless!"

I ran to my room, slammed the door, and cried. Who would take pity on me? Father had always loved me, but why didn't he look out for me this time? Did he not care about me any longer? Was he pleased with my engagement to an imbecile? I hated my teacher. I had to protest.

At school every day, Mr. You showered me with attention, which made me feel disgusting. I thought long and hard about a way out of my predicament, but there was none. Then one day it dawned on me to use my pen as a weapon. I wrote Mr. You a letter condemning what he had done and telling him I was dead-set on rescinding my engagement to Cong. I thought the letter would make him leery of me and consequently give up the engagement. Instead, my teacher became more emboldened.

Mr. You showed the letter to my grandfather and criticized me for being so outspoken. He declared that he would never cancel the engagement and asked my parents to set a date for the wedding as soon as possible. Later Grandfather came to our home and chastised my mother for failing to raise me well. Afterward, Mother stormed to my room in a rage.

"Fengxian, marriage is something to be decided by one's parents. You have no say! Proper girls from wealthy families cannot be betrothed twice. It has already been done. We cannot back out."

At the time, according to traditional customs followed by affluent rural families, once a woman was betrothed, she was forbidden from marrying another man even if her fiancé died before they actually married. Women from poorer families faced less restrictions, but my family was well-to-do and old-fashioned. It seemed that there was no way out of my dilemma. I didn't say a word and lowered my head and cried. Father was not as vocal or opinionated as usual and kept silent.

Later that day Grandfather's concubine came to our home and mocked Mother. "You always think you are so good at educating children, but your daughter is worse than wild girls. Now you have no choice but to confine Fengxian to her boudoir. I have always told you that it is no good for girls to be literate, but you didn't believe me. Now the Chu family prestige has been damaged."

Qie's remarks infuriated me so much that I wanted to hit her. Father was also angry and screamed at her. "Qie, it's none of your business! She's my daughter. We will handle it. Go away!"

Father was still recovering from withdrawal, and the anger made him turn pale. Mother helped him to the study to rest. When she returned, she dragged me to another room and locked the door. Then she picked up a thick rod and spanked me, rebuking me for bringing shame to our family.

"It will be very difficult now for Boya to find a proper husband because of what you have done, Fengxian!" The more Mother yelled, the angrier she became and the harder she hit me. Hearing my screams, father came out of the study to investigate what was happening. He could hear Mother beating me.

"Do you want to kill her?" he screamed at Mother through the door. "You are being barbaric. Open the door!"

Mother wouldn't listen and continued to hit me. Father threatened to have the servants break down the door. Eventually, Mother sat down crying. I opened the door, and Father pulled me to him.

"Fengxian, it's already been done," he said to me in a calm voice. "There is no way to back out of the engagement. Go and rest."

Seeing how hurt Mother was, I felt guilty and went to her side to comfort her. "Don't cry, Mother. I won't fail you again."

Father walked me to my room where Boya had taken refuge. She was frightened by what had happened and feared that Mother would blame her. When Boya saw the bruises on my hands and feet, she also started to cry. Within minutes, Mother was back in our room yelling.

"From now on, the two of you are no longer permitted to go to school. I have always said that girls shouldn't attend school. They should stay at home and learn to embroider and do housework. But the two of you only listen to your father and turn a deaf ear toward me. If you disobey me again, I will beat you to death!"

That evening I fell asleep distressed and in pain. When I awoke, I was overcome with hatred of Mr. You. I was only 12 years old at the time. What kind of world allows someone to be betrothed so young? The more I thought about my situation, the more I wept.

As I lay in bed, I could hear two old women who lived near us pacing back and forth along the path outside Rongxia. They were singing songs describing women of virtue: "Proper girls should imitate their mothers … should not leave their boudoirs … and should not raise their voices."

I knew they were making fun of me, but there was nothing I could do. After a while, they finally stopped.

I wondered why my fate was so bad and not like that of others. Not only had I lost all my freedom, I also had to endure society's criticism. The betrothal had been set, and there was no going back. How would I be able to endure the rest of my life? It would be better to be dead, I thought, yet I was so young. Was my life to be this short? I looked at my battered hands and feet. Why had Mother been so cruel? It is said that a mother's love is the greatest love in the world, but my mother's love could be so hurtful. The longer I reflected on my situation, the more I could see that Mother was just a product of her own traditional upbringing. She had succumbed to that world and had never stepped outside it. She wanted Boya and me to be like her. I could see no way out of this tragedy.

That day Mother refused to speak to me and I stayed in my room. "Don't give Fengxian any food," Mother told Boya. "When your sister is hungry, she will yield."

While Boya was out of the room, I shut the door and windows. I felt as though no one cared about me. I wanted to end my life. Hanging on the wall were several strips of pork that had been treated with chemicals to sterilize the meat in preparation for the Dragon Boat Festival. I pulled down a piece of the poisonous pork and ate it.

As I chewed, I recalled the lyrics of a song I had heard about the difficulties of being a wife. How would I be able to withstand it? The more upset I got, the faster I ate. After I finished one piece, I feared it wouldn't be enough to kill me, so I grabbed another one from the wall. Just then, Boya knocked on the door.

"Fengxian, open the door, please. I have food for you."

"I don't want to eat anything. Go away. I want to sleep forever!"

Boya understood what I meant and became worried. "Fengxian, please, please open the door and let me in."

When I didn't respond, she screamed to our parents. "I don't know what Fengxian is doing. She has locked the door from inside the room."

"If she wants to die, let her die!" Mother yelled.

Father, knowing how stubborn I was, feared that I would do something foolish and ordered a servant to force open the door. By the time they entered, I had passed out. They were horrified to discover me on the bed with the treated pork dangling out of my mouth.

Mother panicked. She took me in her arms and cried out for someone to save me. She apologized repeatedly for her earlier outburst, but I didn't hear a thing. Many relatives came and eventually a doctor arrived.

"Fortunately, Fengxian didn't eat too much," the doctor said. "She is unconscious, but don't worry. It's not too serious." The doctor gave me some herb soup to make me vomit. Slowly, I regained consciousness. I had no idea what had happened, so Boya told me everything. I felt ashamed of my foolishness.

Later my parents told me that as long as Mr. You agreed to dissolve the engagement they wouldn't force me to marry Cong. "Fengxian, we love you and want you to live a happy life. But you are too stubborn. You would rather die than accept this arranged marriage. Even though we fear being laughed at and slandered by our neighbors, we will try to dissolve the betrothal in order to make you happy. You can return to school when you recover."

I was relieved, but at the same time I felt ashamed for disappointing and frightening my parents. Soon news of my suicide attempt spread. It became a topic of all of our neighbors' conversations. My school superintendent and many teachers came to visit. They criticized my parents for being old-fashioned and encouraged me to continue studying. "Society is changing. Today young people choose spouses themselves."

After several days, I returned to school. When I entered the grounds, my heart beat furiously. I was afraid to see my teachers and classmates, especially Mr. You. I went to class as though nothing was wrong and discovered that Mr. You had quit and been replaced. Perhaps he couldn't endure the public outcry or the sting of his own conscience, or maybe he just didn't want to see me. Whatever the reason, I was thankful. I thrust myself into my studies. The end of my last year of primary school was approaching and I intended to graduate.

I don't know where it came from, but a few days later I mustered the courage to write Mr. You another letter. I asked him again to rescind the engagement and to return my crimson card to my father.

For the remainder of the school year, time passed fast. With much hard work, I successfully completed my exams and graduated from primary school. Although I felt sad to say goodbye to my friends, I was glad to put the past year behind me. I looked forward to summer break.

In the middle of the summer, Mr. You gave in to my request to end the betrothal. One afternoon he came to my home to return my crimson card and retrieve his son's. As he was leaving, he angrily rebuked my parents.

"Fengxian has disturbed my peaceful life and made me a laughing stock! If it weren't for my special relationship with you, I would not release her. I never dreamed that a little girl like her could ever cause such havoc."

Pursuing My Own Path

With my engagement over, I felt as if a heavy weight had been lifted from my shoulders. For the remainder of the summer, Father taught Boya and me how to play the flute and Chinese fiddle, how to plant and tend flowers, and how to write essays. As we matured, Boya and I quarreled less with Mother over staying in our room and learning household skills, so we also spent much time that summer studying embroidery and needlework. Our family was close and happy.

When the new school year began, my parents enrolled Boya and me in different secondary schools. They decided I would continue studying at a school in our county while Boya, who was less studious than me, would attend a girls' vocational school in Fengmen to learn Hunan-style embroidery. Both were boarding schools, which meant that we would be living away from home for the first time.

The morning of our departure, Mother helped us pack our bags and arranged for two men to transport us to school by wooden pushcarts. She tearfully hugged us goodbye. "Both of you be chaste. I will arrange to send you home-cooked food every weekend." Mother, Boya, and I cried. Father stood by smiling the whole time and then quietly said, "It's time to leave," and walked us to our carts.

I headed east and Boya west. I had never traveled so far from home alone. Tears streamed down my face as I watched Rongxia fade into the distance. What would the next few years have in store? Although I hated leaving my family, I was full of excitement and extremely thankful to be able to continue my studies. I was confident that my future remained bright.

What neither I nor anyone knew at the time was that, within a few years, our country would be engulfed in war. Unbeknownst to me that fall day in 1937 as I departed for middle school, Chinese troops were staving off an invasion by the Japanese army in the north. Soon our country would slip into the throes of two successive wars. The first, against Japan, would last until 1945; it would be followed by a civil war that would extend until 1949. The chaos of battle would disrupt the dreams and steal the lives of millions of young people, myself included.

As I took in the scenery on my ride to middle school that day, nothing remotely political was on my mind. Huaguo was isolated enough that it often took several days for news of important events like the Japanese invasion to reach us. No family had a radio, and the nearest city with a newspaper was hours away. News usually spread by word of mouth from passengers riding the train through Huaguo. Even then, information was usually only exchanged between men, who rarely discussed current events with their wives or daughters.

After a few hours, the pushcart driver announced that we had arrived at my new school. I looked up and saw a big bright sign atop a black iron gate that read "Central Advanced Secondary School." It was one of the grandest buildings I had ever seen. I felt honored to be walking in the steps of the many well-known local people who had preceded me.

I was orienting myself and wondering what to do next when a girl approached me smiling.

"Are you a newcomer?"

"Yes."

"So am I. My home is very near here, so I know the school well. Let's go see the principal." Her name was Wu. We chatted about where we were from and the schools we attended previously. We hit it off immediately. I breathed a sigh of relief. I knew that everything would be okay.

The principal greeted us and instructed one of the school administrators to lead us to the girls' dormitory where two girls were assigned to each bed. The teacher picked out a bed for Wu and me to share. The pushcart driver set my luggage on the floor. I thanked him and instructed him to return home.

"Tell my mother not to worry about me, that my teachers and classmates are kind, and that they will look after me."

Wu and I quickly became as close as sisters. Because Wu was from that area, she knew the school rules and procedures and helped me learn them. My first major adjustment was eating in the school canteen. At each meal, the students queued and sat in assigned areas. After everyone was seated, a whistle blew and we picked up our chopsticks and ate. The school allotted only five minutes of eating time, after which another whistle blew, and we set our chopsticks down regardless of how full we were. In the beginning, it was difficult to adjust to this strict regimen.

At my first meal, the whistle sounded before I could finish one bowl of rice. Even though everyone else stopped eating, I continued until Wu whispered at me to stop. "Why are you still eating? You will be punished if you are caught by a monitor." It was only then that I put my chopsticks down. "Are you still hungry? Next time don't eat so slowly. Remember to eat fast. Don't be shy. Otherwise, you will go hungry."

On the weekends, the parents of most students sent home-cooked meals. We ate them in our dormitories and shared them with one another. On those days, we could take as long as we wanted to eat and jabbered away happily for hours.

Wu and I were joking on the playground after lunch one day when I looked outside the school's gate and was horrified to see my former teacher, Mr. You, walking toward the school with his son, Cong, my former fiancé. Cong was short and thin, and on his dirty face were two thick streams of snot running from his nose to his mouth.

I watched as Mr. You took a piece of cloth out of his pocket and affectionately wiped Cong's face. I could see how much Mr. You loved his son. I knew he was only trying to do what he thought was best for Cong when he arranged his marriage to me. In a way, I was honored that he chose me, although I was very glad that I didn't have to marry him.

Mr. You and Cong stood outside the gate for several minutes. Mr. You encouraged his son to enter, but Cong didn't want to come inside. Eventually, Mr. You picked up his son and carried him onto the school grounds. Many students swarmed to the gate to watch what was happening. Wu wasn't aware that Cong and I had once been betrothed. She tried to drag me with her to watch, but I stayed put.

When the bell rang, we rushed to our classrooms. As fate would have it, Cong sat right in front of me in class. We didn't say a word to each other. I figured that no one knew we had been engaged, but by the next day all of our classmates were making fun of us. They pointed at us, exchanged whispers, and laughed. Although I felt humiliated, the reality was that we had been engaged, and our betrothal had left an indelible mark on my life.

Cong was more thin-skinned than I. He couldn't bear the ridicule. A few days later, he quit school. Although my classmates continued to make fun of me, I ignored it and focused on my studies. Gradually, the storm subsided, and no one spoke of it anymore.

I was fortunate to have been assigned the best instructor in the school, Mr. Hou (Hō), for my Chinese class. Mr. Hou was a solemn, stern man who rarely joked, but he was an excellent teacher. Mr. Hou taught us how to write essays in vernacular Chinese, which had become increasingly popular after the fall of the Qing dynasty. Prior to that, students primarily learned how to write in the way of the ancient philosophical texts.

Whenever students made grammatical errors in their speech or writing, or if the class was talking too loud, Mr. Hou banged his pointer on a student's desk and frightened us into silence. Although Mr. Hou was strict, his firmness, combined with an abundance of patience, made him an excellent and well-respected teacher among his colleagues and students. Mr. Hou always insisted that our writing be clean and neat.

He pointed out even the smallest of mistakes. Everyone in Mr. Hou's class made great progress in their writing skills.

I excelled in language arts, but mathematics was very difficult for me and always gave me a great headache. My math teacher in primary school wasn't strict with us, and hence I never received a solid foundation in the subject. I was far behind others in my class, which gave me a lot of anxiety. Whenever I was in math class, my heart beat fast, and I was unable to concentrate. Sometimes during exams, I thought about trying to copy other students' answers but never did. I knew that if I ever wanted to find a job in the future I would have to master basic math, so I memorized formulas and asked lots of questions in class. By the end of the semester, I narrowly passed my math exam.

As the lunar year came to an end, the school made preparations to close for the Chinese New Year holiday. The instructors gave us homework to do over the vacation. My parents sent a pushcart driver to escort me home. On the ride back, I reflected on everything I had learned and all of the new people I had met in my first semester away from Rongxia. I had grown a lot during my short time away.

The Magic Man on a Magic Bicycle

I was elated to reunite with my family after being away for so long. Boya and I relayed everything that we experienced during the past semester. Everyone in the family listened intently to our stories. We passed the break playing outside with our younger brothers, who were getting bigger and smarter by the day. Mother also insisted that we practice needlework and embroidery each morning. Boya had become very proficient over the past semester and worked on far more intricate pieces than I did.

During the 15 days of Chinese New Year, it is customary for relatives and close friends to visit one another to pay their respects and exchange good wishes for the New Year. One day my mother's eldest brother came to visit us. Uncle worked as a secretary for a high-ranking local official. He was educated, well-respected, and wealthy. Most importantly, he was one of the few people in the area to possess a bicycle. Back then, people in Huaguo called bicycles "line carts" because they left a line on the ground as they travelled. At the time, it was extremely rare to encounter anyone who owned a bicycle, so the villagers dubbed my uncle "the magic man on a magic bicycle."

I admired my uncle very much. He wrote beautiful calligraphy and was excellent at crafting poems and essays. Whenever he wrote, it seemed as though his brush was dancing with the ink. I dreamed of being as capable as he one day. Uncle worked hard and was always very busy, so he seldom had time to visit us except during Chinese New Year. We always looked forward to his holiday visit.

After uncle arrived, he, Father, Boya, and I went outside to stroll through Rongxia's garden, which was blanketed in frost. The cold north wind was blowing hard, and the flowers and trees, laden with snow and ice, were drooping over. Uncle commented on the beautiful plum blossoms, the only plants in the garden to blossom in the winter. "How brave they are," he said.

I cast my eye on my namesake, the Impatiens, and saw that they had lost all their leaves. Each had only one nude stem left. "Why did you name me after the delicate Impatiens and not the strong, resilient plum blossom?" I asked Father.

"When you were born, it was December of the lunar calendar. I thought about giving you the name Winter Plum Blossom. But after much thought, I thought the name wasn't gentle enough, so I named you after my favorite flower, the Impatiens. I didn't expect…"

"…You didn't expect Fengxian to be so bold and audacious!" Uncle chimed in. We all burst out laughing.

"Maybe one day Fengxian will become as gentle and intelligent as Lin Daiyu, the famous heroine in the novel *Dream of the Red Chamber*," said Boya.

Uncle clapped his hands. "You're right. That may be your father's real intention!"

Father laughed and gently put his arm around me. "No, don't become Lin. She is such a tragic figure. I hope that you will grow to be as gentle and intelligent as her but much happier."

"And what about, Boya?" Uncle asked.

"When Boya was born, I had been spending a lot of time playing the guqin, but I could find no one to appreciate my music. I needed someone who could understand my music as thoroughly as I did. Hence, I named her after China's legendary guqin player, Yu Boya."

"What a pity that Boya doesn't know how to play the guqin," Uncle said. "She only knows embroidery. Why not embroider a beautiful guqin for your father and change your name into Xiuqin?" referring to silk-embroidered guqin. We all laughed.

The wind was freezing cold. We couldn't stay outside any longer, so we returned to the house and prepared a fire in the study. Mother brought some desserts and sunflower seeds, and we all sat around the fire pit talking and laughing. We asked Uncle to challenge us with some Chinese riddles.

"A mountain (山) is linked with another mountain," Uncle said. "The answer is one character." Boya quickly answered, "Chu (出)," which means 'out.'

"Emerging from a field (田)." Once again Boya answered, "You (由)," which means 'from.'

"Four walls on four sides (口) with a man (人) sitting inside." I replied, "Qiu (囚)," which means 'prisoner.'

"Four walls on four sides (口) with ten (十) sitting inside." My eldest brother shouted "Tian (田)," which means 'field.'

"These are too simple. Challenge us," said Father.

"Two 'mu (木)' do not make a forest (林)." We thought about it for quite a while, but no one could come up with the answer, even Father. Then Uncle said, "Xiang (相)." (There are numerous Chinese characters with the pronunciation 'mu.' The 'mu (木)' on the left means 'wood,' while the 'mu (目)' on the right means 'purpose.')

Then Father gave us a very challenging riddle. "Once upon a time, there were two (二) people (人) and ten (十) women (女) in half a field (田). I (我) love riding goats (羊), but that day the goat was riding me. A thousand (千) li linked with the field (田) and with the land (土). The answer is four characters."

The riddle was far too difficult for us children, so we looked to Uncle. "Fuqiyizhong (夫妻義重). A husband and wife remain faithful to each other," he answered. "Very good," Father said and smiled.

"Instead of a riddle, how about a story?" Father asked my siblings and me. We eagerly nodded our heads.

"In ancient times, there was an emperor who one day dreamt of four items. They were light, heavy, red, and white, respectively. The emperor summoned his courtiers to interpret the dream, but no one could. Do you remember this tale, Uncle? If so, you tell the rest."

"Of course," said Uncle. "One of the courtiers said that the light symbolized a wick, the heavy item iron, the red item fire, and the white item snow. The emperor was dissatisfied with this interpretation, after which all of the other courtiers were afraid to interpret the dream. The emperor was furious and said he wanted to kill them all. At that moment, a young man was heard shouting from outside the court. The young man said he was an expert in interpreting dreams. The emperor summoned him inside. When the emperor saw that the man was disheveled, dressed in rags, and barefoot, he accused the man of cheating him. He ordered his guards to kill the man. But the young man replied, 'Emperor, you should not judge a person only by his appearance, in the same way that the ocean should not be measured by a bucket.' The emperor agreed and allowed the man to interpret his dream. The man requested a writing brush and ink, then quickly wrote down the interpretation and read it for the emperor: 'The light represents the winds and clouds crossing over the vast territory under your highness's power; the heavy symbolizes your majesty, which is sure to last forever; the red is the sunlight above this fertile land; and the white is the snow showing a bumper harvest is at hand.' The emperor was very pleased with what the young man had written and wanted to give him a reward. But the man declined any reward and went away. In the end, this simple man saved the lives of all the courtiers."

My siblings and I were engrossed in the story. We begged Uncle to tell us more, but at that moment Mother entered the study and announced that dinner was ready. Out of courtesy, Father invited Grandfather to join us.

According to Chinese custom, guests at any special meal are served by the others as a demonstration of their respect. Neither their bowls nor their cups should ever sit empty. On that day, Uncle was our guest, so Father and Mother continuously picked up food with their chopsticks and added it to Uncle's bowl; they also ensured that Uncle's tea cup was never less than half full. Mother, my siblings, and I finished our dinners well before Father, Uncle, and Grandfather, who lingered there for hours eating, drinking, and chatting about the war and world events.

The next morning, Uncle prepared his things to return home. Mother asked him to take some gifts she had prepared for their parents.

"They didn't instruct me to bring anything to you, so you don't need to send gifts to them," Uncle said to her. "There is no need to be so polite. I really hate some of these old customs. If we could all come and go empty-handed, we could get rid of much of our trouble in this world."

Uncle mounted his magic bicycle, waved goodbye, and then rode away. Knowing how rugged and icy the terrain was, we feared that he might crash, but he fearlessly pedaled on straight and steady. Neighbors stepped outside their houses to watch Uncle ride away. For many of them, it was the first time they were seeing a bicycle. Even many rich people, like Grandfather, didn't own a bicycle. Although it was freezing cold that morning, I stayed outside watching the magic man on a magic bicycle ride away until his figure disappeared into the fog.

Farewell Words

The older I got, the quicker time seemed to pass. Before long, I had completed another year of secondary school and was back at Rongxia helping my family prepare for the most celebrated time of year across China.

At its core, Chinese New Year symbolizes the passing of the old and the coming of the new. We introduce the new year by donning new clothes and cleaning our homes from top to bottom to get rid of the grime of the previous year. People travel to reunite with family members, and children and the elderly are given red envelopes containing cash, called hongbao. It is a joyous time involving much food and laughter.

Chinese people love fireworks and firecrackers, and the smell and sound of both linger in the air for the entire 15-day holiday. The 15th day is known as the Lantern Festival and is the finale of the New Year festivities. On that day, the first full moon of the year appears, and a grand fireworks celebration takes place. We eat rice dumplings filled with sweets and hang colorful lanterns outside our homes and on the streets, which the full moon beautifully illuminates. The following day, everyone returns to their daily routines.

That year I returned to secondary school for my final semester. Because we were nearing graduation, the courses were more advanced, and we had more homework than before. No matter how hard I tried, I continued to struggle with mathematics. At the end of the semester, I narrowly passed my math test, scoring just over 60 out of 100 points. My language arts score was very high, while my scores in other subjects were so-so but sufficient to enable me to graduate.

After commencement, the school held a large graduation party. Students and teachers sang, danced, and played musical instruments. Classmates exchanged commemorative notebooks and wrote words of farewell. Wu and I sang and danced and received much applause. As the party was nearing an end, Mr. Hou called me aside. In his hands was a white piece of paper.

"Ah, Fengxian, time sure flies. I didn't expect we would be parting so soon. I have been very fond of you since you arrived at this school. In fact, I fell in love with you long ago, but I dared not tell you. I am telling you now on this final day of school because I am afraid I will never have another chance. I don't know if you want to or can accept my love, but I feel I must tell you. Here are my farewell words for you."

Mr. Hou held out a piece of paper. I was startled and speechless. Without uttering a word, I snatched the paper from his hand and ran. Wu caught a glimpse of me running and called me over.

"I just saw you talking to Mr. Hou. Show me what he wrote to you."

Wu was eager to read Mr. Hou's note, but after what had just transpired I wondered if I should show her. Before I could answer, she declared that we should first go back to our room, take a bath, then read it. Wu grabbed the paper from my hands, stuffed it in her pocket, and set off for our dormitory.

Wu was a lively girl and loved talking and laughing. She joked about the commencement party the entire way back. Meanwhile, I was silent and in a panic. I had no idea what Mr. Hou had written on that paper, but after our conversation I dreaded that it would make me another laughing stock of the school. I regretted letting Wu grab it out of my hand, yet we were like sisters, and I didn't want to hide anything from her. Soon we arrived back at the dorm.

"Fengxian, you don't look well," Wu said. "Are you tired? Go rest. I will prepare the bath water for you."

I sat on the bed and couldn't stop thinking about what had happened. I believed Mr. Hou was a decent man. I never saw him making fun of others, yet I wondered if on this occasion he was joking with me. Wu called me to the washroom. After bathing, we returned to our room. As soon as we lay down, Wu remembered the paper and quickly sat up. "I almost forgot. We need to read Mr. Hou's words of farewell to you." She took the paper out of her pocket and began to read aloud.

"To Fengxian:
Beyond the curtain, the rain is pattering,
Coming to an end are the colorful hues of spring.
Yet the cold of the morning still penetrates my quilt,
And when I awaken at dawn I recall I was just a passenger.
Last night I drank too much, for I hate goodbyes,
In heaven and on earth, spring ends with withered flowers
flowing in the river.
From Teacher Hou"

"He didn't write this many words to me. Maybe he's afraid I wouldn't understand. In fact, even some of what he did write to me I don't understand. No wonder Mr. Hou always praises you for your writing. You understand what he is saying."

"Actually, what he wrote is pretty straightforward. He is saying that we are parting with one another and don't know when we will meet again. He is trying to demonstrate his sadness and unwillingness to say goodbye."

"I'm tired," Wu said. "Are you sleepy?" With that, she set down the letter and quickly fell asleep.

I, on the other hand, was wide awake and couldn't stop thinking about what had happened. I was very thankful Mr. Hou didn't write anything frivolous on that paper. I had never seen him that nervous before, which I concluded meant that he was telling the truth. I had learned so much from Mr. Hou in my two years at the school. But did I love him? He was my teacher and my elder, and I respected him. After going around and around, I still couldn't figure out if what I felt was love or respect. I recalled how my primary school teacher Mr. You also gave me a similar shock. Why am I destined to encounter this kind of trouble at school? I was glad I would be returning home the next day.

The next morning, Wu shook me awake. "Fengxian, it's late. We must get up right now." We got out of bed and quickly packed our belongings. I said goodbye to my schoolmates and teachers, but Mr. Hou was nowhere to be found.

I was saddened to know that this would be my last time on the school grounds. As I passed through the iron gate a final time, I turned back to look at my beloved middle school. Mr. Hou was standing in the center of the courtyard waving at me. We stared at each other for several long seconds. Then I smiled, waved back, turned and walked away.

Wu and I walked together for a short distance and then parted. Both of us were in tears. I would miss her deeply. "Goodbye, Wu. I don't know when we will see each other again, but we can write letters."

The pushcart driver sent by my parents arranged my belongings in the cart. As I sat down, I recalled the day I departed for middle school, filled with wonder about what the next two years would hold. I glanced back at the school. "Farewell, my school. Farewell, my friends. The time has come for me to leave. I am returning to my boudoir." That was one thing that had not changed.

Sneaking Away to the
High School Entrance Exam

Adjusting to the slow monotony of life at Rongxia took some time. Boya and I had little to do but sit in our room and swap stories from school. Both of us had learned so much. More important, we had experienced a taste of independent life. We were eager for more.

However, by then our brothers were approaching school age. Our parents couldn't afford to educate all five of us, so they decided that Boya and I would have to stay at home. We were crestfallen. Boya had at least learned a skill that would make her employable one day. I had nothing tangible to show from my studies. I began to worry about whether I would be able to fulfill my dream of one day getting a job.

As the summer passed, Boya and I became increasingly discouraged and restless. One afternoon we joked about sneaking away from home to take the high school entrance exam. The more we talked about it, the more serious we became. We reckoned it would be harder for our parents to deny us further schooling if we had already shown we were qualified enough to continue. So on the morning of the exam, we told our parents that we wanted to visit our maternal grandmother for a few days. Mother was pleasantly surprised and agreed to let us walk there on our own.

The exams were held in the town of Hongling (Hōng-lǐng), the capital of our county, which was many hours' walk away. We were excited by the prospect of continuing our studies but a little daunted by the journey. Neither of us had ever been to Hongling. I recalled my classmates saying the main road to my secondary school led there, so that is the route we took.

After walking a few hours, we encountered more and more people on the road, which we interpreted as a good sign that we were on the right path. Soon we came across advertisements for school exams. We decided to take the exam for the Hongling Girls' Normal School and were given directions to the campus. Upon arriving, we were immediately led into a room filled with unfamiliar faces. The exam monitor, who was stern and serious, greeted us and led us to our seats.

Unfortunately, the mathematics exam was first. My heart raced and my hands shook, but I calmed down after a few minutes and worked my way through each of the problems. We handed in our tests when the bell rang and took a brief break. Boya was discouraged and pale. She was unable to finish the entire math exam and felt intimidated by the large number of students.

"Those questions were too difficult," she said. "It's impossible for me to pass." I tried to encourage her by telling her that I also had difficulty, but it didn't do any good.

After the break, we took the Chinese reading and writing exam. I felt very at ease. That was followed by a couple of other exams, which I did reasonably well on. We were quite tired when it was all over.

"If I had to guess, I'd say I passed, but that's just a guess," I said once we were outside.

"I didn't do well at all," Boya said hopelessly. "I'd be surprised if I passed."

That evening, we went to a small restaurant for dinner and then strolled through the streets of Hongling window-shopping. The town was lively and bustling, but we felt ill-at-ease in an unfamiliar place with little money in our pockets. The results of the test wouldn't be posted until the next day, so we had to find a place to stay for the night.

We checked into a small inn, but were too afraid to go to sleep. We decided to take turns being on watch. Boya said she wanted to sleep first, so I sat on my bed staring at the walls. From time to time, Boya shouted or laughed in her sleep. After a while, I got very tired and tried to wake her up to guard the door. But no matter how hard I shook her, she wouldn't wake. She opened her eyes and glanced at me once, but only for a brief moment. I tried pinching her nose and mouth to wake her up, but to no avail. Eventually, I fell asleep.

The next morning, we awoke to lots of noise in the street. We got up and rushed to the school to see the exam results. Posted on the wall was a red piece of paper listing the names of candidates who passed the test. The wall was surrounded by a large crowd. Some people looked at the list and walked away smiling while others were disappointed and sad.

As the crowd slowly dispersed, Boya and I inched our way toward the list. We scanned the paper. "I found my name!" I cried out, jumping up and down. Boya continued searching the list but failed to find her name. She was disappointed but congratulated me.

"Fengxian, your hard work hasn't been in vain. Even though I'm not on the list, I feel very happy and proud of you."

We returned to the inn to wash our faces and brush our teeth. After gathering our belongings, we checked out and went to a small restaurant for breakfast. The waiter insisted that we pay our bill before he would deliver any food. Boya reached into her pocket and discovered that our small pouch of money was gone. She asked me if I had it, but I didn't.

We frantically searched for the pouch, retracing all of our steps that morning. We returned to the inn and asked the innkeeper if he had seen our pouch.

"No, I haven't seen it," he said in an annoyed tone of voice.

"Will you let us back into our room to look for it?" Boya asked.

"There is no pouch in that room. Get out! Stop talking nonsense here."

We felt helpless. Both of us started to cry.

"Do you intend to stay here and cry for the rest of your lives?" the innkeeper screamed.

We had no choice but to leave and begin the long walk home.

Although I was hungry and thirsty, my excitement about passing the exam added energy to my step, so I walked fast. By contrast, Boya was disappointed with herself and walked listlessly. She spent most of her days sitting and embroidering, so she was also overweight. The long journey was more difficult for her. When we reached the halfway point, she called out that she needed a break and sat down beneath a tree. I walked back to accompany her.

"If I knew I would have to suffer this much, I wouldn't have gone to Hongling to take the exam," she said. "If we had more money, we could have separated it into two pouches. If one pouch was stolen, we would still have the other. Then we wouldn't be this hungry."

"I know you're hungry, so am I," I said. "Since both of us are starving, we should hurry home as soon as possible. Otherwise, we will only become hungrier." I stood up and caught sight of a small spring ahead. I raced over, thrust my hands into the cool water, and gulped it down.

"Boya, do you want some water?"

"Of course. Am I an immortal, requiring no food or drink?"

I tore a large taro leaf off a tree and folded it into a small bowl. I filled it with water and carried it to her. Quenching our thirst emboldened us to continue the journey. The sun set a few hours later, but we were still miles away from Rongxia.

"I can't walk any longer," Boya said, looking very pale. I reached out my arm to give her some support, but she collapsed on the ground. I was frightened and cried out for help.

Fortunately, there was a small shack nearby. A girl my age came out to investigate. When she saw Boya on the ground, she rushed inside and came back with an older man. The three of us carried Boya inside.

The old man hurriedly prepared some ginger and brown sugar soup for Boya. After a while, she regained consciousness.

"What are you young girls doing here?" he asked. "Where are you traveling from? Where is your family? Tell me so I can send them a message."

"Our home is not far from here. We went to Hongling to take the high school entrance exam. But we lost our purse and didn't have any money to buy food, so my sister fainted."

"I'll make something for you to eat," said the girl.

"Thank you, but please give the food to Boya first. She needs it more than I do."

The girl, whose name was Lin, prepared a bowl of rice, which I fed to my sister. Slowly, Boya began to regain her strength.

"We only had that one bowl of rice, which was supposed to be my father's, but I have some sweet potatoes you can eat, Fengxian," said Lin. Although I wasn't fond of sweet potatoes, that night I found them delicious. By the time we finished eating, it was pitch dark. The old man said we could stay there for the night and sleep in Lin's room.

Boya was exhausted and quickly fell into a deep slumber. I felt frightened by the silence and wondered if the old man and girl might harm us. Since Boya was asleep, I felt it was my responsibility to guard our safety.

"Where is your mother?" I asked Lin quietly.

Her eyes turned red and welled up with tears. "My mother died in a difficult childbirth not long ago. She gave birth to several sons, but all of them died. I only have one sister, but she has married. Now there are only two of us left in this family — my father who is over 60 and me." I felt very sorry for her.

"Your sister has fallen fast asleep. Why don't you close your eyes and sleep?"

I looked around the room and saw some textbooks and comic strips on a desk. "Are you reading those books?"

"Yes, but they aren't mine. I borrowed them from others. I've never attended school. I want to go very much, but my father can't afford it." Her words reminded me of everything that had happened on our trip. Boya and I had put ourselves at so much risk just for the chance to continue studying. I looked over at the girl and saw that she was asleep. Slowly, I let go of my anxiety and also fell asleep.

"Lin, get up!" the old man shouted outside our room the next morning. I opened my eyes, got out of bed, and opened the door. The old man stood hunched in the doorway puffing on a pipe.

"Lin, prepare some porridge for them so they have the energy to make it back home."

"Thank you, Uncle," I replied. "I will tell my parents to reimburse you for your kindness to us."

"I am old and have many illnesses. Tomorrow I may be dead. If I didn't have my daughter's company, I might have died long ago. In fact, I want to die. Living in this world is too sad for me."

"You still have your daughter. She is not only lovely and lively but also very filial. Look at her. How can you feel unhappy?" The old man coughed several times and then shuffled away. As I stood there watching him, I could see that the weight of his losses was slowly suffocating him. I felt deep compassion for Lin.

"Fengxian, is it morning?" Boya asked. "Last night I fell dead asleep."

"Boya, you are always so carefree and easily fall into slumber, while I was born a worrier and am always tired. Yes, it is morning, and this family is making us some food before we leave for our journey."

"Forgive me," she said and smiled. I could tell that her resentment from the previous day was gone.

I was deeply moved as I watched Lin prepare porridge for us. Although we were strangers, she and her father cared for us as though we were family. After we ate, we thanked them for their kindness and departed.

Energized by the food, Boya and I walked very fast. Soon, we arrived at my former middle school. We were passing the school gate when we unexpectedly ran into my old roommate Wu accompanied by another girl.

"Fengxian!" Wu said. "I have been looking for you. What a surprise that I meet you here. Your mother said you went to visit your grandmother and that she was going to send servants to escort you home. What are you doing here?"

"It's a long story," I said as we sat on the side of the road for a break. "Why did you go to my home?"

"My father and stepmother have betrothed me to a wealthy man twice my age. I don't want to marry him. I know you encountered a similar problem in the past. I thought you could give me some advice. I want to resist this marriage, but I am weak. I don't know what to do."

The girl accompanying Wu chimed in. "I still think that the best option is for you to leave home for a while. You can return after the storm."

"But where can I go?" Wu asked.

"Fleeing is not a solution," I said. "The only solution is to resist the marriage resolutely. They will give in when they see that you will never accept the marriage."

"No, they will never give in. My stepmother is very supportive of the marriage."

"What is your father's opinion? If your father listens to everything your stepmother says, then you have a big problem."

"Fengxian, we need to get home," Boya said impatiently. "You can discuss this later."

As we stood up to leave, Wu changed the subject. "Did you know that Mr. Hou no longer works at our old middle school? He has a daughter but no wife. His wife died a long time ago. Now he is about to get re-married. His fiancé is a teacher in Fengmen. Mr. Hou's paternal aunt introduced the girl to him. Mr. Hou didn't want to marry her, but his aunt threatened to no longer help him look after his daughter. His parents are dead, so he had no choice but to agree to the marriage. Now he has moved to Fengmen and is working there."

Boya became increasingly annoyed. "Fengxian, if you don't want to go home, I will go back myself." Wu and I said farewell, and then my sister and I headed home.

As we walked, I thought about what happened that last day of middle school, when Mr. Hou declared his love for me. Although Chinese society was slowly modernizing, it was still considered inappropriate for men and women to have any close contact. I never knew anything about Mr. Hou's private life. He always seemed so serious to me. Now it all made sense. He was as lonely as a lost, wild goose. He dared not voice his feelings about me until the last moment. I asked God to bless Mr. Hou with a good wife who would accompany him for the rest of his life and give him much happiness and comfort.

"Fengxian, what do you think Mother will do to us if she finds out we sneaked away to take the high school entrance exam?"

"She will scold us vehemently. I don't know if she will beat us. In the end, she is our mother. If she wants to beat us, we must endure it."

As we approached Rongxia, our youngest brother caught sight of us and raced over to greet us. "Have you brought me any candy?"

"No, brother, we haven't had a full meal ourselves for almost two days. We are starving."

Hearing our voices, Mother ran out of the house with tears in her eyes and hugged us. "You said you were going to visit your grandmother and would return after two days. Today is the third day. I sent servants to escort you back, only to discover that you never arrived. I was terrified and beside myself. Fengxian, tell me what happened."

"We want to continue going to school, so we sneaked away to take the high school entrance exam in Hongling. We lost our money pouch, so we couldn't buy anything to eat. We became very weak, and it took us a long time to walk back."

Mother began to scold us, but Father told her to calm down and asked us to continue our story. Soon we were surrounded by many relatives and friends, who listened intently to every detail of the story as though it was sensational news.

"We never would have expected two girls who had spent so much time isolated in their boudoir to brazenly travel on their own to the capital of the county," they said.

"Shame on you!" said Grandfather's concubine. "How dare you girls go to Hongling and sleep away from home. You must have engaged in other disgraceful acts. Shame on you!"

Father asked Qie to leave, but one of her daughters shouted back at him. "Shame on you, Jing! You swindled our money." Father became enraged and shoved them out the door. I had never seen him so angry, but even my good-tempered Father could stand only so much rudeness and contempt from Grandfather's concubine.

"So, how did you both do on the test?" Father asked.

"I failed," Boya said. "But Fengxian passed and has been admitted to Hongling Girls' Normal School."

"I've always known that my Fengxian is a talented girl," Father said, putting his arm around me. "You will have a bright future. I could see it in your eyes when you were very young."

Boya felt humiliated and retreated to our room.

"Father, I studied liberal arts in school, but Boya only learned embroidery. It's natural that she failed and I passed. Don't be too hard on her."

"I was just expressing how happy I am that you passed. I didn't intend to hurt your sister's feelings. Her decision to take the exam with you shows that she is not satisfied with what she has learnt so far." Father called Boya to return. In front of everyone, he made an announcement.

"Boya learnt Hunan-style embroidery in vocational school, and I have decided to send her to an advanced school to further her skills. I hope one day she can become a famous master of it." Boya smiled, and I whispered thank you to Father.

Mother prepared dinner after everyone left. As we ate, she asked us about the family that came to our aid. "I will instruct a servant to deliver some money and rice to express our gratitude," she said. "The next time you go on a long journey, make sure you have enough money. If you had not been saved by Lin and her father, who knows what would have happened."

The next day a couple of servants were sent to Lin's home. Before they left, I gathered some old Chinese language and math textbooks from my years at primary school, as well as some embroidered towels and a pair of embroidered shoes, to give to Lin.

For the next several days, Mother and Father argued incessantly about finances. Mother insisted that we didn't have the money to send Boya and me to school. My siblings and I had been accustomed to an affluent life, so we felt discouraged about our financial situation. Father finally agreed to keep Boya at home, but he continued to argue for me to attend school.

"It's a good opportunity for Fengxian. Even though we don't have the money, we can borrow it. You are her mother. Help her to live up to her potential."

Mother eventually gave in. That fall I entered high school.

Lessons in Sobriety

The next couple of years were uneventful. I felt very fortunate to have the opportunity to continue school, so I buried myself in my studies. Although our family's finances remained tight, my parents always found a way to pay my tuition.

I spent all of my summer and winter breaks at Rongxia. During one summer, an unforgettable spectacle took place that I still remember vividly. That year the government launched a severe crackdown on opium use. One afternoon the police came to search Rongxia for drug contraband. When Qie learned that the police had arrived at our home, she hurriedly gathered her opium paraphernalia and fled into the woods. The investigators scoured every inch of our house and managed to find some traces of the drug still left behind. They imposed a stiff fine on Grandfather.

After the police left, Qie returned from hiding. The moment Grandfather saw her, he flew into a rage.

"Do you know how much money you just cost me?"

"Calm down. Don't worry! We've been fined before. It's not a big deal."

"Not a big deal? Of course it's not a big deal to you. You're not the one who has to pay for this shameful habit. I have had enough of this! You are driving this family into financial ruin. I forbid you from ever smoking opium again!"

"Smoking opium is the one thing I look forward to each day, and you want to take it away? You are heartless! I have been smoking opium for decades. I can't just stop."

"My son was capable of giving it up, and you are, too!"

Grandfather stormed out of the house and ordered some servants to follow him. They went to one of the large Buddhist temples nearby that Grandfather had heard had a very effective method of getting people off opium. He asked the monks for assistance in ending Qie's habit. They agreed to help him in exchange for a large donation.

Late that afternoon, Grandfather and the servants returned to Rongxia accompanied by a monk. The servants carried a large wooden barrel about four feet wide and two feet high. The lid was large and heavy and had a big hole in the center. Grandfather ordered the servants to place the barrel in the garden and to fill it with water. Curious about what was transpiring, the entire family flocked to the garden to watch. As the sun set, Grandfather ordered Qie to stand between him and the barrel.

"Today I visited the temple and requested the help of this monk in ending your addiction to opium," Grandfather said to her sternly. "He has a very effective method. You are to listen and obey whatever he says. Do you understand?"

"What? No! I can stop smoking opium whenever I want on my own. I don't need the help of this monk or anyone else."

"Yes, you do."

"Qie, please take off your clothes and get in the water," the monk said politely.

"No! This is ridiculous!"

"If you don't get in yourself, we will force you in," Grandfather said.

Qie stood there motionless and assessed her options. After a few seconds, Grandfather ordered the servants to pick her up and toss her in the barrel. After Qie was in the water, the monk instructed them to place the lid over her neck, so that her head was sticking out of the hole. The monk secured the lid to the barrel and then took out a large stick and beat the lid while chanting. Periodically, the monk stopped, scooped some water out of the hole, and poured it over Qie's head.

Qie screamed for Grandfather and the monk to stop, but they ignored her. She struggled desperately to get out of the barrel, but couldn't loosen the lid. Eventually, she gave up. Under the moonlight, with her hair matted and wet, Qie resembled a water ghost. She looked pitiful and scary.

The monk stood above the barrel beating and chanting nonstop until 5 a.m. This spectacle went on for seven straight weeks, which in China is the traditional mourning period when a loved one dies. It is believed that during these 49 days, the person's spirit remains in the earthly world. In order to break the spirit of Qie's addiction, the monk forced her to undergo this treatment for 49 straight nights. Sometimes she screamed so loud in agony and frustration that she awakened Boya and me in the middle of the night. Our room was on the northeast edge of the garden. On those occasions, Boya and I got out of bed and peeked at Qie and the monk through our window.

After seven weeks of treatment, Qie's addiction to opium was successfully defeated. The monk returned to his temple. From then on, Qie never smoked opium. Since that summer, I have never heard of or seen this method again.

Shortly after Qie's summer episode, I departed to start another school year. I hadn't been back at school long when my youngest brother Rong became ill. From the time he was a baby, Rong had always had poor health due to a large growth that bulged out of his stomach. As a result, he was unable to play as vigorously as other children. Several times my parents invited a doctor to our home to assess his condition. The doctor decided that Rong needed to undergo surgery.

My parents made arrangements to take Rong by train to Changsha (Chǒng-shǒ), the capital of Hunan Province, where he would have the operation. I was pulled out of school to help Boya look after my two other brothers and care for the house while my parents were away. Rong's treatment was expensive and depleted what little money my parents had saved. I knew I would not be returning to school any time soon, if ever.

While my parents were away, Boya and I looked after our brothers and gave them lessons in reading and writing. In my spare time, I read the novel *Dream of the Red Chamber*, a famous Chinese classic. I became so engrossed in the story that I often stayed up reading into the wee hours of the morning. The more I read, the more I felt as though I were one of the characters. I experienced their pains and joys as though I were there with them. I often smiled and cried as I read.

When Qie's daughters saw how emotionally involved I had become in the book, they told their mother that I had turned into a mad bookworm. Soon the accusation spread beyond Rongxia. I was incensed and confronted them.

"How dare you tell people that I have gone mad and become a bookworm. You are illiterate and don't even know how to read or write!" The girls apologized and promised to stop talking about me that way.

One afternoon they came to our boudoir with a pack of Hunan cards and invited Boya and me to play and gamble with them. We were quickly taken in by the game. We abandoned all of our other hobbies and activities and indulged ourselves in playing cards day and night.

A Hunan deck is composed of cards imprinted with numerical Chinese characters. If you can make a series out of what is in your hand, you win. I was very good at it and frequently occupied the winner's throne. Even after Qie's daughters lost all their money to me, they still insisted on playing. They promised that if they lost they would pay me on the next holiday, when they would receive money. Of course, I agreed because I almost always won.

After several weeks, my parents returned with Rong. We were elated to see our brother doing so well. When Qie's daughters saw my mother, they greeted her politely. She was taken aback. "Since when have you started playing with them? Don't you still quarrel with them?"

"We have grown up," I said. "We understand a lot more now than before. We don't quarrel or fight with them anymore."

The next day Qie's daughters invited Boya and me to play cards, but we had to turn them down now that our parents were home. However, Boya really enjoyed it, so occasionally she and I sneaked away to play in their room. One day Mother discovered what we were up to. She stormed into Qie's daughters' room and dragged us home.

"You should not be spending your time playing cards and gambling! Why not spend your time learning something worthwhile? You worthless girls!"

Mother locked Boya and me in our room for the rest of the day and instructed us to examine ourselves. After a while, we saw how addictive and harmful playing cards could be. We understood why Father had so much difficulty leaving that gambling den and why Qie had become so addicted to smoking opium and playing mahjong. We resolved not to play cards with Qie's daughters anymore. I returned to reading *Dream of the Red Chamber*, followed by its sequel.

During one summer afternoon, I took a break from reading and went outside to enjoy the garden. As soon as I got outside, I overheard Father talking with some friends in the greeting room about the war.

"There is talk the Japanese army may be preparing for another offensive into Hunan Province," said one of Father's friends. "Anxiety in the capital Changsha is high. Japanese soldiers are cunning and cruel. Residents are scared and preparing for the outbreak of war."

The Japanese had tried to capture Changsha three previous times in 1939, 1941 and 1942 but never succeeded. By that summer of 1943, they were gearing up for another attack and had set their sights on seizing control of the Guangzhou (Gwŏng-jō)-Hankou railway, which ran through Changsha and our own Fengmen Station. Father knew that this time the threat was very serious. The war that had seemed so distant could spread to our own backyard.

"We should gather reserves of salt, grain, oil, and other food in case transportation is cut off," Father said. "If Japanese troops make their way to Huaguo, we must take refuge somewhere. Japanese soldiers will be concentrated in the west where the railroad and river are located. There will also be numerous divisions to the north near Changsha as well as possibly the east. Our best option is to flee south and hide deep in the hills. My wife has a sister who lives with her children in a cave in the hills. We can go there and hide."

The idea that Japanese soldiers might encroach on our area terrified me. I sat on one of the stone stools in the garden and began to imagine what might happen if the Japanese army entered Huaguo. Everyone had heard the horror stories of their brutal murders and rapes in Nanjing, but that had all occurred in the northern part of the country. None of us had witnessed such atrocities first-hand. At school, we held many rallies criticizing the Japanese invaders. I told myself not to worry, but it was difficult knowing the slaughter the Japanese had committed elsewhere.

Later Father saw me hunched over crying in the garden. He sat next to me and tried to comfort me, but he was also extremely worried. After a few minutes, we went inside to help Mother prepare for dinner. As we passed the study, I caught a glimpse of a shiny red paper lying across Father's desk with a couplet he had written. I went inside to look at it.

"One of our neighbors asked me to write something as a wedding gift for some newlyweds."

I read it and wondered how it could be considered a wedding gift: "Besieging Enemies from Two Wings Leads to Quick Victory; Breaking Frontlines in the Middle Requires Concerted Action." At the time, it didn't make sense to me at all. In retrospect, I see that Father knew everything was about to change. War was on the horizon, and soon it would infiltrate every aspect of our lives.

A Collegian and a Bride

Although everyone was frightened about the advance of Japanese troops to the outskirts of Hunan, for months day-to-day life remained the same in Huaguo, which was situated far away from the fighting.

One day while I was reading in my room, some of my friends from high school dropped by for a visit. They informed me that a new university named Lakeside College had opened on the banks of the Xiang River in Fengmen. They were on their way to take the entrance exam and invited me to join them. Since I hadn't graduated from high school, I thought it would be impossible for me to pass a college entrance exam. My friends insisted that admission would be easy because the school was new. In the end, they talked me into going with them. "How much harm could be done from just taking the test?" they asked.

I told Mother I was going out for a while and would return later that afternoon. We rode the ferry to Fengmen and then searched for the college, which was located close to Grandfather's former residence. We signed up for the exam and submitted our documents. Because I hadn't completed high school, I had to borrow a diploma from a friend to submit.

As soon as the tests were handed out, I became very nervous. In the end, the questions weren't too difficult and mostly addressed material I had already learned in high school. Still, I thought it would be too good to be true that I would pass the test and be granted admission. We were told that we would be notified of the results by mail once they were tallied.

I didn't say a word about the test to anyone in my family, not even Boya. After a couple of weeks, a letter from the school arrived addressed to my father.

"Congratulations, your daughter has been admitted to college," the mailman said.

"What?" Father asked with a confused look. He opened the letter and read it. "Where is Lakeside College?"

"It's near the water in Fengmen."

Father came straight to see me. He had a big smile on his face.

"There have been many male college students in the Chu family, but now we have our first female college student. How wonderful you are, Fengxian!" Soon I was surrounded by a large crowd of relatives and friends, all of whom were impressed that I could pass a college entrance exam without having finished high school.

"I am very humbled by your praise," I said. "In fact, I am a false college student. In order to take the test, I borrowed a high school diploma from a friend. I have been admitted only out of luck."

"What you did to get admitted doesn't matter," said Father. "What matters is that you are the first and only female college student in our family. Regardless of whether the college is new or old, unknown or renown, I am very happy and proud of what you have achieved."

I had dreamed of attending college since I was a little girl, but it was so rare for women to do so that I never thought my dream could actually become reality. In the end, all of my hard work and battles with Mother had paid off. I was ecstatic.

Mother was also proud of me, but she worried about how she and Father could afford the tuition. "Nowadays, many parents don't have the money to send their sons to college, let alone their daughters." I knew how hard my parents worked to sustain our family. I pledged to always be filial toward them out of appreciation for all they had toiled through to send me to school. I knew how blessed I was to have such a rare opportunity.

The next day I looked at the calendar to see how much time I had left before school started. I desperately wanted to know how my friends did on the exam, but all of them lived far away. There was no way to contact them. I hoped we would be able to remain together. Boya watched as I anxiously paced back and forth across our room.

"Fengxian, you are so lucky to be a college student. Don't pretend to be so unhappy and anxious. I know you just want to show off your good luck in front of me."

"Boya, we studied different things in school. Without your help and companionship through my difficulties, I never would have made it. I owe a huge debt of gratitude to you."

"I was just joking. I'm not jealous of you at all. Instead, I feel very proud of you. I take pride in my own luck to have as good a younger sister as you."

As we were leaving our room to go to the garden, my brother announced that my classmates had come to see me. They were all smiling, which I knew meant that they had also passed the exam. Mother invited them to stay for lunch. Afterward, we discussed what preparations needed to be made before the schoolyear started. They agreed to pick me up on the first day.

Minutes after my classmates left, an unexpected visitor arrived at our home. "There is a very pretty woman outside," one of my brothers said. "Mother and Father don't know her. She is looking for Boya." My sister and I returned to the greeting hall and discovered that it was Ms. Tang (Tŏng), the principal at Boya's embroidery school.

"Boya, I haven't seen you in such a long time," Ms. Tang said. "How are you doing these days?"

"Principal Tang, I'm doing fine, thank you. I never expected you would come to see me. Please don't be insulted that my family has no food prepared for you."

Ms. Tang turned and looked at me. "Boya often talked about her younger sister Fengxian. I am very pleased and honored to meet you in person. You are beautiful."

"Thank you, Ms. Tang."

My parents invited Ms. Tang to sit down and brought her some tea.

"I'm here today to be a matchmaker," she said. "My family owns the large corner store in Fengmen. Currently, my father is suffering from a chronic illness. He has been receiving treatment for a long time, but still he has not been healed. We have decided to arrange a marriage for my brother to dispel the ill omen hanging over our father. We hope this can help my father regain his health. My brother is a high school graduate. He is decent and handsome and a good man. After much consideration, Boya was the only girl I could think of that I would want to be my sister-in-law. She was my favorite student at the embroidery school."

Mother was overjoyed. For years, she had fretted that Boya and I wouldn't be able to marry into good families. "We are honored that you have chosen Boya," Mother said. "We must prepare a special meal to celebrate."

She and Father rushed to the kitchen to begin preparing dinner. Boya and I stayed in the greeting hall to entertain Ms. Tang. I thought I should give them some time to speak alone, so I got up to leave. Ms. Tang insisted that I stay.

"Fengxian, what's your view on this proposal?" she asked. "Your opinion is also very important."

"A girl's marriage is a matter for her parents and the matchmaker. We girls dare not interfere. However, Principal Tang, your brother is not only wealthy but also educated. I'm afraid the status of our family doesn't match yours."

"Don't be so polite. These days I think a person should be able to freely choose his or her own spouse. That's why I would also like to hear Boya's opinion."

"I don't have the right to make such a decision," my sister said. "If my parents agree to it, I will not disagree. I like the idea of free marriage, but so far no one around here has yet to dare break away from traditional customs."

Soon the sun began to set. Father invited Principal Tang to stay for dinner. The table was covered with special dishes.

"I know Boya's grandfather was a famous businessman who exported tea abroad," Principal Tang said. "Your family was very wealthy. Your ancestors were rich, powerful, and educated. I'm afraid my family can't match the Chus."

"No, no, no," Father said. "Currently your family is the richest and most powerful in Fengmen. Your shop is the most well-known in town."

Principal Tang and Father exchanged such praises for quite a long time until both felt comfortable that the other was sincere about the marriage.

"It's a perfect match," said Mother. "Boya is blessed to have the opportunity to be your sister-in-law. Thank you for your proposal. We will discuss it and let you know very soon."

It was dark by the time dinner was over, so Principal Tang stayed the night in one of our guest rooms. She left after breakfast the next day.

As soon as Principal Tang departed, my parents asked Boya what she thought about the proposal. Boya was silent. Mother looked at her in dismay.

"This family is the best in Fengmen. Even if you requested a matchmaker to look for such a match, you would likely never find one. There were many girls at your vocational school, but Principal Tang chose you. Boya, you should feel honored."

Father also expressed his support. "Boya, you learned embroidery at vocational school. You are not like Fengxian, who studied liberal arts. She can further her studies in college, but you can't. You can find an embroidery job, but the work is difficult. Why not choose to be a housewife in such a rich family? You can live leisurely for a lifetime."

I agreed with my parents that it was an excellent opportunity, but I kept my mouth shut. Boya continued to remain silent on the matter, which I found very curious. When we were alone, I asked her what she really thought.

"I know what kind of person I am. I don't have ambitious goals like you, Fengxian. What Father has said is very clear and reasonable. I have no reason to disagree."

"Have you ever seen Principal Tang's brother?"

"It was a girls' school. There were no boys on campus. Of course I haven't seen him."

"What if there's something wrong with him? What if he's disabled in some way? What then?"

Boya was startled at the thought. "That's impossible. Principal Tang wouldn't dare trick me like that."

"In this world, anything can happen."

"Fengxian, you're right. Let's talk to Father before it's too late."

I hurriedly looked for Father and asked him to come to our room.

"Have you and Mother made a decision?" we asked him.

"Since Boya doesn't object to it, we see no reason to turn down the offer."

"Father, Boya is too shy to ask this question, so I will. If there is something wrong with Principal Tang's brother, for example, if he is disabled, what would we do if we have already agreed to the marriage?

It doesn't necessarily mean they don't get married, but shouldn't she know beforehand?"

"I don't think Principal Tang is a duplicitous person."

"Maybe so, but let's play it safe. Why not invite him over for dinner?"

"I doubt your mother will agree to it, but let's go and ask."

Not surprisingly, Mother was completely against the idea. "The Tangs are a wealthy and powerful family. I don't believe they would cheat us. Her brother is rich and has status. Do you think he would be willing to come to our house just to be sized up by you? Making such a request is very impolite. Boya doesn't object to this marriage. I know this must be Fengxian's idea. Don't listen to her."

"Mother, marriage is one of the most important events in a person's life," I said. "If a person doesn't marry well, he or she will never be happy. I don't think it's asking too much to invite him to dinner."

"Your father and I didn't see each other before we married, but you can see we are a perfect match."

Mother clearly wouldn't budge, so Father and I gave up and walked away. The next day, Father went to Fengmen to go shopping. He was all smiles when he returned.

"Boya, Fengxian, can you guess why I am so happy today?" We could smell that he had been drinking. "Today I went to Fengmen to see Boya's future husband. I sized him up and down and saw every detail of him. I even know how many hairs he has on his head!" My sister and I burst out laughing. Mother came to see what the commotion was about.

"Today I went to the Tang's store and bought a few items. Principal Tang's brother was working behind the counter. He is a good-looking man and appears gentle and polite."

"It sounds like you will have a happy marriage, sister," I said.

"Thank you, Fengxian. Thank you for your support."

"I can't believe my little girls are all grown up," Father said, shaking his head and smiling with pride. "It seems like it wasn't that long ago that I was teaching you how to read and write. Soon you will both be gone. One at college and the other married to one of the best families in the area. You have both made the Chu family very proud."

"Your father is right," Mother said, with a sense of calm that I hadn't seen in a long time. "It will feel empty around here without the two of you. But that is the bitter sweetness of being a parent, which both of you will taste for yourselves one day."

PART TWO

Commander Han Arrives

A Surprise Love Letter

Soon the time to depart for college was upon me. The day we were to report to school, my friends dropped by to pick me up. Mother gave me cash to pay the tuition and instructed a servant to carry my luggage to the campus. In the past, whenever I parted with my family, it was a tearful goodbye. This time I felt happy and relaxed. Only Boya was choked up.

"I'll be back before you know it, Boya. Look after our little brothers. I'll miss you," I said as I set off with my classmates.

Each of us was the first woman in our families to attend college. It had been a lifelong dream for all of us. Now suddenly it was a reality. We felt proud and ecstatic and couldn't wait to discover what lay ahead. We were young, eager for knowledge, and determined to make something of ourselves.

After registering, the incoming class gathered in the auditorium to listen to the college president's welcome speech. The president discussed the pitiful state of our country and the world, which were deeply mired in war. He criticized Japanese soldiers for slaughtering and enslaving our countrymen and called upon every student to fight to defend China. He encouraged us to study diligently so we could make a positive contribution to our war-torn world. The speech was inspiring and aroused thundering applause.

In the beginning, I felt self-conscious about not having completed high school and having borrowed a friend's diploma to qualify for the entrance exam. Whenever I spoke with students I didn't know, I ended the conversation quickly because I feared my words might divulge this secret. There were other students who hadn't finished high school, but among them I seemed to have the strongest sense of inferiority and guilt about my dishonesty. My friends encouraged me to relax.

"Fengxian, don't look down on yourself. Otherwise, you will feel depressed and have no enthusiasm to study. As long as you study hard and persevere, you will succeed. There's no need to worry!"

I took their advice. After a while, my anxiety and sense of inferiority eased. From then on, I was always in a cheerful mood.

In the early spring of 1944, my friends and I were strolling around campus one day at dusk when we heard the sounds of soldiers and horses marching on the road next to the Xiang River. We raced to the edge of the grounds to investigate. We saw a long line of Chinese troops for as far as the eye could see. They looked exhausted, haggard, and somber.

"The soldiers have been deployed to defend our area against a Japanese attack," a school administrator informed us.

The terrible war that had seemed so distant had now made its way to our backyard. Everyone felt uneasy.

During a holiday a few weeks later, my fellow students and I took to the streets to demonstrate against Japan's aggression. We sang, danced, and gave other performances, all of which contained a message of resistance against the Japanese. That afternoon we were allowed to go home for a half day to celebrate the rest of the holiday with our families.

On my way to Rongxia, I saw Chinese soldiers everywhere. Many of them appeared to have taken up residence in villagers' homes. I had never witnessed such a scene and began to feel anxious. Suddenly I heard someone calling my name. I looked up and saw father's cousin, Aunt Chen, waving at me from her doorway. I walked over to greet her.

"Fengxian, are you back for the holiday? Come have dinner with us. You can return home later."

"Thank you, Aunt Chen, but my home is very near. I have to return to school tomorrow, so I don't have much time."

Aunt Chen pointed to the troops in her house and shook her head. "Half of my house has been occupied by soldiers. In such a chaotic time, why even bother going to school? You should stay with your family at home where it's safe."

We watched in silence as soldiers walked back and forth across her property, then I said goodbye and left. As I was making my way back to the road, I heard some soldiers laughing. "What a pretty girl! What family is she from?"

Like any woman, I felt proud when I heard someone praise my beauty, but school was my number one priority at the time. I had no interest in men.

As I approached Rongxia, one of my little brothers raced out to greet me. "Have you brought me any candy?" he asked.

I foresaw that this would happen and had prepared beforehand. "Here you are," I said, as I put some sweets in his hand. When I walked into the house, my parents were surprised to see me.

"Fengxian, what are you doing here?" Father asked. "Why didn't you notify us that you would be back for the holiday? We would have sent some workers to pick you up. Today is different from the past. Chinese troops are everywhere. You have to think about your safety."

Mother hurriedly finished cooking, and then all of us sat down and enjoyed dinner together. My parents explained that a number of troops had been stationed at Rongxia and that Boya and I needed to be cautious.

"We don't know whether these men are good or bad," Mother said. "To be safe, don't spend time in the garden or the greeting hall. Stay with your sister in your boudoir."

After dinner, Boya and I returned to our room. I inquired about the status of her marriage.

"We became formally engaged a couple of days ago, so now it's official. The Tang family wants to hold the wedding ceremony soon."

"Boya, you are so fortunate to have the opportunity to marry a good man."

The next morning, I prepared my things to return to school. The servants weren't available to escort me, so Father and Mother offered to accompany me.

"Father, I'm an adult now. I know how to protect myself. Don't be afraid of the troops. I came back alone yesterday, so please let me go back by myself." He eventually agreed but told me to be careful.

As I was walking toward Aunt Chen's house, I saw her waiting on the road. She invited me inside for lunch, but I declined. She walked with me for a while. I could tell she had something she wanted to say.

"Fengxian, when you were here last evening, did you happen to see a machine gun commander? The soldier who was cleaning his gun in front of the door and whose clothes were stained by engine oil?"

"No, I didn't notice any particular soldier. I don't remember any of them."

"After you left, the commander was very excited. He rushed over to your uncle and asked about your name and family. Your uncle told him that you live at Rongxia and are from a wealthy family. Your uncle asked why he wanted to know about you, but the commander grinned and didn't reply. Your uncle was suspicious of the man and told him you are a smart and beautiful girl who is studying at university. He explained that your mother is very old-fashioned and you seldom go out of your boudoir except to go to school. I could tell he was interested in you, so I chimed in. I told him that you are a college student, that many young men from rich families want to marry you, but that you aren't willing to get married right now because you want to concentrate on your studies. I said I doubt you would be willing to be with a soldier like him. His face turned red."

"Aunt Chen," I said, "thank you for telling me, but I am not interested in talking about this anymore." I tried to walk away, but she wouldn't drop the subject. "Aunt Chen, why do you insist on talking about a silly soldier I don't even know?"

"He didn't seem like a bad man. On the contrary, he seemed very decent. And he was handsome. I know you would agree if you ever saw him."

I said I was late for school and rushed away. By the time I arrived back at campus for lunch, I had lost my appetite. Everyone felt anxious after their visits home. That afternoon my friends energetically discussed how we could defend our area from the Japanese, but I stayed quiet.

That evening we were lounging on the grass when, a short distance away, we saw some of our male classmates laughing and waving an envelope. They began to walk toward us.

"Look everyone! Can you guess whose love letter this is?"

We assumed that it was for the oldest girl in our class. However, the boys looked straight at me and shouted, "It's Fengxian's letter!" My face turned bright red, and I felt dizzy. The boys waved the letter in the air and started to open it. Fortunately, one of my girlfriends snatched it from them. My friends and I returned to our dorm.

I looked carefully at the envelope. There was no name or address of the sender. The outside simply read: "To Fengxian … my name is in the letter."

"Fengxian, who is it from?" my friends asked.

"Honestly I have no idea. Maybe it's the man Aunt Chen was telling me about."

"Who is that?"

"I don't really know," I replied. I opened the letter and read it aloud.

"Dear Miss Fengxian, how are you? Since the day I first saw your beautiful face, I have not been able to erase you from my memory. Perhaps, as the saying goes, it is God's arrangement that I should encounter such a beautiful woman as you. If it hadn't been decreed by Providence, surely I would have failed to meet you. I beg you to give me a chance to be your friend, and then from your friend to your companion. I understand that you are a modern girl with a modern mindset. From your aunt and uncle, I know you are a noble girl with an unshakable aspiration to further your studies. I admire your perseverance and determination. Learning is an endless endeavor. Try hard, my friend. I hope you make great progress each and every day. Company Commander Han Weiluan (Hŏn Wā-lwŏn; the name Weiluan means a strong, exceptional man)"

My girlfriends were impressed by the letter and the gesture. They encouraged me to be open-minded about Commander Han.

"There's nothing to be shy of! Just as he said, we are girls of a new generation, so we should break the old shackles and enjoy freedom and equality with men. We can tell he is well-educated and different from those belligerent soldiers who only know how to fight in the battlefield."

I was dumbfounded and didn't know what to think.

"We hope you can become a happy couple in the future."

"A happy couple? I have never even seen him. How can we become a happy couple?"

"This is the evidence," one of them said, as she carefully folded the letter and placed it in my pocket. "Cherish it, Fengxian."

Commander Han Visits Campus

My male classmates teased me endlessly after I received Commander Han's letter. Whenever they saw me, they said, "Mrs. Company Commander, why aren't you on the front lines?" I was mortified.

One day the company commander made a surprise visit to Lakeside College. It was a Sunday, and the atmosphere on campus was relaxed. One of the guards on duty escorted the commander around the grounds as he searched for me. They found me relaxing with my friends under the shade of a large tree, where we had taken refuge after jogging around the school sandpit. The commander walked straight up to us and bowed.

"Hello, everyone. I am Han Weiluan, a machine gun company commander. I've come to visit Fengxian. Please do me a favor and don't leave. Let me join you."

The commander was wearing a military cap and uniform, which had been neatly pressed and was adorned with insignia indicating his rank. A black leather belt and holster were strapped tightly across his waist, and the handle of a pistol stuck out. He was of medium build, neither tall nor short, neither fat nor thin. He stood poised and upright and radiated the demeanor of an officer.

I was so embarrassed that I wanted to bury my head in the sand. My entire body became flushed. Fortunately, my girlfriends were bolder and calmer than I and knew how to handle the situation.

"Commander Han, please sit down and join us," one of them said. "Please don't mind that we don't have anything to serve you."

The commander smiled, took off his cap, and sat on the grass. He asked my friends about the school and our studies. I listened quietly and didn't utter a word. The commander seemed friendly but quiet. He didn't speak an iota of frivolity.

"I'm from Guangdong (Gwŏng-dōng) Province. I'm also a college graduate from the Whampoa Military Academy." From the way he spoke and carried himself, I could tell he was well-educated and an upstanding officer. After a few minutes, the commander stood and said he had to return to his company. He handed me a letter and smiled. He invited my classmates and me to visit him in the field.

As soon as the commander left, the teasing started again. My girlfriends and I took refuge in our dorm. My friends were excited and insisted that I immediately open the letter and read it aloud. This time I recognized the elegant handwriting.

"Dear Fengxian, how are you? This is my second letter to you. I have made up my mind that today I will give you this letter in person. I really want to talk with you. I know you must be surprised to see this strange soldier coming from afar to visit you. But human beings are the noblest creatures in the world because we have affection and the ability to love. When you fall in love with me, you will understand better why I am doing what I am now. Am I right?

You may look down on me because I am just a soldier far away from home. I have asked myself if I can match such a graceful lady like you. I have nothing but a pure heart, which has fallen deeply in love with you, and a sturdy body inherited from my parents, which I cherish. I am a decent, upstanding man, and am proud to say I have few bad habits. I have traveled many places in China. My childhood was good and carefree.

I have never courted a woman. Although some girls have been interested in me in the past, I declined them all as they did not interest me. I never cared. But now I know I've fallen in love. From the moment I laid eyes on you, I was attracted to you. Since then, I haven't been able to think about anything but you and your gentleness and graceful figure. You have left a deep impression on my heart. Now I cannot maintain my reserve, so please forgive my straightforwardness and accept

this heart, which adores you so much. Be my friend, will you?
Yours truly, Han Weiluan"

Commander Han's visit ignited a storm on campus, and I was at the center. The college president called me and my roommates to his office and scolded me severely.

"Fengxian, you should not be wasting your time with a man. I am ordering you to return home. This visit has had a negative impact on other students. Our nation is currently in crisis. People of your generation should be demonstrating their patriotism and focusing on how to contribute to the war against Japanese aggression. The last thing you should be doing is spending time with a man."

I was devastated. I lowered my head and cried. My classmates argued vehemently on my behalf. "Sir, it's not Fengxian's fault. Commander Han initiated all of this. Please give her another chance." They persisted. After a while, the president caved in. He said I could stay as long as Commander Han didn't visit again.

When I returned to the dorm, I threw myself onto my bed. Why was I so unfortunate to keep encountering these romantic situations at school? I pledged to publicly chastise the commander if he visited again. I knew that if my parents ever found out, my situation would be even worse. Mother would force me to quit university. I cursed Commander Han for the trouble he caused, yet at the same time part of me was intrigued by his gentleness, politeness, and persistence.

Fortunately, it was late in the school year and classes soon finished. The commander was unaware of my problems at school and thankfully did not contact me again for the remainder of the school year. At the end of the semester, my classmates and I packed our belongings and returned home for summer break. My parents sent a servant to carry my luggage and escort me home. On the walk back, I asked him if there was any news about Rongxia.

"Chinese soldiers have cut down many of the trees and bamboo in the area to construct defenses against the Japanese, but the large banyan tree on your family's property remains untouched. The soldiers were preparing to cut it down when your father stopped them. To thank them for preserving the tree, your father invited several officers to have lunch today at your home."

As we passed Aunt Chen's house, I noticed that there were no longer any troops on her property. I wondered if they had been transferred elsewhere. Perhaps that was why Commander Han hadn't contacted me again. I breathed a sigh of relief.

As we walked, I saw and heard soldiers building trenches and air raid shelters. Part of a hill across from our house had been leveled to form a training ground. Impassioned anti-Japanese slogans were hanging everywhere. The area was almost unrecognizable. At that moment, the gravity of the situation sank in.

When we reached Rongxia, one of my brothers ran out to greet me and took my schoolbag. We walked hand-in-hand the rest of the way. My parents and Boya also came out to greet me.

"I know it's not great timing," Father said, "but we invited some officers and their wives for lunch today. Boya and you should serve them hospitably. They know all about our family and have been very respectful toward us. We want to maintain a good relationship with the soldiers and offer whatever help we can. Be sure to be polite today."

Boya and I went to our room. Neither of us felt like attending the lunch, but we had no choice. I was tired from the long walk home and year-end exams, whereas Boya was nervous that we wouldn't know the proper way to wait on our guests.

"We have been so sheltered our whole lives that we rarely talk to anyone but our own family," she said. "What if we're too dull and don't know how to entertain them? Maybe they will laugh at us."

"Boya, don't worry. The fact that we have been so sheltered makes us rare and extraordinary. What's so wrong with being extraordinary?"

"You're right. We're pretty and young and irresistible. Wait, maybe that's our parents' aim! Maybe they are trying to show us off. I'm already engaged, so I guess the target is you! If that's the case, we should look our best."

Boya put on a white, flowery cheongsam, light-colored stockings, and white leather shoes. Against this backdrop, her dark hair and eyes sparkled. Boya was more buxom than me, which made her look even more elegant. She tried to talk me into wearing makeup, but I felt it was inappropriate to bring such attention to myself because I was still a student.

"What I'm wearing right now is fine. It's not like I'm going to meet the man I'm going to marry. "

"You must at least change into a clean dress. This one is dirty and sweaty from your walk home."

I put on my yellow school uniform, and then both of us went to the main room. Father introduced us to everyone. Boya and I were too shy to make eye contact with anyone, so we kept our heads down. Father introduced each of the officers to us, announcing their names and ranks. All but one of the officers wore clean, pressed uniforms and shiny black shoes. The last officer to be introduced was dressed in a raggedy, old uniform stained with engine oil.

"This is machine gun company commander Han Weiluan," said Father, pointing to the unkempt man. I immediately recognized the commander, who acted like he didn't know me. I didn't say a word. Boya, Mother, and I sat down at the table reserved for wives and children.

The officers ate and drank heartily the entire afternoon. After a while, many became quite drunk. Some went outside to vomit, while others fainted, laughed, and cried loudly. Father had a high tolerance for alcohol and was the most coherent man at the table. By early evening, all of the men but Commander Han had been carried away by their wives or soldiers.

The machine gun commander was the only officer not to touch a drop of alcohol. While the other men were having a raucous time, he strolled around our house reading the scrolls, appreciating the artwork and furniture, and playing with my younger brothers. Periodically, he sneaked a glance at me, but when our eyes met we said nothing and acted like we didn't know one another. At times, he appeared to be as pure and child-like as my brothers.

"All of the other officers are drunk. Why aren't you drunk?" one of my brothers asked the commander. "Father never gets drunk no matter how much he drinks. You're just like him!" We all laughed. Father stood and asked Commander Han to accompany him to the garden where he introduced the name of each plant and flower.

Boya and I returned to our room, and she rehashed the evening. "Did you see how that one commander was so drunk that he called out for his mother? It was hilarious but also pathetic. Father wasn't drunk at all. I think that made a very deep impression on the officers. Did you notice that machine gun company commander? Everyone was neatly dressed except him. He looked like a dirty soldier. He also looked very young. I don't believe that he is actually a company commander."

The more she talked about Commander Han, the more annoyed I got. I wasn't in the mood to listen to her go on and on. Luckily, at that moment, one of my brothers walked in.

"I like that machine gun company commander. We had a good time playing together. Too bad he had to leave. Fengxian, he asked me to give you this letter." I reached for it, but Boya was closer and snatched it away.

"Fengxian, how could you hide this from me? You never used to hide things from me. What is going on with you and this man? If you don't tell me, I will go and give this letter to our parents."

"Boya, I'm sorry. I didn't tell you earlier because there wasn't any time, and I didn't expect him to be here. I could really use your help in solving this problem."

I explained in detail everything that had happened up to that point. Boya was so absorbed in the story that she didn't say a word even after I stopped talking.

"Boya, say something. Have you been listening to me?"

"Yes, don't worry. I'm trying to think of a way the two of you can have a modern marriage, not one arranged by our parents."

"This isn't a joke. I was severely scolded by the college president. I'm afraid I can't hide this from our parents much longer. Anyway, Mother would never agree for me to marry a soldier. I have never given Commander Han any hope that we could be together. I have never even said one word to him. I think he knows it is unrequited love."

"I can't believe Aunt Chen hasn't spoken to our parents about him. Fengxian, I think you should give this relationship serious consideration. But to do that, you need to get to know one another better, and that means you must write to each other. A person's character and temper are reflected in his words. If you want to know how sincere he is and what kind of man he is, you must write back to him. Brother can deliver the letter to the commander. He'll know not to tell our parents."

It was good advice. Even though Commander Han had already brought me so much trouble, I was moved by his words and his persistence. Boya was right. I needed to know more about this man. That evening I wrote Commander Han my first letter. Brother said the commander was ecstatic when he received it.

After that, Commander Han wrote to me every few days. Soon I had accumulated a large stack of letters, all of which were honest and heartfelt. He wrote about his outlook on life, the war, and his family. None of his words were flirtatious. I could see that he really was a decent man. By then, I had already fallen deeply in love but didn't realize it.

Matchmaker Aunt Chen

That summer everyone in the family was busy in one way or another preparing for Boya's wedding. To pay for the dowry, Father sold a portion of the small amount of land still in his possession after his gambling fiasco, after which our family's finances got even tighter. Mother and Boya created hand-made pillowcases, quilts, bed sheets, clothes, and shoes for the wedding. The pieces were exquisite and colorful. Everyone praised their skills.

Commander Han continued to reside at Aunt Chen's house just down the road from Rongxia. Occasionally, he would come to visit my family, but he never tried to see me alone, which would have been considered inappropriate. The commander's uprightness further strengthened my and Boya's favorable impression of him.

One day, as we were working on Boya's dowry, Aunt Chen came to our home for a visit. She had a big smile on her face and announced to Mother that Commander Han wanted to marry me.

"Aunt Chen, how dare you make such an absurd request. Don't you have any concern for Fengxian's happiness? Soldiers' lives are on the line every minute. No one knows who will or won't be alive tomorrow. Do you want Fengxian to be a young widow? No! I will never agree to this marriage. Don't waste your time talking to me about it." Then Mother stormed out of the room.

I apologized to Aunt Chen for Mother's rudeness. Boya suggested Aunt Chen speak to Father about the marriage. At that moment, Father entered the room to see what the commotion was about. Aunt Chen informed him about Commander Han's marriage proposal.

"How is it possible that this man has fallen in love with Fengxian when she and Boya never leave their room? Fengxian, tell me what's going on. Don't worry. I won't get mad."

I was too embarrassed to speak, so Boya relayed the story from beginning to end. "Fengxian has received so many letters from Commander Han that they fill a whole box!"

"How did he send her these letters? Did he sneak over here on his own?"

"No, Father, brother took the letters back and forth."

"I can't believe what you have done!" Father screamed at me. "There better not have been anything inappropriate. You know your mother could be held to blame for this, too."

Father had never spoken so harshly to Boya and me. We both began to cry. Aunt Chen remained quiet, but I could see the regret on her face. After a few minutes of silence, Father's face began to loosen, and then he smiled.

"Fengxian, I know you are a smart and stubborn girl with modern views. I hope you stay that way. I supported you about school, and I will support you in solving this problem. I now understand the saying, 'though flowers may be locked in a garden, their fragrance wafts far and wide with the spring breeze.' Our flower Fengxian is so charming. She is our mysterious gift from heaven."

"What are you discussing here?" Mother asked as she re-entered the room. "Don't think for one minute that I will agree to this. After all we have done to put Fengxian through school, she engages in this type of behavior. Writing letters to a soldier! It's shameful."

"Don't be too hard on her," Father said. "Our daughter has grown up. It's natural that she has fallen in love and is thinking about marriage."

"Of course I want my girls to marry one day — but not a soldier."

"There are hundreds of millions of soldiers in this world. Not all of them are going to die on the battlefield. Are they to remain life-long bachelors?" Father asked.

"I don't care if soldiers marry or not. I just forbid my daughters from marrying them. On top of that, I have heard many times about how difficult life can be for women in Guangdong Province. I have heard that men and women, young and old, must work in the fields day after day through rain and wind. Their skin is dark, they are dirty, and their personalities can be ferocious. Cantonese men often have three or four wives. Commander Han could already have a wife. Fengxian, if you marry this man blindly, you may toil to death in the field under the summer heat. Have you given thought to any of these things? I gave birth to you and bore the hardship of raising you. I will not let you suffer and die like this."

Mother's eyes were filled with tears. I could see that she was sincere. Much of what she said made sense. Father tried to calm her down. "These problems can be easily solved. We can send someone to his home in Guangdong to look into his background. Then we will know the truth and can make a decision as to whether to go through with the marriage. We shouldn't refuse the proposal outright now."

"Commander Han and his men have been staying at my house for quite some time," said Aunt Chen. "I have asked his men what kind of person he is. No one has ever heard him mention a wife. If you don't trust me, you can go and ask them yourselves. I'm not here to earn money from matchmaking. I just want my niece to marry a good husband."

"Stop fighting!" I screamed. "I've made up my mind not to marry Commander Han. I will stay single and celibate. Don't worry about me." I was sick of listening to them quarrel and left to go to the garden.

For several minutes, I sat alone crying under the shade of a large tree. My tears finally stopped when a beautiful Impatiens in full bloom caught my attention. I approached it and saw that its stem and leaves were withered and dry. I gave it some water. When a breeze came, the flower seemed to nod to me in gratitude. I watched as many butterflies and bees circled the flower to gather pollen. Which one was the flower waiting for?

After a couple of hours, Boya joined me in the garden. She informed me that Father had sent word to our maternal uncle to come help him resolve the dilemma over Commander Han. "Don't worry, Fengxian, you will marry him. Mother always listens to her big brother."

I was grateful to Father for always supporting me. Usually it is fathers who are strict and mothers kind, but in our family it was the opposite. When Uncle arrived on his bicycle, we immediately went to greet him.

"Fengxian, your father told me everything about Commander Han," Uncle said. "Do you love him? Do you think his love for you is true? This is very important. Don't be shy."

"Uncle, Commander Han is a good man. I believe his love for me is true. I have never spoken one word to him. We have only written letters expressing our attraction to one another. I admire him, but I have never promised him anything as I knew there would be huge resistance to this marriage. Don't worry, I don't intend to marry him."

"Fengxian, I'll try to persuade your mother. Your mother never went to school. She is illiterate, old-fashioned, and stubborn. Don't blame her. Is there any mother in this world who doesn't want her children to be happy? Now, show me all the letters from Commander Han. Your father and I will read them and make a decision."

After Uncle and Father read all the letters, they agreed that Commander Han was from a good family and was a decent, well-educated man with a sincere heart. They believed we would be a good match. The problem was convincing Mother to allow me to marry him. Uncle called her to join us.

"Brother, I will never agree to this, so don't try to persuade me. I would rather die than allow Fengxian to marry this officer."

"Sister, listen. During my time in the army and then as an accountant and political secretary, I've been to many places in this country, including Guangdong. I have many Cantonese friends and colleagues. They are polite, traditional, and gentle. Sun Yat-sen was from Guangdong and so are many rich tycoons in Hong Kong and Southeast Asia. The province borders the sea and has abundant, delicious seafood. People there are well-fed and well-educated and have good manners. Their houses are equal to, and sometimes better than, those in Hunan. Commander Han comes from a well-to-do family. Both of his parents are doctors. They don't need to worry about what to eat or what to wear. Their family is a perfect match with yours. Don't listen to the rumblings and rumors about what farm life is like in Guangdong because Fengxian won't be living in such a home. Don't be so stubborn. Otherwise, your feudalistic thinking may destroy Fengxian's golden opportunity of marrying a good husband. Sister, look around this room. It is filled with items for Boya's dowry, which has brought this family close to bankruptcy. If you were to marry Fengxian to a similarly rich family, how much would it cost? You don't have the money to marry Fengxian to another wealthy family. If Fengxian marries Commander Han, you can be free of the burden of a dowry. All you have to prepare is some bedding and clothes. There is no question that they will be a happy couple. Please, consider what I am saying."

"If all of you are for this marriage, I alone cannot reverse the result. Clearly, no one cares about my opposition. You have made your decision." She stood up and angrily left the room.

For a few seconds, there was silence, and then everyone smiled and congratulated me. Aunt Chen returned home to inform Commander Han of the good news. Father and uncle wrote letters to the commander's mother and brother requesting their approval of the marriage.

Up to that point, I had avoided thinking about the prospect of marrying Commander Han because I didn't want to be disappointed. Now it appeared that my secret wish was coming true. I couldn't believe it. My parents had actually consented to my marrying a man of my own choosing — not theirs. I was going to be the first person in the Chu family not to have an arranged marriage but rather one built on friendship and love. Chinese society really was changing.

Marching Orders

Ill of us anxiously awaited the reply from Commander Han's family. Father feared that he had sent the letters to the wrong addresses and returned to the post office repeatedly to inquire about them. Each time he returned with no information. We began to wonder if the commander's family was against the marriage. Eventually a letter arrived. We all rushed to Father's side as he tore it open and read it aloud.

"Respected Mr. Chu Jing, we appreciate your letter. Thank you for allowing your daughter to marry my younger brother, Weiluan. I am happy and grateful to hear the news. Our family is not rich and has little to boast about, but there is no worry about food and drink. Our Mother is aged. She misses my brother Weiluan very much and hopes the war will end soon, so he can return to our hometown and we can all be reunited.

I am the eldest of my living siblings. Weiluan is the youngest. He also has an older sister and another older brother. Weiluan has never been married. He joined the army to make his contribution to the war against Japanese aggression. He has been away at battle for many years and hasn't had the opportunity to search for a wife, which has always been a big concern for my family. Now, with God's providence, he has fallen in love and found a girl to be his wife.

The properties of our family are sufficient for the couple to live a comfortable life here. They include two houses, several acres of wet rice paddies and dry fields, and a pharmacy in a nearby town. Our loving mother has been thrifty since her childhood and has saved some money. If my brother can marry a virtuous girl like your daughter, I'm sure they will live a happy life here in Guangdong. All the best to your family. Han Weiluan's fourth brother"

Father was elated after reading the letter. Mother dared not say anything against it and kept quiet. I felt as if the clouds had broken, and I was finally seeing blue sky. Later that morning, Father went to Fengmen to purchase some fish, pork, and sweets for an engagement luncheon that would make the betrothal official. Invitations were sent to all of our friends and relatives. By the time the guests arrived that afternoon, the dining table was full of delicious dishes and wine. Uncle and I chatted while Mother and Boya entertained the guests.

"Fengxian, after you get married, you can continue your college studies. With Commander Han's income, tuition shouldn't be as much of a burden as it is now for your parents. After you graduate, you can find a job. I believe the two of you will live a happy life together," Uncle said.

"Thank you, Uncle. It has always been my dream to work in an important job like you. You know I admire you very much."

The climate was festive and joyous, but one key person was still missing: Commander Han. He had been instructed to report to division headquarters that morning, so he didn't arrive until late in the afternoon. He carried an armful of gifts, and his face was drenched in sweat. There was an aura of seriousness about him. I felt bashful when I saw him, so I took refuge in my room.

Commander Han sat down. Father showed him his brother's letter. After reading it, he stood up and asked to speak with me. A servant came and got me, and I went to the greeting hall. As I walked toward the commander, he picked up the gifts and handed them to me. "I bought these items for you, Fengxian. Please accept them."

I took the gifts from him and saw his eyes welling up with tears. Then he made an announcement to everyone.

"My company has received orders to depart for the battlefield at midnight tonight." My heart sank. I looked at the clock. It was already 5 p.m. A couple of the gifts fell out of my arms. I sat down in shock.

"I apologize to all of you for this. This meal was meant to be an engagement banquet for me and Fengxian, where we could express our gratitude to all of you. But now I have been called off to battle. I don't know if I will make it back alive. If I were to die on the battlefield, Fengxian would become a widow and, according to custom, would not be permitted to marry again. That would be unfair to her, so I've decided to call off the engagement for fear of destroying her happiness. Fengxian, I bought these gifts for you as an apology. You can remember me by these souvenirs. I hope we can still be friends."

The room was silent. Commander Han and I looked into each other's eyes, but neither of us uttered a word. I asked God why this was happening to me. Aunt Chen broke the silence.

"Commander Han, you spent so much money on these gifts for the engagement. If the engagement is canceled, how can we accept them?"

Uncle gave his support for the engagement to continue. "Commander Han, you are a good man with a good conscience. We are moved by your decision, and I believe God would also be moved by you. It's not too late for the engagement. You won't die in the battlefield. Fengxian will always be your wife."

Commander Han smiled and shook his head. "Okay, okay. If you say so, we will go ahead. Thank you."

I walked to Commander Han's side. The servants lit several special red candles, a ritual when paying respects to one's ancestors. The commander and I bowed to heaven and earth, paused, then walked to the family altar and bowed to our ancestors. We then went and bowed before my parents, followed by each of our elders. (Chinese religion represents a mixture of Taoism, Buddhism, and Confucianism, combined with folk beliefs and practices that include worship of ancestors and deities of nature. Fengxian, Weiluan, and their families often exhibit a more monotheistic perception of God than typically would have been found in rural China at the time. The origins of this are unclear.)

After this brief ceremony, our family and guests feasted in the hall, while Commander Han and I went outside to the garden. We sat on a bench and looked at the flowers. It was the first time in my life that I had sat beside a man and had such close contact with him. My entire body felt electrified and feverish. I didn't dare raise my eyes and look at him. The commander took my hand, put a gold ring on my finger, and then kissed my cheek.

"Fengxian, now that we are formally engaged, please call me Weiluan. Tonight I leave for battle. If I don't return in one year, don't wait for me any longer. Find another good man to be your husband. Don't grieve for me, for I will have died a glorious death on the battlefield."

I didn't know what to say and began to cry. He ran his fingers through my hair and put his arm around me. I glanced up and saw that tears were also streaming down his face.

"Why must we have such bad luck?" I said. "I want to go with you to the battlefield. I want to be with you, life or death."

"War is cruel and no place for a gentle woman like you. I will not let you come with me and make you endure that kind of horror and hardship. You must stay at home and wait for me."

I asked him to wait in the garden. I rushed to my room to fetch a pair of cloth shoes, a handkerchief, and a wool sweater that I had made for him. After I handed them to him, I took off the silver necklace that I had worn since I was a young girl and put it in his hand. "This is my engagement gift for you."

"I will cherish this necklace dearly, Fengxian. Whenever I look at it, I will think of you smiling at me."

We left the garden hand-in-hand and returned to the banquet hall. As midnight approached, we heard Weiluan's troops lining up on the path outside Rongxia. A few minutes later, one of the platoon leaders knocked on the door.

"Sir, it's time to go. We can't stay here any longer."

My family and I escorted Weiluan to the road. One by one he said goodbye to the guests and my parents. By the time he got to me, tears were dripping onto his shirt. "Goodbye Fengxian. Know that I love you."

We looked at each other in silence; then he turned away, mounted his horse, and charged off into the black horizon. The guests returned to their homes while my family and I stayed several minutes staring quietly into the darkness.

Eventually Boya took my hand, and all of us slowly walked back home. We returned to the banquet hall, which just minutes before had been bustling but was now empty and silent. Uncle tried to comfort me.

"Fengxian, Commander Han will come back soon. I was really moved by his love for you. I hope you think I did the right thing by suggesting that you go through with the engagement."

"Uncle, we are very grateful for your care and consideration. Without your help, we might never have gotten engaged. If that was the case, we both would have regretted it for the rest of our lives. Even though we have had to part so soon, it's still better than not ever having been able to be together at all."

It was after 1 a.m. We were all exhausted and went to bed, but I couldn't sleep. Whenever I closed my eyes, I would see Weiluan's image. It wasn't until the sun began to rise that I finally fell into slumber. Later that morning I was awakened by my mother calling my name outside my room. When I opened the door, I saw Weiluan's orderly. He bowed and handed me a letter. I immediately opened it.

"My unit arrived at 2 a.m. We are currently residing on a high mountain. We will stay here only one day and then move to another place. We have already engaged in battle with the enemy, but our casualties have been low. Don't be sad, Fengxian. I will come back for sure. Take care of your parents and teach your brothers to read and write. I have enclosed some money in this letter to ease some of your expenses. I have to end here. I will write you again soon. Weiluan"

Lonely Days

For the next several days, everything in my surroundings prompted recollections of Weiluan: the greeting hall and garden at Rongxia, the anti-Japanese banners draped across the center of town, the trenches and bomb shelters strewn across the countryside that had been constructed by his troops. I could still picture and hear the soldiers exercising on the training ground across from Rongxia under Weiluan's command and his calls, "one, two, three, four." The memories saddened me deeply.

As the war drew nearer, more Chinese troops flooded the area. Shops and schools closed, my brothers returned home, and Lakeside College sent word that fall classes were cancelled. After all I had gone through to continue my education, the war was interrupting everything.

With no schoolwork to focus on, Weiluan and his safety was all I could think about. Mother also worried about Weiluan. She expressed this by complaining incessantly that I never should have gotten engaged to a soldier. Qie and her children gloated over my misfortune. I didn't care what they thought, but Mother hated losing face.

"I predicted this very problem before you ever agreed to marry Commander Han," Mother said. "How many soldiers return from the frontlines? I told you this time and again, but you refused to listen. Now your entire life may be ruined."

"Mother, don't listen to what other people are saying. They are just trying to make us upset. If Commander Han is killed in action, and I am unable to marry, so be it. I knew the risk when I agreed to marry him."

I suppressed my sorrow and fear to comfort Mother, yet deep inside I was terrified Weiluan might not return. I lost my appetite and was unable to sleep. I stayed in my room day and night. I read each of Weiluan's letters over and over again and stared at his photos. He looked so strong, poised, and valiant. I told myself repeatedly that God wouldn't allow a man like him to be killed on the battlefield. To help me get through that difficult time, I scribbled all of my thoughts on paper. Every day I wrote and sang, wrote and sang. I could think of nothing else.

At the time, Boya and Mother were busy preparing for her wedding. Boya became increasingly upset that I wasn't accompanying her in her final days at home. One day she pounded on the door until I responded.

"What do you want?"

"Fengxian, your loneliness is making you ill. You must shift your mind to something else. Soon I will be married. I am anxious and nervous and want you by my side. Please unlock the door."

I began to feel guilty for being so self-absorbed and opened the door. Boya gazed at the letters and writings strewn across my bed, desk, and floor. She shook her head, grabbed my hand, and led me to the room where she and Mother were preparing her dowry. It was filled with silk cloth, beautiful bedding, clothes for each season, wood furniture embedded with painted glass, ceramics, and baskets of shoes decorated with delicate silk embroidery. Most of the cloth items had been made by mother and Boya, while the rest had been purchased by Father. It was clear that my parents had spent a fortune.

As was customary at the time, the groom's family sent my parents some money to pay for the privilege of Boya's hand, but it was well below what my parents had spent on her dowry. There are many old sayings in China about the high cost of marrying off a daughter, which is one of the reasons girls are deemed inferior to boys. As I stood there looking at Boya's dowry, I understood why Uncle had said my parents didn't have the money to betroth me to a rich family after Boya.

"Why do we have to prepare so much?" I asked Father.

"This is an old custom. If you want to marry your daughter to a wealthy family, you must prepare a rich dowry for her. Otherwise, the groom's family may not go through with the wedding, or she will be looked down upon and be treated badly by his family. If you want your daughter to be accepted, you must follow this custom. As parents, we must try our best to prepare a plentiful dowry even if it means selling our fields. We don't want to lose face."

"What a ridiculous custom!" I said. "Someone needs to change this."

"Times are changing, Fengxian. Your modern, unarranged engagement to Commander Han is an example. Slowly, you and others like you will help us shed this heavy burden."

"I'm afraid that I may not have the fortune of marrying Commander Han in the end. I may be single for the rest of my days."

"Bite your tongue!" Mother said.

That night we went out to dinner and spent the entire meal talking about Boya's wedding. When we returned home, Boya and I gazed at the letters and papers strewn across our room. I picked up a few and set them in a pile. Boya picked up one of the pages I had written and began to read it aloud.

"When will I be lifted from this sadness and suspense? Every day I long for you but cannot see you. When night falls, the loneliness is compounded. When will you return, Commander Han? The shadows cast by the candles at our engagement ceremony and the loud bugle calls before your departure that evening have left a permanent impression on my soul. Only your photos, letters, and engagement ring can comfort this broken heart."

"Fengxian, I admire you so much," Boya said. "What you have written is so touching. No wonder Commander Han traveled far and wide but didn't fall in love with anyone until he met you. If he could see these verses, so touching and full of love, he would be so happy. Although I have a plentiful dowry and am marrying the son of a rich family, our relationship isn't built on a foundation of love. Without love, where is the meaning in life? My marriage is simply a business transaction between two rich families. When what the Tang's have bought becomes old and rotten, they will throw it away. I would prefer to have no dowry and marry a man like Commander Han, who loves me from the depths of his heart. But I don't have this luck. I'm not as intelligent as you. This is my fate."

On the morning of Boya's wedding, Rongxia's courtyard overflowed with guests. A wedding band played several joyful tunes. As I listened, I couldn't resist feeling sad. I was losing my sister, my closest friend. I couldn't keep myself from crying. When I looked at Boya, I saw her eyes were also filled with tears.

"Fengxian, I don't want to part with you and the rest of the family," Boya said. "This is my home. I don't know if I'm prepared to be a wife." We hugged each other and cried some more. After a while, we both calmed down.

Soon a young woman came to accompany Boya through the traditional pre-wedding ritual, which included bowing to pay her respects to heaven and earth, our ancestors, and our parents. Afterward, the woman led Boya to the sedan chair that had been sent by the groom's family.

Boya climbed into the chair, which was then hoisted onto the shoulders of several men, who would carry her to the groom's home, where the formal wedding would take place. Behind the sedan chair followed a long convoy of family, friends, and dozens of servants, who had been hired to carry food, wine, cake, and Boya's large dowry. The procession began with the sound of a large firecracker and was lavish and boisterous.

The groom's family was pleased with the size and quality of the dowry my parents prepared. They warmly welcomed Boya and my parents. Everyone in our family was relieved that the long period of preparation was over and that we had met the expectations of the Tang's.

That night, when we returned to Rongxia, the house felt quiet and desolate without my sister. I looked forward to seeing her again in three days' time when, according to Chinese tradition, it is customary for a newly wedded couple to return to the home of the bride's parents to pay their respects.

That day Boya and her husband arrived mid-morning in sedan chairs. We all missed her deeply and were overjoyed to be reunited. They brought gifts for everyone. All of us were comforted to see how gently and considerately Boya's husband treated her. After a hearty, joyous lunch, the newlyweds returned home. Boya's eyes filled with tears as she said farewell. None of us knew when we would see her again. According to tradition in the countryside at the time, wives were forbidden from visiting their families without their husbands' approval. It wasn't uncommon for a married woman to see her family only once a year during Chinese New Year. Some women never saw their families at all after they married. My parents, brothers, and I still had each other, but Boya was alone with a new family, all of whom were strangers. I could feel the deep sadness in her heart as we parted.

Life Under Japanese Occupation

By early summer 1944, the Japanese had penetrated the northern and eastern borders of Hunan. Having failed to capture our provincial capital Changsha on three prior occasions, the Japanese army was determined to succeed this time. An all-out attack was devised to seize control of Changsha and much of the Guangzhou-Hankou railway, which was the line that ran right through Fengmen Station.

This time battle-weary Chinese troops were unable to fend off the attack on Changsha. On June 19, 1944, our capital city of Hunan fell into Japanese hands. Afterward, the Japanese army pushed south along the

Xiang River. As the war inched closer to Huaguo, anxiety in the village intensified. Every shop, school, and business closed. Even the highly anticipated Dragon Boat Festival was cancelled. Most villagers, including my family, spent their days and nights close to home. Life came to a complete standstill.

Although I was afraid, I remained preoccupied with Weiluan and his safety. To cheer me up, one day one of my brothers invited me to fly kites with him at the military training ground across from our house. I didn't have anything better to do, so I agreed to go.

It was a windy day, and my brother and I managed to maneuver one of the kites high into the sky. For a long time, we guided it through the open air, but eventually the wind became too strong, and the kite crashed to the ground. As we were running to fetch it, we suddenly heard loud rumbling all around us. We looked up and saw Japanese fighter planes roaring over our heads. Dozens of bombs fell from the sky and exploded all around us.

For a few moments, my brother and I stood frozen in shock. It seemed as though bombs were dropping everywhere. Thankfully, none hit the ground where we were standing. I grabbed my brother's hand, and we raced down the hill back to Rongxia. On the road, we encountered Father, who was coming back from town.

"What are the two of you doing outside? Get back to the house now! The Japanese have invaded Fengmen. It won't be long before they reach Huaguo. People are running for their lives. We have to hide and take refuge in the hills immediately."

Father relayed the news to our neighbors. Everyone panicked. Some people immediately charged toward the hills but then turned around after a couple of minutes when they realized they had no provisions. Some of the braver villagers slaughtered their animals and began to make a hearty feast, hoping to eat their fill before they had to flee. Father chastised them for being so nonchalant. "If you continue to stay here and take your time to eat, the Japanese invaders may eat you!" After hearing my father's warning, the villagers shoved what they could into their mouths and pockets and left the rest to rot.

Grandfather, Qie, and their children had already fled a few weeks earlier to a friend's house several villages away. Father ordered our servants to escort my mother and brothers to a cave in the mountains, where he believed we would be safe. Because Mother's feet were bound, she was unable to stay behind and assist Father in gathering provisions, so I accompanied him. Fortunately, Father had been expecting the invasion for a while and had sent some food, salt, oil, and other important items to the home of one of our relatives in a nearby village for safe keeping. As we headed there, I realized that I had left behind all of Weiluan's letters and photos. I turned around and raced back to Rongxia.

"Fengxian, what are you doing?" Father screamed. "Do you want to get yourself killed?"

I didn't respond and kept running. Father had no choice but to follow me. When I entered my room, I quickly gathered all of Weiluan's letters, photos, and my verses, tossed them into a big bag and slung it over my shoulder.

"Fengxian, it's fortunate that you did a lot of exercise at school. Otherwise, you might not be able to outrun the Japanese devils!" Father joked.

Father and I fetched the provisions and immediately headed for the cave. About halfway there, we stopped to have a rest. Villagers were scrambling everywhere. The elderly and sick groaned as they struggled to walk, children cried, and adults complained. We had yet to encounter any Japanese soldiers, but I was already overcome with fear. I realized then how cowardly I was.

"We need to get out of here," Father said. We followed a narrow path through the woods. After a while, we saw my mother, one of my brothers, and another woman standing near a cave-like structure beckoning us. As we approached, I saw that the woman was my mother's sister, who I hadn't seen for several years. She had a big smile on her face and clenched my hands.

"Fengxian, the last time I saw you, you were still a toddler. You have grown into such a pretty and elegant girl. You look beautiful."

"Thank you, Auntie. It's good to see you after such a long time."

Until then, I hadn't known that Mother's sister was living in such poverty. She also had bound feet and wasn't able to travel far. Her husband had been forced to join the Nationalist KMT army several years ago and never returned. She didn't know if he was dead or alive. Auntie was raising her four children on her own. Her life was extremely difficult. She had aged much more than Mother. When we were alone, I asked Mother why I had never heard about Auntie's situation.

"My sister is very independent and doesn't like to impose on her family. Your grandmother, your uncle, and I help her when we can. Without your uncle's assistance, she wouldn't even be able to live here. Auntie is too ashamed to visit our home, which is why you haven't seen her in so long. Without a husband, a woman is doomed and destined to be bullied and mocked by others."

The cave wasn't a traditional stone cavern that jutted into the earth, but rather a man-made cave that was nestled at the bottom of several hills and surrounded by tall trees and thick foliage. Some poor families who couldn't afford regular homes resided there. They constructed makeshift huts out of tree branches and dried straw, which made the structures indistinguishable from their surroundings. The area was shady, quiet, still, and remote. It was a perfect place to hide. The only problem was that other villagers had also fled there. We feared that all of the activity might divulge our location to the Japanese, so the men agreed to take turns guarding the cave.

A couple of days later, Father announced that he was going to return to Rongxia to protect our house from being looted. We begged him not to go, but he was insistent and fearless.

"We can't afford to lose everything in our home. Take care of each other. Fengxian, help your mother look after your brothers and be careful."

Father feared that if Japanese soldiers discovered us, they would rape us, so he instructed us to make ourselves look as undesirable as possible. "Take off those beautiful clothes and put on something shabby. The dirtier, the better. Rub some dirt on your face to make yourself look ugly."

Mother and I only had the clothes on our backs. We had nothing shabby to change into. Auntie didn't have any extra worn-out clothes, either. She asked some of her neighbors, but they had their own relatives who had fled there and were now wearing their ratty clothes. Eventually, Auntie managed to track down some tattered shirts and pants for Mother and me.

After we changed our clothes, Auntie handed each of us some black soot from the campfire. She dumped it in our hands and instructed us to rub it on our faces. She spread the soot over her entire face until everything was black except for her white teeth. She looked like a disheveled madwoman. Auntie's daughters did the same. After Mother rubbed the soot onto her face, I could hardly recognize her. Everyone looked so awful that we couldn't help laughing.

When my turn came, I took the soot into the Auntie's hut and set it on the ground. I couldn't believe that our lives had come to this. No matter how ugly we make ourselves look, I thought, we won't be able to escape the evil of the Japanese soldiers. I took out some paper and wrote out my anger about what the Japanese were doing to our country.

After a couple of hours, Mother came to check on me. "Fengxian, have you painted your face?"

"Not yet."

I put down my pen, looked in the mirror, and shook my head. Then I dug my fingers into the black soot, smeared it across my cheeks, and went outside to join everyone.

Mother was increasingly anxious that Father had not yet returned. I offered to look for him, but Auntie insisted that one of her sons go instead. Her son knew the route well because every day he chopped wood and hauled it to town to sell. After her son set off, we burned some incense and prayed for God to protect my father and cousin.

After a few days, neither Father nor Cousin had returned. We feared the worst. Auntie visited her neighbors to see what news they might have heard about the Japanese. One neighbor told her that Japanese soldiers had entered Huaguo a few days earlier. Many houses were set on fire, and the entire village was ablaze. The neighbor heard that Rongxia had been ransacked but didn't know if it had also been burned to the ground.

Mother, my brothers, and I were devastated when we heard the news. Not only was Father likely dead, our house had also been pillaged. Auntie tried to comfort us, saying that Father could have escaped. "With God's blessing, I believe he will come back safe and sound. Your father is a good man, and he will turn ill luck into good luck."

We didn't know what to do. The fact that the Japanese had made their way to Huaguo meant that they weren't too far from the cave. Leaving the refuge of the woods could put our lives in danger. Yet we couldn't just stay there and do nothing. We were discussing our options when someone saw my cousin in the distance carrying Father on his back. We rushed to help them.

Father was bloody and unconscious. We laid him on a bed in the hut and covered him with a thick blanket. I stroked his face, but he didn't respond. "Father!" I cried. "Wake up. Your children can't live without you. Please, Father, answer us!"

Auntie prepared some ginger and brown sugar soup, and we forced it into Father's mouth. Mother wiped the blood off his face and hands and put some ointment on his wounds. Slowly, Father regained consciousness. All of us breathed a sigh of relief. Auntie prepared more soup for him, this time with ginseng. After a few hours, Father opened his eyes wide, looked at us, and told us what happened in a weak voice.

"I was attacked in our home by Japanese soldiers. I was injured so badly that I could barely move. For days I laid there hungry and cold. I thought I would never see any of you again. I never expected someone would come to my rescue." He was extremely pale, and his eyes filled with tears.

"You should thank Auntie's son," Mother said, pointing at my cousin. Father nodded at him and gave him a weak smile. Then he closed his eyes and fell back asleep. We left the hut to give him some peace and quiet. Once we were outside, we asked cousin to tell us what had happened.

"I sneaked through the hills on a special path to get to Huaguo. The village was empty when I arrived. There wasn't a single sound. I became very frightened. As I made my way toward Rongxia, the sun was setting. Once inside the house, I quietly called out for your father, but there was no reply. I searched the grounds outside, but I still couldn't find him. Because I hadn't seen him on the path in the hills, I figured he was probably still in the house somewhere. It was getting dark. There was some charcoal still burning in the stove, so I set some bamboo on fire to use as a torch. I went through the house room by room. I could hear intermittent groans but couldn't see anyone. I feared that it might be a ghost. As I was preparing to leave, I tripped over some broken furniture. I stopped to take a look and saw a large sack moving slightly. I tore it open and found Uncle inside. His limbs were tied up, and a big, heavy stone was on his chest. His face was caked in blood, and his lips were badly split. I found a pair of scissors and cut the rope. Then I removed the heavy rock from his chest. He was extremely weak and on the verge of dying. I hoisted him over my shoulder and ran back as fast as I could."

We thanked Cousin for being so brave and for carrying Father all the way to the cave. After a few hours, Father awoke and asked for some food. Auntie made him some congee. After he ate, he got some energy and came to life.

"The day after I left here, the Japanese entered Huaguo. They burned down houses, killed dozens of villagers, and raped several women. Everywhere people were screaming in misery. I knew it was extremely dangerous and was preparing to flee when I encountered some soldiers. They weren't in military uniforms, so they took me by surprise. They asked for gold and silver. I told them I didn't have any, and they began punching my face. Then they asked for some pretty girls. I shook my head and said there were no pretty girls. Then they beat me some more. After a while, I fell on the ground. They tied up my hands and feet, stuffed me in a large sack, and dropped a very heavy stone on my chest. I could hardly breathe. They stood there laughing and laughing, then left. After two days of lying there in pain without water or food, I resigned myself to the fact that I would die there. Eventually I lost consciousness."

In the ensuing days, Father slowly recovered. But soon we were confronted with a new challenge: our provisions were dwindling. My family was fortunate to have stockpiled enough food that we could bring what we needed for several weeks to the cave. Other families weren't so fortunate. They had to risk their lives each day to return to the fields to gather something to eat. After a few weeks, we were on the verge of finishing all of our rice, salt, and oil. We could borrow rice from others and cut back on oil, but salt was essential. With no salt, everyone was losing their strength. Other refugees at the cave dug for salt from the earth. They boiled what they collected to get something approximating salt, but it tasted very bitter.

Father understood how desperate the situation was. He insisted on returning to Rongxia to fetch some of the extra salt that Mother had purchased and hid in the ground. Knowing that he hadn't fully recovered from his injuries, Mother and I were reluctant to let him leave. However, Father was determined to return. We had no choice but to agree to let him go. This time Cousin accompanied him from the start. All of us prayed that they wouldn't encounter any Japanese soldiers.

After a couple of days, Father and Cousin returned with salt, oil, rice, chicken, goose, duck, and pork. Their backs were hunched over from carrying the heavy loads. We helped them set everything down and urged them to sit down for a rest. They were both silent and traumatized. After several minutes of silence, Father began to talk about their journey.

"When we arrived at Rongxia, more goods had been looted, and some furniture and other items were broken and burnt. We were fortunate to discover these meats left over by the Japanese soldiers. The most horrifying sight was of the stream in front of our house. It had turned red from our fellow villagers' blood. All of the elderly, sick, and pregnant people, who were unable to escape, had been killed and tossed into the stream. The women were raped first. We saw one woman, who had just given birth, running with her baby toward the hills. Some Japanese soldiers saw her and chased her down. One of them stabbed the baby with his bayonet and then lifted the bayonet upright toward the sky. He twirled the baby around and around while he danced. The soldiers raped every woman they came across. We watched them scour the nearby hills for villagers. They followed the cries of one baby, found dozens of people, and killed them all. There was so much blood in the stream that it had turned red."

Father's story was so vivid that by the end everyone was in tears. All of us were terrified and enraged. I thought about the painful final minutes of our neighbors' lives and hoped that they had now found peace. I prayed that their souls would protect the safety of everyone else in Huaguo.

For the next several days, we talked about how evil the Japanese soldiers were and how their crimes must be avenged. We vowed never to forget what they had done until the day justice was brought to our countrymen who were killed and raped. Regrettably, sometimes blood can only be repaid with blood.

Autumn and Winter at the Cave

Time passed very slowly at the cave. There was nothing to do each day except listen to the bombings of fighter jets, the shelling and shooting of soldiers, and the cries of children and their mothers. The sounds pierced the hearts of everyone.

When the mid-autumn festival arrived, Mother and Auntie did what they could to prepare a special celebration, but I wondered how we could enjoy anything amid so much loss and destruction. They made special dishes out of the meats Father and Cousin had carried back. After dinner, we nibbled on peanuts and soybeans while we watched the moon. It was a clear, bright night. The prior mid-autumn festival my parents, siblings, and I had sat in the garden after dinner appreciating the flowers in the moonlight. Father played the guqin and the flute. It was so peaceful.

So many thoughts ran through our minds, but no one had anything to say. For a long time, there was silence. Father eventually murmured a few words of nostalgia and then lowered and shook his head. "I never would have dreamed we'd be seeking asylum here for this long." Father's words made me more saddened. I got up and walked to where I could sit alone. I missed Weiluan deeply and wondered how he was spending the holiday. After a while, Father and one of my brothers came and sat beside me.

"Fengxian, we are now living in a period of national crisis," Father said. "People are unable to lead a peaceful life. I would rather be a dog in peace time than a person in war time. Common people like us don't have weapons, so we are bullied by the Japanese and can't defend ourselves. How I wish I had a gun so I could fight back! If Commander Han were here now, I would join his troops to defend our land. Don't worry about Commander Han. He is a good man. He won't die on the battlefield. You'll see that I'm right when he returns."

"Maybe, but it's also possible that he's unable to hide from all of the bombs and bullets and becomes injured or dies. I worry about him day and night."

"I know you do."

It was chilly that evening. Mother came and picked up my brother, who had fallen asleep on Father's lap. She brought Father and me blankets and told us not to stay up too late. Father and I sat there quietly for several minutes.

"Fengxian, it's been so long since we've spoken about literature and poetry. How about you write me a poem about the mid-autumn festival?"

"Father, I'm not a poet. You write much better than I do. How about you write me a poem?"

Father fetched some paper, ink, and a writing brush. "Write down anything that comes to mind," he said to me.

For a while, I couldn't think of anything to write, but seeing Father's kind face and smile reminded me of his boundless love. I jotted down a few lines about how fortunate I was to have such a kind Father, who was my greatest champion, protector, and savior. I read it to him. He gave no response. After another several minutes of silence, he began to talk to me about the importance of being literate.

"In life, it is inevitable that one encounters unexpected disputes and conflicts. You must struggle to the end, not with your fists, but nonviolently through writing. It is important that you be brave enough to defend yourself with your writing brush, much like the people who come to me asking me to write legal complaints for them. Do you understand what I'm saying, Fengxian?"

"Father, I'm just a woman. I don't think I'll ever have a dispute with someone to the point that I need to pursue a lawsuit."

"Just remember what I said about writing. Some day in the future your ability to write may be your savior."

"Okay. I won't forget."

We both got up and went to bed.

Autumn passed quickly, and the icy cold bitterness of winter arrived. Because we were hiding deep in the hills, firewood was plentiful, so we spent most of our days sitting next to the fire. By then, we had exhausted most of our provisions. We were subsisting on a simple diet of rice and vegetables. Around Chinese New Year, Father learned that a new public security committee consisting of several local villagers had been set up to restore order in Huaguo and liaise with the Japanese. Most of the Japanese forces had moved farther south and west, and soldiers were returning to Huaguo only every three to five days to ransack the village. As a result, increasing numbers of villagers sneaked back to their homes each evening after sunset to till the fields and rebuild their homes. They would return to the hills at daybreak to avoid the Japanese soldiers.

On the final day of Chinese New Year in 1945, Father decided it was time for us to return to Rongxia. We departed the cave in the middle of the afternoon and arrived around 7 p.m. For months, all of us had been wondering how much damage had been done to Rongxia. We knew it would be bad, but we still weren't prepared for what we saw when we arrived.

Nearly everything in the house had been broken in one way or another. Paintings were torn, vases smashed, furniture shattered, linens and embroidery burned and stained. The most revolting of all was the residue of Japanese soldiers' urine and excrement everywhere. We toiled the entire night cleaning the soldiers' waste and trying to restore some semblance of order.

When the sun rose, we returned to the hills. Father searched for a safe place where we could hide until the next evening. We took refuge atop a hill adjacent to Huaguo. From there, we could see all of the comings and goings in the village. Early that afternoon, we watched as members of the security committee led Japanese soldiers into the village. The soldiers unleashed their machine guns randomly across the landscape to instill fear into everyone. Then they went from house to house robbing each family of their food. They left around 4 p.m. When dusk arrived, we and other families snuck back to our homes.

We lived under this routine for several weeks. Every day was intense and filled with fear and anxiety. Because Mother's feet were bound, she had an extremely difficult time walking long distances, particularly in rugged terrain. I tried to help her as much as possible. During the day, I often lay under the shade of a large tree, watching the sky and listening to the sad songs of birds and the murmuring of trickling streams. Everywhere I went, I brought Weiluan's letters and photos with me. They were my only source of consolation in exile and gave me the courage and optimism to go on each day.

"Fengxian, are you daydreaming again?" Father said. "Don't be so anxious and sentimental. You will harm your health and emaciate your body. Come eat lunch." He had a big smile on his face, which I hadn't seen in ages. I knew something was up and joined my family for lunch.

"These days Japanese soldiers no longer enter our village because they are afraid of our guerillas. Now it is much calmer and safer. This afternoon we will return home for good. However, we still must be cautious and careful."

That evening we spent our first night in the garden in more than a year. All of the flowers had been destroyed and the pots shattered. The only thing left unscathed was a large Camellia tree that remained lush and green. It quietly swayed in the breeze as though it was patiently awaiting our return.

"This tree was planted by your great-grandfather," Father said. "It's like a family heirloom. Perhaps it was the souls of our ancestors who protected this tree. Maybe they wanted to show us that we will not be defeated."

I loosened the soil around the trunk and fetched some water for the tree, while my brothers fixed the broken flower pots. A couple of hours later, Father announced that he found some old flower seeds and rushed to the garden to plant them. My mother, siblings, and I chipped in. We took great care with each seed, hoping that in a few months' time new life would begin to spring forth from all of the destruction.

As I lay in bed that evening, I realized that it had been over eight months since I had slept in my room. Everything seemed so different now. Mother had tried so hard to shelter Boya and me from the world by confining us to that room, but in the end, our only protection lay in abandoning it. Without my sister's laughter and chatter, our room felt quiet and desolate. I recalled the many good times Boya and I shared there. But every time a happy memory emerged, I was flooded with flashbacks of how the room looked the first day we returned from the cave: everything shattered and upturned, all of Boya and Mother's embroidery stained with human waste, and urine and excrement everywhere. That night I cried myself to sleep.

Rebuilding was a challenge for every household. Goods of all kinds, including food, were in short supply, and prices for everything were volatile. All businesses and shops remained closed. It was nearly impossible to find the materials to reconstruct furniture, etc. The small amount of money my parents had hidden was barely sufficient to put food on the table. Still, we were fortunate. Many families didn't have a cent, while others were grieving over family members who had been raped and murdered.

Several days after returning, I heard one of my brothers excitedly calling my name. "Fengxian, Father wants you to come to the gate! There's a soldier in a uniform across the road. Father thinks it might be Commander Han, but he's not sure." Brother grabbed my hand, and we ran toward the gate.

"Fengxian, look at that man and tell me if you think he's Commander Han," Father said. As the uniformed man walked closer and closer, it became clear to all of us that it was Weiluan. My heart began to beat fast, and I had butterflies. Villagers swarmed to him on the road and thanked him for fighting for our country. It took him a long time to make his way to Rongxia. I was overjoyed to see that he was unharmed, but I didn't know what to say to him. I was so nervous that I fled to my room.

Neighbors, friends, and family escorted Weiluan onto the grounds of Rongxia. Their happy voices filled the house. I listened as they asked him questions about the fighting. They informed him about everything that had happened to our village since the evening he left. Weiluan had not only returned safely, he also brought with him a level of energy and discourse that had been absent in our community for nearly a year. Relief and joy resonated through Rongxia, breaking the long silence of the invasion and occupation.

After a while, Mother came to my room to check on me. "Almost all of our blankets were burnt by the Japanese. Fengxian, you should give your blanket to Commander Han to use tonight."

"Is that all you have to say right now?" I asked in amazement. "Don't worry about the blanket!"

"I know you are happy that Commander Han is back. But I must remind you that you are still an unmarried woman. It's improper for you to be conversing with a man, even if he is your fiancé. You are to stay in this boudoir. I forbid you to speak with him lest you spark gossip among the neighbors. Don't worry. Soon we will arrange an auspicious day for your marriage."

After all the trauma our country, village, and family had experienced over the past year, I couldn't believe that Mother's traditional mindset hadn't changed at all. Father was my only hope. I listened as he and Weiluan spoke about the war and the events of the past year. Father instructed one of my brothers to bring me to see Weiluan, but Mother forbade it. After a while, Father realized why I still hadn't come to greet Commander Han, so he came to my room to bring me to see him.

As soon as I entered the main hall, Weiluan stood up and smiled. "Fengxian, we finally see each other again." He had lost a lot of weight and looked haggard and tired.

"Congratulations. You have managed to return safely."

"Thanks to your blessings, I have made it back alive from the battlefield. I was shot in my right kneecap. After treatment in a hospital, I was discharged. Fortunately, the bullet mainly destroyed flesh. The bone wasn't badly hurt. I am okay now, but sometimes the pain is still intense." His story sent a chill up my spine.

That evening we shared a leisurely, hearty meal together. Father invited the orderly accompanying Weiluan to partake with us. "Join us, soldier. Don't be so polite. We're like family. At the dinner table, there is no difference between an officer and a soldier."

Golden Bracelet

About a week after Weiluan returned, Mother invited a fortune teller to visit our home and select some auspicious dates for our wedding. She deliberated about the selections for days until one morning she declared that we would wed a few weeks later on March 26 on the lunar calendar. Once the date had been set, the focus shifted to making preparations for the ceremony and dinner. Money and food — the two most critical ingredients for any wedding — were in short supply at the time. Weiluan didn't have any cash, and my parents' savings had dwindled.

"I don't have a cent now," Weiluan said. "I feel it's not right for me to marry Fengxian until I find a job and have some savings."

"We've already waited a long time for Fengxian's marriage," Mother said. "How long are you going to make us wait? Do you really think you can find a job during the occupation? That's impossible."

"My wife and I have the money to pay for the wedding banquet," Father said. "But we must keep it as small and informal as possible. I doubt that many people will come anyway out of fear of the Japanese soldiers. Commander Han, we definitely can't afford any dowry to give you."

"Jing, what are you talking about?" Mother said. "This is our daughter's wedding. We must invite many relatives and friends. I don't want to lose face. No matter how poor we are, we must put on a good wedding."

Mother and Father argued like this for quite some time, which made Weiluan feel embarrassed. After a while, he put his hand in his pocket and pulled out a beautiful gold bracelet. He placed the bracelet in my mother's hand.

"The reason I don't have any money now is because I spent my savings of many years to buy this gold bracelet, which was going to be my wedding gift to Fengxian. But now I want you to use it to pay for the wedding preparations. I will buy another one for her in the future."

"Commander Han, don't worry about the wedding," Father said. "We will solve this problem. Save the bracelet for yourself and Fengxian. Besides, we are under occupation. There is no jewelry or pawn shop where we could exchange it."

The next day Aunt Chen came for a visit. All Mother could talk about was the wedding. Seeing how anxious Mother was, Aunt Chen suggested borrowing some items from Boya for my wedding so we wouldn't have to buy everything. All of us thought it was an excellent idea.

While discussing the plans, we heard a neighbor cry out that some Japanese soldiers were approaching. We had been so engrossed in discussing the wedding that everyone was stunned. We quickly fled outside and up the hill behind Rongxia. Mother had a difficult time walking, so Weiluan carried her on his back.

By nightfall, the Japanese soldiers had left. We inched our way back home in the darkness. The house was a mess again. As we sifted through the debris, we came across remnants of the military uniforms of Weiluan and his assistant. The Japanese soldiers had discovered the uniforms hanging on the clothes line and had ripped them into shreds. Upon seeing that, Father was convinced that it was no longer safe for us to stay there. We made preparations to return to the cave. Weiluan initially wanted to stay behind to protect Rongxia, but eventually he agreed to accompany us.

When we arrived at the cave, Auntie was happy to see us, but also very concerned as she knew we wouldn't have come back unless something bad had happened. Mother explained the situation and then introduced Weiluan. They exchanged greetings and some small talk.

"Fengxian, you are a lucky girl. Commander Han is so handsome and strong. He really deserves the title of officer."

The next day Father took Weiluan to see some of the local cliffs and caves, while Mother, Auntie, and I stayed behind and discussed wedding preparations. Mother insisted on going through with the ceremony on March 26.

She instructed the servants to go to Boya's house and borrow some items from her dowry. When the servants returned, they explained that most of Boya's dowry, which Mother and Father had spent so much time and money on, had been buried in the ground when the Japanese soldiers arrived. As a result, much of it had been ruined by insects and water.

Whatever items remained in good shape they brought back to the cave. Mother was disappointed but felt that it was better than having nothing.

Mother put Father in charge of purchasing food and other items for the ceremony. Several days in a row, Father journeyed to various villages searching for the items we needed. Every night he returned exhausted. Eventually he was able to purchase everything.

A couple of days before the wedding, Father, the servants, and Auntie's children returned to Rongxia to prepare the house for the ceremony. Most of our relatives had managed to get word to us that they would attend. But the two people I desperately wanted to be there — Boya and my dear maternal uncle — were unable to make the journey. Boya had recently given birth to her first child, while Uncle had taken refuge in a place far from Huaguo. Grandfather said he would return to Rongxia alone for the ceremony. I was glad to hear that Qie wouldn't be attending.

On the day of the ceremony, we departed the cave after lunch. The weather was good, and I recall bright sunlight beaming through the shade of the trees. Weiluan carried Mother most of the way, which slowed us down considerably. We didn't arrive at Rongxia until 7 p.m. By then, family and friends had been waiting for quite some time. They had already lit the red candles in the greeting hall, which are used in traditional Chinese weddings as a symbol of respect to the gods.

Aunt Chen and some other women whisked me away to bathe, change clothes, and put on makeup, while Weiluan donned his military uniform. We met in the courtyard and walked into the greeting hall side by side. We bowed first to heaven and earth, then to our ancestors, parents, elders, relatives, and finally to each other. We were then guided to our bridal room where we spent a few moments alone. The bed was draped in mosquito net and covered with embroidered pillowcases. We sat on the edge of the bed. Weiluan lifted my veil and handed me the gold bracelet.

"I hope we can live happily together for the rest of our lives and love each other in life or death." I didn't know what to say, so I kept silent. "Fengxian, I never expected we would be getting married during the occupation. I had hoped we would wait until we won the war, so I could invite my mother and siblings to Hunan. But these are the circumstances we are in. I'm sorry that you have to have such a simple wedding."

After a few minutes, we returned to the celebration. There were five tables of guests. As soon as we entered the hall, Weiluan and I toasted all of the guests. We thanked them for their presence during such a difficult time. The room was festive and full of laughter. The banquet lasted until midnight, after which the guests accompanied us to the bridal room to extend their congratulations and blessings for a long, loving marriage. They tossed red dates, peanuts, longans, and lotus seeds onto the bed to symbolize a fruitful marriage with children. A cousin related to one of grandfather's brothers said some brief words on behalf of the family.

"This is the first time that a daughter in the Chu family is marrying a military man. It's also the first unarranged, modern wedding in the family. The two of you have broken the chains of the old society and found each other by falling in love. With time, the love between you will become even more precious. Fengxian is a role model for the daughters in the Chu family. All of us here wish the two of you everlasting happiness."

Everyone clapped. Weiluan expressed his gratitude to my cousin by lighting a cigarette and handing it to him. A few children climbed onto the bed to snatch the red dates, and we all laughed. Then Aunt Chen announced that it was time for everyone to leave because we had to get up early to return to the cave. After we said goodbye to everyone, Weiluan and I sat on the bed.

"I owe so much to your parents for putting on a wedding like this at such a difficult time. I will never forget this moment or what they have done today. This is the most significant and meaningful day of my life. I feel ashamed for having no money to fulfill my responsibilities in holding this wedding ceremony. Money has never been something important to me. As a soldier, I had many opportunities to make money through crooked means, but I have always stuck to my principles of honesty and hard work to maintain a clear conscience. That's why God blessed me and enabled me to return to you. Still, I hate to look at these items on the bed and know that they are used and were borrowed from your sister. I never would have dreamed that I would be penniless on my wedding day."

"Weiluan, don't be so hard on yourself. I don't blame you for such a simple wedding. Our love should never be measured by money. Marriage is the integration of our hearts and bodies. Luxuries are superficial and only provide physical pleasure. They do not bring happiness. I am more interested in marrying a good man than having expensive gifts."

"I'm glad you are understanding and think this way."

As the wedding candles began to flicker out, we got into bed and spent the night together for the first time. The next morning, we were awoken by Mother's knocking on the door.

"Get up quickly. It's almost time to go. Gather your things and have some breakfast. We need to leave soon for the cave."

Within an hour, a long line of family members and servants was trekking up the hill. Everyone's arms were full of items and food left over from the wedding. There was a quiet sense of relief among all of us that we had succeeded in holding the ceremony without any problems. Everyone seemed more relaxed, and everything on the mountain — the trees, flowers, streams — seemed more beautiful. Mother smiled all day that day. That evening she called Weiluan and me to come sit with her.

"The two of you are now married," she said. "You are bound to each other for the rest of your lives. You must share everything, stick together through good and bad times, and care for each other in sickness and in health. Commander Han, you have stayed with us long enough to know the kind of background Fengxian has had. She comes from a well-to-do family where she has never lacked food or other necessities. Most important, she has never had to work in the fields. I have often heard people say that in Guangdong, in rain and in wind, young and old, men and women, must toil in the fields. Often people there have to endure such hardship that they become ferocious. I know you are a good man, but I still have my concerns about Fengxian's future. Please remember that no matter how difficult and hard your situation is, don't let Fengxian suffer and never abandon her."

"Mother-in-Law, I assure you that I will love and care for Fengxian forever. Thank you for your kindness in allowing us to marry. Hunan is my second home. Perhaps I will wind up spending the rest of my life here. I will not let Fengxian suffer. I will find a job to support her. She will never toil in the fields."

Father and the servants tried to allay Mother's worry by telling her about how upstanding and unique Weiluan was, but I could see she was still anxious. In the end, almost all of Mother's concerns would come to pass. Later I would replay this scene over and over in my mind. Mothers have a unique ability to sense when their children are in danger, and children, out of a naïve sense of invincibility and longing for autonomy, rarely listen.

Despite the fact that we were in exile deep in the woods, Weiluan and I were intoxicated newlyweds. We spent every moment side by side. We walked hand in hand along the hilltops and streams and watched the sun set behind the hills at dusk. By early summer, Japanese soldiers were entering Huaguo less frequently, so we and other villagers returned to our homes.

Upon our arrival, Father put each of us in charge of restoring a part of Rongxia. Weiluan and I helped Father revitalize the garden, which had been destroyed yet again. We picked weeds, trimmed broken tree limbs, and planted new flowers. Mother and my brothers cleaned the house and fixed the furniture, while the servants got the rice paddies and vegetable plots back into operation. The fields had been left barren during the war and required several weeks of work. My parents hired some additional laborers to assist the servants.

Until the fields began to yield harvests, we were unable to collect any rent from our tenants. As a result, our finances remained extremely tight, and food was in short supply. Mother tried her utmost to sustain all of us. She cut back on the amount she ate so the rest of us could eat more. Mother always put others before herself, which was one of her many good qualities.

A few weeks later grandfather, his concubine, and their children returned to Rongxia. Although it was nice to have the house full again, it wasn't long before Qie's jealousy casted a dark shadow over our family. When Weiluan was introduced to her, Qie responded with some snide remarks and a look of contempt, then turned her back and walked away. My family and I were used to her rudeness, but Weiluan was very insulted by it. Often Qie would come to our wing of the house and criticize Mother and Weiluan.

"You thought marrying your daughter to an officer would lead to a life of power and luxury, but God has made a joke of you by sending you an officer without a penny to his name. Why did you spend so much money on the wedding banquet? Now you can't put enough food on the table for your family. How ironic and funny!"

Our family had two sources of solace to allay the stress from Qie's squabbling and the war. The first was music. Every evening in our garden, Father played the Chinese flute, accompanied by Weiluan on the erhu. The countryside was so still and silent at night that neighbors a mile away could hear their songs. Father was a jovial, optimistic man, but his songs carried a deep feeling of sadness. The melodies resonated in the hearts of many friends and neighbors, who joined us in our garden each night. All of them praised and admired our family's musical ability.

Our second source of solace was the discovery that I was pregnant. As soon as we learned that I was with child, everyone in my family became more cheerful. It was a poignant reminder that, even in the midst of death and destruction, life would go on. Eventually, new life would begin to fill the void left by the war.

However, having a baby on the way introduced new complications. Money was already scarce, and Weiluan became increasingly anxious about how he would support me and our child.

"Your parents have already been extremely generous," he said. "We can't depend on them for the rest of our lives."

Weiluan felt it was time to begin looking for work. One morning he got up early and said he was going to Huaguo and Fengmen to inquire about the state of the war and what, if any, job opportunities were available. Newspapers weren't distributed to locations as remote as ours, and no one had a radio, so it often took weeks for news of major events to make their way to Rongxia.

When Weiluan hadn't returned by the next day, my mother and I became very worried. Father went looking for him, but no one had any information. That night we were discussing what to do when Weiluan suddenly barged through the gate of our house with a big smile.

"I heard some great news! The Japanese are retreating. It looks like they might surrender!" Everyone was elated. As Weiluan walked over to hug me, he noticed that Mother and I both had red, swollen eyes. "Why have you been crying?"

"They were worried about you," my brother replied. "When you didn't come back, they were afraid that you had been caught by the Japanese, or that you had fled because you couldn't bear the hardship here."

"I'm not a boy. I know how to protect myself. I'm very happy here. I don't feel any hardship or bitterness. And even if there was some, it would be worth it."

A few weeks later, in August 1945, the Japanese army officially surrendered, and the war came to a close. At that time, access to information was so limited that we had no idea what prompted the sudden surrender after so many bitter years of fighting, and no one really cared. All that mattered was that it was over. We could finally begin to rebuild our lives. Prior to the arrival of Japanese troops, I had been happily studying at university. Since then, I had married and was now pregnant. Even if Lakeside College reopened, I knew it would be impossible to return. After all of my impassioned efforts to continue my education, in the end I would become a housewife.

With the war over, Weiluan decided it was time to travel to some larger cities to search for work. I dreaded being separated from him, but knew that we needed some form of income to provide for our child. My parents gave Weiluan the money for the journey, and one of my cousins walked him to the train station. The day he departed, we had an emotional goodbye. He had a hard time leaving me behind and turned back several times to tell me to be careful for the baby.

That afternoon I sat alone under the shade of the banyan tree, gazing at the pond. We had often sat there together. Weiluan would pick lotus flowers from the pond and give them to me. Once he put my brother in a tub and pushed it into the middle of the pond. When my brother got scared and stood up, the tub capsized. Weiluan rushed into the water and carried Brother back inside. He had only been gone a few hours, and I already missed him.

Worry Begets Illness

Without Weiluan by my side, I felt empty, sad, and alone. Every day I eagerly awaited a letter from him. One finally arrived after a month. Weiluan explained that he was staying with some friends in Changsha, who were helping him look for a job. All of us were relieved to hear some news, but Mother remained worried about the future of me and my baby. This anxiety, on top of the nonstop criticism she received from Qie, weighed on Mother's spirit. Soon she fell ill.

Father hired many doctors to treat Mother, but nothing helped. Each day she got worse. Soon she was bed-ridden and required around-the-clock care. Mother eventually was diagnosed with uterine cancer, which was nearly impossible to cure back then, particularly in the countryside. Father sold many of the items still in our possession to raise money for Mother's treatment, but she remained in constant pain. Her body became frail and emaciated, and her skin turned a grayish pale. She was just 45 years old, but she looked like an old woman.

I took on the daily responsibility of looking after Mother. This included feeding and bathing her as well as giving her herbal concoctions. Boya had seldom come home since she had been married, but when Mother became sick she returned a couple of times to check on her. However, my sister made no real effort to care for Mother. Neighbors and relatives praised me for being so filial and said that my efforts would be repaid one day because God always blesses filial children.

Even on her death bed, Mother remained concerned about my and Weiluan's future. She worried about the baby in my belly and that my body might not be able to handle the burden of nursing her day and night. She often looked at me with tears. Every day she asked if there was any news from Weiluan.

"Why isn't Commander Han back yet? Has he found a job?"

Mother fell ill in October. By December, she was on death's doorstep. She knew more clearly than we did that the end was near, that the time for treatment was over, and that it was time to begin saying goodbye. However, Father continued to race from one place to another looking for a doctor who could cure her. Eventually, he learned of a hospital in Changsha that had expertise in uterine cancer. He had already spent all of the money from selling Mother's jewelry and other household items, so he decided to borrow money from friends to take Mother to Changsha. When Mother learned of his intentions, she refused to go.

"I know the condition of my body. If you try to send me there, it's very likely that I will die in transit, which would be a miserable death for me. Please allow me to spend my final days at home." Father was devastated to see that Mother had resigned herself to death, but he agreed to abide by her wishes.

"Fengxian, I worry most about you. Commander Han has been gone for months now, yet we have received no word. You are pregnant, alone, and have no one to depend on."

I wanted Mother to die in peace and to stop worrying about Weiluan and me, so I made up a story that I had just received a letter from him with lots of good news. I pointed across the room to the letter he had sent me two months ago.

"That paper over there is a letter I just received from Commander Han. In it, he says he has found a good job and will come back to see you soon. He also sent some money to cover your medical bills."

"Really? That's wonderful! If I am to die right now, I no longer have anything to worry about. I can die with a peaceful heart."

In fact, Mother was right. Weiluan hadn't written for months. I was as scared as she was about my future, but I suppressed my feelings. Every day I cried quietly behind her back. Mother was so ill that her impending death weighed on me every minute to the point that I became deeply depressed.

Mother hung on through Chinese New Year 1946. During that time, many friends and relatives came to say goodbye, including her beloved older brother, who had traveled from afar to bid farewell to his sister. By the time Uncle arrived, Mother could no longer speak and could barely move. Yet her eyes opened wide when he entered the room. She had been holding on just for him.

Uncle walked straight to Mother's side. He gave her a loving smile, stroked her hair, and whispered some final words to her. They stayed there in silence for a while, then Mother motioned to me to come to her. I could see in her eyes that this was our last goodbye. I began to cry, and she touched my hand. She nodded for my father and brothers to come over. She gave each of them the same loving look of farewell and touched their hands as a final goodbye.

We stood around her bed in a circle and watched as her eyes fell into a blank gaze. After several minutes, her body jerked, and she stopped breathing. Her eyes were still wide open. We cried out to her, but there was no response. She was gone. Mother died mid-afternoon on January 19 of the lunar calendar.

All of us wept. I looked around the room and knew that Mother must have felt comforted and grateful to have us there. But one key person was missing: Boya. I felt angry that my sister made no effort to be there, even though I knew she was under the control of her in-laws and couldn't come and go as she pleased.

"No more tears, everyone," Uncle said after several minutes. "To die is to be human. I asked some very renowned doctors about this disease. All of them said it's incurable. There is nothing any of you could have done. You shouldn't blame yourselves. Sister was such a worrier that over time her anxiety had built up to such a level that it began to sap her health, making her vulnerable to this disease."

While Father had the final say on all matters, Mother had been the core of our household. Without her, everything felt amiss. My three brothers were still young; they were devastated. Father had never borne the responsibility of managing the family and felt overwhelmed. Worst of all, every penny we possessed had been spent on Mother's treatment. By the time she died, no money was left to bury her.

I felt lost and overcome with guilt. What Uncle had said about Mother's worrying being the source of her illness was true. Without a doubt, I had been the biggest source of worry in her life since the day I was born. I recalled all of the arguments we had had about my betrothal to Cong, attending school, marrying Weiluan. There was nothing I could do to change the past, but I did have the ability to give her the grand funeral she deserved. I decided to pawn the gold bracelet Weiluan gave me as my wedding gift and to use the money to cover Mother's funeral expenses. I believed he would agree that it was the right thing to do to repay my mother for her kindness and care.

Friends and relatives could see my distress and tried to comfort me. "Fengxian, your mother's death is not because of you. You did your best to nurse her. Her disease was too serious. Everyone must die someday. Don't burden yourself with too much grief and sadness. Remember, you are going to give birth to your baby soon." They were kind words, but I was inconsolable. I cried until I was so exhausted I could cry no more.

At the time, the tradition in our hometown when someone died was to let the coffin lie in state in the main hall of the house for as long as it took the deceased's relatives to pay their respects. During this time, the coffin would be accompanied around the clock by a member of the deceased's immediate family. The coffin was not to be left alone for any reason. With Boya absent and my brothers still young, the burden of accompanying the coffin fell to my father and me. Seeing how exhausted and depleted I was, and knowing that I would soon be giving birth, Uncle suggested that we bury Mother after two weeks since all of her important relatives had already paid their respects. We agreed to bury her in early February.

Many friends and relatives came. Boya and her husband didn't attend the burial, but they sent gifts. The hall was full of funeral wreaths and couplets expressing grief and sorrow. There were also numerous items made of colorful paper, all of which would be burned for Mother so she could enjoy them in the next world.

I felt anxious about the lie I had told Mother about Weiluan getting a job. I feared burying her without this worry of hers being resolved. Then auspiciously, just before the funeral began, someone announced that a letter and parcel had arrived from Weiluan. I quickly opened it, then explained the situation to the Taoist monk in charge of the ceremony. The monk told us he would immediately give the message to Mother and quickly started the proceedings.

The monk walked over to Mother's coffin, began to beat a gong and drum, and chanted to Mother's soul that Weiluan had returned in spirit.

"Your son-in-law, Commander Han ... has sent some money and silk cloth to express his grief and sorrow ... Please accept it and rest in peace ... Under the care of Commander Han ... your daughter will live a life of everlasting happiness ... Do not worry about them ... Please rest in peace."

I knelt in front of the funeral altar as he chanted. Whenever he paused, I bowed. After the monk was finished, I could sense Mother smiling at me from heaven. Her final wish had been satisfied. I thanked God for releasing Mother from her last earthly burden. After the ceremony, we carried Mother's coffin up one of the hills behind Rongxia and buried her with our other ancestors.

After the funeral was over and the guests had left, Father became pale and weak. My own sadness was so heavy that I could do nothing but go to my room and lay on the bed. After a few hours, I reopened Weiluan's letter and parcel. In fact, he had no idea that Mother had died or was even sick. It was just a fortunate coincidence that his note arrived the moment before her funeral.

"Fengxian, I'm now in Hankou in Hubei Province. I haven't yet found a good job. If it's not a good post, I don't want to do it. Although I'm not beside you, my heart is always with you. Don't worry too much. Take care of our baby, which is the manifestation of our love. I borrowed some money from an old friend. I am using some for my daily expenses. The rest I have used to buy some silk cloth for you and the baby. I am also sending you a money order, which is enclosed. Please inform me as soon as you receive the money. Please let me know the situation at home. Your parents have treated me so well. Their love and care are as deep as the ocean. I will repay them one day. Please take good care of them. I will return once I find a good job and settle down. Please wait for me patiently. Weiluan"

As I was reading the letter, Uncle and Father entered my room. Uncle asked me if he could look at the letter, so I handed it to him. He shook his head after he read it. "It's very difficult right now to find a good job. He should find a job first, and then look for a better one. Waiting like this is not a solution. If you want to look for your lost horse, riding a cow is better than walking."

I handed the money order to Father.

"Fengxian," Uncle said, "I have to return home now as I have a business trip in a few days. Take care of yourself. Help your father manage the family and teach your brothers to read and write. Don't be too sad. For every person, death is inevitable. Restrain your grief and accept this loss." As Uncle was speaking to me, tears were streaming down both our faces.

We accompanied Uncle to the front gate, where we said farewell. We watched in silence as he climbed onto his magic bicycle and pedaled away.

Sunshine Follows Rain

The next day Father went to the post office to exchange Weiluan's money order for cash. There were no banks in the countryside, so everyone used the post office for financial transactions. When Father returned, he handed all of the money to me, but I was so deep in grief and uncomfortable with the pregnancy that I told him to use it for whatever our family needed. Seeing how distraught I was and knowing I would soon give birth, Father hired a middle-aged woman to nurse me and asked Aunt Chen to periodically check on me.

As soon as I could muster the energy, I wrote a letter to Weiluan informing him of Mother's passing. Later that night I woke up feeling an urgent need to urinate, so I went to the outhouse. When I didn't return for some time, the nurse rushed and told Aunt Chen, who quickly deduced that I had gone into labor. They assisted me back to bed and informed Father, who instructed one of the servants to find a midwife.

The pain of childbirth was worse than I ever imagined. After several hours, I finally gave birth to a white, plump, beautiful daughter. It was mid-February 1946, around 10 p.m. Grandfather named her Zijiao, which means "born beautiful," or Zi (Zǔ) for short.

After giving birth, my health deteriorated and I lost my appetite. I had a nasty cough and was afflicted with rubella (German measles). My head and face became swollen, leaving me with only a small line of vision. I often fainted. Fortunately, my body was still able to produce enough milk to feed Zi. Father invited many doctors to treat me. I eventually recovered after a few months.

By then, it was summer, and the annual Dragon Boat Festival was approaching. I received a letter from Weiluan informing me that he would be home for the holiday to pay his respects to Mother.

"I never expected Mother would pass away so abruptly. I couldn't believe my eyes when I first read the news. I thought you must have written it wrong, or I must have read it wrong, but after reading it over and over I had to accept that this great tragedy was true. I am so sorry about Mother. When she was dying, she was still worrying about us. I didn't have the opportunity to return to see her one last time. I owe so much to her. It is a debt that I will never be able to repay. I regret this deeply. If Mother were still here, I would beg her to forgive me, her unfilial son-in-law. I will never forget Mother and her words to me. I will take good care of you, Fengxian, to try to make up for my mistake.

I am currently working as a Nationalist KMT military staff officer at a command post in Hankou. I will return to Rongxia for the Dragon Boat Festival. I must visit Mother's tomb to pay my respects to her spirit. Please make the necessary preparations for me to visit Mother's grave. After that, I will bring you to live with me in Hankou.

Has our baby been born? I worry very much about you. Please convey my best wishes to Father-in-Law. I have much more to tell you, but will save it until we see each other face-to-face. Weiluan"

Father and I were still deeply grieving, but we took comfort in the news that Weiluan had found a good job. His impending visit injected much-needed energy into our household. We considered the news of Weiluan's employment, along with the birth of Zi, as "double happiness" for the family, a term commonly used in China to represent good fortune.

When Grandfather learned that Weiluan was working as a military officer in Hankou, he dramatically changed his attitude toward me and my family. Previously Grandfather ignored us, but now he frequently came to see and hold Zi and sent many tonics to help my body heal. Between the failure of his tea business, Qie's opium habit, and the Japanese occupation, much of Grandfather's fortune had been lost. He viewed my moving to Hankou as an opportunity to reconnect with old friends and start anew. He asked me to satisfy his wish and say some good words about him to Commander Han.

"Grandfather, we have no money aside from Commander Han's salary. We are unable to support you for a long visit. If you want to visit for a couple of weeks, that is fine, but it is impossible for us to support you for a long time. I just want to be frank with you."

"Of course, I wouldn't stay for long," he replied curtly.

Weiluan arrived a couple of days before the Dragon Boat Festival. He didn't say any words of greeting or even request to see or hold Zi. He only asked to be led immediately to Mother's tomb so he could pay his respects. Father ordered a servant to carry items he had prepared at Weiluan's request to the graveyard and to set them in front of Mother's tomb. All of us followed and knelt in front of the tomb. Weiluan took out a piece of paper from his pocket and handed it to me. "Here is a funeral oration that I wrote for Mother. Please read it aloud on my behalf."

"Today is May third on the lunar calendar in the 35th year of the Republic of China. Mother-in-Law, the news that you passed away shocked me greatly. Today I have returned to pay my respects to your spirit before your tomb. Spirit of Mother-in-Law, I have prepared delicious dishes, wine, incense, and white candles for you. Now, as I kneel before you, I pray that you can enjoy them. Alas, how sad I am! Here, through this ritual, I can only express part of my grief and sadness. These acts cannot make up for the debt I owe you for your kindness, which I will regret for the rest of my life. I feel so sorry and shameful to face your spirit. But there is nothing I can do but to look up into the sky, beat my chest, and shed tears of blood.

Please drink this first bottle of wine and eat these dishes. If your spirit can hear me, Mother-in-Law, please forgive me. In the next life, I will surely repay your love and care. I will never forget what you said to me. Your words have been engraved on my heart, and I will follow them with the best of my effort. Do not worry about this.

Please drink this second bottle of wine and eat these dishes. As I kneel down here, Mother-in-Law, I promise to never forget your virtues and strengths. I can still see your face in front of me. Your greatest wish will be realized soon. After the Dragon Boat Festival, I will take Fengxian and our daughter to live together with me in Hankou. From now on, we will never be separated. Without your help, I couldn't have married your daughter. How pitiful it is that I cannot repay this debt of gratitude to you.

Now, all I can do is to cry out your name with my broken heart. Please drink this third bottle of wine and eat these dishes. Mother, if your spirit can hear me, please rest in peace. Alas, how sad I am. Written by your son-in-law, Weiluan, in grief"

Everyone wept as I read the letter. After a few minutes, we all stood up and regained our composure. However, one of our old servants remained distraught and was overcome with tears.

"I have been a servant in the Chu family for my entire life. Your Mother always treated me well. She never looked down upon servants and always helped us solve any problems we may have had. Why has God let such a good person die so young? Now the Chu family is reunited with Commander Han, but your Mother is absent." As I listened to the servant's words, I couldn't help crying. Mother's humility and kindness toward others were her greatest attributes.

Three days later, Weiluan and I left Rongxia for Hankou. Our luggage consisted only of some embroidered pillowcases, blankets from our wedding, and a few items for Zi. After breakfast, we said farewell to our family, neighbors, and friends. Servants carried our luggage to Fengmen Station, while my family and I trailed behind. Father and my brothers were heartbroken to see me go; I felt awful leaving them. Our family had been confronted with too many goodbyes recently. The sadness was overwhelming for all of us.

As soon as we boarded the train, I rushed to a window seat and waved. "Farewell, everyone," I shouted. "We will surely see each other again someday."

"Take good care of yourself, Fengxian," Father yelled back.

I watched out the window until I could no longer see anyone. During the train ride, Weiluan played with Zi while I quietly reminisced about my family. I thought about Boya, whom I was so close to when I was young. I wondered if my sister and I would ever see each other again. I began to cry.

"Fengxian, every party has its end. Friends and loved ones inevitably must part. But the closest relationship in the world is that between husband and wife. Don't shed any more tears."

Weiluan insisted that I eat something so I would be nourished enough to nurse Zi. Afterward, I silently gazed out the window. Isn't this the day I have been dreaming of for so long? I should feel happy instead of sad, I thought. What I know now, but was only beginning to learn then, is that every new beginning brings a close to what went before it. With the start of a new future comes the end of the past.

PART THREE

Salvos of a Young Couple

Getting Started

For China, World War II had been a temporary distraction from the larger clash over control of our country between the Chinese Communist Party (CCP), led by Mao Zedong, and the Nationalist Party (Kuomintang or KMT), led by Chiang Kai-shek. The two sides had engaged in numerous skirmishes since the late-1920s. A few months after Japan's surrender, the CCP and KMT, which had fought side by side against Japan, resumed battling each other.

As the civil war intensified, the KMT required more personnel, which created numerous job opportunities for former KMT officers like my husband. Weiluan secured a job at the KMT's army base in Hankou mapping and plotting the battlefield topography for the director of the base, General Cheng Qian (Chŭng Chē-ĕn). The job gave Weiluan high visibility with senior officers, but the pay was low.

We spent one day and night on the train from Huaguo. When we arrived in Hankou, Weiluan hired two rickshaws to take us and our luggage to our apartment. We arrived at a one-floor bungalow tucked away on a remote road. The neighborhood was away from the action of the city center but near the KMT army base.

The front door of the building opened into the middle of a vestibule leading to two apartments. A family from Shanghai was renting the apartment on the left side of the bungalow, and our quarters were on the right side. The door of our apartment opened into the living room, which was flanked on the left and right sides by bedrooms. Behind the living room was the kitchen, and beyond the kitchen was a small pond with many lotus flowers. As with most city dwellings, the apartment had no toilet, shower, or running water. We used an old wooden bucket, called a matong, as a toilet. Every evening a worker emptied the matong in exchange for a small fee. We purchased water every few days from neighborhood salesmen who strolled through our area announcing, "water for sale, water for sale." We used this water to drink, cook, wash clothes, and sponge bathe.

The apartment was completely bare, without even a stool to sit on or a place to put our clothes. Our new housemates were very friendly and invited me to sit and chat while Weiluan went shopping for furniture and other necessities.

A couple of hours later, Weiluan returned with some kitchen supplies, two long wooden benches, and a large piece of wood that formerly had served as a door. He placed the benches in the middle of our bedroom, laid the door on top, and announced that it would serve as our bed.

"Fengxian, I'm sorry I can't give you a comfortable life right now, but don't worry. We will have a happy family for sure. Believe me, the current situation won't last long."

"It's also my responsibility to create a happy family," I replied. "We are husband and wife. We must stick together through thick and thin. We must work together to overcome our difficulties."

That evening I covered the wood with the elaborate silk bedding I had brought from Hunan, which had been hand-embroidered by Mother and Boya. The bed resembled a flower in cow dung. As I looked around the bare apartment that night, it began to sink in that life with Weiluan was going to be very different from the comfort and simplicity I had been accustomed to at Rongxia. I was now a wife and mother. It was going to be my job to make that empty place into a home. I knew we would face many challenges, but at least Weiluan and I were together, and that was what mattered most. True love between a husband and wife cannot be measured in riches. I knew that Weiluan was doing his best to support us, so I never complained about our circumstances.

Hankou was a bustling city, but I rarely stepped foot outside. After years of being confined to my boudoir, I had grown accustomed to spending most of my time in the house. I spent my days looking after and playing with Zi, cooking meals, doing laundry, and cleaning. Every evening Weiluan brought home fresh produce, meat, or fish, which I prepared for dinner. Occasionally, he splurged on some cloth, which I used to make clothes for Zi and me. We couldn't afford a tailor, so I did all of the sewing and needlework myself. The first garments I made were cotton tops and bottoms for Zi. They looked surprisingly good, which gave me confidence to tackle more difficult items. Later I made a silk cheongsam for myself.

After a few months of thriftiness, we accumulated a small amount of savings. One weekend Weiluan took Zi and me window shopping at one of the more popular areas in Hankou. That evening, we visited one of the night markets, ate noodles with shredded chicken and beef at a small restaurant, and then walked home hand-in-hand.

When Weiluan had spare time, he helped me with housework, including washing Zi's diapers. He often told me to rest while he did the chores. He even offered to make clothes, but we both laughed at that proposition. Our small amount of savings still wasn't enough to buy furniture, so our home continued to be bare. Nevertheless, we were a happy couple and a happy family, and Weiluan was a good, hard-working husband. I felt fortunate.

A few months later, we received a surprise visit from my grandfather, who was under the mistaken impression that Weiluan and I were living a luxurious life in Hankou. As soon as Grandfather arrived on the train, he went straight to my husband's office. That evening they came home together. Grandfather was stunned when he entered our apartment and saw how bare it was.

"I just came to visit some old friends," he said. "After that, I will return to Hunan."

"Grandfather, our life in Hankou is nothing compared to yours when you lived here. I know you aren't used to this kind of austere life. We have nothing to entertain you with, and there is no place for you to sleep but the floor. Nevertheless, we will try our best to support you during your stay because you are my grandfather, after all. The one precondition is that you must not complain."

"I understand," Grandfather replied. Rather than impose on us, after dinner Grandfather left to stay at a friend's house.

The next weekend, we felt we owed it to Grandfather to show him a good time, so we took him to the night market and the movies. It was the first time I had ever been to the cinema. We watched *The Secret History of the Court of the Qing Dynasty*; I was enthralled. Afterward, we bought some small gifts for Grandfather, my father, and brothers. By the time Grandfather left, our small savings had been depleted.

"Just when we had finally accumulated some money," Weiluan said, "it is suddenly used up by your grandfather."

"I know, but we had no choice," I said. "We had to entertain him out of respect."

Weiluan's meager salary was a source of anxiety for both of us. Because it was war time, he often worked long hours, which prevented him from doing additional work on the side. Consequently, the only way for us to accumulate any savings was to spend as little as possible. For that reason, we rarely left the house or engaged in the fun activities other families did for entertainment. Fortunately, we didn't have the burden of paying rent each month. Our bungalow previously belonged to a man who sympathized with the Japanese and committed treason against China. The KMT confiscated the bungalow when they captured the man. They rented out half to the family from Shanghai and allowed us to live in the other half for free.

When winter arrived late that year, the cold was like nothing I had experienced before. The wind crossing the Yangtze River sent a bone-chilling shiver up my spine that didn't relent until spring. There was no heat in our apartment, so I had to wash clothes and do other chores in the freezing cold. Often I was so frozen that I could barely move my limbs or walk. Zi was so uncomfortable during the winter that she cried incessantly. At times, I didn't know if I would be able to endure, but I didn't have a choice.

As Chinese New Year approached in 1947, I desperately wanted to send money to my father, but we hadn't accumulated enough savings. I felt ashamed not being able to fulfill what our family considered to be a filial obligation of every child living away from home. I hoped that Father would understand. Instead, I wrote him a lengthy letter. Weiluan could tell I was deeply homesick, so he tried to cheer me up with some stories about his own difficult experiences living away from home.

"Several years ago, while I was away in the army, my hometown suffered a year of terrible weather. A horrible famine ensued. I knew that 2,000 kilograms of rice were being held in a nearby military reserve, so I arranged with my nephew, Dong (Dōng), who was also in the military at that time, to send some rice to my family. Many times in the past I had rescued my nephew from various entanglements, so he agreed to repay me by helping me ship the rice home. I wrote a letter to my family telling them that some food would be arriving shortly. A few weeks later, I received word that the rice never arrived. I confronted my nephew. Dong concocted a story about the ship breaking down and the water spoiling the rice. I knew he was lying. I couldn't believe he would dare steal grain at such an urgent time. Where was his conscience? After that, I began to wonder if my nephew was so unreliable, could I ever rely on anyone? Luckily, all of my family members survived that famine, but other people in my hometown died that year of starvation and disease."

I shook my head and sighed. "Even though we may share the same blood with a person, sometimes he can feel as distant and foreign as a stranger on the street."

"Fengxian, I know how helpless a person can feel when he is so far from home and unable to help his family. Don't be too hard on yourself."

"I know. Leaving home is never easy."

That was how I spent my first Chinese New Year away from Rongxia: in a frigid, barren apartment chatting with my husband on a bed constructed from a door. But none of that mattered because I was young and in love.

Shortly after Chinese New Year in 1947, I came down with another bout of rubella. My body became frail and I occasionally fainted. Because I was home alone all day, Weiluan became worried and hired a doctor to evaluate me. To our surprise, the doctor informed us that I was pregnant again. I was stunned and didn't know if the news was good or bad.

At one point, I became so weak that I couldn't get up from bed, so I wrote a letter to Father requesting that my eldest brother Liang come help me care for Zi. Liang dropped out of school and rushed to my aid. My brother added another mouth to feed, but his presence was a great help around the house and gave Weiluan much peace of mind.

Later that spring, Director Cheng promoted my husband to Lieutenant Colonel. Weiluan deeply admired Director Cheng and worked diligently for him every day. Director Cheng's son was working in the same department as Weiluan. Although they were from different social strata, they became close friends. They discussed political affairs and shared midnight snacks when they worked late. Director Cheng's son often gave Weiluan a ride home in his car. I felt proud to see Weiluan with Director Cheng's son.

One winter evening, while opening the door to greet my husband, I doubled over in pain. Weiluan knew instantly that I was going into labor and rushed back to his friend's car to seek help. Soon he returned with a doctor. Around 1 a.m. in late October of the lunar calendar, I gave birth to my second daughter. We named her Tianjiao, which means "natural beauty," or Tian (Tē-ĕn) for short. Her arrival brought us great joy.

With a new baby, our daily expenses increased. The small raise Weiluan received with his promotion was quickly used up, and he became increasingly discouraged about our financial situation. Director Cheng could see that something was bothering my husband.

"Lieutenant Colonel Han, how is your family these days?"

"They are doing well, but my newborn daughter has added another mouth to feed. I can hardly bear the heavy burden of supporting them now."

Director Cheng smiled, picked up a pen, and scribbled a few lines on a piece of paper.

"Go buy some tonics to nourish your wife's body, so she has enough milk to breastfeed your daughter."

"Sir, I can't possibly impose on you like this."

"This is a special allowance for your family that all staff members in difficult situations are entitled to. Please accept it."

"Thank you for your generosity, sir. Not only are you very smart and capable, you are also very compassionate. No wonder you have been so successful."

Weiluan returned from work that day with a big grin.

"What are you so happy about?" I asked.

He handed me the slip of paper. I unfolded it and saw that it was a note signed by Director Cheng permitting him to receive two months of additional salary.

"This is wonderful! You know the saying, 'Whatever concerns the man who pays you must concern you.' Well, now that Director Cheng has been so generous to us, you must be loyal and work hard for him."

After breakfast the next day, Weiluan went to the accounting department of the base to pick up the money. He decided to use some of the money to purchase a proper bed for us. We gave the benches and door panel to my brother, who was very easygoing and hard-working and never asked for anything.

An Overnight Windfall

After living one year in the bungalow, Weiluan was assigned a larger, more beautiful apartment in a livelier neighborhood close to the city center. Previously, a senior Japanese officer had lived there. The KMT inherited the apartment when the Japanese army surrendered. The new apartment was far superior to where we had been living, but it felt empty without all the furniture and fancy decorations to go with it.

Less than a month after moving in, Weiluan suggested that we sell the apartment to a rich businessman and pocket the proceeds. At the time, it was common for KMT officers to liquidate assets seized by the army and keep the money for themselves.

"We can get a large sum of money and move back to our old apartment."

"Hasn't the bungalow already been rented out to other people?"

"No, not yet. If I say I want to move back, no one will stand in our way."

"Well, if you think it's feasible, and you won't get in trouble, then sure, let's go ahead. It's not a problem for me."

A couple of weeks later Weiluan sold our new apartment. Overnight we became rich. The money we earned was a windfall for us, but it was paltry compared with the large fortunes other officers amassed.

I continued to be thrifty, only spending money on items we absolutely needed. At first, Weiluan was the same and only used the money to purchase food and furniture. But after a while, he began to waste more and more money on jewelry and expensive clothes.

Weiluan bought me a new gold bracelet to replace the one I pawned to pay for Mother's funeral as well as a gold ring, ruby ring, and gold necklace. He arranged to have a green sapphire-colored plush coat tailor-made for me. I went several times to the tailor shop to be measured. The coat was very formal and elegant and worth more than 100 grams of gold.

Weiluan also bought me many other clothes as well as cotton and leather shoes for all seasons. He purchased fine, expensive military uniforms for himself and bought clothes for our daughters and Liang as well. On Sundays, he often took me to the cinema, followed by dinner in a fancy restaurant. It was the first time we had enjoyed such a laidback, luxurious life since being married. Dressed in that expensive coat and adorned with gold jewelry, leather gloves, and high-heeled shoes, I was transformed overnight into an elegant, upper-class woman. Weiluan also looked very handsome in his new uniforms. Everywhere we went we attracted attention.

One evening Weiluan arranged for us to go out to dinner with some of his colleagues. The minute they spotted us on the street, they chuckled and shouted at us to come over.

"Lieutenant Colonel Han, when did you become a tycoon? Your wife looks more luxurious than Director Cheng's! Have you received some kind of windfall?"

I never liked attention, and listening to them joke about the way we looked made me blush and uncomfortable. When I took off the coat to sit down for dinner, my new, bright-colored cheongsam immediately caught their eyes.

"Lieutenant Colonel Han, your wife is so beautiful. No wonder we seldom see her on the streets."

"It's not that I don't want to take her out. The true reason is because we never used to have the money."

"Don't worry. You don't have to act like you are poor in front of us. We won't ask to borrow money from you!"

"No, what I said is the truth. Just a couple of months ago, Fengxian and I barely had enough money to get by each month."

"So how did you manage to strike it rich overnight? Please tell us, so we can learn from you and do the same!"

Weiluan explained that he had sold the luxurious apartment he had been given to a rich businessman. His colleagues thought it was a brilliant idea and admired his foresight.

On our way home from dinner that night, we ran into some other colleagues of my husband, who also were taken aback by our dress and asked if we had struck it rich. By the time we returned home, I was fed up with all of the gawking and sarcasm. The second I walked through the door, I tossed my coat onto the bed.

"I will never put on such a luxurious coat again, so that I can be made fun of by others. That coat and I don't mix well at all."

"Fengxian, I bought these things for you. How can you be angry with me? If I didn't buy them for you, you might say that I was not good to you."

"I never asked you to buy such expensive clothes. I will not wear them again."

"I wanted to show you and your family that I am taking good care of you and that your life has become better, not worse, since marrying me. I couldn't contribute one cent to the cost of our wedding, and we had no money to send your father for Chinese New Year. Until recently, Liang has had to sleep on the floor. I don't want your family to think of me as a worthless soldier. If you don't want to wear the clothes, then we can save them for our daughters."

"Fine. Save the clothes for them. I don't want them."

Weiluan had been so irresponsible in managing the money we earned from the sale of the apartment that, before the end of the month arrived, he had to ask for an advance from his paycheck in order to put food on the table. The only reason he could get it was because he had become such good friends with the head accountant of the base, who had also grown up in Guangdong Province.

In the span of a few months, we had gone from poverty to affluence and back to poverty. After this incident, it became clear to me why

Mother had always insisted on managing the financial affairs of our family: many men, if left to their own devices, will squander away the largest of fortunes to salvage their face or pride. Sadly, I learned that Weiluan was no different.

Family Rumblings

As with my grandfather, many of our relatives were under the mistaken impression that my husband and I were living the high life in Hankou. Although we enjoyed a brief period of extravagance, we quickly returned to living from one paycheck to the next. Not having seen for themselves how austerely we lived, many family members assumed that Weiluan's high-ranking job under Director Cheng, who was well-known throughout southern China, meant that we were in a position of wealth and power. Nothing could have been further from the truth. Nevertheless, we began to receive frequent correspondence and visits from family members on both sides, most of whom were seeking jobs in the city.

After helping us care for Zi and Tian for more than a year, Liang was itching to start his own life. He decided he wanted to attend radio technician school and asked Weiluan for assistance. My husband made several inquiries and was able to secure my brother a spot at a good school in Nanjing.

After Liang left, the full burden of child-rearing and housework fell back on our shoulders. Life became extremely busy and difficult for both Weiluan and me. Overwhelmed by everything that had to be done each day, I wrote to my father and asked that my middle brother, Dian, who had just graduated from high school, come to help me look after the girls.

I hadn't seen Dian in a few years. When he arrived at our apartment, I was surprised to see that he had grown into a tall, strong young man. It was immediately clear to my husband and me that Dian didn't belong cooped up in an apartment with us and two little girls. Weiluan made some inquiries and arranged a place for my brother in the next entering class at Whampoa Military Academy in Nanjing. Dian was extremely appreciative.

In the spring, Weiluan received a number of letters from his family. They were the first opportunity I had to get a glimpse of the people in his life before I met him; I enjoyed reading them. Weiluan was the youngest of his father's nine children, five of whom were from his father's first wife and the remaining four from his father's second wife. All of the first wife's children had either died or moved away, leaving only the second wife's children in his hometown.

Weiluan's father had been a doctor and owned a successful pharmacy in a small town outside their village. The family had been quite wealthy and well-known in the area, until one year when they encountered several tragic misfortunes. It all began with the embezzlement of a large sum of money from the pharmacy by a local warlord. Because of the warlord's power and political connections, Weiluan's father had no way to retrieve the money. Shortly thereafter, the pharmacy suffered a devastating fire and burned to the ground. Deeply distraught and depressed by the loss of everything he had worked for, Weiluan's father killed himself by overdosing on some pills. Weiluan was just a few years old when his father committed suicide.

Without a breadwinner, the family's financial situation rapidly deteriorated. Weiluan's mother reopened a smaller pharmacy in the spot where the original shop used to be, but it didn't earn nearly the same revenue. Putting Weiluan through school was a struggle.

"I was too poor to eat three meals a day at school," he said, "so all I ate for dinner each evening was a single piece of preserved tofu. If I was able to get my hands on some peanuts, I felt it was the best enjoyment in the world."

One day we received a letter from Weiluan's mother asking him to return immediately to his home in Guangdong Province. She informed him that his fourth brother had usurped the new pharmacy and had expelled her along with his seventh brother. They had been banished to the family's old rundown property outside the town center. Fourth Brother had torn down the sign of the pharmacy that bore his father's name and replaced it with a new sign bearing his own name. Weiluan's mother pleaded with him to return quickly, so they could appeal to the local authorities to divide the property equally among them.

"I am not surprised to hear this news," Weiluan said shaking his head. "I have always felt from the time I was little that my fourth brother didn't like me and wanted to usurp the pharmacy. That is one reason I didn't want to stay there and chose to leave and join the army. He cares nothing about brotherhood and kinship. This has always distressed my mother. Mother is now asking me to return, but I can't leave you and the girls alone. I don't know what to do."

"Weiluan, you have your own life here. You don't need to get involved in their troubles. Let your brother do whatever he wants. These kinds of things are dictated by fate and cannot be changed by your interference. A rich inheritence isn't what makes a man good."

"I don't care about the money. I am only concerned about my mother. It's unfair to her and my seventh brother."

"But what can you do for them? Do you think your mother would like to come here? Maybe we can bring her here once our financial situation improves."

"My mother would never agree to come here."

A few days after receiving his mother's request, a letter arrived from Fourth Brother. Weiluan was reluctant to open it, expecting the letter to be filled with petty arguing over the pharmacy. Instead, it was bad news. He had written to inform Weiluan that, shortly after taking over the pharmacy, his youngest son had fallen ill and died. "I am so sad that I long to be a monk living a secluded, isolated life. Lately my thoughts have become negative and pessimistic." Both Weiluan and I immediately thought that it was fate's retribution for his selfishness.

News of the death of Weiluan's fourth brother's son put him in a predicament. He was saddened by the loss. But if he showed too much compassion, his mother and Seventh Brother would interpret it as a sign that he was siding with Fourth Brother and was not interested in helping them. The conflict weighed heavily on my husband, who was conscientious and took everything to heart.

"Fengxian, what do you think I should do?"

"Weiluan, I don't have any opinion. I have never been to your home or met any of these people. It's too entangled for us to know who is right and who is wrong. However, family members should never seek money and property at the expense of family ties. I believe that you should not offer to do anything that you don't intend to follow through on. Otherwise, you will cause more trouble for yourself and be seen as going back on your word. That's all the advice I can give you. Beyond that, I have to say that what I have learned about your family over the past couple of weeks is very different from the picture you painted when you were trying to convince me to marry you. Your father had two wives. Is that the kind of family you are from? Do you also intend to take a concubine? Like father, like son?"

"Fengxian, I am not that type of man! I am a gentleman with a good conscience. I'm not like my brothers and father. That is one reason I left. I never felt I belonged there."

I smiled and apologized. Weiluan was a good man. If he wasn't, he would have taken even more advantage of his position in the military to make a fortune as others had done. Instead, he labored away honestly every day, and we lived a poor but honorable life. I admired him and loved him and felt fortunate to be his wife.

I didn't know it at the time, but the letters and visits from Weiluan's family painted an accurate picture of what his family was like: self-serving, petty, cruel. Within a couple of years, I would learn for myself just how different my husband was from the rest of his family. But by then, it would be too late to do anything.

An Electoral Defeat

By 1948, the Communists were gaining momentum across the country, and the civil war had begun to cause disorder in the top leadership of the KMT. In April, the KMT held an election for the post of vice president, a position second only to Chiang Kai-shek. On the ballot were several prominent KMT figures, one of whom was Director Cheng. Weiluan desperately hoped his boss would win because it would improve his career prospects and, more important, our financial situation.

On the day of the election, Hankou was teeming with activity. For days, the streets and alleys had been plastered with posters and advertisements featuring the candidates. At nearly every sidewalk, stoop, and storefront, large crowds of men gathered to discuss the election. Newsboys barked out new developments, which would then spark a frenzy of conversation. The streets were so overfilled that the cars of local officials and businessmen couldn't budge, resulting in a long queue that stretched for several blocks.

At the time, I was completely absorbed in caring for my daughters and had no interest in the election. Weiluan rarely spoke about politics or the war at home. To me, what was taking place on the streets was another world. The morning of the election, Weiluan could sense the intensity building outside and instructed me to stay in the apartment the entire day. "The streets are in chaos, and the girls could get lost. We don't want anything to happen to them, so don't go out."

"Don't worry, I won't leave the apartment," I assured him. "I am accustomed to staying in the house from all of the years I spent cooped up in my room. I can imagine the noisy scene outside without having to watch and listen first-hand."

Weiluan didn't return home until very late that night. As soon as he entered the apartment, I could tell from his demeanor that Director Cheng had lost. "Why does God always ignore my prayers?" Weiluan asked in frustration. "I wanted so much for Director Cheng to win."

"He may have lost the election, but he is still a prominent, high-ranking official," I said, trying to comfort him.

"Yes, but if he had won, I could have moved into a much higher position, and our future would be brighter. Don't you understand that?"

"Of course I do. But whether a person is rich or poor, powerful or powerless, is predestined by fate. Don't get too upset over this because there is nothing you can do to change fate."

"I know, you're right," he said. "It's just that we could really use the money."

After several moments of silence, I replied delicately, "Well … I could work and earn some additional money for us." I had proposed the idea of working once before when the army base was searching for teachers. Weiluan was adamantly against it and refused to allow me to interview for the job. I thought now was a good time to bring it up again. This time he responded even more angrily than before.

"Fengxian, I know you don't like it that I won't allow you to work. Don't you understand that you are a mother? Your place is at home with the children not somewhere outside working. That's my job. I don't want to talk about this ever again!"

Weiluan was usually quite open-minded and reasonable, but on this particular issue he was unyielding. From then on, I dared not speak again of my desire to work.

A couple of months after Director Cheng's electoral defeat, the KMT undertook a reorganization of its military and political structure in the central and southern part of the country. Director Cheng was assigned to a new post as governor of Hunan Province and head of the KMT's thousands of soldiers in that theater. He asked several members of his staff to accompany him to his new post in Changsha, including Weiluan. I was overjoyed when my husband informed me that we would be returning to Hunan. I hadn't seen my family in more than two years and looked forward to being closer to home.

In the summer of 1948, we sold our furniture, packed our belongings, and moved to Changsha. The KMT gave us some money to cover the cost of relocation. Between this subsidy and the money we earned from selling our furniture, we had a fair amount of cash in hand. After living a brief time in a small apartment, we moved to a nicer home on the second floor of a private hospital next to the army base. It was an exquisite, small Western-style building.

Because we were now living so close to my family, Weiluan felt he needed to give the impression that we were well off in order to save face. He purchased some expensive furniture, and we decorated the apartment to look elegant and beautiful. In reality, Weiluan's salary remained modest. Nevertheless, in order to preserve our dignity and mask our true situation, we did what Chinese people aptly call, "beating your face swollen to appear to others as fat (打肿脸充胖子)."

Numerous family members and friends visited us after we arrived in Changsha. It felt wonderful to be reunited with everyone, but entertaining the guests raised our expenses by half. These additional costs quickly pushed us back to living from one paycheck to the next.

Voiceless, Oblivious, Replaceable

Shortly after returning to Hunan, I began to feel under the weather again. I lost my appetite, felt uncomfortable all over, and constantly wanted to sleep. My body became weak and thin, and my complexion turned yellow. When the symptoms didn't subside after several days, I knew it could mean only one thing: I was pregnant again.

Upon hearing the news, Weiluan was ecstatic. I was not. I was already exhausted and overwhelmed from looking after Zi and Tian. I didn't know how I could cope with another baby. We were barely making ends meet as it was and couldn't afford another mouth to feed. I began to feel as though I were no different from an animal on a farm, a mother pig breeding lots of little piglets — the old ones tugging at my skirt and the young ones clinging to my feet — each new piglet adding to the already heavy weight I had to bear each day.

Since ancient times, it was believed that a Chinese woman's sole purpose was to produce sons to carry on her husband's ancestry. Women had no rights, and we were given little respect. In all aspects of life, men were exalted and women belittled. Such beliefs were deeply rooted in the fabric of the old society, and women lacked the voice and power to change this mentality. During the day, we labored nonstop tending to our children and homes, and at night we served as sexual toys for men. Where was the pleasure in this kind of life?

During my youth, I was more fortunate than the vast majority of Chinese women of my generation, most of whom were never given an opportunity to attend even one day of school. I was blessed to have a father who believed in gender equality and who permitted me to find and exercise my voice. But the day I became a mother, all of that ended. Prior to marrying Weiluan, I naively believed that after we married I would be able to finish college and find a job. It never occurred to me that I would be confronted with motherhood so soon, and that the day I became a parent my children would take priority over everything else.

Weiluan was a good man, who respected me, but he believed strongly that a woman's only place was in the home, particularly if she was a mother. I cherish each of my children and my husband, and, if given the choice, I would do it all over again. Yet the moment I became a wife and mother, I lost a part of myself and my dreams that I have never been able to recover. I was among the first generation of Chinese women to be given an opportunity for a different, more independent life. However, society had still not evolved enough to allow that opportunity to become a reality.

After a week of feeling discouraged about the pregnancy, I resigned myself to accept my fate. I had never heard about contraceptive methods, so I was unaware that couples had other options. Who was I to question whether I should have another child or not? If I was to bear another child, I would give birth to it. If I was to die during childbirth, I would accept it. Fate cannot be defied nor can one's husband.

Weiluan was overjoyed that I was pregnant again. He, like most Chinese men at that time, believed the more children a couple had, the happier the family. Even though supporting a larger family would add more financial strain, no number of children was considered too many for my husband. During those months, Weiluan was always smiling. Because I was so weak, he took over many of the household chores and never complained. He never said so, but I suspected he believed I would be giving birth to a son.

About a month after Chinese New Year in 1949, I gave birth to my third daughter at 10 a.m. on February 6 of the lunar calendar. She was healthy and lovely, but I felt disappointed when I learned that I had given birth to another girl. I had been married four years and still had not fulfilled my single most important duty as a wife. How much patience would Weiluan have with me?

I knew Weiluan was also disappointed, but he shook his head and grinned. "Let's call her Yanjiao! It means a beautiful, winsome smile. Smile reflects happiness, and isn't it happy to have another daughter?" In this way, he tried to comfort me, but I knew he felt unspeakable anguish inside.

The arrival of Yanjiao, or Yan (Yěn) for short, turned our already disorderly household into further chaos. Day and night the apartment reverberated with the sounds of children crying or laughing. I was so weak that many of the chores had to wait until Weiluan returned from work each day. Sometimes I would sit in the apartment during the day and wonder how we would survive. Over time, I regained my strength and was able to cope.

Weiluan was sitting on the bed one day quietly looking at our three girls when Yan cried for milk. I climbed onto the bed to breastfeed her, and Zi and Tian rushed to my sides. Weiluan looked at the four of us and began to laugh.

"What's so funny?" I asked.

"Before I turned 30, I was preoccupied with winning over two breasts. But now at 30, I find that my bed is full of breasts, and there is a pair of large breasts at the center of them all!" There was a tone of bitterness in his sarcasm, which made me start to cry.

"I never thought you were actually such an ugly man. If girls aren't what you want, why didn't you marry a man? You were given life by a woman. I know girls are more burdensome to you than boys, but what choice do we have? Now you are beginning to complain about me and get fed up with me, right?"

"Fengxian, don't be so narrow-minded. I was just kidding and trying to make you laugh. I didn't expect that I would stir up such a storm. I will never say this again. Please forgive me."

I felt guilty about getting angry with him. Weiluan really was a good husband and father. I knew life was difficult for him. He was more willing than most men to help around the house. Looking at our three daughters on the bed, it was understandable that Weiluan wasn't pleased with me. I was fortunate to have a husband who didn't have a mindset of valuing boys over girls, but it was reasonable that he wanted a male heir.

I handed Yan to him and apologized silently with a small smile. His face relaxed when he could see I was no longer angry.

"Is this our winsome smile?" he asked with a big grin as he took Yan into his arms.

A few weeks later, Weiluan returned home from work one day and handed me a letter. "Read this. It's good news."

The letter was from my father, so I rushed to open it. Father explained that he had met another woman and that he wanted to marry her. She was a year younger than me and already had her own children. Her husband had died in the war. The fact that her family was allowing her to remarry suggested that they were poor — and hence less adamant about following old customs that barred women from remarrying.

"I don't know if this is good news," I said. "I'm not sure I can support this. It may create an unfavorable environment at home for my brothers."

"Didn't you read the part where your father says 'without a female master, a home is not like a home?' Should we insist that he remain alone the rest of his life? As his daughter, you shouldn't stop him from doing this. Instead you should sympathize with him and agree to this marriage."

I thought about what Weiluan said and recalled the many instances in my childhood when father stood up for me. He supported my efforts to continue my education and to marry Weiluan. Opposing him on this new marriage would be unfilial. I decided that I should not only agree, I should also give him my congratulations in person. However, fate interrupted my plan.

Soon after receiving father's letter, Yan came down with an acute form of pneumonia. Several attempts at treatment failed, and she was hospitalized. Then, after living only 50 days in this world, our beautiful baby girl died.

Although I had been hesitant in the beginning to have another child, Yan quickly won over my heart. Her death was a painful loss for both of us. Weiluan took Yan's death even harder than I did. My husband cried so hard that his shirt became soaked with tears. I was so angered by Yan's death that I initially lashed out at Weiluan and blamed him.

"Why did you have to make jokes about Yan? Your callousness is the reason our baby girl didn't want to live with us and left!"

The wives of some of my husband's colleagues tried to console us.

"Yan was as weak as an elderly person with one foot in the grave. There was no way she could survive. Don't be sad. This was her fate. Don't cry anymore. Let's play mahjong!" The last thing I felt like doing was playing mahjong, but Weiluan agreed to play to get his mind off the grief.

We were too depressed to attend father's wedding, so we bought some gifts and asked someone to deliver them to Rongxia, along with the news about Yan's death. A few days later, father, my new stepmother, and her two daughters came to express their sympathy.

My stepmother was attractive but plain. She had indeed been brought up in a poor family, which is why she wasn't held to the same standards about not re-marrying. Father was very kind and attentive and seemed content with his new life. Yet I couldn't help thinking that it should have been mother who was there comforting me after the loss of my daughter. They stayed with us for a few days, which helped to temporarily distract us from our loss.

On the last day of their visit, I suggested we go shopping, so we could purchase some gifts for them to take home. We walked to the local flower market, which was always packed with small peddlers, and noticed many of the salesmen carrying large stacks of silver dollars. When we tried to pay for a few items, we discovered that the prices we were accustomed to had gone up multi-fold.

"What's going on?" Father asked one of the peddlers.

"The KMT government refused to accept the peace terms laid out by the Chinese Communist Party, so Communist troops have restarted their attacks. In the last 10 days, they have taken over Nanjing and Hangzhou, and they are making their way west and south toward Hankou and Hunan. If the KMT is defeated, their money will become completely worthless!"

The banknotes issued by the KMT government seemed to have completely lost their value and turned into slips of waste paper. Luckily, Weiluan's salary was paid in silver dollars, but even the purchasing power of that had declined significantly. I had never encountered such hyperinflation.

"If you think this is expensive now, wait until the end of the day. Prices are climbing by the minute!" said one peddler.

Because I was a woman, no one, including my husband or my father, ever talked to me about the war or our country's political situation. We didn't own a radio, and newspapers were a luxury purchased and read by men. It sounds absolutely absurd now, but at the time I wasn't even aware precisely which factions were battling it out in China or the reasons for the conflict.

Although Weiluan was involved with the civil war on a daily basis, he never spoke one word of such matters to me. As a woman, my world was centered entirely on my husband, children, and home. Anything outside this was considered the domain of men. Consequently, when I heard that the Nationalist KMT might be defeated and that the Communist CCP might take over the country, I didn't grasp the significance of what such a turn of events might mean. I had no idea that, within a few years, our world would be turned upside down and that our lives would never again resemble their current shape.

Because of the hyperinflation, we purchased only a few gifts for Father and his new family before we escorted them to the Changsha train station. As I waved goodbye, my mind was flooded with memories of Mother. She had worked so hard raising my siblings and me. She had never enjoyed a day of leisure in her entire life. She died too early. It wasn't fair.

"Fengxian, your father was very gentle toward Stepmother," Weiluan said. "We should celebrate this. The family has been re-energized and resumed its original look."

"Yes," I said, "it's nothing for a man to lose his wife. When the old wife dies, he can re-marry a younger one. When the ugly wife dies, he can re-marry a prettier one. A man will never be afraid of losing even eight or 10 wives. But for women from traditional families like mine, we don't have the ability to marry again. If we lose our husbands, we are forbidden from re-marrying and must suffer on our own like my Auntie at the cave without even a job. If I died now, I'm sure I would be quickly replaced, and you would re-marry another woman."

"Fengxian, why do you hurt me by saying such words? People are not grass or trees. We have affections and emotions. You are my only love. If you die, I will not re-marry. Believe me."

"When I die, I will know nothing. I will not know if what you said now is true or not. You can promise everything now, but I know how things work in this world. Whatever a man wants, he gets."

Retreat to Snow Peak Mountain

The weeks following Yan's death were marked by successive military and political victories for the Communist Party. By mid-1949, the CCP was in command of most of northeast China and was quickly pushing its way into the south and west. The Communists were not only triumphing in nearly every military skirmish, they were also winning the battle for the hearts and minds of the people, who had become fed up with the corruption and poor leadership of the KMT. Since the overthrow of the Qing Dynasty in 1911, Chinese people had been thirsting for revolutionary change in society. We were about to get it.

Despite all the violence and turbulence around me, I remained oblivious to what was happening. My two daughters and Weiluan were the center of my world. I paid little attention to anything else. In the summer of 1949, I became pregnant again. This time I was feeling much stronger. With the pain of Yan's loss still so vivid, I was more open to the idea of having another child.

Then one day in late-July, the world as we knew it changed forever. It was mid-morning, and Weiluan had frantically rushed home from work, his face covered in sweat. He ordered me to pack all of our belongings immediately.

"The Communists are advancing on Changsha. It's very dangerous. I can't look after you right now. We have no time to talk. Just do what I say and pack. I will go find some porters to carry the luggage to the trucks."

As he was speaking, a siren and emergency order came over the loudspeaker on the base: "All personnel must evacuate immediately with their families to the trucks parked at the rear of the compound."

I was so ignorant about the war that the evacuation had taken me totally by surprise. People were scurrying everywhere. The atmosphere was buzzing with anxiety, but I had no time to feel afraid. Weiluan raced off to find porters. I grabbed our luggage and packed whatever would fit into the bags. By the time Weiluan returned, I had everything prepared.

"Let's go," he said. "We need to get out of here."

"You're coming with us, right?"

"No, I'm not. I can't leave with you. I must stay behind and accompany Director Cheng. My colleagues' wives will be with you. I will return to your side when my work is completed."

"But I see many soldiers getting on the trucks with their families. Why can't you come with us?"

"They don't work as closely with Director Cheng as I do. I must stay with him."

I panicked. I didn't know how I would be able to manage the girls and our luggage on my own in an unfamiliar setting — plus I was pregnant. Weiluan was trying to calm me when my brother, Liang, fortuitously appeared at my side.

"Fengxian, what's going on?" Liang asked.

"Liang, what are you doing here?"

"The radio school in Nanjing was disbanded, so I got on a train to return to Huaguo. The train stopped in Changsha, and everyone was ordered to get off. I decided to come to the base to see you and Commander Han."

"Brother-in-Law," Weiluan said, "I'm so glad you are here. Director Cheng has ordered an emergency evacuation of the entire base. I was about to put Fengxian and the girls on a truck. Can you accompany them? Fengxian is pregnant, and I'm afraid it's too much for her to handle on her own."

"Of course I will accompany her. Don't worry. I will look after them."

"Thank you so much. I will join all of you when I can."

Weiluan helped us climb into the back of the truck and asked his colleagues to look after us. "Fengxian, please be careful and watch over my beloved little girls. I will return to you soon."

"You be careful, too," I replied.

Before we could say anything else, the truck sped away.

No one on the truck except the driver had any idea where we were going. Zi and Tian could sense the anxiety among the evacuees and were restless and crying. The combination of the pregnancy and motion made me dizzy. I felt like vomiting but thankfully didn't. What distressed me most was the chaos and fear I saw among the KMT soldiers on the ground. Troops and equipment were moving in all directions with no semblance of order. I wondered if that was the type of situation Weiluan would soon be in.

After a couple of hours on the road, someone in the truck announced that we had arrived in another county. We exited the truck to stretch our legs and eat lunch and then resumed traveling. Soon we entered a well-known area in western Hunan called the Snow Peak Mountains, which are renowned for their tranquility and beauty. The road became very narrow. As the truck zigzagged up the mountain, the people below became as tiny as flies. Ahead of us, another truck had flipped over and was teetering on the edge of the mountain. Several passengers yelled at the driver to be careful.

"Shut up and calm down!" he shouted at us.

I tried to focus on the serene atmosphere to allay my fear. I admired the tall, ancient trees, whose limbs reached high into the clouds, listened to the melody of the birds chirping, and inhaled the delicate fragrance emanating from the flowers. The mountain was wrapped in a fog that blocked the peak and the mountain's full grandeur, but through the mist I could still see a silvery waterfall cascading over the rocks. For the first time that morning, I felt calm. As the truck crossed the summit and began to descend, I turned back and watched the scenery slowly fade away.

"The girls have fallen asleep," Liang whispered. "Wrap them in this blanket." I had been so engrossed in the view that I momentarily forgot about my daughters. I smiled at my brother and thought about how fortunate I was to have him by my side.

By the time we reached the foot of the mountain, the sun had set and the sky was black. We stopped at a small restaurant in town, where scores of other military vehicles and passenger cars were parked. The scene was chaotic. Some trucks were carrying equipment and supplies, while others, like ours, were packed with the relatives of KMT officers. Fighter jets roared back and forth, adding to the already high level of anxiety. Was the civil war going to encroach on the very place we had sought refuge?

As we sat watching and waiting, someone in the crowd announced that a famous KMT chief of staff had been captured by the Communists. Hearing that such a respected man had been arrested evoked resignation among the KMT soldiers with us. If such a powerful officer could be captured, what hope was there for anyone else? Panic erupted. People started to flee every which way. Liang and I had no idea where to go, so we stayed put.

As I watched the mayhem around me, I recalled Weiluan saying that the Communist Party may one day replace the KMT in China. I also remembered my grandfather once mentioning that Mao Zedong could come to power someday, and that Chiang Kai-shek could fall from grace. It was a profound thing for Grandfather to have said when the revolution was so young. At the time, I did not comprehend the context of either comment, so I ignored them. Was this what was happening now before my eyes? Would the victors become the new emperors?

The drivers of the trucks unloaded everyone's luggage and quickly sped away, leaving all of us behind. Scores of people queued at the bus station to buy tickets that would take them farther away from the fighting. Most people were trying to go farther south to the next province or even to Vietnam. Only senior officers were permitted to travel in the passenger sedans, which soon fled, leaving everyone else to wait patiently for buses and new military trucks. I feared straying too far from Weiluan, so we stayed put.

Many days elapsed, but no trucks arrived. We decided to move to a nearby temple with some wives of my husband's colleagues. The local residents in that area were destitute. Corn and sweet potatoes were the staples of their diet. Rice was scanty and of poor quality, and there was no oil to cook with. The majority of families lived in shacks constructed out of bamboo and straw, while a few lived in sheds built of mud and low-quality timber. There was no furniture or other belongings in their homes. Their clothes, made of rough cotton, were extremely worn. To our astonishment, they had no shoes and walked barefoot on dirt paths full of pebbles and brush. They didn't seem bothered at all by walking barefoot, which impressed us deeply. If there were any wealthy people in the area, they were gone by the time we arrived.

"Mommy," the girls cried, "we want to go home. We want our daddy. This isn't our home."

"I know, but it's not safe at home. We have to stay here. Daddy will join us when he's finished working." I also longed to be at home with my husband. I missed him so much and worried about his safety.

After several days, most of the families that had taken refuge with us had managed to purchase bus tickets and left. As our numbers dwindled, I fretted about what would happen if no trucks came to evacuate us and if Weiluan never returned. I began to resent my husband for only caring about his work and abandoning us. We were strangers in this place. Who would help us? Would I ever be reunited with Weiluan? I was at a loss as to what to do. Fortunately, Liang was with us. I appreciated his help but wondered if we would be able to survive without Weiluan.

"Mommy, we're hungry," Zi cried. "We want to eat some rice. We don't want to eat more corn and potatoes."

I asked several families from that area if they would sell us some rice, but all of their rice been confiscated by soldiers. The girls wouldn't stop crying, and I felt embarrassed. An old woman heard their cries and invited us to her house.

"I have a small amount of rice left that I can cook for your daughters," she said.

"Thank you," I replied. "I am so grateful for your help."

The woman took out two kilograms of un-husked rice and ground it by hand with two stones. I had never seen anyone use such primitive tools. When she finished cooking the rice, I hurried to offer her some money, but she declined.

"It was predestined that we should meet here," she said. "Let's cherish this arrangement of fate."

I smiled and asked about her family.

"In that deep valley ahead is a group of bandits. They beat my husband to death because he refused to join their group. Then they kidnapped my only son. He tried to escape, but he was discovered. They beat him so severely that now he is disabled." She pointed to a lame man sitting across the room. "My grandchildren are now 10 years old. When they grow up, they are doomed to be taken away by those bandits. There is no end to our torture."

"Why don't you move somewhere else?" I asked.

"It's not that simple. This entire area is full of bandits. Wherever you go, you cannot escape this fate. What about you? Where is your husband?"

"My husband is still fighting on the frontlines in Changsha. He said he would join us when he is finished. I hope he returns."

I thanked the woman profusely for her kindness. She wouldn't accept any money, so I gave her a few items from our luggage. We returned to the temple for the rest of the evening. The stories about the bandits terrified me. How would we survive their wrath without Weiluan?

We were passing time sitting idly in the temple one day when Liang announced that a man resembling Weiluan was approaching. "Sister, look, I think Commander Han is back!"

"What?" I asked.

I stood up and saw my beloved husband walking toward us. Tears streamed down my face, and the girls jumped up and down. I knew we would be safe now.

"I've been looking for you for days," he said. "Are all of you alright?"

"Yes, we're fine. Are you okay?"

"I'm fine. Changsha has been taken over by the Communist Party and liberated. We can return. Director Cheng and I defected to the Communists. We peacefully handed over Changsha to prevent unnecessary bloodshed. As a result, the Communist Party has rewarded Director

Cheng by allowing him to stay on as part of the Hunan Province leadership. If we return to Changsha soon, I will be able to secure a job on his team."

"That's great," Liang said. "How are we going to get there?"

"The roads and public transportation have been completely destroyed. We have no choice but to walk."

"Walk? That is going to take forever, Commander Han. Changsha is more than 200 miles away, we are traveling with two little girls and a pregnant woman, and we have to traverse a mountain range."

"I know. We will pace ourselves, but we have no other choice."

Because we had evacuated by truck, we had brought a fair amount of luggage with us. Now we wondered how we would be able to carry it all back. Weiluan and Liang gathered our bags and strapped them onto two shoulder poles. Meanwhile, I tried to prepare myself mentally for the journey. Not only was I pregnant, I was dressed in a silk cheongsam that was tight and constraining. I hadn't thought to bring anything else more comfortable. I opened one of our bags and put on the most comfortable pair of shoes I had: ankle-high boots lined with thin fur. The men picked up the shoulder poles while I led Zi and Tian by hand.

Our immediate concern was safety. Many people had warned us that the mountains were filled with bandits and disbanded soldiers of the KMT who were mugging travelers everywhere. Weiluan was a resourceful man. He found out where the bandits headquartered themselves, went straight to one of the leaders, and made a deal. In exchange for some money, the bandits promised to let us pass safely and to provide us with two strong men to help haul the baggage. After we safely passed the danger zone, Weiluan tipped the two men and let them return. For the remainder of the day, we rested.

The next morning, we set off at daybreak. To our dismay, this area also was filled with bandits. Soon nearly all of our money was stolen. The bandits only cared about our cash and left our belongings untouched. They had no interest in hauling anything around that rugged terrain.

After several days, the long walk had begun to take a physical toll on all of us. The baggage was too burdensome for my husband and brother to carry, so we decided to get rid of some of the heavier items.

We placed them in a stream so that no one would see what we left behind and mistakenly think we were wealthy. The water quickly carried the items away. The next day we thinned out our belongings even more. We couldn't lighten our load too much because we would have to exchange clothes for food and shelter.

We passed through many places in Hunan during the journey. Occasionally, we encountered other people on the road, but for the most part the streets were empty. However, bandits and criminals were everywhere. Every minute we were on edge. All of us had moments of intense frustration. My husband, in particular, was aggravated with how slowly we were moving. He feared that we wouldn't return in time for him to secure a new job with Director Cheng. Often, he steadfastly pushed ahead while we slowly trailed behind.

We continued walking like this for months. Our feet became blistered and swollen and ached terribly. At one point, Zi and Tian came down with nasty colds, high fevers, and diarrhea. We were forced to stop and rest for several days. Tian became so ill that she needed to see a doctor. Weiluan still had a little bit of cash, but feared taking it out because he knew we were constantly being watched and would immediately be robbed. Instead, we rummaged through our belongings to see what we could sell. We still possessed several items of value, including some of my gold jewelry and an expensive Parker pen Weiluan had purchased on his spending spree. However, we were in a remote area with no pawn shops, and no one was interested in buying anything that expensive if it couldn't be re-exchanged easily. We were at a loss as to what to do when suddenly Liang's shoes caught Weiluan's attention.

"There is one item we may be able to sell," Weiluan said.

"What?" I asked.

"Liang's leather shoes."

"Commander Han," Liang said. "Are you crazy? My feet are killing me. I need these shoes for this walk. They are my favorite pair."

"Brother, please think of my daughter. She needs to see a doctor. We have other shoes you can wear. I promise to replace them. We have no other choice."

Liang reluctantly agreed. We gave him a pair of Weiluan's cloth shoes, but they were nowhere near as sturdy as his leather ones. From then on, every step my brother took carried an aura of resentment.

By the grace of God, the girls eventually recovered. Despite my pregnancy, I didn't experience any serious health problems throughout the long trek. We had started our walk in September 1949 and completed it in December. We arrived in Changsha weak, weary, and with bloodied feet. I was six months pregnant when we finished our march.

When we arrived in the city, Weiluan tore away the strap from one of the bags and pulled out our few remaining silver coins, which he had carefully hidden inside. "We're lucky to still have these coins. Let's buy some food and find a place to stay. I will visit Director Cheng tomorrow."

That night we stayed at a small temporary shelter for travelers near the train station. All of us collapsed. We were physically and emotionally drained.

"Things can only get better," I repeated to myself before I fell asleep. "Things can only get better."

A Tired Bird Returns to its Nest

The next day Weiluan visited the home of the former staff director of the KMT military base and explained our circumstances. He pleaded with the man to find him a job in Director Cheng's new administration. Although the man sympathized with our plight, no openings were available for former KMT officers who hadn't been through formal re-education by the Communist Party. He put my husband's name on a list for the next entering class at the University of Military Affairs and Politics, but it would be several months before the next class started. The first group had already begun several weeks ago, and it was too late for Weiluan to join that group.

With little money left, we weren't sure what to do. After a decade of war, the economy was in disarray, and the CCP was only beginning to organize the new government. Millions of people were unemployed, and it was unlikely Weiluan would be able to find other work in Changsha. It seemed our only option was to return to Rongxia and wait for the second group of students to start university. However, Weiluan was reluctant to impose further on my family. That afternoon he suggested we visit a fortune teller, who might be able to advise us.

Fortune tellers are popular in China, and many different techniques are employed to read a person's fortune. The first man we visited read fortunes by examining the components of Chinese characters that subconsciously popped into customers' minds when they entered his shop.

As soon as we sat down, the fortune teller asked Weiluan to give him a Chinese character to analyze. "Don't think about it too much. Just tell me what character comes to your mind first."

"Hong (鸿)," replied Weiluan.

"Hmm. Officer, I can see that you have been working outside your hometown for a very long time. It is time for you to return home. Your mother is waiting for you."

"Yes, my mother asked me to return a long time ago. Master, what I want you to tell me is whether it is appropriate or not for me to return."

The master picked up a writing brush, dipped it in black ink, and wrote the character on a piece of snow white paper.

"Look, hong (鸿) means riverside (江) bird (鸟). We often say 'a tired bird returns to its nest.' You have come here to ask me to analyze a character and tell you your fortune. I will say to you, officer, that it is time for you, the tired bird, to go back to your nest. You should return home as soon as possible."

Weiluan thanked the man and gave him his money. He didn't have much confidence in what the fortune teller said, so we visited another one. This man used the precise time of a person's birth to read his fortune.

"Officer, please tell me the year, month, date, and time of the moment of your birth on the lunar calendar."

Weiluan gave him the information. The master did some calculations with his fingers and then shook his head. "Officer, to be frank with you, according to the eight characters in your birth date, your fate is very common. You are to encounter many difficulties and misfortunes in your life, and your family will be of no help. Luckily, there is no risk of losing your life, but inevitably you and your wife will encounter harm.

Any fortune you might have will be lost. This fate has been arranged by heaven. You cannot avoid it, so take care of yourself."

We paid the fortune teller his money and returned to the hotel discouraged and listless. That evening Weiluan decided it was best for us to return to Rongxia and wait for the second university class to start.

Father was elated to see us. During the first couple of days, there was a festive mood in the house, but soon the rest of my family began to resent us. As usual, Grandfather's concubine and her children were rude and cruel. A rift also developed between me and my new stepmother. Her two daughters were the same age as Zi and Tian, and our children often quarreled over toys and food. The children's arguments often spilled over into arguments between us.

In addition, Liang continued to harbor bitterness toward Weiluan for forcing him to sell his precious leather shoes during our long trek to Changsha. On several occasions, Liang joined stepmother in chastising my daughters; in one instance, he and I fought so intensely that Weiluan, the girls, and I had to move into a room on Grandfather's side of the house. Rongxia may have been my childhood home, but I was beginning to feel like an intruder.

During those weeks, we pawned some of my gold jewelry in order to buy food. As our resources dwindled and tension at Rongxia festered, Weiluan suggested that we return to his hometown in Guangdong Province and wait there for the next class to start university. I was afraid I wouldn't fit in and felt reluctant to leave. I didn't understand the Cantonese dialect and wasn't familiar with the local customs. More importantly, I feared that what mother had said about life in Guangdong being unbearable might be true.

"Fengxian, going back to Guangdong would just be temporary. We can take advantage of this opportunity to visit my loving mother and other family members, whom I haven't seen in many years. After you give birth to our baby, it will be time for me to start university. Once I finish school and am assigned a job, you can come to Changsha to live with me."

I dreaded the idea of leaving Hunan again, but as Weiluan's wife, I had no authority to defy him. I had to go along with his wishes. My husband chose an auspicious date for us to depart after the new year, which would allow us to spend one more Chinese New Year with my family in Hunan. The holiday was bittersweet.

Despite the recent tension in my family, everyone was tearful on the day of our departure. At some level, all of us sensed that our country was on the verge of a major transformation and that we may never see each other again. Numerous family members and neighbors came to say farewell. Father was extremely sad. As we walked out of Rongxia's grand red gate, he began to cry.

"Fengxian, your mother had always been afraid of your moving to Guangdong. We quarreled many times about this. At the time, I thought she was overly concerned. I didn't expect that it would become a reality in such a short time. Yet no matter how high a tree is, its leaves must fall and return to its root. Weiluan must return home. Write to me as soon as you arrive, so I know you are safe. We may only be able to communicate through letters in the future. Your father is getting older. I don't know when or whether we will meet again."

"Father, don't be so sad. I will come back and see you soon. Take care of yourself." I turned to my stepmother and said, "Mother, please take good care of Father." It was the first time I addressed my stepmother as Mother. I hoped that in doing so she would be good to Father. Zi and Tian clung to my father tightly and didn't want to part with him.

"Commander Han, I hope you will return soon," my beloved maternal uncle said. "Fengxian and the girls aren't familiar with the Cantonese dialect and the people there. Please take good care of them. The world is changing so fast. We have finally rid ourselves of foreign aggression but now are beset by internal problems. The Communist Party has come. They are the people's saviors. You have a difficult and long journey ahead of you to Guangdong. In many places, the bridges and roads have been destroyed. Please be careful. Fengxian, you are very dear to my heart. I will miss you deeply."

"Thank you, Uncle. Thank you for your special care. We appreciate it very much," I replied.

"Fengxian, you and the girls need to get into the sedan chair," my youngest brother Rong whispered in my ear. "You don't want to miss your train." I waved goodbye to the many friends and relatives who had gathered on the large meadow in front of Rongxia and then slowly waddled, pregnant and potbellied, toward the sedan chair.

The chair-bearers carried me and the girls while Weiluan, Father, Uncle, and other friends and relatives trailed behind. I silently bade farewell to my precious hometown and the beautiful, familiar scenery.

"Goodbye, my beloved Huaguo, this fertile land along the Xiang River, so picturesque and tender. I love this place wholeheartedly. Goodbye, my wonderful father, who raised me from a little girl into a woman. Now I am a wife with my own children and must follow my husband. Hence, I must leave you, even though it breaks my heart. Farewell, my family, who have given me companionship and so many happy memories. Farewell, my beloved garden. How I wish I didn't have to leave you lovely trees, flowers, and grass, who are smiling in the spring breeze and wave to me in silence."

As we headed to the train station, many neighbors and friends rushed out to say goodbye and join the procession. I overheard many of them gossiping during the walk.

"If Fengxian's mother hadn't died, perhaps she wouldn't have to leave for Guangdong ... Her mother was afraid of allowing her to marry a Cantonese because she feared Fengxian would have to bear great hardship, but Fengxian's uncle and father agreed to the marriage ... Aunt Chen also wanted Fengxian to marry Commander Han because she thought he was a wealthy, powerful officer. Now where is Aunt Chen? Why hasn't she come to see off her niece? It's said she fell ill. I think she must feel ashamed to come here and see her poor niece leaving for a strange place far away from here ... Fengxian could be bullied to death in Guangdong because she has no relatives or friends there to protect her. Poor Fengxian!"

The gossip was loud and endless. My family tried to drown out the jabbering with heavy footsteps, but it didn't work. I heard it all.

When we reached Fengmen Station, I wiped away my tears and stepped out of the sedan chair. Aunt Chen was there waiting on the platform with a large bag of eggs, salted pork, and fish.

"Fengxian, I'm really sorry to see you leave so soon for Guangdong. I didn't expect this would turn out this way so quickly."

"I know. Neither did I, Aunt Chen. I will miss you."

"Commander Han, farewell. Please take good care of Fengxian and her children. Promise me that you will never abandon them. Please come back as soon as possible." As Aunt Chen spoke, tears streamed down her face onto the platform. We clutched each other's hands and waited in silence.

When the train arrived, we hurried aboard. The girls and I rushed to some seats near a window while Weiluan organized our luggage in the racks. We left many of our belongings with my father.

"Take care," everyone shouted and waved.

I pressed my face against the window, smearing it with tears, and waved back. As the train departed, I looked across at Weiluan, put my arm around my daughters, and sighed. I thought about what mother had said about life in Guangdong Province and prayed to God that it wouldn't be true.

PART FOUR

Into the Vortex

Returning to Guangdong in Glory

My husband's hometown was only 400 miles from Huaguo, but it took us more than a week to complete the journey. As Uncle had warned, the railways and other public transportation were in tatters. We frequently had to stop and switch from the train to a bus and vice versa. The temperature rose as we inched farther south. Overnight the climate changed from winter to summer. When we left Huaguo, I was wearing a cardigan sweater, a coat, and leather gloves. That was far too much for the warm temperatures in the south. Each of us shed several layers, which added significantly to our luggage.

Tian's body had yet to recover from our long trek to Changsha. She became ill after a couple of days on the road. We took her to a doctor as soon as we crossed into Guangdong Province. The medical fees and cost of the hotel burned through the little money we had brought with us. There was nothing left to purchase the medicine she required, let alone finish the journey to Weiluan's home, so we rummaged through our luggage to see what could be sold. I still possessed a few small items of gold jewelry, but there was no pawn shop to exchange them. No one was interested in buying any of our clothes, but someone was interested in the Parker pen Weiluan had purchased on his brief spending spree a few years earlier. The proceeds were enough to purchase the medicine Tian required and get us at least as far as Guangzhou, the capital of the province. Once there, Weiluan hoped to track down some relatives and borrow money.

The transportation in Guangdong was as bad as in Hunan. It took us several days to get to the capital city. "I can't believe we're finally here," Weiluan said when we set foot in Guangzhou. "We're safe now. Fengxian, you stay here at the bus station with the girls. I'll find my nephew, then come back and bring you to his home, where we can stay for the night. Don't worry. It's a reliable plan."

I was exhausted. My daughters and I waited at the station several hours. Weiluan eventually returned frustrated and disappointed.

"When a person is having a run of bad luck, he encounters obstacles in everything he does and can find no one to help him. I am having a run of bad luck."

"Were you unable to find your nephew?"

"He's away at his father's pharmacy near my hometown. Only a servant and his children were at home, but they were unwilling to lend me any money. Maybe that fortune teller was right. Maybe it's my fate to have no relatives who are able or willing to help me out of difficulty."

"I guess that means we have no choice but to stay in a hotel. Fortunately, we still have a little money left," I replied.

Weiluan found a porter to carry our bags. As soon as we entered our room, my husband collapsed on the bed. I tried to keep the girls quiet while he rested, but all of a sudden he sprang up.

"Fengxian, don't worry. Worrying is of no use. Where there is a will, there is a way! Tonight we will visit one of my cousins who lives in Guangzhou."

"If you can't get your nephew to help, do you really think a cousin will help us?"

"I don't know, but don't dampen my enthusiasm with cold water. Have faith! If we are going to visit my family, we should be dressed in our best clothes. Put on a nice cheongsam and wear that green, plush coat I had tailor-made for you."

"The one I refused to wear ever again?"

"Yes, that one. I want to give them a good impression of us."

I understood my husband's aim and did as he instructed. Weiluan desperately wanted to give the impression that he was returning to Guangdong in glory. He didn't want others to know how poor we really were or they might look down on him. Even though we were penniless, we weren't so desperate as to risk losing face in front of his relatives. For Chinese people, maintaining face is everything.

Dusk was approaching by the time we left the hotel. It had just rained, so I had a good excuse to wear the coat that evening, which otherwise would have been inappropriate in such a warm climate. Weiluan's cousin lived only a few blocks away, so it didn't take us long to reach his home. His cousin was taken aback to discover us on his doorstep, but he and his wife were warm and welcoming. Their home was elegant and beautifully decorated. They invited us to join them for dinner.

Weiluan and his cousin enjoyed catching up. I stayed silent most of the time because I didn't know any Cantonese. At the end of the evening, we thanked them for their hospitality and returned to our hotel.

"I couldn't bring myself to ask them for money. It would have been too humiliating," Weiluan said.

"I know. I understand. At least we were able to enjoy a hearty meal," I said. Both of us chuckled.

The next day the four of us visited Weiluan's nephew's home, only to discover that he still had not returned from the pharmacy. We had two legs of the journey left — a boat ride from Guangzhou to Pingyang (Pǐng-yǒng) and another boat ride from Pingyang to Weiluan's hometown of Donghu (Dōng-hū). We went to the docks and inquired about the next boat, which we were told departed at 6 a.m. the next day. We had just enough money to pay for a second night at the hotel plus the boat ride to Pingyang, so we returned to the hotel to rest.

At dinner time, we fed Zi and Tian the few odds and ends left from the food Aunt Chen had prepared for us. It wasn't nearly enough, but we had nothing else. That night the girls cried themselves to sleep in hunger. Weiluan and I didn't eat at all that evening.

At dawn the next day, we checked out of the hotel and headed to the pier. We had a few cents left after purchasing the tickets, so we bought the girls steamed buns for breakfast. The sunrise that morning was stunning. The sunlight glistened on the water, illuminating the city skyline in a beautiful orange glow.

During the ride, the girls meandered around the boat while Weiluan and I sat in silence thinking about what might lie ahead. My husband's face was bitter and sad. He was as worried as I was about our future. But on top of that, he had to bear the shame of returning home after years away without a cent in his pocket and three mouths to feed, all of whom were female. The girls bombarded Weiluan with questions about Donghu, but his only response was a sour smile that was so unnatural that I will never forget it.

When we arrived in Pingyang, we unloaded our luggage onto the pier. Weiluan instructed me to stay at the dock with our bags while he went to inquire about the next boat to Donghu. The girls and I were sitting on the dock when two husky men approached us, snatched our luggage, and started to walk away. I screamed at them to put down our bags, but they ignored me. Thankfully, my husband saw the men and called out to them. They tossed our belongings on the ground and ran away laughing.

"You're not a local, so they figured they could bully you," Weiluan said.

"I can't believe how brazen they were!" I replied. If this is what Cantonese people were like, I wondered how long I could last. I suddenly understood why my relatives in Hunan feared I might be bullied to death in Guangdong.

The next boat to Donghu was departing soon. My husband picked up half of our luggage and asked a porter to help him carry the rest to the next pier. We had just gotten settled on the second boat when the owner walked up to Weiluan and patted him on the shoulder.

"What a wonderful scene! It appears our old friend has returned. Manfu (Mǒn-fū, my husband's nickname in his hometown), you've been working away from home as a military officer for over a decade. Now you are returning with your family. How glorious and happy you must feel!"

"Uncle Shao, it's so good to see you. This is my wife Fengxian, and these are my two daughters, Zi and Tian. I am no longer an officer, and I have no money, so it is by no means a glorious return. I am ashamed to see you and my relatives and friends this way."

"You don't need to say that you are poor. Don't worry, I won't borrow any money from you!" Uncle Shao said and chuckled.

We were the only passengers on board. As I gazed at the landscape, everything — the people, the terrain, the climate — seemed so different from what I was used to in Hunan. My eyes filled with tears.

"Fengxian, don't worry. When we arrive at my home, you'll see that life in Guangdong isn't that different from Hunan. Women in wealthy families here don't toil in the fields, either. They enjoy leisure and joy at home, just as in Hunan."

After we passed the last shoal, the men took out some food and began to cook. They offered to prepare a meal for us for a small fee, but we didn't have a cent.

"Thank you for the offer, but don't bother to cook for us," Weiluan replied. "Soon we will be arriving at home. We can eat there."

My husband tried to distract the girls from the food by pointing out scenery, but they were starving and intoxicated by the smell. They ran up to Uncle Shao and asked for something to eat.

"I really apologize for this," my husband said. "My daughters are young and have no patience."

"Don't worry, Manfu. They are small and don't eat much. We won't charge you for this."

Luckily, I found a few crackers someone had left on the ship and nibbled on those.

"You're the only one with nothing to eat," I whispered to my husband. "Are you okay?"

"I was a soldier. Hunger was commonplace. On the battlefield, sometimes I went without eating for two or three days. I'm used to it. Don't worry about me."

As we approached the dock in Weiluan's hometown, I fretted over how we would pay for the ride since neither of us had a cent. I was thinking about what we had in our luggage that we might be able to give Uncle Shao when Weiluan suddenly turned to me and said, "Fengxian, pay the fare."

I looked at him as if he were crazy. He knew I didn't have any money. Why was he asking me to pay the fare? Did he think I had the magical ability to turn objects into cash? Then suddenly I came up with an idea.

"Right now, I'm more worried about how we're going to deal with this luggage. First, go ashore and find someone to help us carry our bags. Once we get everything off the boat, then we can pay."

Weiluan grinned at me and ran ashore. He returned half an hour later with money and bread that he had borrowed from relatives. He paid the fare, and then we sat on the pier to rest and eat.

"I think we managed to escape that situation without Uncle Shao knowing we were penniless," my husband said and chuckled.

"Yes, they are still under the impression that you are coming back in glory. In the end, we overcame all of our difficulties and arrived here safely."

"You are so clever, Fengxian. That was a great idea about finding someone to help with the bags, so I could get off the boat and borrow some money. I know you are good at solving problems, so I figured you would have some idea about how to solve the issue with the fare."

"In the famous Chinese essay *Thirty-Six Stratagems*, the last strategy is to run away. It doesn't mean you should disappear to avoid facing the problem, but rather running away should be part of the solution."

A Less Than Warm Welcome

Soon a group of relatives arrived at the pier. We exchanged greetings. A few of the men carried away our belongings, while others escorted us on the walk to Weiluan's home. By then, Zi, Tian, and I were exhausted, so Weiluan and his relatives walked ahead while the girls and I slowly trailed behind.

At one point, the men stopped to greet an old woman. She wore a coarse linen scarf wrapped around her head and a knee-length, black cotton smock. What stood out most were the woman's glaring bare feet, which were large, filthy, and rough. In Hunan, women that age wouldn't dare display their feet in public. The woman hugged my husband and caressed his face. I knew then that she was Weiluan's mother.

"Mother, your unfilial son is finally back," Weiluan said. "I've been away for so many years. I'm very sorry that I didn't have the opportunity to attend to you. This is my wife Fengxian," Weiluan said and stepped aside.

I bowed silently and respectfully, and then Weiluan's mother grabbed my hands.

"There's no need to keep bowing, Fengxian," she said.

"Mother, these are my two daughters, Zi and Tian," Weiluan said.

"They are adorable. Why didn't you write ahead to inform us that you were coming? We would have made special preparations."

"I hadn't planned on coming back right now, but we need a place to stay. There was nowhere else to turn."

"That's our home," Weiluan said to me, pointing at a quaint U-shaped building ahead of us. In front of the house was an open lawn with green grass. The left and right perimeters contained small vegetable gardens. Behind the house stood a large, old tree and numerous, tall bamboo stalks. Unlike Rongxia, which was nestled in the hills overlooking the rice paddies, Weiluan's home was located in a valley amongst a cluster of houses on level ground with the paddies. The home appeared quiet and peaceful.

We stood on the lawn visiting for nearly an hour. During this time, many villagers came to inquire about the commotion. They stared at me and I stared back. Their clothing was less formal than what I was used to, and they spoke a different dialect of Chinese that I didn't comprehend. What shocked me most were their enormous, protruding bare feet. I had never seen so many exposed feet before. In Hunan, everyone wore socks and shoes no matter the season. Women's shoes were often decorated with delicate silk embroidery. People cared very much about their dress and appearance. If I wasn't dressed in my school uniform, I wore a skirt or silk cheongsam. In Donghu, everyone wore field clothes and went barefoot.

As soon as the women of the house learned that Weiluan had returned, they began preparing a special feast. We were taken on a quick tour of the house before sitting down to eat. The home was divided into two wings, which together formed a U-shape: the right wing belonged to Weiluan's seventh brother, Qige, and his wife Qisao (Chē-gǔ and Chē-sao; 'Qi' means seven, 'ge' means older brother, and 'sao' means sister-in-law), and was where Weiluan's mother lived; the left wing belonged to his fourth brother, Sige, and his wife Sisao (Seu-gǔ and Seu-sao; 'Si' means four). In the middle of the two wings was a small outdoor courtyard that led to the lawn and path in front of the house. The home was comfortable, but it didn't come close to the grandeur of

Rongxia. The floors consisted of dirt, the windows contained no glass, and the walls were dusty and bare.

After the tour, a joyful reunion dinner was held in the home of Qige and Qisao. The table was covered with savory dishes and wine. Weiluan hadn't been back in a decade, so there was lots of news to share. The discussion was lively. Every now and then my husband translated for me, but most of the time I left him alone to catch up with his relatives while I looked after the girls. The atmosphere was warm. I felt comforted. This is my new family, I told myself. I should cherish this family, respect the old, look after the young, and be a good daughter-in-law.

After dinner, we were led to a nine-foot-square bedroom in Qige's wing of the house. It was smaller than the boudoir Boya and I shared at Rongxia and contained only a bed, a table, and a bench. There was a small window on the back wall, which let in a small amount of sunlight and air, but it was too high for anyone to look out. When we were alone, Weiluan shook his head and sighed.

"The room is a little small, but we can decorate it into something beautiful," I said to cheer him up.

"Fengxian, I know you have the talent to turn nothing into something, so please try to do it again. I have to return to the sitting room to entertain our guests."

I pulled out the beautiful bedding that had been handmade by my mother and Boya and draped it over the bed. Weiluan's mother came by with a broom and sat in the room while I swept the dirt floor. We couldn't understand each other, so we did a lot of nodding and gesturing, which made us both laugh. After she left, Weiluan returned.

"Wow, Fengxian, you really have the magic to turn bad things into good. Look at the change in this room."

All of us were exhausted from the long journey, so we lay down and quickly fell asleep. After a few minutes, someone knocked on the door. Weiluan opened it and saw Seventh Brother's wife, Qisao.

"Manfu, your mother eats with me every day, and you and your family will also eat with us. The family has encountered many difficulties recently. My husband, your seventh brother, has become addicted to opium, and we have fallen into the abyss. He steals anything he can to feed his addiction. The house has been almost emptied by him. Manfu, now you are back. All of us are so happy! We are all looking to you to bring us a better life."

"Qisao, thank you for looking after my mother for so many years. I wish I could repay you. I'm willing to make my due contribution to improving our lives. This is my responsibility."

Mother-in-Law overheard us speaking and came to our room. "Qisao, don't bother Manfu with these issues right now. Let them rest. They have had a long journey."

"It's no problem, Mother," Weiluan said. "In fact, I'm glad you're both here. Please come in." He opened our luggage and took out the contents. "Mother, do you think it's appropriate for us to give some of these items as gifts to our relatives?"

"Yes, that would be very kind."

"Then can you please invite everyone into our room?"

Moments later our small room was packed with family members. With our suitcases wide open, Weiluan handed out yarn, cloth, leather hides, and sweaters. Everyone received something. The most precious items we had were two pairs of ivory chopsticks, which we set aside for Fourth Brother, Sige, and Seventh Brother, Qige, neither of whom was present.

"Please accept these small items as symbols of our appreciation and respect. I have been working away from home for a decade, but I don't have a cent of savings. What I earned was barely enough to make both ends meet. Hence, there's no extra money in my pocket. I will try my best to solve this problem."

As soon as Qisao heard that we had no money, she immediately stood up and left. Everyone else thanked us and told us to rest. I was awakened in the middle of the night by one of the girls crying and noticed that Weiluan was still awake.

"Fengxian, I fear that my family isn't going to treat us well. You saw how Qisao reacted when I said I had no money. That's why I invited everyone into our room. I wanted them to see all of our belongings and understand that we didn't come back with much. Otherwise, tomorrow they may ask us to begin paying for our meals. Do you think I did the right thing?"

"Yes, you did. The items we gave them didn't amount to much, but they were a kind gesture. It gave us an opportunity to convey our situation frankly, namely, that we are poor and have many mouths to feed."

The next day Weiluan announced that he wanted to take Zi, Tian, and me to visit his fourth brother, Sige, at the family pharmacy in the town of Gaoshui (Gao-shwā), which was located a few miles outside of Donghu. Mother and Qisao were preparing to accompany us when Fourth Brother's wife, Sisao, arrived.

"I don't think you should all go together," Sisao said. "Manfu, your wife is pregnant, and your daughters are young. They should stay at home. You should go alone."

"Sisao, thank you for your concern, but we can manage," Weiluan replied. "We will be taking the boat, so the journey shouldn't be difficult. Sige has never met my wife and children, so we must pay a formal visit to him. We'll only stay a few days and then return."

Realizing that Weiluan wasn't taking the hint, Sisao became firmer. "Well, it's not convenient for Sige and myself. There aren't many rooms in the pharmacy, and your brother dislikes children because they are noisy and bothersome. Fengxian and the girls can visit another time. Please follow our wishes."

"Sisao," Mother-in-Law said, "Weiluan hasn't seen his brother in a decade. It's necessary for him and his family to pay a visit to Sige."

Sisao didn't respond. I could taste the standoff in the air among her and Weiluan's mother. It was clear that Sisao was deliberately trying to prevent us from going to Gaoshui as a family. I didn't know why, but I suspected that she feared the girls and I would like it better in Gaoshui and try to convince Weiluan to settle there rather than in Donghu.

Weiluan broke the silence. "Mother, what Sisao has said is right. We are quite tired after our long journey. Please take Fengxian and the girls to rest. I will visit Sige on my own." Sisao smiled, and Weiluan departed on his own for the pier.

Without my husband around to translate, I was unable to communicate with anyone. I felt isolated and alone. When I initially saw the house and met everyone, I was comforted by their warmth and believed that our families matched well. Now I was getting worried. Weiluan had told me before how cruel Sisao was, but I never expected her to act that way so soon. We had been there only one day, and already she was dictating where we could and couldn't go.

Weiluan returned a few days later. "Fengxian, please don't be angry with me for leaving you alone in this strange house. There really was no other option. Sige is the only person in the family with any money. I didn't want to go against his or his wife's wishes. I hope Sige will treat me as his brother and give us some financial assistance that we can live on. I am so ashamed to face my family members, but what other choice do I have?"

"I understand. You explained the issues in your family a long time ago. How was the trip to Gaoshui?"

"The pharmacy looks pretty much the way it used to, except that Sige tore down the sign my father had hung and replaced it with a new sign bearing his name. What mother and Qisao have been saying is true. Sige has totally usurped the pharmacy for himself. I understand the pain my mother feels and why she has repeatedly asked me to come back to divide the shop. But to be honest, I don't want to see the pharmacy divided. It's the fruit of my father's life-long efforts. I don't want to destroy it, or our family ties, by splitting it up. I've never been interested in inheriting any property from my father. Right now, my sole hope is that Director Cheng will contact me soon, and we can return to Changsha. Then we can leave here and live independently."

When Mother-in-Law saw that Weiluan had returned, she came to our room to inquire about his visit. "Son, was your brother happy to see you? What did you think about the pharmacy? The shop has now become the sole property of your fourth brother. It's because of this that your seventh brother began to smoke opium. With Qige in the abyss and you not around, there were no other men who had a right to criticize Sige, so he was able to do whatever he wanted. Now he has even turned a blind eye to me and barely treats me as his mother."

"Mother, please don't be so angry and sad. Sige is a doctor. He needs the pharmacy more than I do. He's also your son. I don't care if he controls the shop. If we split it, it will only destroy our father's life-long business, so please forgive Sige."

Qisao's room was right next to ours. She had been listening in on the conversation from the start. When she heard what Weiluan said, she rushed into our room and laid into him.

"Brother Manfu, how eloquent you are! You are a good, virtuous man, who couldn't care less about money. What kind of secret deal did you strike with Sige during your visit to Gaoshui? Your seventh brother isn't as competent as you and has been victimized by Sige. If he hadn't stolen the pharmacy, my husband would still be a healthy man. How come you aren't helping the victims and instead are conspiring with the criminals? We asked you to come back to help us punish the criminals and reverse the injustice done to my husband. It will not only benefit us, but also you. Do you understand that? You are our only hope."

The louder and longer Qisao spoke, the more intimidated Weiluan became. Soon his hands and arms began to shake. Qisao was an intense, cruel woman — much worse even than Grandfather's concubine Qie — but watching my husband get so unsettled and frightened by her was disconcerting. If he couldn't stand up to a nasty country girl like her, we didn't stand a chance of surviving in this crazy family. My husband may have been a soldier, but at that moment I learned that he wasn't a fighter. He was a peacemaker. He always took the moral high ground, even if it meant others would walk all over him and our family. They were some of the qualities I admired most in Weiluan, but they could also be incredibly frustrating. In a family like his, I could see how they could also lead to many headaches.

"Manfu, what Qisao said just now is very reasonable," Mother-in-law said. "You should listen to her and take action." She walked out the room. Weiluan shook his head and didn't say a word.

I was exhausted, so the girls and I went to bed as soon as they left. I had only been sleeping a short while when Weiluan shook me awake.

"Fengxian, wake up, wake up. Please find a solution for me. Tell me how to deal with this family."

"No matter how difficult the situation is, we can overcome it. But it's your family, and I don't have any opinion about how to deal with them. I'm just a daughter-in-law and a newcomer."

"We should never have come back. I knew this family was a hot potato. I managed to get rid of these chains in the past. Why did we come back this time? I guess I expected that things would have changed by now. Instead, the situation has gotten worse. They are forcing us into the vortex of this family dispute. To make matters worse, we are penniless. You heard Qisao say that living here is already very hard for them. Now here we are adding more mouths to feed. Plus, you're about to give birth to another baby. What should I do?"

I didn't have an answer for him and turned over and went back to sleep.

The next morning, Mother-in-Law announced that she wanted to take us to the local Buddhist temple to express appreciation to the gods for reuniting the family. At the temple, we burned incense and lit firecrackers, a common Chinese custom when families are reunited after a long separation. The firecrackers attracted many people, all of whom were looking at me. I could hear many of them murmuring about the cheongsam I was wearing, which was standard attire in Hunan but fancy for that area.

After we visited the temple, Mother-in-Law took us to see the family's second home, a mansion, which was located on a nearby mountain. During the walk, Mother-in-Law explained the history of the house.

"The mansion was constructed by Weiluan's father and his first wife when the pharmacy was doing well and the family had a lot of money. However, the first wife didn't follow the feng shui master's instructions about building the house at a lower location on the hill. Instead, she selected a site high on the mountain. That placement disrupted the feng shui of the building. Shortly after moving into the home, the family suffered successive misfortunes. The pharmacy burned to the ground, Weiluan's father committed suicide, then nearly all of the first wife's descendants died one after another. People became convinced that the mansion was cursed. Despite how beautiful and luxurious the house is, no one else in the family dares to live there. Since then, the house has sat abandoned, except for some distant relatives who have been hired to stay there and look after the property."

The house was surrounded by spectacular, lush scenery and was magnificent and spacious. In front of the building was a pond containing green willows, and behind it stood dozens of fruit and bamboo trees. Weiluan's family clearly had been very wealthy before his father died.

First, we visited the alter honoring the Han family's ancestors to pay our respects. Then Mother-in-Law took us on a tour through the entire complex. The tour ended behind the house at a small, flourishing orchard of lychee trees. The girls loved the orchard and ran through fields chasing dragonflies and butterflies.

"Son, you have been away from home for a decade. Many things happened while you were gone. The worst was your seventh brother's addiction to opium. In order to get money to feed his addiction, your brother has repeatedly snuck into this beautiful house, demolished the rooms, and exchanged the items for opium. If this structure weren't so solid, it might have fallen down by now." Mother-in-Law burst into tears.

It was getting late, so we decided to return home. During the walk back, the girls jabbered about the dragonflies and butterflies they caught that afternoon while the rest of us quietly listened. The second we arrived home, the storm started again.

"Manfu, did you see what Qige has done to your father's beautiful house?" Sisao asked. "It's grossly unjust and deserves everyone's condemnation. He has taken it apart and sold the red bricks, green tiles, carved wooden beams, and marble to buy opium. How does it make you feel? Will you criticize Qige for his actions?"

"Sisao, what you said is right, but so far I haven't had the opportunity to see Qige. When I see him, I will surely condemn his opium smoking and try to persuade him to give it up."

"Son, don't worry," Mother-in-Law said. "You will get a chance to see your seventh brother. He is probably ashamed to see you, which is why he hasn't come by the house. When he does return, you must keep your eyes and ears open to prevent him from stealing anything from you. Once he stole a pair of Qisao's trousers and sold them. That became a big joke in the family."

"At least you can still visit the mansion," Qisao said and sneered. "Unlike the pharmacy, which has been completely stolen from us."

"Sisters-in-Law," Weiluan pleaded, "we are a family. Please forget the unhappy past. Let bygones be bygones." His request fell on deaf ears, and all of us retired to our rooms for the night.

Brotherly Love

The next evening we were preparing dinner when a short, disheveled man approached the house. First, he greeted Mother-in-Law, then he walked up to my husband.

"Brother Manfu, when did you come back?" he asked.

"Seventh Brother!" Weiluan said and clutched his brother's hands. "Qige, it's so good to see you! How are you doing? I haven't seen you in over a decade."

Qige looked at the ground and didn't answer.

"Look at yourself, what an unworthy opium addict and rascal you are!" Mother-in-Law screamed at him. "You must be out of money. Otherwise, why would you be here? Do you have face to see your brother? Now that Manfu is back, he won't tolerate your criminal behavior and allow you to continue to tarnish the reputation of the Han family."

"Mother, don't be so angry," Weiluan said. "It's of no use to be so angry. The only solution is to be patient and persuade Qige to give up opium."

"What are you doing here, you worthless husband?" Qisao shouted when she saw Qige. "Get out now! You're not welcome! Everyone else, dinner is ready."

I agreed with Weiluan that treating Qige so harshly wouldn't solve the problem. When my own father struggled with opium addiction, what he needed most — and responded to best — was patience, love, and persistence, not anger and condemnation.

During dinner, Weiluan asked Qige many questions about his life, but Qige didn't acknowledge a word Weiluan said. Instead, he kept his head down and focused on eating. At one point, Qige made eye contact with me. I wanted to say something, but I barely knew any Cantonese. He was very handsome, and his eyes were bright and sparkling. I wondered what had prompted him to turn to opium. Qisao and Mother-in-Law had said repeatedly that Sige had turned Qige into an addict. There must be a reason for them to say that.

Qige stood up to leave after he finished eating.

"Where are you going?" asked Weiluan. "You just got here. We haven't had a chance to catch up."

"Don't ask so many questions," Qige said. "Now you are a high-ranking officer returning home in glory. Do you still remember your seventh brother? If you still cherish our brotherhood, you will give me some pocket money."

"Sorry Qige, I only have a few cents that I received from Sige," Weiluan said, handing him some change.

"So little? Sige has a lot of money. He often gives a lot of money to others. Why didn't you ask for more? Manfu, Sige usurped the pharmacy from us. Now you are back. It's time for us to get even with him! Then neither of us will have to worry about having no money. Let's divide the pharmacy."

"Qige, Sige is our brother. Brotherly love is precious. Don't split the pharmacy. Please do me a favor and don't mention this anymore. If a battle is started, it will harm both you and me. I have never been interested in dividing the pharmacy. The purpose of my returning home now was to see all of you because I have been away for so long. I intend to return to Hunan soon. Qige, there is something I want to say to you from the bottom of my heart. Please, give up opium and change your ways. Together we can rebuild our family. We must restore the harmonious atmosphere in this family. As the saying goes, harmony brings about fortune."

Qige didn't utter a word and walked away.

"Manfu, I have tried numerous times to persuade my husband to change his ways, but he has always turned a deaf ear to me," Qisao said as she stood up to clear the table. "For such a person, the best outcome is that he meets an early death. You should know that Sige and Sisao made him this way."

After dinner, Mother-in-Law accompanied us back to our room. She and Weiluan sat on the edge of our bed talking, while I tucked in Zi and Tian.

"Manfu, while you were away, so many changes took place in this family. It's time for me to tell you what happened," Mother-in-Law said in tears.

"Mother, don't think about those unhappy things anymore. Please throw them into the ocean and let them be submerged by water. Let the family revive in happiness in the future. Your son and his family are back."

"Manfu, I have waited for this moment for so long. Because of these things, my hair has turned grey. I have so much bitterness. I can no longer bury these memories in my heart. Please listen. Fengxian, now you are a member of this family, so you also need to know what happened."

"I apologize, Mother. Please tell me if it will make you feel better."

"I want to start from the beginning, when your father died, because there are so many things I kept from you when you were young. When the pharmacy burned down and your father committed suicide, we ran short of money. Fortunately, we had no debt. Your father had taught me some medical skills, so I re-opened a small clinic. However, the income wasn't enough to sustain us. I tried to borrow money from your father's elder brother, but he refused to give me any unless I gave him your eighth sister to be his maid. He wanted me to sign a contract saying that if I didn't repay him by a certain time, your sister would become his maid forever. I would rather die from hunger than sign such a contract, so we were left to fend for ourselves. During this difficult period, you were just three or four years old. The poverty was too much for your little body to handle. You became ill with dysentery and otitis media. Your eighth sister and I took care of you during this time, and fortunately you recovered."

"Yes, I remember Eighth Sister sitting by my bedside and telling me many stories," Weiluan said. "She helped me laugh and kept me from getting bored while I was bed-ridden. I am very grateful to her. She is my favorite sibling."

"Somehow, we managed to scrape by during those years. When your fourth brother got older, he wanted to study medicine in Guangzhou. I knew it would be a great help in reviving the pharmacy, so I did everything I could, including foregoing meals, to pay his tuition. As your seventh brother got older, he was able to help me at the clinic. Qige was an extremely hard worker and bore much hardship to help us save money. He often went with no shirt or shoes, so we could save the expense of buying clothes for him. Due to his sacrifice, over time our lives became easier. At that time, Western medicines weren't available anywhere except Hong Kong. I thought that selling Western medicines would be a good business opportunity for us, so when Qige got old enough I began to send him to Hong Kong to purchase the medicine and bring it back to our pharmacy. He got up very early in the morning so he could make the trip to Hong Kong in one day. He brought bread in case he got hungry, and if he was thirsty he drank from the streams. He bore these hardships in silence and never complained about them. If he was injured on the trip, he treated his wound and hid it before he saw me to save me the worry. On one of his trips, the weather was very bad and he returned sick. It was only then that I learned about all of the pain and hardship he bore for this family."

"I remember Qige working a lot when I was young," Weiluan said and shook his head. "I thought nothing of it. I had no idea he sacrificed so much for us."

"Selling Western medicine was very lucrative. Our finances improved greatly. We were able to send Eighth Sister and you to school. After a few years, you left to join the army. When your fourth brother graduated from medical school, he returned to the clinic. Business got even better. Everything seemed to be going well, until one day Sige returned to Guangzhou to meet some of his old classmates. While he was there, he met a woman, Sisao, and fell in love. They got married, and she returned with him to Gaoshui. Sisao's father was wealthy. Sige borrowed money from his new father-in-law to refurbish the pharmacy. People flocked to this new shop that sold both Chinese and Western medicine. The family became richer and richer. With money came power. Soon Sige was elected head of Gaoshui Township. Sige and Qige got along, but weren't close. The more successful the pharmacy became, the more Sige turned to outsiders to help him with the business. This hurt Qige's feelings. None of us realized it at the time, but your fourth brother had already started in motion an elaborate plan to get Qige out of the picture."

"So is this where the opium comes in?" I asked Mother-in-Law.

"Yes, one day Sige asked Qige to come to the pharmacy. He gave Qige a large wad of cash and asked him to go to Guangzhou with some servants to procure some medicine and supplies. Qige was overjoyed that his brother was turning to him for such important business and immediately went to Guangzhou. Shortly after, Qige got engaged. Sige spent a large amount of money on the wedding ceremony. By then, Qige was convinced that his relationship with his brother had turned the corner. While the couple was still immersed in newlywed bliss, Sige asked Qige to go to Guangzhou again. However, this time Sige secretly instructed the servants accompanying Qige not to spend the money on medicine, but to do everything they could to corrupt and ruin his brother. The servants took Qige shopping and whoring and introduced him to opium. Day and night they lived debaucherously. When the money was used up, they returned to Gaoshui. Sige criticized Qige for squandering the pharmacy's money. A few weeks later Sige said he would give Qige another chance and sent him to Guangzhou again. The servants were given the same instructions. This happened a few times until Qige had become completely addicted to opium. Once Qige had fallen into the abyss, Sige was able to cut him out of the business completely without criticism from anyone. Sige usurped the pharmacy for himself. He took down the old sign with your father's name and hung a new one bearing his name. When Sige first took over, I wasn't aware of how he had manipulated your brother. I tried to talk him into giving your brother another chance, but Sige called Qige an unworthy son and accused me of taking sides. He said he would no longer give a penny to Qige or let him near the business. After that, Qige stole things to feed his addiction. The last person Sige needed to get rid of was me." Mother-in-Law sobbed.

"Mother, you can finish this story another time if it's too much for you," Weiluan said.

"No. No, I want to finish it now. Sige got rid of me by telling me it was time for me to retire and to stop visiting the pharmacy. He persuaded me to move into this house with Qisao full-time. At this point, Sige is the only person in the family with any money, so all of us, including me, have to do what he says. Now everyone looks down on your seventh brother, who has lost his dignity and is a ghost rather than a human being. Yet few people know that Qige was deliberately manipulated into addiction by Sige. Several times I have raised the issue of dividing the pharmacy, but Sige has money, power, and social status. No one would dare go against him. Manfu, now that you are back, will you help your mother redress this injustice?"

I looked at Weiluan. He didn't know how to respond after hearing such a heart-wrenching story. He wiped the tears from his mother's face and tried to comfort her, but she pushed him away.

"Manfu, what do you intend to do?" she asked impatiently. "Will you divide the pharmacy?"

Weiluan lowered his head. "Mother, please don't force me to do anything. The pharmacy has been under the control of Sige for a long time now. Qige, Qisao, and you have been struggling to win it back, but you haven't succeeded. There is no way that I, who have been away from home for so long, will be able to do it. I don't know a thing about the shop. I don't want to fight with Sige over it."

As she listened to Weiluan, Mother-in-Law's hands trembled. "You are a coward and a useless man! You are frightened to fight with your brother. Okay, let's wait and see what magic you have to feed your wife and children! The money that Qisao and I live on comes from the profit of that pharmacy. Qige has sold every valuable item the family possesses to buy opium. Do you think I have the money to support your family? You had better think about this carefully." She stood up and angrily stormed out of our room.

I could see the deep hurt in Weiluan's eyes. After several minutes of silence, I walked over to my husband and sat next to him on the bed.

"Weiluan, let's leave here. This is the kind of place where one is apt to get into serious trouble."

"We don't have the money to leave here and support ourselves. The economy is in tatters, so it would be impossible for me to find a job. We already wore out our welcome with your family, so we can't go back to Rongxia."

"I know, but the world is so big. Why do you think we can't find a safe haven in it?"

"No. Now is not the right time to leave. Soon you will give birth to another baby, and we already have the girls. Don't talk anymore about leaving. I will not agree. Our only hope is Director Cheng. Eventually, the second group will get called on to attend training. At that time, we will return to Hunan. My mother will calm down. Be assured, Fengxian, my family will not starve you and our children to death."

A few days later, Mother-in-Law walked up to me while I was outside playing with the girls and hastily handed me a pair of work pants and a work shirt. "It's time for you to stop wearing that beautiful silk cheongsam, Fengxian," she said. "It's not appropriate here." I looked at the garments, which were the same simple clothes worn by every woman in that area.

"Yes, Mother, thank you," I replied. I carried the clothes to our room and tossed them on the bed. I had no desire to wear them. For as long as I could remember, I had worn either a cheongsam or a school uniform. Mother-in-Law came to our room a few minutes later. She was enraged when she saw that I hadn't changed.

"Change your clothes now!" she ordered. I had no choice but to put them on and began to undress. When Weiluan heard the ruckus, he returned to our room. He tried to comfort me by telling me how beautiful I looked in the clothes, but I knew he was lying. When Qisao overheard the commotion, she came to our room with some shoes.

"Those nice leather shoes don't match your new clothes, Fengxian. Put on these wooden clogs." Qisao tossed the shoes at me. I bent down and slipped them on. "Ah, now you are finally beginning to look like a member of this family. You've been here a long time now. It's time for you to begin working like the rest of us. Your family came back here without a cent. Do you intend to continue being freeloaders?"

Soon Sisao came to our room and added more fuel to the fire. It wasn't long before the three women began fighting again over the pharmacy. Their quarreling was so loud and intense that it drew many neighbors to our home. The girls and I hid on the sidelines. Weiluan blushed and apologized when he saw the neighbors.

"Everyone, I'm sorry. It's all my fault. I shouldn't have come home. My return has ignited this storm. Mother, Sisters-in-Law, please don't quarrel any more. Go back to your rooms."

Then someone in the crowd yelled out, "Manfu, it has nothing to do with you. Before you came back, they were constantly fighting over dividing the pharmacy. Each time your mother said, 'When Manfu comes home, we will divide the shop.' So, now you're back, are you going to divide the pharmacy?"

"I didn't come home with any intention to split the pharmacy. I just wanted to see my mother and my family. Soon, we will return to Hunan." After hearing that, the crowd dispersed and returned home.

"Manfu, why are you so frightened of arguing?" Mother-in-Law asked.

"I feel it is a great shame. Quarreling is not a solution. The more we quarrel, the unhappier the family will be. Let's figure out a way to patch up our family ties. Don't worry about me. I will find a way to support my family."

"You can begin by exchanging Fengxian's gold jewelry for money!" Qisao said and sneered.

I wondered how Qisao knew about the jewelry, which I kept hidden. Then I recalled her peeping at me the previous night while I was taking a bath. I felt embarrassed and wondered what kind of sister-in-law she was.

"Manfu, your wife has gold jewelry?" Mother-in-Law asked. "Why didn't you tell me this? You are an unfilial son!"

"Mother, they are very small pieces that are worth little. We have kept them to this day only because we haven't come across a pawn shop where we could exchange them. Believe me, I want to contribute to our daily expenses."

"I don't believe you. Fengxian, come here," Qisao ordered.

"Call her Manpo (Mŏn-pō). She's Manfu's wife," Sisao said.

I reluctantly walked over to Qisao. She removed my gold necklace. She and Sisao examined it and then tossed it back at me.

As the women mocked me, my mother's warnings before my engagement to Weiluan raced through my mind. "I am worried about Fengxian marrying a Cantonese," Mother had said. "I have heard that people in Guangdong often have to endure such hardship that they become ferocious ... I fear Fengxian could be bullied to death ..."

In the end, it turned out Mother wasn't paranoid — she was right. But it was too late to turn back. Now the only question was how far the bullying and ferocity would go. Was there a line, as Weiluan had indicated, that his family wouldn't cross? "Be assured, Fengxian, my family will not starve you and our children to death." Or would Mother turn out to be right about that, too?

Alone with the Wolves

The standoff over the pharmacy weighed on my husband day and night. He lost weight, and his face became sad and depressed. I hated seeing him this way and tried to think of a solution to our dilemma. If leaving wasn't an option, we had to find a way to survive amid this insanity.

"Weiluan, I think I know how we should proceed. It's not really a solution but rather a guiding principle for how we should try to deal with this problem."

"Tell me. Your insight is always very helpful."

"Well, the most important priority for us should be seeing that our daughters' basic needs are met. This, of course, requires money. Sige is the only person in the family with money. I fear that if we offend him, we will be left with nothing to eat. So we should try our utmost not to offend him or his wife Sisao. This means not taking any action to divide the pharmacy."

"But then how do we deal with the pressure from Mother and Qisao?"

"The neighbors said the family has been bickering about this long before we returned. They have gotten used to it, and we need to also. We need to adapt ourselves to this quarrelsome atmosphere. Every day that we endure is one day less we have to stay here. When you are contacted about training, we can leave."

"So I should try to get close to Fourth Brother? That may be the correct approach, but I'm afraid Sisao won't allow me to do so."

"Don't be so stupid as to do it openly! Do it delicately."

As we were talking, we heard some commotion outside our room. Weiluan peeped outside. "Speak of the devil, Sige is home," he said with a grin. Because I hadn't been allowed to accompany Weiluan when he previously visited the pharmacy, I had never met Sige. Weiluan rushed out to meet his brother, while I cleaned up the girls. I had just stepped foot into Sige's wing of the house when his wife Sisao stopped me in my tracks.

"Manpo, there are many guests here. It really isn't convenient for you, Zi, and Tian to be here right now," Sisao said condescendingly. "Please go cook something for your daughters to eat. We already have so many guests. I'm afraid that the presence of you and your girls may interrupt my husband's conversation with others."

I couldn't believe what I was hearing. I was meeting my husband's brother for the first time but was being prevented from even saying hello by his domineering wife. She opened the door and gestured for me to leave. To maintain peace, I did as she asked. On our way out, Sige instructed his wife to give a few candies to the girls. Once outside, the girls were excited and smiling about the candy, but I was seething about how rudely I had just been treated. I wondered if our plan to cozy up to Sige would work.

Due to the demands of the pharmacy, Sige spent almost all of his time in Gaoshui, while Sisao split her time going back and forth between the pharmacy and our home. However, that evening they both spent the night. The next morning they were unnaturally cheerful and invited Weiluan to accompany them back to the pharmacy. My husband was taken aback by the offer and wasn't sure how to respond. He came to our room to discuss the situation with me.

"The proposal came so suddenly that I haven't had time to think about it carefully," my husband said. "I can't say no. But if I go, you will be left here alone and face more bullying. Fengxian, what's your opinion? Please find a solution for me."

"I don't have an opinion. This is a family affair. Here comes your mother and Qisao. Ask them what they think."

"Son, did your brother ask you to go to Gaoshui with him?"

"Yes, but I don't know whether I should go or not."

"In my view, it's a good opportunity," Qisao said, butting in. "If you go to the pharmacy, you don't need to worry about food and lodging. You can even go sightseeing. If I were asked to go, I would fly there immediately because it's like paradise for me."

Mother agreed with Qisao, so Weiluan accepted the invitation, even though I could see he was reluctant. "I'll only be gone a few days. Take good care of our daughters and the baby in your womb."

During the first few days Weiluan was away, Mother-in-Law was very kind to my daughters and me. She told me she thought I would be giving birth to a son. When she found a chicken that had drowned in heavy rain, she saved it for me to eat. "It's very nutritious and will make the fetus in your womb healthier," she said.

However, when Qisao learned that Mother-in-Law didn't share the chicken with her, she became jealous and made a fuss. Qisao screamed so loud that several neighbors came to investigate. To maintain peace, I returned the chicken and instructed Mother-in-Law to give it to Qisao. Some of the neighbors followed me to my room, where they tried to cheer me up.

"This family is always quarreling and in a mess," one of the neighbors said. "Giving a chicken killed in the rain to a pregnant woman should be indisputable. They should be killing more chickens for you to eat, yet instead they argue about it."

Hearing others' sympathy gave me comfort, but in the end there was nothing anyone could do to change our situation. I felt discouraged and helpless. At night, while everyone else was asleep, I cried and cried until my pillowcase was soaked.

Weiluan had been gone several days when Uncle Shao, who operated the ferry that brought us to Donghu, came to our house for a surprise visit.

"What is the occasion for this visit, Shao?" Mother-in-Law asked.

"I'm here to inform you that Manfu has gone to Hong Kong to look for work."

"What? Why is he in Hong Kong?" Mother-in-Law asked.

"Your son Sige suggested that Manfu go to Hong Kong to find a job, so he wouldn't have to support Manfu and his family any longer. He gave Manfu enough money to cover his travel expenses. On the ferry, Manfu told me he had no option but to obey his brother's request. He said he would return as soon as possible. He asked me to come here and inform both of you. Now I must get back to work."

Mother-in-Law and I escorted Uncle Shao to the courtyard.

"Manpo, did Manfu tell you that he wanted to go to Hong Kong?"

"No, he never mentioned it. He has always been focused on returning to Hunan to work under Director Cheng."

"This must be another evil plot of Sige and Sisao. By sending Manfu to Hong Kong, they can get rid of another eyesore and end any plans to divide the pharmacy. Now you and your daughters are left here alone. What will you do?"

I didn't know how to answer her and stayed silent.

Later that week we were all sitting outside watching the girls play when Qisao leaned over and murmured something in Mother-in-Law's ear. She pointed at me and began to laugh. "Manpo, your husband was an officer in the KMT. You must have led a comfortable, wealthy life. Why didn't you save any money? If you had, you could be leading a leisurely and comfortable life now."

I wanted to explain our situation, but my Cantonese was too weak to say much. "Weiluan's salary was very low. We were actually very poor at that time."

"Listen to her, she says she was poor! Do you really believe that? What a cunning woman she is. Clearly she can't be trusted. She is neither virtuous nor filial and has the gall to come here and depend on your meager income, Mother-in-Law. How shameful!"

"Qisao, you are right. Your words have awakened me. Without these new mouths to feed, we wouldn't have to bear the hardship we are now facing. Manfu listened to his brother and went to Hong Kong, but he turned a deaf ear to me. Manpo, you'd better find a solution to help yourself."

Both of them stood up and left. I saw that they were heading to the kitchen, so I followed them to offer my help. Since I had grown up with servants, I had never learned how to cook properly, but I was very familiar with maintaining the fire, so I thought I could be of some assistance.

I entered the kitchen, rolled up my sleeves, and grabbed one of the matches. When Mother-in-Law saw me, she yanked the match from my hand, tossed it into the stove, and vigorously stirred up the ash, causing it to blow in my direction. The ash flew into my eyes, and I could barely open them. Then Mother-in-Law muttered something and pushed me backward onto a pile of hay, while Qisao began screaming at me.

"What a shameless woman you are, Fengxian!" Qisao yelled. "I have told you time and again not to come to the kitchen to steal food. Why don't you listen to me?"

Zi and Tian saw me lying on the ground and raced over to help me. "Grandma, please don't beat Mother!"

As my daughters were helping me stand, Qisao slapped both of them across the face. "You devil's spawn! No one beat your mother. It's she who fell carelessly."

I dusted myself off and took the girls to our room. I was so furious that I began crying. I felt so helpless and alone. I didn't know what to do.

As the days passed, I lost weight and became increasingly depressed. I contemplated suicide on many occasions, but couldn't bear the thought of leaving my daughters alone in that prison. If I died, it would only worsen their hardship, so every day I told myself to be strong and accept whatever insults and difficulties I was confronted with.

When Qisao and Mother-in-Law were away one day, a middle-aged woman who I had never met sneaked into my room. She must have been from Hunan because we understood each other perfectly. She wouldn't tell me her name. The woman informed me that every day while everyone was working in the fields, Qisao scolded Mother-in-Law for treating us too kindly. Qisao would get on her hands and knees, and, in tears, plead with Mother-in-Law to be harsher toward us. The woman feared getting caught speaking to me, so she didn't stay long. I thanked her for making the effort to tell me.

This new information explained Mother-in-Law's recent change in attitude. She was being victimized the same way we were. Qisao was employing the ageless strategy of holding the emperor hostage and acting in his name (挟天子以令诸侯). I was comforted to know that other people took notice of the dirty tricks Qisao played, but this was a family situation. No one outside the family dared to get involved.

A few days later, my greatest fear came true: Qisao and Mother-in-Law began using food as a weapon against us. They gave my daughters and me unclean, rancid food to consume. We would starve if we didn't eat it, but if we did eat it we would become ill. After more than a week of this, I came down with serious diarrhea. I became so weak and dizzy that I could no longer walk the short distance to the outhouse, so I had to start using a matong in our bedroom. Fortunately, my daughters were still healthy, but they were young and didn't know how to help me.

At one point, my daughters became so anxious about my condition that they screamed out the window for help. Our bedroom faced a road, so many people outside heard them. They came to our house to investigate. When they saw how sick I was, they immediately became worried about me and my fetus. They raced to the fields to find Mother-in-Law and Qisao. Mother-in-Law dropped what she was doing and started to rush back, but Qisao couldn't have cared less.

"Why are you going back?" Qisao asked her. "Fengxian isn't going to die. She must be playing dead. You should look out for her tricks."

"You are the one who is good at tricks!" a neighbor replied. "It's you who made this woman from Hunan so miserable. If her husband and parents knew you treated her like this, they wouldn't take it lying down."

Sisao also worried about my condition. She feared that she and Sige might be criticized for sending Weiluan away at such a critical time. She dispatched someone to Gaoshui to tell her husband to come to Donghu immediately. In the meantime, she cooked some congee and other food for me, but I had completely lost my appetite. I was so weak that I didn't even have the energy to speak, so I pointed at the food and then to the girls to signal that I wanted her to feed my daughters. I felt comforted watching Zi and Tian eat their fill.

Sige arrived at dusk. He said I was suffering from acute gastroenteritis. "If the diarrhea can't be stopped soon, your body will become fatally dehydrated, which is extremely dangerous. At that point, the baby in your womb can't be saved. Then the lives of both you and your baby will be in danger."

Sige gave me a shot and some medicine, but it did nothing. Then he gave me some salt water to drink, but that only worsened my condition. Sige's expertise was pediatrics. He wasn't familiar with treating adults and was at a loss as to what to do. As a last resort, he gave me some opium pills. After a short while, the diarrhea miraculously stopped. Sige instructed Qisao to clean my room and to treat me more hospitably.

After this incident, Mother-in-Law changed her attitude toward my daughters and me. She frequently checked on how we were doing and prepared fresh, decent food for us. I was very polite and thanked her for her help, but I wondered how long this newfound kindness would last.

Happiness from Heaven

Weiluan returned from Hong Kong after being gone one month. The girls jumped up and down when they saw their father.

"Daddy, you're back! Please don't leave us again. Mommy just narrowly escaped death!"

"Fengxian, are you okay? What happened?" Weiluan asked me.

"I'm fine. Go greet your mother. We can talk later."

Weiluan found his mother and invited her to our room. Qisao followed them to see what, if any, money and goods Weiluan had brought back from Hong Kong.

"Manfu, I see you have come back with a large bag," Qisao said as she entered our room. Without asking, she grabbed it and pulled out several pieces of women's and girls' clothing.

"These appear to be only for your wife and daughters. Why didn't you come back with anything for your mother?"

"These clothes are from Fengxian's Uncle Jusheng and his wife. They also gave me some pocket money. I know we desperately need cash, so I didn't spend a cent to buy anything for anyone. I apologize, Mother. Please take this money and buy something to eat."

"Thank you, son. How much money did you manage to earn in Hong Kong?"

"Manfu has been gone so long that he must have brought back a lot of money," Qisao said, "but I'm not sure if he is willing to give any to you, Mother. Maybe he wants to give it to his wife to be her private money."

"Qisao, Mother, trust me. I don't have a cent in my pocket. The money I just gave to Mother was actually from Uncle Jusheng. Let me tell you what happened while I was away. While I was in Gaoshui, Sige suggested that I look for a job in Hong Kong to support my family. It was a good idea, but when I got there I couldn't find anything suitable. I didn't want to accept a low-level job that would make others look down on me. I visited many relatives and friends, but most of them are just simple hawkers without any roof over their head. They keep their shops open until 1 or 2 a.m., then they find an empty place in the shop to lie down and sleep. Life is very hard for them. The wife of Uncle Jusheng teaches in a primary school. After classes are over, the family of three pushes some desks together to serve as their beds. It's relatively peaceful there, so I spent many nights with them. Uncle Jusheng gave me some money to give to Fengxian. His wife also gave me some of her old clothes as well as clothes that her daughter had outgrown."

"I know a man who works as an unskilled laborer in Hong Kong," Qisao said. "The money he earns is enough to support his wife and children. Manfu, you are young and strong, why don't you do the same?"

"My son was an officer in the military," Mother-in-Law said. "How can he accept a job as an unskilled laborer? No matter how difficult our circumstances, we must still save face and not let others look down upon us."

"Thank you, Mother, for understanding my dilemma," Weiluan said.

That evening I told my husband everything that had happened since he left. He felt awful and embarrassed about how his family treated me, but he wasn't surprised. Before we went to sleep that night, he patted my belly and spoke to the baby.

"You must be a good boy. Please achieve honor for your father."

"And what if it's another girl?"

As soon as I asked the question, the baby kicked my belly, which startled both my husband and me. Soon I began to feel intense pain. I knew I was going into labor, so I told Weiluan to inform the family. Mother-in-Law fetched a midwife, who happened to be the woman who had secretly visited me a couple of weeks earlier. I felt comforted to have her by my side.

Around midnight on February 20 of the lunar calendar, I gave birth to a beautiful baby boy. I was so overjoyed and relieved that I forgot about the pain. Weiluan was ecstatic when he heard the news. Everyone except Qisao was in a joyful mood. When Sige and Sisao heard that I had given birth to a healthy boy, they purchased some special food to nourish my body, so I would have milk to feed the newborn. Weiluan named the baby Haoran, which means "an upright man." We prayed that Haoran, or Hao for short, would bring us good luck and blessings from heaven.

At the time, it was customary in Donghu to hold a special celebration upon a baby boy's one-month birthday. Weiluan and I had no money to hold such a feast, so Mother-in-Law talked Sige into paying for it. Many relatives and friends were invited. When it was over, Qisao lashed out at Mother-in-Law for being so kind to us.

"You no longer care about me and my children," Qisao said. "I have made up my mind that I want to divide the family property and live separately from Manfu and his family. They will take care of themselves, and I will take care of myself."

"Qisao," Mother-in-Law said, "Manfu fathered a baby boy. Isn't that worth celebrating? I know why you've been so angry since the day Manfu arrived. It's because of Manfu's land, which I have allowed you to live off for the past decade. You fear it might be taken away from you if he stays here. Well, you're right. I won't allow you to use it anymore."

When Qisao heard Mother-in-Law say this, she flew into a rage beyond anything we had witnessed thus far. Her plot had been exposed. Later that afternoon, Mother-in-Law came to our room with a small packet of papers. They included the deeds to all the family properties as well as a special booklet predicting Weiluan's fortune that his parents purchased for him when he was just two years old.

"Manfu, this booklet is very precious. It's the guidebook of your entire life. It records fortunes and misfortunes. We invited a famous fortune teller to write it for you when you were a toddler. It cost two silver dollars at the time, which was very expensive."

Weiluan and I were both very curious, so we immediately read it. We were surprised to find that what was stated in the booklet was in line with his life up to that point, including the fact that he would be a soldier. The booklet ended when my husband was 65 years old. For that year, the fortune teller wrote:

> "After bitterness finally comes sweetness ... The wick is lifted higher, the silver lamp becomes brighter ... Looking backward, I can only see the clouded Qinling Mountains, but not my home beyond those hills... Looking forward, I can only see the snow-capped Blue Sky Pass, but whether to step forward, my horse hesitates ... Around my ears, the crying of my wife and children still echoes."

After reading it, Mother-in-Law handed Weiluan all of the deeds.

"Son, this is the deed to our fields, these are the deeds to the mansion and orchard built by your father, and this is the deed to this home. The deeds of all our family's properties are here. Promise me that you will never lose them no matter what happens. They are the foundation of our life."

"I promise to take good care of them," Weiluan said.

"Now, I have some other things I want to tell both of you. You heard Qisao say earlier this evening that she wants to divide the family property. My biggest concern about doing this is your family. You are in a very difficult situation. You have nothing to depend on for a living. You are not strong enough to work in the fields, and you have many young children that require care. Manfu, I have missed you day and night for over a decade. I never would have imagined that you would return home like this. You were an army officer, but that was just in title. You were too honorable to use that title to seek benefits for yourself. Previously, Qisao had pinned high hopes on you. She thought you would be the savior of the family since her husband had fallen into the abyss. Now it turns out that you are in a worse predicament than she is in. That's why she has been so cruel to you and your family. When you left a decade ago, you said you weren't interested in inheriting any of the family property, so Qisao made arrangements to have her son informally adopted by you. This enabled her to reap all the benefits from your land. The value is not low and amounts to thousands of kilograms of rent grains per year. I permitted this while you were away, but I always told her that one day you would return, and this arrangement would have to end. I have always kept the deeds hidden from Qisao, so she could not get her hands on them. Your two brothers and their wives are not good-hearted people. They are all selfish. Only you, Manfu, don't put money first. If Qisao insists on splitting the family property, she will no longer receive your share of rent grains. This will make her life more difficult. I'm sure she understands this. For this reason, I think she won't go through with the threat, but we'll see. I hope you can put family harmony first and try to tolerate her. Son, you said that you will go back to Hunan in the near future. Is that true?"

"Yes, Mother, it's true. Don't worry about me. I'm sorry for making you so anxious about my situation. I am an unfilial son and can't help you to solve these problems. Please forgive me for this."

Later that night, we were finishing dinner when we saw Sisao and Qisao leave the house together. They were laughing and jovial.

"Those two have been at each other's throats for years," Mother-in-Law said. "Now suddenly they are friends. What is going on here?"

"We should feel happy for them that they have patched up their relationship," Weiluan said. "Now we won't have to listen to them fighting every day. Our lives will be much quieter and happier."

"You don't know those women like I do," Mother-in-Law said. "I am certain they have something up their sleeves."

That night the two sisters-in-law returned all smiles. Qisao told Mother-in-Law again that she wanted to split the family property.

"Qisao, are you sure you have thought that through?" Mother-in-Law asked. "What will you rely on for a living once the family is split up?"

"Don't worry about me. That's my business. If you are smart, you will choose to live with me and my sons in the future, and you will have a comfortable life. Don't you love your grandsons any longer?"

"Qisao, you know I love my grandsons. But Manfu is my youngest son. I can't see his family suffering in such poverty and do nothing."

Weiluan felt very ashamed and lowered his head when he heard his mother say those words. "Mother, don't worry about me. I will find a solution."

A Family Divided

The next morning the bickering among Mother-in-Law, Qisao, and Sisao continued. After the sisters-in-law left, Weiluan's mother announced that she was going to visit the family elders. "I will arrange for them to come and witness the splitting up of the family property. I see no other way out of this tempest."

Weiluan and I felt devastated seeing his family fall apart and knowing that we were the source of the conflict. We had arrived at Weiluan's home penniless and with five mouths to feed. After two months, no one wanted to carry the burden of supporting us any longer. The strategy was clear: sever all ties with us and leave us to survive on our own. That way, if we starved to death, they wouldn't be held responsible.

"Weiluan," I said, "how are we going to survive in the future?"

"Fengxian, our only hope is to wait for the order to return to Hunan for training. I never expected my family would disintegrate like this. No matter how heavy our burden, I will shoulder it. Don't worry. As long as we are together, I will never have any regrets, even if I starve to death one day."

"But I have never worked in the fields. How can I handle it in addition to caring for three young children?"

"Believe me, the message from Hunan will arrive soon. Then we will be saved."

Mother-in-Law returned from the family elder's home that afternoon. He informed her that Qisao had already visited him requesting to divide the family property. She had no authority as a meager daughter-in-law, so he ignored her. Now that Mother-in-Law was making the request, he would abide by her wishes and visit our home the next day with several elders.

"Ma'am," he said, "before you leave, you should know that Qisao told me that Sige and Sisao promised to look after her once her fields were transferred to Weiluan. It seems your fourth son is hanging his younger brother Manfu and his family out to dry. I hope they can survive."

"So do I, so do I."

Weiluan was hurt and angry when he heard that the families of his brothers had allied against him. "Have I done anything to harm them? No, I haven't! Why are they treating me like this?"

"Weiluan," I said, "don't you remember what the fortune teller in Changsha said? He said that you are bound to encounter many difficulties and that no relative will come to your rescue. This is your fate. You can do nothing but accept the arrangement of your destiny."

The next day the family patriarch and many neighbors came to our home, but Weiluan's two brothers were absent. Mother-in-Law asked the guests to listen, watch carefully, and serve as witnesses. She ordered someone to bring out all of the family's dishes, utensils, and cooking ingredients. Weiluan and I received a few bowls, some salt, a dozen kilograms of rice, a half-liter of oil, a dull kitchen knife, Mother-in-Law's tiny wood-burning stove, and a small cooking pot.

"Everything else is mine!" Qisao said.

As for the property, Weiluan was given full control of the fields under his name, and a small area in Qisao's wing of the house was to be blocked off and given to us to reside in. The patriarch and elders agreed that this division of property was fair.

The proceedings then shifted to which son Weiluan's mother would reside with.

"I will live alone," Mother-in-Law said. "I don't want to live with any of them."

"In my opinion, you should continue living with Qisao, not only because that is the current arrangement, but also because your fourth son Sige told me that he would not give you any money to cover your daily expenses unless you lived with Qisao."

"So now my fourth son is forcing me to give up my freedom?"

"It's not like that. You have been living with Qisao for a long time. Her rooms are more spacious than Manfu's. Manfu also has several young, noisy children. He and his wife have enough of their own problems. It's better that you not add more burdens on them."

"I earn rent grains from my own fields. I won't be a burden to anyone."

"Manfu," the elder said, "you've been silent this entire time. You are an intelligent former officer and must be good at settling things. What do you think is the best solution?"

"I am a useless son. I feel ashamed to face all of you. I can't even feed myself, let alone my family. What you said earlier, patriarch, is correct. I don't want to put my mother through poverty and starvation with us."

"Okay, then it's settled. Your mother will continue living with Qisao."

Everyone dispersed, and we returned to our room. I had never witnessed an event like that before and was in shock. I couldn't believe that relations between family members could disintegrate to the point that people were dividing their cooking oil and salt. Was love within a family really that fragile? How did Weiluan's family get to this point? Little did we know that in a few years an even larger redistribution of the possessions of every family in the village would take place, led not by family elders but by the Communist Party.

In addition to our small bedroom, we were given two additional rooms from Qisao's wing of the house: a narrow 5-foot-by-12-foot room to be carved out of Qisao's living room by a thin partition, which we would use as our kitchen and living room, as well as a 12-foot-by-9-foot attic that was only accessible from a steep ladder in front of our bedroom.

Qisao and her sons put up a large wooden partition in her living room to separate our part of the room from hers. The partition only went two-thirds of the way to the 15-foot ceiling, and there were several large cracks in the wood. Hence, even though we were physically separated from each other, Qisao and her family could still hear everything we said in our kitchen and living room. They often peeked at us through the cracks. The tiny room was only marginally wider than a hallway and felt extremely confining.

Weiluan and I stared at our bare brick walls and dirt floor and cried. Our biggest sorrow was the loss of Mother-in-Law's presence. We worried about how Qisao would treat her, especially after she had spent so much time recently looking after us. Qisao wouldn't allow her kindness to go unpunished.

Mother-in-Law came to visit that afternoon sad and in tears. I could only imagine how much pain she felt seeing her sons destroy her family in this way.

"Manfu, your fourth brother Sige and his wife are so shameful and evil-minded. They know you have many mouths to feed and not one penny, yet they didn't give you a cent. Sige didn't even attend the meeting. They didn't make any effort to seek an arrangement for you. How can Sige be so cruel to his younger brother? They simply want to force you to die or at least to drive you mad. As your mother, I feel unspeakable pain watching this happen to you."

"Mother, please sit down. Don't be so sad. Otherwise, your unfilial son will feel guiltier."

"Manfu, your number one priority should be putting food on the table for your family. I want you to come with me now to the house of one of the tenants on your fields. She is due to submit another 100 kilograms of rice to us. This rent rice should help you for a while. We also need to recover the fields from them so that you can take over management. This way you will have some food to eat in the future."

Qisao had been listening to us through the partition and suddenly stormed into our room. "Those rent grains are mine! Manfu doesn't have the right to collect them."

"As of today, they are officially his," Mother-in-Law replied. "You have been collecting rent from his property for a decade. You are so disgraceful!"

After seeing Qisao get angry, Weiluan hesitated about accompanying Mother-in-Law to the fields. I wondered if my husband would ever be able to stand up to Qisao.

"Weiluan, that rice belongs to us!" I said in dismay. "How dare you not collect it when we have nothing to eat. Do you really want to starve us to death?"

Weiluan mustered the courage to go to the fields with his mother and carried back an armful of rice still in its husks. The rest was brought later that day by one of the tenant's sons. The boy was shocked to see how destitute we were and that we possessed no container for the rice. "I can lend you two bamboo baskets," he said. We thanked the boy for his kindness.

We had received quite a lot of grain. Fortunately, the husks had been dried, but the rice still needed to be cracked open before it could be eaten. The next morning Weiluan asked Qisao if he could borrow her grindstone. Surprisingly, she consented. Weiluan carried the grain to the small room where the processing machine was. Zi and Tian were curious and followed him. As soon as they entered the room, the girls were beaten and bullied by Qisao's children, so Weiluan carried the girls back to me. When he returned, he discovered that half of our grain had disappeared. My husband was infuriated but too timid to confront Qisao directly, so he approached his mother about it.

"Mother, did you see anyone enter that room?"

Mother-in-Law didn't dare reply. Instead, Qisao shouted back. "I allowed you to use our grindstone out of good intention, but now you accuse me of stealing your grain. What is the point of being nice to you? I won't lend you anything anymore. Get out of here!"

Weiluan returned home frustrated.

"Since the stolen grain can't be recovered, why didn't you at least grind the remainder before coming back?" I asked him.

"We can crack it open by hand on our own."

As we pounded the grain that morning with our feet and hands, our new reality began to sink in. From then on, life was going to be very different. We would have to rely on ourselves for everything. Neither Weiluan nor I had any experience farming. Could we succeed in sustaining our family? If we failed, we faced certain starvation. By the time we finished opening enough grain, I was exhausted and sweaty, and a large piece of skin had torn off my foot. But the next meal was on the table, and that was all that mattered.

Fire Sale

The next few days Weiluan and I learned how to do a number of tasks that in the past had always been done for us. When we needed water, we fetched it from a well near the river. When we required wood or hay to fuel the stove, Weiluan chopped some from the bushes on a nearby hill. Each time he returned with bloody hands and feet.

Some of our neighbors took pity on him and suggested I make some clothes for them in exchange for hay. They gave me the material, and we agreed on a date when I would finish the pieces. Unlike Huaguo, the women in Donghu never learned how to sew or do needlework. I felt happy to be able to contribute to our family in this way. However, the arrangement didn't last long. Nearly everyone around us was poor; few could afford material. Soon demand for my sewing services dwindled.

Day and night we pondered a way out of our situation, but there simply wasn't any. The economy was in a mess from more than a decade of war. Few job opportunities existed anywhere, particularly in the countryside. Our only options were to make a go at farming or ask Sige to take mercy on us and find Weiluan a job. Weiluan understandably had no faith in his brother.

"If Sige cherished our brotherhood, he wouldn't have treated me this way from the beginning. He would have come back when the family was splitting up to make an appropriate arrangement for me so that we can survive. Giving me a small amount of money would have been nothing for him. He is the head of Gaoshui Township. He could easily have helped me find a job. The fact is he doesn't care about me at all. Mother was right. Sige doesn't want to help me. He is only interested in seeing me die. Then he can get rid of another threat to his pharmacy. We must depend on ourselves. With our hands, sweat and courage, I'm sure we can create a happy family."

"I agree, but we need some kind of foundation to build on," I said. "We need money so we can buy the tools to do farming. We will never succeed with courage and sweat alone. Why don't we ask Sige for help? Perhaps he will lend us some money to get started or even give you a job as an assistant in the pharmacy. No matter how small the salary, it would still put food on the table."

"Neither Sige nor Sisao will let me near the pharmacy. It's impossible that they would help me by lending us money. This is just your own wishful thinking."

"So are we to sit here and wait to starve to death just because you are too full of pride to ask for help? You haven't talked to Sige yet. How do you know he won't agree?"

"Fine. I'll go and talk to him." Before Weiluan left, he opened enough grain for the girls and me in case we got hungry. He set off for Gaoshui on foot since he had no money for the ferry. He didn't return until it was dark. He immediately collapsed on the bed in tears when he entered our room. Clearly, it didn't go well.

"Weiluan, being a human being in this world isn't easy. Survival is difficult. But no matter how hard our life is, we must summon the courage to never give up. Look at our beautiful, innocent children. For them, we must survive."

Zi and Tian ran to their father with smiles and goaded him into playing with them. Eventually he sat up. I prepared dinner as they played. Listening to Zi and Tian giggle momentarily eased our anxiety, and we were able to enjoy a few moments of bliss. After the girls went to sleep, I asked Weiluan about his visit.

"The trip was a total failure. Sige didn't agree to either request. Instead, he scolded me. He said, 'You are a man. You shouldn't stay at home with your wife every day. Our family has split up and gone its separate ways, yet here you are asking me for help. Manfu, you must muster the strength to rely on yourself. I'll give you 50 cents to buy some oil and salt. As for the money you requested, I will not give it to you. Go home and don't come here again!' I told you Sige wouldn't help us."

The grain we received from the tenants didn't last long. Soon we were running low on food. Weiluan began losing weight and became ill. I knew he needed to see a doctor, but he refused to spend the money. Every day he got weaker. I was at a loss as to what to do.

After a few days, I decided that our only option was to sell some of the items we had brought from Hunan. I discussed the idea with my husband, but he didn't want to sell anything. I pleaded with him to reconsider.

"Weiluan, where there is life and health, there is hope. Isn't life more precious than these belongings? We will not only be saving your life but also the lives of everyone in this family. I'm determined to do this whether you agree or not."

"Fengxian, you're not familiar with this area. You don't speak the local dialect. I really don't want you to go out and be seen in public alone. This will not only erode my dignity but also make you feel humiliated."

"It doesn't matter. In order to save this family, I can bear anything."

"Fengxian, I feel so terrible that I have let down your mother. I am so useless. I hate to see you suffering like this for me."

"Don't worry about that. What matters right now is getting you healthy and putting food on the table for our daughters and son."

I didn't admit it, but I was nervous about roaming the streets of an unfamiliar place alone. Given my education and privileged upbringing, I never dreamed that one day I would have to resort to pawning my belongings on the sidewalk. Yet if I didn't do so, what other choice did we have? How important were the words "ashamed" and "save face" in our current situation? I knew that survival should be our number one priority. I rummaged through our bags, pulled out the items we would miss the least, and then set off for the market.

"I'm leaving now. Weiluan, please look after Hao. If he gets hungry before I return, you can feed him some hot water. Zi, Tian, take care of your father and brother. Mother will be back soon."

The first, fourth, and seventh day of every lunar month were market days in Donghu. On those days, people from surrounding villages convened to peddle their items. As I was walking to the market, I encountered dozens of other people carrying bags, baskets, and shoulder poles full of items to sell. Half of them were women, which gave me comfort.

When I arrived at the market, I took notice of how everyone else was selling their items and imitated them. I found an empty spot on the ground and laid out our clothes, bed sheets, quilts, etc. so that customers could see them clearly. It was the first time I had ever tried to sell anything in a market. I felt very shy. Other people were yelling out what items they had to attract customers, but I was too timid to say a word. I felt embarrassed even raising my head to look at anyone.

Hours passed, and I still hadn't sold a thing. I began to worry that I would return home empty-handed. Weiluan and the children were waiting for me to return with good news. I didn't want to disappoint them. I slowly abandoned my inhibition and mimicked the other peddlers' shouting. I attracted the attention of many shoppers because my announcements were in Hunanese rather than Cantonese.

Soon a large crowd was surrounding me. They inspected everything I had for sale, but no one inquired about the prices. After the crowd dispersed, a man my age came forward and spoke to me.

"Why are you selling these items?"

"I live in a home with four bare walls, I have many children, and my husband is ill. I don't have the money to provide my family with three meals a day. That's why I'm here selling these items. It's for my family's survival."

"I can tell from your accent that you are from Hunan. Are you the wife of Han Manfu?"

"Yes, I am."

"Manfu left over a decade ago. I thought he was leading a good life away from here. He was a high-ranking officer in the military. Why did he come back?"

"My husband was an officer, but, unlike many others in the military, he was honest and upright. He never used his position to amass ill-gotten gains. As a result, we never attained the wealth of other officers' families. After the civil war, Weiluan lost his job. Burdened by me and our children, he had no option but to come home. We never expected that upon our return his family would split up. Now we have no means to sustain ourselves. That's why I'm here."

"Manfu's brother owns a pharmacy and is the head of Gaoshui Township. Why haven't you sought help from him? He has a lot of money."

"We've asked him for help many times, but he has refused us."

"That's outrageous! Sige often comes to the aid of strangers, but he won't help his own brother."

The man took 50 cents out of his pocket and handed it to me. I felt ashamed taking a handout from a stranger. I thanked him for his kindness but refused to accept it. The man left. By early afternoon, I still hadn't sold anything. Other people were gathering their items and preparing to return home. I also wanted to go home, but how would I buy the rice, oil, salt, and firewood to make dinner? I stayed and prayed that a buyer would come my way.

After a while, the man who had spoken with me earlier returned with a friend. "I brought someone who is interested in buying your fox fur mattress pad."

I smiled with excitement and handed him the mattress pad to examine. The man asked me how much I wanted for it. I had no idea what it was worth, and, to be honest, I didn't care. I just wanted to earn something.

"I don't know how much it's worth now. What price are you willing to pay?"

"How about five yuan?"

I thought five yuan was too low but didn't say anything. The man I had spoken with earlier saw that I was reticent.

"Manpo, I brought this buyer here. He's my friend. You are so poor. This is a good opportunity. If you miss it, you may not have another chance."

I thought about it for a few seconds and then finally agreed. Regardless of whether the price was too low, we would get some money to hold us over for the next few weeks.

"What's your name?" I asked the man as they were walking away.

"I'm from Gaoshui. Your husband was my classmate. I haven't seen him in over a decade. I'm sure he wouldn't remember me. My name isn't important. Goodbye."

I hurriedly packed my items and headed home. I wanted to bring back some food as a surprise, so I traded some small items for stuffed buns on the way. Zi and Tian rushed to greet me when they saw me approaching the house. Zi was carrying Hao on her back. He was crying.

"Hao, don't cry. Mother has returned," Zi said. "Now we have food to eat!" It broke my heart to hear Zi say that. I hated watching my children go hungry. I handed the buns to the girls and took Hao into my arms. I breastfed him as soon as I went inside.

"Why are you so late?" Weiluan asked. "Did you sell anything?"

I took out the five-yuan bill and handed it to my husband. It was a new note recently issued by the Communist government. We studied the front and back.

"What did you sell to get so much money?"

"Of course, our precious fox fur mattress pad."

"What a pity. That was my favorite."

"I know, but compared to your health, it's much less important. When some families are in difficulty, they have to sell their children to survive, but we only sold a fox fur mattress pad. It was worth it. It was one of your old classmates who bought it. He wouldn't tell me his name. Without him, we wouldn't have sold it."

For the next few weeks, we survived on that five yuan plus some additional money I earned from selling other belongings. Weiluan still refused to see a doctor, so his illness worsened. One day a neighbor invited a doctor to her home to examine a family member. When I caught wind of it, I hurried to the neighbor's house and asked the doctor to come evaluate my husband.

The doctor informed us that Weiluan was suffering from malaria. He said that it must be treated quickly or Weiluan could die. He prescribed several Chinese herbs. I was walking him out the door when the doctor took me aside and whispered to me in a low voice.

"Half of your husband's illness is due to sadness and anxiety. If you want him to recover quickly, tell him not to think about things that make him sad and to take things as they come. Try to comfort him whenever possible."

I thanked the doctor and gave him his fee of 0.2 yuan. Then I hurried to Donghu to buy the herbs. When I returned, Weiluan tore into me.

"Don't squander our money on me! This money was hard-earned. Do you really think this small amount of herbs can cure my illness? I don't believe it." I tried my best to persuade him, but Weiluan refused to take the medicine.

With my husband bed-ridden, the burden of keeping the family going fell to me. Between market days, I would tend to the vegetables in our small garden, fetch water, gather firewood, cook, and clean. After several weeks, I had sold almost everything we had except for a few items. All of the customers in Donghu had seen my goods, so I was forced to take the items to other markets that were farther away. The round trip to those markets took an entire day. If I was lucky and sold something, I was able to buy food on the way home to fill my stomach and give to my family. But if I didn't sell anything, I walked all the way home on an empty stomach.

As winter approached, Weiluan's malaria worsened. His face became haggard and thin. I had also lost a lot of weight, but fortunately I had not fallen ill. I firmly believed that life would eventually turn around for us. Weiluan was a pessimist. Soon he was unable to get out of bed. I could see that he was on a slow path to death and insisted he see a doctor.

"Fengxian, I know this illness well. I will not recover. I'm sorry to put you through such suffering."

"How can you say such words at this moment? You're always so pessimistic. Now you are looking to death to extricate you from these difficulties. What a coward! You have let down me and your children. For the sake of the entire family, you must see a doctor."

"Chinese medicine won't work for this, but I will see a Western doctor."

I immediately rushed to Donghu Hospital and asked a doctor in Western medicine to come to our home. He examined Weiluan head to toe.

"Mr. Han, you are suffering from malaria. This disease is very harmful and infectious. Why didn't you see a doctor earlier? If your children become infected, the consequences will be very serious. This can't be cured in a couple of days. You need some special injections. It will cost a lot of money."

"No matter what it costs, we will pay the fee," I replied.

The doctor gave Weiluan an injection, prescribed some pills, and instructed me to return to the hospital with him to fetch some disinfectant to kill the germs in our home. Fortunately, we had enough money left to pay for everything. On the way to the hospital, the doctor and I chatted.

"I heard many times about a Han Weiluan who had left Donghu and was working as an officer in the KMT. I had always been under the impression that he was wealthy and powerful. I had no idea that your home would be so bare and that you would be so destitute. How do you make a living?"

I explained to the doctor everything that had happened to us over the past year — the emergency evacuation to the Snow Peak Mountains, our several-month trek on foot to Changsha, the difficulties living with my own family in Hunan, our journey to Donghu, and the nasty in-fighting between Weiluan's family. The doctor took pity on us and didn't charge me for the disinfectant or pills.

"Your husband's face is full of sadness and anxiety. Anxiety is very harmful to one's health. Try to keep your husband calm and comfortable. I will visit him again tomorrow."

I thanked the doctor for his kindness and generosity and hurried home with the disinfectant and pills. I cleaned our home top to bottom. After a few hours, Weiluan began to talk with more energy and enthusiasm than I had seen in weeks. The injection was clearly working.

"In the past, I was very strong. I wasn't afraid of rain or wind and didn't fall on the battlefield even under heavy gunfire. I never expected that one day I would be confined to bed like this. Now I'm a fallen soldier afflicted by poverty and disease."

"Everyone has his own fate. Perhaps you are doomed to encounter many adversities now. Even so, we must have the courage to overcome this present difficulty. Weiluan, from today on you must find the will to struggle out of these challenges and to be a good, resilient husband and father. Abandon your negative and sad feelings and adopt an optimistic attitude toward life. For the sake of our family, for our happiness, you must commit yourself to what you said on our wedding night. Do you still remember what you said?"

"That we would stick together through thick and thin and be together until our deaths."

"Yes, but that wasn't the most important thing you said that night. When I married you, you were penniless, and I had no dowry. At that time, you said, 'A wealthy father is not what makes a man good.' And I replied, 'And a rich dowry is not what makes a girl good.' Both of us had nothing at that time. We promised to create our own happiness with our own hands. How happy we were!"

The more we spoke, the more Weiluan perked up. "But we have been struggling for so many years. Now our children must suffer through these difficulties with us."

"Yes, but there are children who are worse off than they are. The most unfortunate children are those without parents. As their mother and father, we cannot disregard our children's needs and their survival. We must struggle on."

After reflecting on my words, Weiluan sat up. He still looked very ill, but he was more energetic than he had been in weeks. I wondered if it was the medicine or our conversation that was breathing life back into his veins.

"I'm really hungry," he said. "I need to eat. I want protein."

I heard someone peddling tofu outside, so I ran out and bought five cents' worth. That night Weiluan slept soundly. I didn't hear him moan at all. I knew then that he was going to be okay.

The doctor returned the next morning. "Mr. Han, how are you doing?"

"I feel much better. Thank you so much, doctor."

"That's great to hear. You need to receive another injection today and tomorrow, and then you should be cured."

"Fengxian, hurry and give the doctor his fee."

"There's no need," the doctor said with a smile. "The drugs aren't expensive. Save the money and buy some food to nourish your husband." That day the doctor didn't charge us a cent. We thanked him for his generosity. Strangers had more sympathy for us than our own family.

Day by day, Weiluan slowly regained his strength. I feared he might relapse if he didn't consume more nourishing food, so I looked around our barren room to see what we could sell. It was winter, and quilts were hot items in the markets. I decided to sell one of our two remaining quilts along with a silk duvet. I hated to part with them because it would leave us with just one quilt for five people, but I had no choice.

I took the quilt to Donghu market, but no one was interested. The next day I decided to take it to Gujing (Gū-jǐng) market. I had been to Gujing before, but had forgotten the route. After wandering around for a while, I eventually came across a path that I thought led to Gujing. When I encountered an old man, I asked him the name of our location.

"Wandering girl, the name of this place isn't important. You don't need to know the name of this road. You can explore your own road."

"Thank you, old man," I said, smiling and nodding politely.

A few moments later, some strange men approached me. They asked where I was from and where I was going. They could tell from my accent that I wasn't from that area. They began to tease me. They asked what I was carrying and if I was going to Gujing market. I feared they may rob me or harbor other ill intentions, so I quickly ran away.

When I reached the market, I laid the quilt and duvet on the ground and began announcing what I had for sale. Many people were attracted to the duvet and came to inspect the items, but no one was interested in buying them. Later that day, the men I had encountered on the road came to examine the quilt. They said they wanted to buy it, but something about them made me nervous.

"Your quilt and duvet are beautiful. We know this is worth a lot of money. Sell it to us. We're not poor people. Why won't you sell it to us?"

I didn't know how to answer them, so I kept quiet.

"Since you brought these things to the market, you must want to sell them. What are you hesitating about? Are you reluctant to sell them?"

"Yes, I am reluctant to sell them. Please go."

After the men left, many other people came to admire the quilt, but no one wanted to buy it. By the afternoon, I began to regret not selling the quilt to those men. The weather had become colder, and there were few people left in the market. My stomach was rumbling, so I decided to return home.

As I approached the area where I had met the men earlier that day, I became anxious. I feared encountering them again and walked as fast as I could. Then, suddenly, I heard a woman calling my name.

"Manpo, are you coming back from Gujing market?" the woman asked. She was one of Sige's servants. "Please come in and have a cup of tea. I apologize that I don't have anything special to offer you," she said as she placed some hot tea and a bowl of sweet potatoes in front of me. We chatted for a while; then I explained that I needed to get back before dark.

"What's in your bag?" she asked as I was leaving.

"A quilt."

"Don't sell your quilt. You'll need another one when your children get older."

"I know, but we have sold everything else. This is all that's left. If I don't sell it, we will starve."

The woman took pity on me and gave me a bag of sweet potatoes. "Take these. This can solve your hunger problems temporarily."

As we were saying goodbye, one of the men who had teased me earlier walked up to us.

"Auntie, do you know this woman from Hunan?"

"Yes, her husband is the brother of my master."

"I'm still interested in buying your quilt," the man said. He offered me three yuan, but I insisted on five. After a lot of back and forth, he eventually agreed to give me five yuan. I felt so relieved and walked the rest of the way home smiling. Not only did I have five yuan in my pocket, I was also bringing back a bag of sweet potatoes that I had gotten for free.

When I arrived home, the girls ran up to me. I handed them the bag of sweet potatoes. They jumped up and down and immediately began biting into them. During dinner, I explained the day's events to Weiluan. He gave me a bowl of congee, but I passed it to the girls. "I'm already full from all of the sweet potatoes I ate," I said. In fact, I was still hungry. I wanted to eat that bowl of congee, but it was more important to see that my daughters not go hungry. Those days, unless I felt unbearable hunger, I refrained from eating.

One Rock at a Time

After a couple of weeks, Weiluan recovered from the malaria. Soon he was helping me with the chores. As the spring planting season drew near, we began to prepare for our first endeavor with farming. Rice was the staple crop in that area. It not only served as the main source of farmers' incomes but also was what the government required families to submit for taxes. There were two seasons for rice: February to early June and late June to October. In addition to owning rice paddies, most families also possessed dry fields, where they would plant vegetables, potatoes, peanuts, beans, and gourds. Often, if a family suffered a bad rice harvest, they would have no rice left after paying the grain tax. In these instances, the food harvested from their dry fields was their only means of avoiding starvation.

The day after Chinese New Year in 1951, the tenant who previously rented our fields came to our home to return the land to us and pay us our final rent grains. Mother-in-Law, one of the family elders, Weiluan, the children, and I accompanied the tenant to the fields. Mother-in-Law and the tenant pointed out precisely which areas were ours. There were eight different plots, some nearby, and others as far as a 45-minute walk away. Altogether, we took possession of nearly two acres of wet rice paddies and two acres of dry fields. The tenant asked if we would be willing to continue renting some of the fields. I thought it might not be a bad idea because it would be difficult for Weiluan and me to cultivate such a large area on our own, but he disagreed. He insisted on recovering full control of all the fields.

Both of us were daunted by the task ahead. Our financial worries would disappear if we could reap decent harvests. But would two novices like us be able to achieve that? We still lacked seeds and an ox and didn't possess a single tool necessary to do the work.

Weiluan consulted the older men in the village about how to construct the tools from scratch. The edges of our rice paddies were adorned with small clusters of bamboo trees, which Weiluan cut down with our old, dull kitchen knife. He crafted the bamboo into makeshift tools and baskets using their instructions. The items didn't look as professional as others', but they worked. We were encouraged by this success.

When the planting season arrived, Weiluan went out every day to learn the ropes from friends and relatives. He watched closely as other families plowed their fields and planted rice in small, dense incubator patches. After a few weeks, the seedlings would be transplanted from the incubator patches to the wet rice paddies. Weiluan explained our situation to everyone he talked to, hoping that someone would take mercy on us and lend us some seeds and an ox.

One morning Weiluan announced that he would go to Gaoshui to ask Sige to lend us some money to get started. I was glad to see my husband get over his fear of approaching his brother for help. I prayed that Sige would cherish their relationship enough to extend a helping hand. However, he was only willing to give my husband two yuan. It was better than nothing but far from enough.

I was beginning to doubt that we would be able to plant anything that season when Weiluan returned home one day very excited.

"Fengxian, I have some good news! I heard that there is a gold shop in Pingyang. We can go there to exchange your necklace for money."

"That's great! I don't know if we'll get very much, but even a small amount will help."

The next day Weiluan got up early to begin the long walk to Pingyang. He received only a few yuan for my necklace, but that, along with the five yuan from the sale of the quilt and the two yuan from Sige, was enough for us to buy seeds and an untrained calf. Both of us felt hopeful.

We believed we would succeed by making progress little by little, just as the mythical Yu Gong had done. (In a famous Chinese fable, a man named Yu Gong manages to deconstruct a mountain one rock at a time.)

We were getting ready to go to bed that evening when we were startled by a knock on our door. As soon as Weiluan opened the door, Sisao barged in carrying a bright lantern.

"How dare you go to Gaoshui and ask for money from my husband!" she screamed. "We owe you nothing. I heard you went to Pingyang and exchanged your gold necklace for money. I know you have more than enough money to repay me right now. Give me my money!"

Weiluan didn't know how to respond.

"We didn't borrow any money from Sige," I yelled. "He gave two yuan to my husband because he still cherishes their brotherhood. The money wasn't borrowed. It was given to us. We don't need to repay you at all."

Not surprisingly, Qisao raced to our room when she heard the commotion, adding more fuel to the fire. "Sisao, demand your two yuan back. If you give it to them, they won't be grateful. It's better that you give it to me, so I can buy some healthy food for our mother-in-law."

Both women screamed at us for several minutes while Weiluan and I sat there silently. Sisao eventually got tired and gave us one last order.

"I'm instructing you to never again visit the pharmacy. You are not to see my husband for any reason. Our family is now living separately. Therefore, anything given to you must be repaid. Are you clear?"

My husband nodded yes. The two sisters-in-law slammed the door and left.

"I have never encountered such evil women," Weiluan said. "I have never done anything to offend them. In the 10 years that I was gone, I didn't spend a cent of this family's money, while they reaped all of the proceeds from my fields. I never complained about it."

That night neither of us slept well. In the morning, Weiluan was still upset. "Fengxian, we have only one way to go."

"Go? That's great! The earlier we leave here, the less we have to endure. Where are we going to go?"

"I don't mean leaving here. I mean there is only one path of survival for us. That is to get called back to Hunan by Director Cheng. I am going to write him a letter right now." Weiluan jotted down a few paragraphs and then gave it to me to review.

"Respected Director Cheng, it has been over a year since I bade farewell to you in Hunan. I wish you good health and happiness in your work and life. As for me, I am young and strong but have no other virtues to brag about.

I still remember the years when I worked as your subordinate. Your support, care, and patient teaching have been deeply engraved on my heart. I admire your nobility of treating everyone the same, no matter if he is rich or poor, and helping people when they are in difficulty and danger. I have learnt a lot from you. However, I am afraid I cannot repay my debt of gratitude to you in this life. In the next life, even if I have to work as a beast of burden, I will do everything I can to support you to achieve your goals.

After my children, wife, and I returned to my home in Guangdong, we witnessed a sudden, terrible change in my family. I wish so much that I could work under your leadership again. I hope you can help me do so. This is what I pray for now. Sincerely yours, Han Weiluan"

Weiluan raced to the post office and sent the letter by registered mail. We prayed we would hear from Director Cheng soon. In the meantime, we had no choice but to proceed with farming. Fortunately, one of Weiluan's cousins learned of our predicament and arranged for us to borrow rice seeds from one of his friends. We were already behind schedule, so the minute we received the seeds we planted them in the incubator patch.

After planting the rice, Weiluan used the money we had accumulated to buy additional tools and an untrained calf since the money was insufficient to purchase an experienced adult ox. The calf hadn't been tamed and ran wild whenever it encountered strangers. Weiluan spent hours every day teaching the animal commands. But he was a novice and the calf was stubborn, so their progress was slow. In the past, Weiluan had commanded hundreds of soldiers and horses on the battlefield, but now, no matter how hard he tried, he couldn't control this one animal.

About a month later, it was time to transfer the rice seedlings from the incubator patch to the wet paddies. Some neighbors who had already finished their work offered to help us transfer the seedlings and till and plant our dry fields in exchange for a liter of rice and two meals a day. We desperately needed help and accepted their offer.

Picking the seedlings out of the incubator patch was easy but time-consuming. Transplanting them into the wet paddies was much more challenging because the paddies were packed with ferocious leeches. The skin on my and Weiluan's feet and legs was thin and tender, so the leeches flocked to us. We had been in the water only a few moments when they attacked us. Both of us rushed out screaming. We tore the bloodsuckers away, which left streaks of blood running down our legs. The farmers in nearby fields burst into laughter.

"Don't be frightened. They won't kill you. Try wearing socks. Maybe that will help."

Weiluan and I went home to tend to our wounds and eat lunch. That afternoon I returned to the fields in socks. I naively thought the socks would protect me; instead, the leeches were just as vicious. I could feel them digging into my flesh as soon as I stepped into the paddy. I rushed out of the water again. I was tearing the leeches from my feet and legs when Qisao arrived.

"Why are you helping these two imbeciles?" she asked the people we had hired. "You will only make this lazy woman from Hunan lazier. Right now she is putting on a show. Why are the leeches only biting her? I have worked in these fields for years. I have never been bitten by leeches."

I was watching Qisao rant when, out of the corner of my eye, I saw Weiluan approaching her carrying a shoulder pole full of seedlings. Both baskets were loaded, and he was struggling to maintain his balance.

"This Hunan woman is playing tricks!" Qisao yelled. She turned to leave just as Weiluan was taking an unsteady step in her direction. The two of them collided. Qisao grabbed hold of Weiluan's torso to keep her balance, which made his full weight fall into her. The shoulder pole and seedlings went flying. The two foes crashed into the muddy water face-to-face in a tight embrace. They looked like clay figures when they stood up. Everyone was hysterical.

"Manfu got up right after he fell," one farmer said, "but Qisao didn't. It seems Qisao is the one who is putting on a show!" Flustered and embarrassed, Qisao cursed my husband and angrily stormed away.

The incident kept everyone laughing for the rest of the day.

After we finished transferring the seedlings and planting the dry fields, we thanked the workers for their help and paid them. Neither of us had realized just how much rice we would have to pay out when we hired them. In the end, we handed over nearly 10 liters, which made a huge dent in our reserve. We stretched out what little rice we had left, but eventually we ran out. Unlike other families, who had reserves of vegetables and potatoes from the previous season to get them through hard times, we had nothing to fall back on since it was our first season farming. The slow, agonizing process of starvation began.

We had gone two days with nothing to eat when Weiluan suggested that we sell our new calf to purchase rice. I hesitated because I knew we would need it to plow the fields after the harvest. It would be impossible for us to buy another animal in the future. We decided to hold off. Day by day our bodies became more weak, pale, and emaciated. Mothers have an innate instinct to feed their children. Seeing my children go hungry and lose their rambunctiousness and enthusiasm broke my heart.

I was outside grazing the calf one day when Liu (Lē-ō), a widow from the village who was about 10 years older than me, approached me with a basket of leaves. "Manpo, I have watched you and your children getting thinner and thinner each day. I know you don't have any food. Children can't bear starvation like adults. I've brought these bean leaves for you to cook for your children. Of course, they don't compare with rice, but they taste decent. My children and I have subsisted on this off and on for more than a decade. It's the only thing that has kept us alive."

I broke down as Liu talked. For the first time in a long while, I felt like someone could truly see and understand my situation. "Thank you so much for your help, Liu. You are so kind and thoughtful."

I was moved that this destitute widow and her children — the poorest family in Donghu — had taken mercy on us and tried to help us. Everyone else, including our own family, couldn't care less about us. They had no qualms about watching us die. Only people who have experienced such desperation can know the bitterness of it. I immediately felt a close kinship with Liu.

"After my husband died, we were destitute," Liu said. "I didn't have an ox. No one ever helped me. Every day I led my children to the fields, where we toiled by hand. It was unbelievably difficult. I'm surprised we survived."

I thanked her again and rushed home to cook the leaves for my family. They were coarse and bitter, but at least they filled our stomachs. I was glad to learn that this type of leaf could be eaten. However, they were in short supply and couldn't provide a reliable source of nourishment. My husband and I racked our brains about other ways to get food. A couple of Weiluan's cousins ran a small business producing and selling tofu during the down season, so my husband paid them a visit. He begged them to give us the mushy soy bean dregs left at the bottom of the pots after they made the tofu in exchange for firewood.

"Cousins, please, have mercy on us. My family is starving."

"Manfu, we understand your predicament, but we're sold out right now. Many people buy tofu dregs to feed their pigs. First come, first served."

From then on, Weiluan would awaken every morning at 3 a.m. and rush to his cousins' homes to get tofu dregs. They tasted awful, but they were nourishing and kept us alive. On days when no tofu was made, Weiluan returned empty-handed, and we went hungry for the entire day. During the busy season, tofu production was halted completely, so we went without food day after day while at the same time laboring in the fields. All of us became extremely weak and gaunt.

After a few weeks of living this way, it became clear to Weiluan and me that if we didn't begin to ingest some decent food soon, illness and death would be imminent for all of us. We decided we had no other choice but to sell our young calf. That afternoon Weiluan went to fetch the animal from the hills, but it was nowhere to be found. He frantically raced home.

"Fengxian, the calf is missing! I've looked everywhere for it, but I can't find it."

"Where did you last leave it?"

"On the same hillside I take it to every day."

Neither of us said a word. We immediately rushed to the hill and began searching for the animal. Because I was so malnourished, my legs began to tremble after running a short distance, so I stopped to rest on the grass while Weiluan continued searching. I felt so frustrated and angry that I began to cry.

"God, why are you torturing us like this?" I asked aloud. "Are you really able to bring justice to the world? My family is starving. Can't you see this? People say that the more hurtful one is toward others, the less God will bless him. We haven't done anything to hurt anyone, yet you don't bless us. Please, please send us our calf."

The sun set after an hour. It was impossible for us to find our calf in the darkness, so I yelled out for Weiluan to return. I received no response. I knew the children would be scared at home alone in the dark, so I stood up to go back. At that moment, I heard a cough and a moo. I thought it might be Weiluan, but instead it was another man from the village.

"Manpo, your calf and my ox walked off together to a distant hillside. Your husband has retrieved your animal. He is resting behind me. He is very weak and walking slowly."

I thanked God for answering my prayer and shouted out to my husband.

"Fengxian," he shouted back, "what are you still doing out here? Go home to our children. It's late."

When I arrived home, Zi and Tian rushed to me in tears. I hugged them and told them not to worry. "Daddy found the calf. He'll be home soon."

Weiluan returned exhausted. Seeing how pitiful and haggard we all were, he shook his head. "I'll go borrow some rice from a neighbor. I'll repay him tomorrow after the calf is sold." None of us had eaten a proper meal in weeks. We were elated to have the opportunity to eat some rice.

Weiluan used some of the money from the sale of the calf to purchase vegetable and other seeds to plant in our dry fields. But without the calf, the two of us had to till the soil by hand. Liu saw us struggling and offered to help. She had recently purchased an adult ox that her eldest son used. We asked her son to help us till our dry fields in exchange for three meals a day. Liu also pitched in, but she never asked for anything in return. Her younger son often picked wild berries for my daughters. Liu and her sons didn't have a stitch of decent clothing, so to express our appreciation, I gave her a shirt with cotton padding that I had made a while ago.

"Thank you so much, Fengxian. Your sewing skills are excellent. I wish I could sew like you."

"The shirt isn't new. I've worn it before, so it's not worth much. You and your sons have helped us so much in the fields. We owe you a lot."

Once the seeds had been planted in our dry fields, Weiluan and I moved on to the task of watering the crops. Every morning we carried dozens of barrels of water from the trenches surrounding the fields to our plots. The used barrels we purchased were of very poor quality and leaked profusely. By the time we reached our plots, often there was little water left to pour on the crops. Weiluan fretted that it might be too dry for the plants to grow. However, a couple of months later, we reaped a bumper harvest of kidney beans and gourds from our dry fields, which we ate three meals a day for several weeks.

Even though we now had kidney beans and gourds to eat, our diet was unbalanced. We were constantly exhausted and often felt light-headed. One day Weiluan was on his way to the attic when he became dizzy and fell off the ladder. His hand came smashing down on a glass bottle and was badly cut. Blood gushed everywhere, and he lost consciousness. My children and I panicked and screamed for help.

Sisao heard us and rushed over. She immediately fetched a bottle of iodine, put some on my husband's hand, and instructed her servants to carry Weiluan to our bed. She bandaged the cut and strung up his hand to keep the blood flowing downward. Word was sent to Sige, who instructed some servants to bring Weiluan to Gaoshui by boat. He stayed there for several days.

I asked Sisao many times to take us to Gaoshui to visit Weiluan, but she refused. I thought about sneaking behind her back to visit him, but I knew that if I angered Sisao or Sige it would be counterproductive for Weiluan's treatment. I decided to wait patiently at home.

Weiluan finally returned after 10 days. Uncle Shao insisted on accompanying him home from the ferry because he was so weak. When I opened the door and invited Uncle Shao inside, he was shaken and stepped back.

"My god, Fengxian, look at how you have changed!" he said, shaking his head. "When you and your children arrived here on the boat, you looked so elegant and graceful. How could you change so much in just a year and a half? If I saw you on the street, I wouldn't recognize you at all."

"It's all my fault," Weiluan said. "I'm so useless that my family must suffer and starve with me. Our home no longer resembles a home, our family no longer resembles a family, and we no longer resemble people."

Uncle Shao shook his head and sighed. "This world of ours is constantly changing. You must be patient. A good man must know how to endure when faced with adversity. Life will get better one day."

Coward

With the help of Liu and her sons, we completed the summer rice harvest. It wasn't a bumper harvest, but the paddies yielded enough to give us comfort that the hard work was paying off. Weiluan invited Liu and her sons to dinner to express our appreciation. He instructed me to go to town and exchange some rice for pork and fish, which we hadn't eaten in ages.

"How about we invite your mother, too?" I proposed. "We haven't had your mother over for dinner since the family was divided."

"I don't want to trigger another episode. Even if we invite her, she may be unwilling to come, or Qisao may forbid her from coming. I think it's better to invite her another time."

That afternoon Liu, her sons, and I continued harvesting, while Weiluan stayed at home with the children and prepared dinner. We returned home at dusk. When we entered our house, the smell of the food was intoxicating. Everyone's mouths were watering. We had just sat down to eat when Qisao and Mother-in-Law barged in.

"Now you are enjoying pork and fish and don't even invite your mother," Mother-in-Law said. "What an unfilial son you are! I should beat you to death!" She charged at him. Fearing the two women might attack his injured hand, Weiluan stepped away from the table.

"Mother, please, please forgive me."

Neither Mother-in-Law nor Qisao were interested in what he had to say. Instead, they grabbed the table and turned it upside down, spilling all of the precious dishes we had worked so hard for onto the dirt floor.

"Now enjoy your food!" Mother-in-Law screamed.

Tian ran to pick up the fish and pork, but Qisao trampled on it so no one could eat it. I was so angry that I was at a loss for words. Feeling uncomfortable and out of place, Liu and her sons quickly left. Weiluan and I felt so embarrassed. Curious about the noise, a cousin named Dafa, who lived nearby, came over with his wife. He was enraged at what he saw.

"You old woman!" Dafa screamed at Weiluan's mother. "Manfu almost died from an injury, yet you, his mother, don't sympathize with him. Now you become angry just because his family has some pork and fish to eat? Do you want them to eat tofu dregs every day?"

The evil pair left. Zi and Tian scraped up the pork and fish and cleaned off what they could. They ate most of what was left and handed the few remaining pieces to Weiluan and me. We were no longer in the mood to eat.

"People always say a mother's heart is good, but where is your mother's goodness?" I asked.

"Mother is good. It's Qisao who has influenced her. That woman is as evil as a wolf and as fierce as a tiger. She holds mother hostage to act in her power."

"Do you really think your mother is completely free of blame?"

"It's all my fault. If I had listened to your advice and invited Mother, this wouldn't have happened."

"I don't think so. Even if we had invited her, they still would have found a reason to fight with us. In the end, they wanted to prevent us from being able to enjoy such a special dinner. Those two women want us to die! Then Qisao can take back your fields. Her only objective is to usurp everything we have. She is an evil woman, and your mother has become just like her."

"It's not Mother's fault, Fengxian. I hope you can show respect to my mother."

"A fish rots from its head."

Weiluan and I eventually calmed down and ate what remained of the meal. Then we gathered our composure and headed to Liu's house to apologize for the fiasco. They were just finishing dinner when we arrived. Liu and her sons were kind and understanding, but, like everyone, they were flabbergasted at Weiluan's timidity.

"Manfu," Liu said, "if you continue to be such a coward, you will be bullied for the rest of your life. Don't you get angry and upset when your family treats you this way?"

Weiluan talked on and on about how evil Qisao was, how she had brainwashed his mother, and how there was no way to get through to someone like her, which was all true. But as they listened, I could see in their eyes that they thought what everyone else thought: Weiluan had brought on a lot of the trouble himself by being so meek.

That fall our harvest was decent enough that we had a fair amount of rice left even after paying the grain tax. I was relieved to not have to worry about food. But within a couple of weeks, Weiluan announced that he wanted to sell most of the remaining grain to buy a new ox. I was hesitant.

"Fengxian, it's too hard for us to farm without an ox."

"I know, but if we exchange our rice for an ox, what will we eat? Our children narrowly escaped dying of starvation the last time we ran out of food. I can't bear to see them suffer from hunger like that again. On top of that, you and I have to toil in the fields every day during the busy season. If we don't have rice to eat, we won't have the energy to work."

"In the off-season, we can eat other things. We can save what rice we have for the busy season. I have made the decision to buy it." As his wife, I had no choice but to go along with him. In order to save money, Weiluan purchased another young calf, so we had to spend a lot of time training the animal. Nevertheless, it was a ray of hope.

As winter slowly settled in, the days became shorter and cooler. That year we were confronted with a particularly harsh winter with extremely cold temperatures and sleet, rare for the south. The grass in the fields and on the hills turned yellow and dry, making it difficult for farmers to graze their oxen. Many animals, including our new calf, became malnourished and emaciated as the frost destroyed pasture. It wasn't long before the frigid temperatures and lack of food claimed the life of our new calf.

In order to recover some money, Weiluan's cousins suggested that we slaughter the animal and sell the meat. In the end, we recovered only half of what we paid for it. Now we were without rice or an ox. I was beside myself.

"It seems like the poorer we become, the more misfortunes we suffer," I said. "We gave up all of that rice for nothing. Now it's certain that we will starve."

"People must adapt to change. I never expected that purchasing the calf would turn out this way and worsen our situation. But this will not stop me."

"We already exchanged all of our rice for that calf. What do you intend to do now, exchange one of us?"

"No! I want to use the proceeds from the meat to purchase a piglet, which we can raise at home and exchange for a calf when the pig is fully grown."

It didn't sound like a bad idea, so I went along with it. The next day Weiluan went to the market and brought home a piglet. The animal was very docile. Whenever it was full from eating, it immediately went to sleep. Zi and Tian enjoyed playing with it. After several weeks, the piglet grew much bigger. Weiluan's plan appeared to be on track.

The pig was roaming around outside one day when it returned groaning and with a broken leg. After a few minutes, it keeled over and died. It was clear that the pig had been beaten. The most likely culprit was Qisao or one of her children, but we had no evidence. Neighbors heard the groaning and came to see what had happened.

"Manfu," one of the neighbors said, "your family is so poor and unfortunate. Several of your livestock have died recently. Were they killed by God or a human? If they were killed by God, we have nothing to say. But if they were killed by a human, this person must be very vicious and evil. Let us avenge you!"

As the neighbor spoke, cousin Dafa ran toward our house from the fields. "I can be your witness. It was Qisao and her two sons. I saw them beat your pig with my own two eyes. I would not fabricate such a story."

The neighbors suggested that we confront Qisao. "Bring her here and insist that she compensate you with another pig. Then she won't behave like this again."

"Thank you for your care and sympathy, but the animal has died," Weiluan said. "The pig cannot be revived. My mother lives with Qisao, so I must put up with this. It's just another misfortune. We must accept this reality."

The neighbors shook their heads in dismay. "Manfu, you are so cowardly. You are hopeless!" They left in frustration. I was also upset that Weiluan wouldn't fight for us on this occasion.

"This time we have the support of so many people. Why not demand that Qisao compensate us? If she isn't punished, she will continue to act like this in the future."

"We should forgive others whenever possible," Weiluan replied. "Qisao and mother are hiding in their room. What are we supposed to do, break in? Mother is Qisao's shield. If they were to deny that they attacked the pig, how would the situation be resolved? I couldn't bear humiliating Mother like that. Forget it. Since none of the neighbors are interested in buying the pork, we can eat it ourselves, so it isn't a total loss."

"Now we have lost our rice, ox, and piglet. What will be next?" I asked.

Chinese New Year in 1952 came and passed uneventfully. That Spring Weiluan and I noticed our neighbors and friends acting more insular than before. Everyone held their heads low to avoid making eye contact with anyone. Even Liu and her sons, who previously were so warm, suddenly said they could no longer help us. Because we were outsiders, people rarely spoke with Weiluan and me about village affairs, so we weren't sure what was happening. Weiluan made some inquiries one day when he went into town.

"One of my friends told me that the Communist Party is preparing to roll out several new policies in the countryside," he said. "Some people will be selected as targets of persecution. People are afraid to associate with each other right now because they don't know who will be targeted. They want to look good in front of the Communist Party and don't want to be seen as consorting with undesirables. Many people are talking about fleeing to Hong Kong. My friend asked me to go with him."

"Are you going to go?"

"Of course not! Who would take care of you and the children? It wouldn't be fair to you. I would never do that."

"I think it's not a bad idea. You can earn some money to buy another ox and farm tools. The children and I can take care of ourselves. Don't worry about us. If God thinks our lives still have purpose and value, he will protect our safety. When you have saved enough money, you can come back. It's no use staying in this house and waiting for a solution to present itself out of thin air. If we continue like this, our lives are in danger. We are on a slow path to death. Think of our innocent children."

Weiluan finally agreed, albeit hesitantly, to go to Hong Kong to find work. He borrowed a small amount of cash from one of his cousins to cover his travel expenses. The children and I escorted him part of the way to the train station and said a tearful goodbye.

"Don't think about saving face," I said. "Do whatever work is available to earn some money. When you get tired, rest."

"I know. I will try my best. Pulling a rickshaw would be a good way to earn money quickly. Since I used to be in the army, I'm strong and should be a good rickshaw puller. Take care of the children."

The children and I had been home just a few minutes when Weiluan suddenly appeared before us.

"What are you doing here?" I asked.

"Fengxian, please forgive me. I really don't want to go to Hong Kong alone. I will be lonely away from you and the children."

"Okay, if you don't want to go, I won't force you. We can die together in this wretched place. You are such a coward!"

Although I was angry, part of me was relieved that Weiluan would remain by my side. The work that had to be done in the fields was overwhelming, particularly now that we had lost the help of Liu and her sons.

Weiluan tried on two more occasions to go to Hong Kong, but every time he couldn't go through with it and returned home to me and the children. On his last attempt, he arrived home with some fish.

"While I was on my way to Hong Kong, I came across some people doing commercial fishing. I thought it would be wrong to just jump in the water, take some fish, and leave, so I offered to help them. They gave me a few fish in return."

"That sounds like hard work, Father," Zi said.

"Yes, but it was worth it. As long as my wife and children can eat fish, I feel very happy."

"Fengxian, please don't blame me for not going to Hong Kong again. I just can't bear to leave this family. You must think that I'm an incurable person."

"Okay, then this will be your grave. We can all die here together! I have tried and tried to persuade you to earn money for us, but you have been such a coward and cheated me time and again. Why couldn't you follow through just once? What is it about this place that you can't leave?"

"I'm not reluctant to leave this place. I'm unwilling to leave you and the children. I don't have the ability to take you with me and support you, and I don't want to go alone."

I shook my head and walked to the kitchen to clean the fish. As I watched my husband chat with the girls, I could see that he was right: he was incurable, incurably devoted to us. I was fortunate to have such a caring man as my husband and the father of my children. I knew he must have given serious thought about leaving. What I and others saw as cowardice might actually be farsightedness. Perhaps Weiluan could foresee how difficult life would be for us without him. Better that we suffer together than alone. I decided to stop pressuring him to go to Hong Kong.

The Dung Collectors

Cultivating so many fields without the help of Liu, her sons, and her ox was extremely draining. With no one to help us, we had no choice but to make Zi and Tian pitch in. On days when we didn't require help in the fields, our daughters prepared lunch and delivered it to us. On their way home, the girls would carry back anything that had been reaped that morning. During harvests, the girls made numerous trips hauling heaps of rice husks back to our home. Every husk had to be dried before being cracked open or else it would rot, so the girls also saw to it that all of the husks were properly dried in the sun. It pained us to make the girls work so young, but we had no choice.

Exhausted after weeks of plowing our fields by hand, Weiluan awoke one morning very frustrated. "I don't think farming day and night can solve our problem. I want to go to the market in Donghu and see if I will be lucky enough to find a solution."

"By luck, you mean borrow money. You still haven't repaid the money you borrowed from your cousin to go to Hong Kong. You can't keep borrowing money from people. That is not a solution. We must overcome our weaknesses by working diligently. Don't go to the market. Come to the fields with me."

On the way to our plots, we unexpectedly ran into Weiluan's nephew, Dong, who had previously served in the army with him. Dong had been living outside Donghu for years and had just returned. I was unkempt and dirty and felt embarrassed when Weiluan introduced us. Dong invited us back to his home. Weiluan went with his nephew, but I continued on to the fields. That evening I inquired about his visit.

"Is Dong back to see his family?"

"No, he has returned to settle down. The rumor is that he struck a fortune and wants to build a new house here."

"That's interesting. Does he still remember what he did in the past?"

"What did he do in the past?"

"Don't you remember? You helped him several times when you were both in the army. On one occasion, he embezzled a large quantity of grain from you that you were trying to send to your family."

"I had completely forgotten about that."

"He could be our savior. Why don't you ask him for some assistance?"

"I'm a man. How can I beg for help from others?"

"I'm not asking you to beg for help. Rather, ask him to reciprocate his debt of gratitude to you."

"It's still hard for me to broach such a subject. How about we visit their home together? You can meet his wife. When the two of you get closer, you can bring it up."

"Okay, I guess."

The next day I washed myself and Hao, then the three of us went to visit nephew Dong and his wife. Dong was away when we arrived, so we sat down and chatted with his wife, Li.

"Manpo, have you become accustomed to life here in Guangdong?" Li asked.

"Yes, I have."

"She's now a full-fledged rural woman," Weiluan said. "I feel sorry for how hard she has to work."

Weiluan and Li spoke for a long time about the family. He filled her in on recent events. Dong arrived after an hour. We introduced him to Hao, chatted some more, then returned home. As we were leaving, Dong and his wife handed us a few candies to give to the girls.

A few days later I was doing housework when Li dropped by our home for a surprise visit. She was astonished at our tiny house and austere living conditions. I explained how difficult it was for us to make ends meet.

"Is there anything we can do to help?" Li asked.

"Thank you so much for asking. We could use help buying an ox. We never seem to be able to save enough money to buy a decent ox. We would repay you after the next harvest."

"Of course. That shouldn't be a problem. Let me go home and discuss it with my husband. Tomorrow you and Weiluan can come to our home to finalize the arrangement."

Weiluan was exhilarated when I told him the news. Both of us felt like we were finally seeing some light at the end of the tunnel.

The next morning we arrived at Dong's home. Everything had already been arranged. The money was sitting on the table, along with an IOU. Some government officials also were present to serve as witnesses to the deal.

"Uncle Manfu, you helped me a lot in the past. Please forgive me that I couldn't reciprocate your kindness then."

"Nephew Dong, don't worry. Let bygones be bygones."

"Uncle Manfu is an intelligent, capable, and magnanimous person," Li said. "You were a heroic and commanding officer. I recall many girls falling in love with you. I never expected that you would travel all the way to Hunan to find a wife, but I can see now that she is a very good woman. She knows how to endure hardship and is willing to learn new things. These are rare virtues in a woman."

"Fengxian is from a wealthy, scholarly family. She is well-educated and even attended college briefly. She is a modern woman who hasn't forgotten what it means to be a decent person. She has never complained about my bad fortune. She always puts our family first. I am very lucky to have her support."

"Yes, you are, Uncle Manfu," Dong said. "Now let's get down to business. My wife told me that you need some money to purchase an ox. I have 50 yuan here to lend you. I hope you don't mind signing this IOU."

"No, of course not. This is a very large sum of money. We must repay you."

After Weiluan signed the IOU, Dong took it and tore it in half. He handed the pieces to the cadres for inspection. After approving it, they handed one half to us and the other to Dong. We thanked the couple repeatedly for their assistance and returned home.

"You should have written him the same kind of IOU when you gave him that batch of grain years ago! Then today he would have to return a large sum of money to us, and we would owe him nothing!"

"Fengxian, be quiet! Only the two of them and the two of us know about that grain. Don't speak of it to anyone else. Otherwise, Dong and his wife might get angry and stop helping us. Right now, they are the only ones around here who are still good to us."

"I know it's just between you and me. I won't say a word to anyone."

Weiluan promptly went to the market and purchased an adult yellow ox. All of us were excited. When the time came to transplant the rice seedlings, we worked in the fields from dawn until dark. We had become true Chinese farmers. We had tasted for ourselves the meaning of the poem:

"Hoeing the crops under the noonday sun,
His sweat drips on the ground beneath.
Who knows that on his dining plate,
Each grain was wrought from such hardship?"

With the help of our new ox, we reaped a bumper harvest. But after paying the grain tax, exchanging some rice for fertilizer, and repaying our IOU to nephew Dong, little rice remained for our family. We desperately needed to find a way to put more food on the table.

In between busy seasons, villagers shifted focus from working in the fields to preserving food, gathering firewood, and collecting dung to make into manure. It took me a long time to become familiar with the landscape and how to identify the best locations for firewood. Even after I became familiar, often I was unable to gather as much wood as others because of how weak and malnourished I was. I moved so slowly that I was frequently left behind in the hills after everyone else returned home.

I was walking home from the mountains alone one afternoon when I slipped on something wet. I stopped to look at what it was and realized it was a gold-coin turtle, just like the ones Grandfather used to keep in the drainage pool at Rongxia. I picked up the turtle, wrapped it in the cloth I carried each day to wipe away my sweat, and rushed home.

"Weiluan, look at this, what do you think it is?" I asked as I unwrapped the creature.

"It seems like a stone, but I can tell it's not. What is it?"

I set the turtle on the floor. When it didn't budge, I worried that I had killed it when I stepped on it. Then suddenly it moved. Weiluan picked up the creature to study it. "It's a gold-coin turtle!" he shouted. "These are very rare and expensive."

Many people came to our house to see the turtle when they heard about it. "The Hunan woman can't chop wood, yet she managed to find a gold-coin turtle!" they said in amazement.

"There is no way you caught that turtle," Qisao said. "People much more skilled than you have been unable to catch one. Do you expect us to believe that a novice like you caught a gold-coin turtle on your own? You must have stolen it from someone else."

Qisao's insults raised doubts in the villagers. I had to find a way to make them believe me.

"No matter what Qisao says, the truth is that I caught this creature on my own. The turtle was in the middle of the path, just waiting to be stepped on. I caught it without any effort. We used to have many gold-coin turtles at my home in Hunan. Turtles are intelligent animals. This turtle waited on the path just for me so it could reciprocate my kindness to it in its previous life."

The villagers were impressed with my defense. "The Hunan woman is really good at speaking. She is even talking about this life and the last life. Many people walked that same path, but none of them enjoyed the bliss of catching a gold-coin turtle. It was Manpo's fate to catch the turtle."

Weiluan's cousins suggested that we kill the creature and eat it, but Weiluan and I agreed it would be better to sell it and purchase rice with the proceeds. We would get much more food that way. Weiluan quickly took the turtle to the market. He sold it for 1.58 yuan, which was enough to put food on the table for a few weeks.

As the money from the turtle sale dwindled, Weiluan proposed that we direct our energies into making fertilizer. "It's the down season, so we have a lot of time on our hands. I can go out every day and collect as much dung as possible. Then you and the girls can mash it into fertilizer at night. We can purchase rice with the money we earn."

"That sounds like a good idea. Let's try it," I said.

From then on, every afternoon Weiluan and our ox scoured the hillsides, mountaintops, and riverbeds in search of dung. At night, my daughters and I took the droppings he collected and broke them into small pieces which I took to the market the next day and sold. We earned 0.2 yuan for each basket. It wasn't a lot, but it was enough to put food on the table and keep our children from starving.

After a couple of weeks, whenever the villagers saw Weiluan, they waved and shouted "dung collector, dung collector" and pointed to places where they had seen droppings. I was happy to see Weiluan set aside his pride and do whatever was required to support our family. The man who a few years earlier had turned up his nose at any job he thought was beneath him had now become the village dung collector. We had both learned a lot about hard work, perseverance, and humility.

"I never expected that I would live in such circumstances," my husband said one night when he came home. "When I am out there alone on the hilltops, I alternate between laughing and weeping about what I'm doing. This week I made up a song about it, which I sing when I am lonely and collecting dung."

"A song? What kind of song? Sing it for me."

"Dung collector, dung collector
Many mountains you have climbed
Oxen are everywhere, dung only here and there.
The mountains are high, the grass green
Oxen come here to feed, I come here to reap
Accompanied by my ox, how happy I am

The collector's life is hard, yet he is satisfied
In my youth, I, too, was nourished by these hills
Now I am scorched by sun, tattered by rain and wind
My skin wrinkled, back hunched, vision blurred.
One day I fell into a ravine, stood up and soldiered on
But perseverance is hard to muster, so I sing to survive

The more dung I gather, the happier I am
With full bags, I resemble three persons,
Neighbors joke, my family split their sides
Hearing their laughs, my hardship fades.
For a decade I battled the Japanese accompanied
        by soldiers and horses
Now I walk these hills, an ox my only companion
Yet I love my family, so here I collect dung

Dung collector, dung collector
I sing loudly on the hills, my voice echoes in the clouds
Through these shouts I vent my complaints
I hate that I am a tiger away from my terrain,
        where even a dog dares to bully me
I hate that I am a caged bird with two wings, but cannot fly
I hate that I am a dragon trapped in shallow water,
        laughed at by shrimp.
But because I love my family, I happily bear this hardship
        for I am now the village dung collector

As the dung collector sings, his family chuckles
He is happier than a king even without three meals a day
But who can taste the bitterness in his happiness?
Only oxen are willing to listen, only birds sing to me
Why am I alone on this hill? Even the animals have left
It is time to return home, the only comfortable place for me"

"Weiluan, you are so talented. Your song is so beautiful and vivid. I'm sorry we have made you into a dung collector. I really appreciate what you endure every day for me and the children. I really am very sorry."

"You are the wife of the dung collector. You also work hard every day. I know life is very difficult for you, too. At night you pound droppings, and the next day you sell the manure in the market. Your contribution is as big as mine. Regardless of his job, a man's success rests on his wife. Our work isn't prestigious, but we manage to succeed and survive. This shows that I have a good wife. Fengxian, I will also marry you in my next life."

After a couple of months of this routine, we had filled a small storage area in the attic with extra dung. Our house smelled awful, but we were able to repay all of our debts. Perhaps our string of misfortunes was finally over.

PART FIVE

Bad Elements

Left for Dead

On October 1, 1949, in Beijing's Tiananmen Square, Chairman Mao proclaimed the founding of our new People's Republic of China to a massive, roaring crowd. The night before, in a speech to the first session of our new Communist Party government, he declared, "We, the 475 million Chinese people, have now stood up. The future of our nation is infinitely bright." For decades, the Communist Party had been promising to kick out foreign imperialists, modernize society, and improve the lives of hundreds of millions of destitute peasants. Now the party finally had its chance.

Up to that point, scores of revolutions had occurred in our country's long history, but the end result was always the same: the substitution of one ruling family for another. The impact of dynastic change rarely trickled down to rural families like us apart from perhaps new policies on grain taxes or the conscription of men for an emperor's army or work projects. However, in 1949, all of us sensed that this particular revolution was different, yet few foresaw the magnitude of change awaiting us.

In its first two years in power, the Communist Party focused on restoring law and order, stabilizing the economy, and creating a new bureaucracy to administrate policy from Beijing. Daily life in rural areas remained largely unchanged. During this time, Weiluan and I were engrossed in acclimating to our new lives as farmers and keeping our children fed. Completely cut off from all forms of media, we gave no thought to the goings on of the new government. It wasn't until Chairman Mao's campaign to revolutionize the countryside reached our small village of Donghu, that we finally took notice.

At its core, communism is a theory of how to structure an economy and society to attain greater equality among citizens and free workers from exploitation. But, as we were about to learn, achieving this can be an ugly, arduous process. To begin, all existing personal wealth must be confiscated by the state and redistributed from those with plenty to those with little. Next, ownership of all private businesses must be seized by the government to prevent such inequalities from re-emerging. The culture of individualism must then be replaced with a new culture of the collective in which the interests of the group trump those of individuals. Finally, all previous social hierarchies must be eliminated to free the poor and exploited from the mentality that they remain weaker than and beneath others. All of this requires a government capable of and willing to use violence and indoctrination to break the citizenry's old mindset and squash contrarian views. Control over the media and all flows of information are critical in this regard.

At the time the Communist Party seized power in 1949, few of us understood communism. All we knew was that the Communist Party had promised to be "the savior of the poor." By then, our population was a half billion, of which nearly 90 percent were poor peasants. Precisely how the Communist Party intended to save so many destitute farmers like us was unclear, but the fact that the well-being of the lowest rungs of society was now forefront in the minds of policymakers was a sea change in Chinese politics and history. Relieved that 12 years of war and turmoil were finally over, citizens were willing to give the new leadership the benefit of the doubt.

Our first indication that the political and social climate were changing came with the establishment of the new Donghu Poor Peasants Association, a small group of destitute local farmers handpicked by the Communist Party to help it implement reforms in our village. This association, together with local Communist Party representatives and civil servants, formed the backbone of the new administration in Donghu. Never before had the poor been given such voice and authority. It was a poignant demonstration of the Communist Party's pledge to lift the destitute from oppression. Many people interpreted it as a promising sign of things to come.

The establishment of grassroots groups like the Poor Peasants Association brought Communist Party rule into citizens' lives in a deeper and more personal way than any dynasty that preceded it. The old saying, "the mountains are high, and the emperor is far away (山高皇帝远)," no longer applied.

Our family's first experience with our local Poor Peasants Association came one morning during a heated dispute between Weiluan and

Qisao. They were arguing over how to share the cement sunning ground in the family courtyard. Qisao was using the entire area to dry hay to fuel her stove and selfishly refused to give us one inch of space to dry our recently harvested rice.

"First come, first served," Qisao said. "Why should I bother to empty a place for you?"

"Qisao, you're just drying hay for the fire, while we need to dry our rice husks so they don't rot. Otherwise, we will go hungry. Please let us dry our rice."

"If I don't have hay, I can't cook dinner, and then your mother will go hungry. Is that what you want?"

The more Weiluan and Qisao argued, the louder their voices became. This attracted the attention of some neighbors who were members of the Poor Peasants Association. Soon the association and some government cadres were at our home inserting themselves into our family dispute. The association listened intently to both sides, then discussed their views and made a ruling.

"The sunning ground is to be divided in half," they authoritatively announced. "Each family will use one half. Qisao, move your hay. We will not leave until we see that this has been properly divided."

Qisao angrily shook her head, murmured something under her breath, and then removed her hay.

Weiluan and I thanked the association members for their help. Finally it seemed someone was standing up for us. If this experience with the new government was any indication, perhaps brighter skies were ahead.

"Maybe the Communist Party really is the savior of the poor," I said to Weiluan that night as we got ready for bed.

"Perhaps," he replied as he closed his eyes.

As with everything else positive in our lives at that time, this encouragement was short-lived. Soon we began to get glimpses of the darker side of utopia. One of the first stages of transitioning to communism is the identification of those people who will be elevated and those who will be denigrated under the new system. If society is to be entirely reshaped, it is important at the start to define those characteristics and behaviors that are desirable and should be fostered as well as those that are undesirable. At that time, landlords and wealthy farmers — who were considered to have attained their wealth through the exploitation of others — fell into the undesirable bucket and were labeled "bad elements," followed by anyone perceived to be against the Communist Party's new vision of society. Because of Weiluan's many years of service in the KMT army, he, and by extension our family, was at risk of falling into the ostracized category.

The first indication of our shifting social status was the sudden change in our neighbors' and friends' attitudes toward us. Overnight, people who previously had been friendly now turned away whenever they saw Weiluan or me. Even Liu and her sons scurried away whenever they saw us approaching.

"Weiluan, have you noticed how everyone seems to be avoiding us lately? Do you think it's related to the new government policies you mentioned before?"

"You know all of those political meetings people have been going to that we haven't been invited to?"

"Yes."

"Apparently the Communist Party has launched two campaigns called 'Land Reform' and 'Class Struggle.' That's what everyone discusses when they go to those meetings. People like us, who used to be connected to the KMT, aren't allowed to participate. In fact, people like us often are the subject of criticism in the meetings. Our neighbors and friends are probably afraid to associate with us because it might tarnish their image in front of the Communist Party."

I felt hurt to hear that our friends and neighbors thought so poorly of us, but I was too busy and exhausted to spend much energy worrying about it. By then, it was summer, and working in the fields was like being slowly cooked alive in an oven. Every day we were sandwiched between the scorching sun and piping hot water in the rice paddies. That particular summer the heat was unusually intense. After spending a few hours bent over in such conditions one day, I became dizzy and fainted in the rice paddy. When Weiluan noticed me lying on the ground, he raced over and tried to wake me.

"Fengxian! Fengxian, are you okay? Fengxian? Help! Help! Someone please help!"

Weiluan screamed repeatedly, but the people nearby stared at him blankly. Not one person budged or made any effort to assist us. When Weiluan realized that no one was going to help, he decided to carry me home on his own. Unfortunately, we were in one of the paddies farthest away from our house. He dragged my body out of the field and hoisted me onto his back. Weiluan was also weak and dizzy from the heat, but he managed to carry me the entire distance. I finally awoke when he laid me on our bed.

"Fengxian, Fengxian, can you hear me? Are you okay?"

"Yes. Did I faint?"

"Yes, you collapsed in the rice paddy. I screamed for someone to help us, but everyone just stared at us. No one moved an inch. For all they know, you could have been dying, but they didn't care. Human beings can truly be as cruel as animals. You stay here while I make you something to eat."

As my body cooled and I put something in my stomach, I began to feel better.

"I'm so glad you're okay. I don't know what I'd do if I lost you."

"I'm fine now. Don't worry. I'm sure it was just the heat."

My husband couldn't stop brooding over the way we were treated. "Why didn't anyone help us? We have never done anything to harm them. Why would they treat us like this? I know we shouldn't depend too much on other people, but they easily could have helped us for a few minutes."

"I don't know why they didn't help us, but I have decided that I am going to return to the fields with you this afternoon."

"No! You should stay here and rest. You just collapsed!"

"Time is too precious. We have so much work to do. I feel fine now."

Weiluan knew I was right. We had a massive amount of work to complete. That afternoon we returned to the fields together. When the villagers saw me walking on the path, they immediately began to whisper to one another.

"Wow! Two hours later the Hunan woman has come back to life after death! Was she faking it? Is she made of iron? It's unbelievable and admirable!"

I listened to them gossip but didn't say a word. Like my husband, I was incensed that they didn't lift a finger to help me. In the past, they had been kind and welcoming. We often chatted and joked. They taught us how to do everything in the fields. Now they had turned their backs on us and had left me for dead. It seemed as though the ground had shifted overnight.

Land Reform

The first stage of the government's plan to transform China's countryside into a communist utopia was called "Land Reform" and involved confiscating private assets from the wealthy and redistributing them to the poor. The campaign began with a visit to every household by local government officials, who took a painstakingly detailed tally of every piece of property possessed by each family. Everything imaginable, no matter how trivial, was counted, including land, animals, tools, grain, seeds, furniture, pots and pans, dishes, toys, books, clothing, pens, jewelry, cash, gold, silver, etc. Equipped with this information, government cadres then categorized each family into four economic classes based on their wealth: landlords, rich peasants, middle-class peasants, and poor peasants. The Communist Party glorified poverty, so the lower one's economic class, the better they were treated by the new leadership.

Land reform got fully underway in our area around 1952. Not surprisingly, it caused a lot of anxiety and upheaval among the wealthy families in our area, who feared the confiscation of their money and valuables. As a result, rich families pondered elaborate ways to hide their possessions before the inspections.

Sisao was one of the wealthiest women in Donghu. In addition to owning many fields, she possessed a large collection of gold and silver coins, jewelry, silk, and expensive furniture, as well as dozens of kilograms of grain. Fearing that her belongings would be confiscated by the government, Sisao instructed her servants to dig ditches and construct false walls in her home so she could hide her valuables. The servants followed her orders, but Sisao's possessions were so vast that, even after doing all of that, a number of items still remained in plain view.

Knowing that our home was completely bare, Sisao decided that the perfect place to hide her remaining valuables was in our living room. One day, when Weiluan and I were working in the fields, Sisao and her servants stashed her leftover belongings in plain view in our home. When we returned that evening, we discovered our living room filled with expensive silk, rice, and other items. Weiluan and I were incensed when Zi explained what had happened. Fearing we would be punished if the inspectors discovered the items in our home, we charged across the courtyard to Sisao's wing of the house and demanded that she remove everything.

"Sisao, take your things out of our home," Weiluan said. "You are risking our safety. If Communist Party comrades come to investigate, they may think we stole the items. We could be severely punished."

"Don't worry. You used to be a high-ranking officer in the KMT. If they find the cloth, just say it's yours from the past. If they ask about the rice, you can explain that you are in the midst of harvesting your fields. They will think it's reasonable and won't continue to interrogate you."

"Everyone knows we are destitute and have sold everything we own. They know that after paying the grain tax we often don't have a single grain of rice left for ourselves. They will immediately be suspicious of where those items came from."

"Don't forget that I saved your life when you fell and cut your hand, you ingrate! If I knew you would forget my kindness, I would have let you die then! You should reciprocate this debt of gratitude."

"Sister-in-Law, please don't put us in this quandary," I pleaded. "My husband and I won't forget to repay our debt of gratitude to you. But we can't do it now, not like this."

"You should repay it now!" Sisao shouted.

As we were arguing, the land reform inspectors arrived. First, they inspected Sisao's home, and afterward they came to our home. The minute they entered our front door, they were taken aback at the sight of our living room full of rice and other expensive items.

"Where did all of this come from?" one inspector asked sternly.

We didn't know how to reply, so we kept our mouths shut.

"I said, where did all of this come from?"

When the inspectors could see that we weren't going to answer, they left. I prayed that they would be able to see through Sisao's manipulation. Soon after the inspectors departed, Sisao and her servants returned to retrieve her belongings.

"Since you put all of these things in our home, they should be ours now," I quipped.

"Absolutely not! You have no right to them," Sisao said as she filled her arms with her riches.

Weiluan and I sat in silence as we watched Sisao and her servants carry everything away. After they finished, we discussed how to handle the situation.

"Fengxian, the inspectors saw all of those valuables in our home. We could get in very big trouble."

"I know, but everyone around here knows how destitute we are. They must know that those items aren't ours. Don't worry. I believe people's eyes are sharp enough to distinguish what is true from what is false."

Later that evening, the inspectors returned to our home. When they saw that the items were gone, they shook their heads and looked at us with even more suspicion.

"Mr. Han, you are ordered to write an official explanation for all of the items that were here earlier. If you don't explain the situation fully and truthfully, you and your family will have to face the consequences."

Weiluan deliberated long and hard about what to write. "Why are we so unlucky? Misfortunes seem to strike us one after another. Every day we have to worry about having no food to eat and tattered clothes to wear. Now we have this to add to our concerns. Why do the rich add more suffering to the poor? Fengxian, what do you think I should write?"

"Write it as it is. Be honest and frank and explain everything clearly, so they can investigate it further and know the truth. Even if we allow ourselves to be Sisao's scapegoat, the truth will eventually come out anyway. But by then, no one will believe us. That is an even worse outcome."

"I am afraid Sige will be angered and encounter trouble if I write the truth about what his wife did. We are brothers after all."

"I have told you what I think. Ultimately, it's up to you to decide what to write."

After several hours of going over and over it in his head, Weiluan finally settled on writing a truthful account of what happened. "Forgive me, brother," he said when he finished writing and set down his pen.

"Why are you asking for Sige's forgiveness? Don't you remember how he has treated us? If he cherished your brotherhood at all, he wouldn't have turned his back on us the way he has so many times."

"Yes, but we are still brothers. I should look out for him regardless of whether he does the same for me."

A few days later, Weiluan and I had just returned from the fields for the evening when we heard heavy footsteps in our courtyard. We peeped outside and saw several Communist Party cadres standing outside Sisao's door, which was located directly across the courtyard from our door. They were demanding that she hand over her gold and silver. Sisao acted as though she didn't know what they were talking about, so the cadres angrily stormed into her house, tore down the false walls her servants had built, and uncovered stacks of valuables. They hauled away everything they found, including several pieces of Sisao's expensive furniture. After they finished clearing out Sisao's belongings, the cadres moved on to Qisao's home. From there, they removed additional pieces of expensive furniture as well as a large amount of rice. The cadres were harsh and intimidating. Even though Sisao and Qisao were upset, neither of them put up much resistance. Later, everything that was confiscated from wealthy households was redistributed to poor families in the village. Unfortunately, we received nothing due to Weiluan's past ties to the KMT.

We feared that the representatives might eventually come to our home, although we didn't have much to lose because we didn't possess a thing that could be considered valuable. In the end, no one ever came.

"Weiluan, I think this means that the Communist Party believes we truly are poor, property-less people, just like the kind they exalt!"

"Yes, and don't forget I also fought side-by-side with Director Cheng when he defected from the KMT to the CCP and peacefully handed over Changsha. We also helped bring the CCP to power."

"Why hasn't Director Cheng replied to your letter? Is it possible he never received it?"

"He must have received it. I sent it by registered mail."

"It would be wonderful if he asked us to return to Hunan," I said. "I would finally be able to visit my family."

"Director Cheng put a lot of effort into training me. He knows I am a talented man. I believe he won't turn a deaf ear to my request."

Director Cheng was our only hope of escape.

Time to Confess and Be Punished

About a week later, Weiluan and I accidentally overslept one morning. We were preparing to head to the fields after breakfast when a young man knocked on our door. We invited him inside. He looked around stealthily and approached my husband.

"Manfu," he whispered, "now is the time of Land Reform and Class Struggle. Recently the new Communist Party government in Donghu has begun to shift its attention to men and families that used to be associated with Chiang Kai-shek's KMT. People like you. I have overheard them talking about a new campaign called the 'Suppression of Counter-revolutionaries.' It's aimed at eliminating the threat to the Communist Party from former KMT supporters. I heard them say, 'Han Manfu is masking his true intentions with farming. Don't be deceived by appearances. He is intelligent and resilient. He pretends to be very poor and work hard, but we should watch out. He used to be a KMT officer. He is a danger to the Communist Party.'"

"Thank you for coming to tell me, young man," Weiluan said.

"Manfu, I admire you very much. A hero like you is resilient in adversity. That's why I took the risk to tell you, but I must leave now."

At that moment, we knew for certain that Weiluan's past involvement with the KMT was the reason everyone's behavior toward us had suddenly changed. The Communist Party was turning everyone against us. The young man's words frightened me. I saw how ruthlessly the Communist Party cadres treated Sisao and Qisao. What would they do to us if they thought we were a danger to them?

"Fengxian, don't get anxious. I have never done anything evil. I am clean and decent and have nothing to fear if someone knocks on my door at midnight. Come on, let's go to work."

We arrived at the fields mid-morning. Because we were racing against time to plant the next crop, we didn't have the luxury of dwelling on other matters. The young man's visit quickly fell into the background. For hours, Weiluan and the ox trudged in front of me churning the earth, while I followed behind spreading fertilizer.

Later that afternoon, a middle-aged man neither of us recognized stopped us in our tracks as we were working. The man blocked the path of our ox and charged up to Weiluan.

"Sir, or shall I call you KMT officer? Why do you pretend to be a poor farmer? Are you trying to win sympathy from others? In the past, you drank the blood and sweat of the Chinese people. I guess you never expected a day like today. Now it is time for you to confess and be punished for your sins of the past! Even though you may be laboring exhaustingly, that does not exempt you from punishment!"

"I have never pretended anything. We are tilling the fields to support our family. We lack manpower. If we don't work this hard, what alternative do we have?"

The man gave us a snide look and left. Between his words and those of the young man that morning, we sensed trouble was looming.

"We must finish planting these seeds as soon as possible," my husband said. For the next several days, we worked around the clock.

A couple of weeks later, some land reform comrades and a representative from the Poor Peasants Association visited our home. Zi and Tian invited them inside.

"Mr. Han, the time has come for you to be re-educated, to confess what you have done in the past as a member of the KMT."

"Okay," Weiluan said. "Where should I go to do this?"

"Someone will come this afternoon to take you. You will be going to a Communist re-education center in Hongli (Hōng-lē)," they said.

Their stern tone frightened me. Not knowing when my husband would be led away, I rushed to make lunch so he could leave with a full stomach.

"Fengxian, don't worry. Nothing dangerous will happen. I know how to handle it. Just take care of the family while I'm gone. Do the farm work little by little. Your health and our children come first. Try not to get angry with the girls. They have already suffered so much with us."

"I know. Since we can't defy it, we must accept it."

"Fengxian, it will be your responsibility to look after our ox. Taking care of the ox is more important than anything else because we can't survive without it."

As we were saying our goodbyes, some young people came to take Weiluan away. They belittled my husband and called him a "bad element." When I saw that Weiluan was leaving empty-handed, I rushed to hand him a change of clothes, a towel, and a toothbrush.

"I'll return soon. Don't worry about me."

The rest of the day I felt extremely uneasy and sad. I thought about the many times Weiluan had tried to flee to Hong Kong. Each time he returned because he couldn't bear leaving the children and me. This time he had no choice. For years, Weiluan had worked like a slave. He never complained and accepted the hardship willingly. I knew I had not married the wrong man. Weiluan was a devoted and faithful husband. Even though I had to work hard, I felt it was worth it.

After several days, my husband still had not returned. I got worried. I tried to inquire about his situation with numerous people, but everyone I approached turned their back and wouldn't speak a word to me. At that moment, I realized that Weiluan's troubles were not just his, but our entire family's. All of us had been officially outcast. No one wanted to associate with a bad element family lest it tarnish their own reputations. If I wanted any information about my husband, I would have to find it myself.

The next day I decided to go and search for my husband. I recalled passing the village of Hongli on my way to sell clothes and dung at Gujing market. Although I had never been there, I believed I could find it. The more important question was whether anyone would be willing to let me see him or give me information. Nevertheless, I felt I must try.

That morning I instructed Zi to look after the ox and told Tian to take care of Hao. I cooked some soybeans and vegetables for my husband and set off. I arrived at Hongli without a glitch. It was a relatively small village, so it didn't take me long to cover the entire place. I couldn't find anything resembling a re-education camp anywhere, so I decided to search the outskirts of the village.

I was walking on the main road when I saw a number of haggard men in the distance walking listlessly back and forth in a large, fenced yard. I carefully scanned the group but couldn't see my husband among them. Nonetheless, I surmised that must be where they were keeping Weiluan.

I approached the building but was fearful of entering. As I stood outside the door thinking about how to proceed, a man came outside with a handful of vegetables.

"Is this the re-education camp?" I asked him.

"Yes, why do you want to know?"

"My husband is here. I have come to visit him."

"Go ahead inside."

As I approached the door, a guard suddenly burst outside. "Stop! Who are you? What are you doing here?"

"I'm here to bring some food to my husband."

"What is his name?"

"His name is Han Weiluan."

"Wait here," he ordered and went back inside.

After a few minutes, Weiluan appeared at the entrance. He was unkempt, dazed, and appeared totally drained. His eyes, dark and sunken, were lifeless, and his body was frailer than when he had left. When he saw me, he pretended to smile, but I could tell that nothing inside him felt like smiling. I had never expected him to look so aged and worn in such a short amount of time. I took out the soybeans and vegetables I had prepared and handed them to him.

"Wait!" the guard shouted. "They must first be checked for poison."

"He is my husband. Do you really think I would poison him?"

"Those are the rules. Anything that is brought here must be checked."

Another guard came to inspect the food. He instructed me to eat a few bites before I could hand it to my husband.

Weiluan looked at me blankly, took the food, then turned and walked away without uttering a single word. His entire demeanor had changed. I became even more worried.

On the walk home, I wondered if my husband would be able to endure the process of re-education. I had no idea what was going on inside that facility, but I feared that he might not be strong enough to prevail and would become ill. No matter how hard we worked in the fields, the family was always together and we were happy. But now, after only a few days of re-education, more years had been added to my husband's face than the last two years of hard labor and malnourishment. What were they doing to him?

When I arrived home, I was comforted to see that Zi and Tian had followed my instructions. Everything was under control.

"How is Father?" Zi asked. "Is he okay? When will he come back?"

"Your father is doing very well. He has fish and pork to eat, and he doesn't need to do any farm work."

"Maybe he will bring back some fish and pork for us!" Tian said. "It's good that he can rest."

On the surface, I was smiling, but inside I was weeping. I preferred hard labor over psychological torture. I feared that when Weiluan returned he might no longer be himself. He might be permanently changed. Was that their intention?

From then on, I visited my husband every two to three days. The guards became accustomed to me and no longer inspected the food I brought. After a few visits, Weiluan and I were allowed to speak briefly with one another. I comforted him as much as I could.

"Just accept things as they come and be as candid as possible so you can return home and be reunited with us."

"I know," he said and sighed. There was a long pause after every sentence Weiluan uttered.

"Fengxian, you don't need to visit me so often. You should be looking after our children. You are their only source of support."

"Yes, but you also need my support."

"I feel I have let down you and your mother. I promised her that I would take good care of you, but I couldn't keep my word. I apologize for making you suffer so much hardship with me. Please forgive me."

"Mr. Han, your time with your wife is up," a guard announced. "Your wife must leave now. It's time for you to return to your interrogation session."

Without saying a word of goodbye, Weiluan stood up and headed inside. I watched him walk back, his head bent low, and hoped it would all be over soon.

Class Struggle

During the time Weiluan was in Hongli, the government intensified another campaign called "Class Struggle" aimed at helping the poor shed their mentality of inferiority and subservience toward the wealthy. This mindset of being beneath one's masters and the rich was deeply ingrained in the psyche of Chinese peasants and had been passed down for generations. Confiscating money and possessions from the affluent and giving them to the poor helped lift millions of families out of destitution, but it did nothing to change these deeply ingrained beliefs. If land reform was to be a revolution and not just a re-distribution, the entire social order had to be upended and destroyed. The Communist Party believed that, unless the poor themselves actively seized their position atop the new social hierarchy, society could not be successfully reshaped.

While Weiluan was away, the Communist Party ordered that "struggle sessions" be held multiple times a week in every village and town in the country. During these sessions, people considered to be from the exploiting classes, i.e., landlords and rich farmers, were put on display and subjected to fierce criticism by the exploited, i.e., poor peasants. Crowds of poor people were mobilized to attend the struggle sessions and encouraged to stand up, "speak bitterness (诉苦)," and seize control from their former masters.

Unleashing resentment that had been bottled up for centuries was a horrid process. Frequently, the shouting led to mass beatings. When the sessions were over, landlords and rich farmers often crawled home beaten and bruised physically and emotionally while the poor returned home empowered on an adrenaline high. In some villages, struggle sessions reportedly became so intense that destitute peasants, after verbally expressing their pent-up anger and resentment, were given free rein to kill the accused. The belief presumably being that nothing could be more empowering than giving someone the ability to take the life of his oppressor.

Nothing that violent occurred in Donghu, but the struggle sessions were still brutal. Thankfully, I was banned from participating because of Weiluan's ties to the KMT. It was a blessing to be able to stay away from such a cruel and poisonous environment. Nevertheless, families like ours still came under attack. Class struggle frequently spilled outside the formal sessions and into everyday interactions between villagers. Soon it became acceptable to harass and assault anyone deemed to be against the Communist Party's new vision of society. Families like ours with KMT ties were particularly targeted.

One day, I had just returned home from visiting Weiluan at Hongli when I found Zi and Tian crying. They raced into my arms when they saw me.

"What's wrong? Why are the two of you crying?"

"While we were grazing our ox, a boy in the neighborhood came and bullied us," Zi explained. "He tied the ox to a tree and beat it. I ordered him to stop, but he grabbed my hair and spit in my face. Then he stuffed hay in my nostrils, picked up some ox dung, and forced it into my mouth.

He said 'you should be used to eating bullshit!' He forced me to kneel down before him and call him master three times before setting me free. We ran home, but he followed us. Then he beat Hao."

"When he hit Hao, I bit his hand, and he ran away," Tian said proudly.

"We're afraid he might come back," Zi said.

At hearing this, I became infuriated. I wanted to rush to the boy's home and tell his parents, but I knew they wouldn't listen to a word I said. He wouldn't be punished. In fact, telling his parents might only embolden him. Times were changing. Chinese society was being turned upside down, and families like ours had sunk to the bottom. We were powerless. I could do nothing but comfort my daughters.

"Try to be tolerant and resilient. If you can endure, the storm will eventually subside. Then you can enjoy some peace. Remember, it's best not to fight or quarrel with others."

"But why should we stand by and let others bully us?" asked Tian. "Why are you on their side? Why don't you stand up for us?"

"I am on your side, and I will protect you. You won't be bullied again. Go wash up. I'm going to prepare lunch for you."

"How is Father?" Zi asked. "When will he come back?"

"He is doing fine. Don't worry about him."

"When Father was here, no one dared bully us," Tian said. "But after he left, now bad people come and bully us."

As I prepared lunch, I wondered if that would still be true when Weiluan returned. Would he be able to protect us in the future? The world was changing and so was my husband.

We were preparing to head to the fields after lunch when nephew Dong's wife, Li, dropped by for a surprise visit. She had joined the Communist Party and was now a member of one of the local party committees.

"Aunt Manpo, how is Uncle Manfu?"

"I'm worried about him. He looks very worn out. His eyes are sunken and dark, and he is very thin. He barely says a word during our visits."

"Don't worry. He's strong. He will endure."

"I hope so. He instructed me to contact you if I need any help."

"Of course, if you have any difficulty, please let me know. I will try my best to help you."

"There is one issue you might be able to help me with. When I returned this morning from visiting Weiluan, I found my daughters crying. They said they were bullied by a boy from the area. He beat our ox and my children. He even forced Zi to eat dung and stuffed straw in her nostrils."

"That's outrageous! How could such a thing happen? I will speak to his parents. Even though Uncle Manfu may have made some poor choices in the past, this has nothing to do with his children. God will punish those people for their evil deeds for sure."

I thanked Li and hoped that her political connections would help resolve the situation. In the meantime, I decided to follow Weiluan's advice and spend more time with the children rather than visiting him. The time to harvest peanuts was upon us. For 10 days, the girls and I worked in the fields while Hao played in a nest of peanut leaves we made for him. We stayed in the fields from dusk to dark, eating as we worked, to ensure that our peanuts weren't stolen. When the girls got tired, they took a nap. Each night after we returned home, I went to town and traded some of the fresh peanuts for rice and salt.

After the harvest was completed, I cooked some peanuts and went to Hongli to visit my husband.

"Fengxian, you've done a good job looking after the children and completing the peanut harvest. Now I can rest assured that everything at home is okay. How are our children?"

Weiluan had enough on his mind at Hongli. I didn't want to burden him further by telling him about the bullying. "They are doing well. Don't worry. When do you think this re-education will end? When can you come home?"

"I don't know. I hope soon."

We were never allowed to converse for very long, but even a few words were better than none. We said goodbye, then I rushed home, worried that the children may be getting bullied again. When I arrived, I couldn't find the children anywhere in the house and panicked. I screamed their names, but there was no response. Then, after a while, I saw them skipping on the path toward our home accompanied by Li.

"Mother," Tian said, "Li came to visit while you were gone. She was afraid we might be bullied again if we stayed at home alone, so she invited us to go to her house and play. We weren't bullied at all."

I smiled. I was very thankful for Li's help. She was the only person in the village not afraid to have contact with us. She really was a considerate and good-hearted woman. I admired her courage and nobility.

"Li, thank you so much for looking after my children."

"Of course. It wasn't a problem. A few days ago I went to the home of the boy that bullied your daughters. I told his parents what he had done. I asked them to talk to him about not treating others like that again. His parents couldn't have cared less. On the contrary, they said, 'Do you know what time it is now? It is time for the poor to rise over the rich; it is time for us to get our revenge! The Communist Party has overthrown the warlords and landlords, who for centuries ate the rice produced by the hard labor of peasants. Don't my children now have the right to beat the children of warlords and landlords? Don't interfere with our business!' I couldn't believe what they were saying. Children are naïve and ignorant, but parents are adults and should know right from wrong. Fengxian, I'm sorry I wasn't more successful in helping you solve this problem."

"Li, it's we who should be apologizing to you for putting you through this trouble. Thank you for trying. Don't worry about us. Everything on Earth is predestined by heaven. We can blame no one. It's all because of our ill fate. I hope our bad fate doesn't bring any bad luck to you."

"Of course not. Don't worry about that. Aunt Manfu, I also want to inform you that your two sisters-in-law, Sisao and Qisao, and Uncle Manfu's mother were taken to a struggle session yesterday. They were interrogated and criticized at length. It's very serious. Apparently, all of them have been classified as landlords."

"And what about Weiluan and us?"

"I haven't heard anything about your family. Anyway, you must tread carefully these days."

"Yes, we will. Thank you."

After Li's visit, I fretted about what the future held in store. The Communist Party was turning society on its head. Li had reason to be worried about us. The fact that we were destitute and that Weiluan had defected to the Communist Party with Director Cheng didn't seem to make much difference in the eyes of the new government.

"Mother," Tian said, "if anyone dares to come here and beat you, we will fight back together and beat him to death! The last time when that boy came and hit Hao, I bit him and he ran away."

"Your mother isn't afraid of being beaten by others. It's too complicated for you to understand right now. We can talk about it when you get older. Now it's time to go to the fields."

Zi went outside to retrieve the ox and discovered it was missing. She quickly searched the area but found no trace of the animal and raced home. I panicked when she relayed the news. I hurriedly tied Hao's leg to the kitchen table, which was common among families who couldn't arrange child care and had to leave their little ones at home. Then the girls and I frantically searched for the animal. It was nowhere to be found. I was deliberating what to do when a man appeared out of nowhere with our ox.

"Manpo, I discovered your ox eating some of my rice. It was already ripe, so you must compensate me for it."

"Thank you so much. I'm so sorry. Of course, we will compensate you when we harvest our crops. I will tell my husband to compensate you."

"Okay. Be careful. If your ox had eaten others' rice, they may not have returned the ox to you. They might even beat you to death. These days all types of violence against people like you are acceptable. Do you understand?"

"Yes, I understand. Thank you. I really am very sorry."

The girls and I breathed a sigh of relief and then headed to the fields. We were chatting along the way when a band of youngsters approached us.

"How did you find your ox? We unleashed it and beat it."

"So this was all your fault?" Zi screamed back. "Because of you, now we have to compensate other farmers for their rice!"

"Ha-ha, you deserve it! But that's nothing compared to what we do during struggle sessions against landlords. Even though they are nearly beaten to death and their bodies are stained with blood, they dare not utter a word of disagreement. How about we show you?"

I was so incensed that I couldn't hold back my anger. "How dare you children beat people for no reason! If you want to fight, let's fight! Zi, come here and take the ox. We have had enough of your harassment. We will not take it lying down. Now, either you die, or I die!"

The youngsters scurried away when they saw my anger. Some farmers who had watched the entire episode from the fields laughed. "We have never seen this Hunan woman get so angry. We didn't know you could be so tough!"

"I had to be that way. I will not take others' harassment lying down."

I had been successful in driving away the youngsters on that particular occasion, but I knew I couldn't prevent it from happening every time. Our fate was in God's hands, not mine.

We walked the rest of the way to our plots in silence. I was so confused about what was happening. Previously, the Poor Peasants Association had stood up for Weiluan and me in our dispute with Qisao over the sunning ground. But later I had been abandoned in the fields and left for dead. Now it was considered acceptable to beat anyone in our family to death. The Communist Party's goal of empowering the poor and lifting them out of their misery sounded appealing, yet in reality they seemed to view many poor families like ours as enemies. Rather than condemn violence, they encouraged it. We were more destitute than many other families. Why weren't they interested in being our savior?

I was deep in thought when I heard one of my daughters shout, "Look, Father! Father is back!"

I raised my eyes and saw a slim figure walking toward us in the distance. I couldn't believe the girls were able to make out that it was Weiluan from so far away. I smiled as I watched them jump up and down.

"How is everyone?" Weiluan asked with a smile. "Let's go home and celebrate."

The girls ran into his arms. "Father, we are so glad you are back. Some bullies attacked us while you were gone!"

I didn't want to burden him with our problems the minute he returned, so I hurriedly cut in. "Don't listen to them. They're just children. They don't understand much. You must be tired. Let's go and rest."

My husband quietly smiled. For the first time since he left, I could see that the old Weiluan was back. I breathed a sigh of relief as the four of us walked home hand-in-hand.

An Ink Spot on a Snow-White Shirt

That evening I made a special dinner to celebrate Weiluan's return. I exchanged some soybeans for tofu and prepared fresh vegetables and peanuts. After dinner, Weiluan and Zi took the ox to graze. Zi relayed everything that had happened since he left. Weiluan listened quietly and then examined the animal. The ox was thinner than before and had an injured leg. When they returned, my husband prepared some sweet potatoes for the animal.

"Weiluan, what are you doing? We don't have enough food to feed the family. We shouldn't be giving precious food to the ox."

"We can manage by eating thinner porridge, but if the ox doesn't have enough to eat, it will become even thinner. Then it won't be strong enough to plow the fields, and we will have no rice to cook porridge. This ox is our lifeline. We must look after it, even if it means we go hungry."

After the children went to sleep that night, Weiluan told me about his experience in Hongli.

"Do you recall that young man who came to warn us one morning about the 'Suppression of Counter-revolutionaries' campaign?" Weiluan asked.

"Yes, I remember him."

"Well, it turns out he was right. The Communist Party decided several months ago that all previous KMT soldiers, officers, politicians, and bureaucrats must be screened to determine who may still pose a threat to the new regime. All former KMT staff in this area were taken to Hongli.

For weeks, we were interrogated about our pasts and political views. Those of us considered not to be a serious threat were re-educated and encouraged to turn over a new leaf and be reborn as new men."

"When I visited you that first week you looked dreadful. You had me really frightened. What were they doing to you?"

"The first couple of weeks we spent most of our time split up in separate rooms. Day and night I was subjected to intense questioning about my past. I was prevented from sleeping more than a few minutes at a time, and sometimes they bound me in restraints. The interrogators constantly ordered me to 'reveal and recognize your crimes ... fully and honestly confess everything about your personal history.' They made me go into painstaking detail about my entire life from the time I was young to today. I always told the truth. Yet every time I finished 'confessing,' they told me I hadn't been clear or sincere enough and to come clean about myself. Then they would make me start all over again. It was as though nothing I said, even about the most trivial, irrelevant things, could satisfy them. They questioned everything. After a couple of weeks, most men reached their breaking point. I became so delirious that I was willing to say anything to make it end. Then one day the intensity suddenly eased, and I was finally allowed to rest. After that, some days I was verbally questioned while other days I was told to write lengthy self-criticism reports for the interrogators. I wrote dozens of such reports. I always spoke and wrote the truth. If I hadn't been so candid, they probably wouldn't have let me return home today. They allowed me to come back to you only because I was open and honest and had never done anything evil."

"What about the other men? Were they also allowed to return today?"

"No, a lot of men are still there being interrogated and re-educated. Some were sent to prison. I heard that others may have been killed."

"Killed? For what?"

"I don't know. Each man's story and situation are different. Perhaps those men refused to submit and talk openly about themselves. Perhaps the Communist Party cadres felt they still posed a threat to the new regime. Perhaps they wanted to scare the rest of us — killing the chicken to warn the monkeys (杀鸡儆猴)."

"So what exactly did you write?"

"I wrote the truth. I explained that I joined the KMT army when I was very young, and that for the next eight years I risked my life to protect our country from the Japanese. I was injured on the battlefield. After the war against Japan, I worked under the direction of Director Cheng. When Director Cheng defected and switched sides, I didn't hesitate to follow him. I helped Director Cheng peacefully turn over Changsha to the CCP. I explained over and over that I wasn't against the Communist Party. They also instructed me to write about my life after you and I returned to Guangdong in 1950. I explained how we arrived penniless, how my siblings and mother did nothing to help us, and how our family and home were later divided. I described how every day we live on the brink of starvation, and how our home consists only of four bare walls. I wrote every detail of my life from the time I was in school to today. I dared not omit anything. Not only did I write about what happened, I also wrote my thoughts and reflections looking back on my life. The psychological weight from re-hashing so many details of the past was heavier than a year of hard labor."

"It sounds like all they did was interrogate you. Why do they call it 're-education'?"

"The re-education comes later. After about a month of making us re-hash our past, some of us began attending group study sessions where we were taught the central tenets of communism. We were shown how our previous ways and thoughts were errant and exploitative. Every day we had to identify and criticize elements of our past and identify ways to improve ourselves. We were taught to view the world through a new communist lens. I understand more now than I did before about the belief system and objectives of the Communist Party. They really do seem sincere about wanting to help the poor. I see now how a critical weakness of the KMT was that we lacked this type of unifying ideology and set of objectives. We seemed to be fighting to stay in power just for power's sake, but the Communists have a true vision they want to achieve for Chinese society. Maybe they really are the people's savior."

As I listened, I thanked God for allowing my husband to return safely. He still looked drained, but he was more talkative and energetic than he had been on any of my visits to Hongli. It was comforting to finally have him back by my side.

The next morning my husband awoke early and prepared hot porridge with peanuts for me and the children. It was one of his favorite meals. He was anxious to see how the crops were doing, so we quickly headed to the fields. The next harvest was upon us, and we were already behind schedule.

After a few grueling weeks, we completed our work, but, because we were late, lacked manpower, and hadn't spent money on decent fertilizer, it was a poor harvest. After submitting what we owed to the government for the grain tax, we didn't have a single grain of rice left over to carry us through the winter. We had no choice but to begin collecting dung again during the down season.

That winter, the Communist Party rolled out the final stage of its land reform campaign, which involved the seizure and division of landlords' and rich peasants' land and homes. Fields owned by Sisao and Qisao were among those confiscated and given to poor people.

Fearing she would soon lose everything, Sisao one day tried to sneak her remaining stash of silver coins to her husband's pharmacy in Gaoshui. On her way, she was intercepted by the leader of the Poor Peasants Association. Her money was confiscated. Sisao returned enraged and immediately stormed to our home to blame us.

"Everything in my possession has now been confiscated! How is it that all of my belongings have been taken away but none of yours? Manfu, it must be due to the report you wrote about my hiding things in your home. If you hadn't written the truth, none of my things would have been taken away. I never knew you were such an evil and sinister man! Now I possess nothing. Are you happy? From now on, I forbid either of you from visiting the pharmacy in Gaoshui ever again! You are forbidden from seeing your brother Sige or seeking his help. He knows the tricks you have been up to."

As always, Sisao's shouting caught the attention of Qisao, who immediately rushed to our home to join in the criticism.

"It's because of your fields that I was labeled a landlord!" Qisao screamed. "If I hadn't cultivated your fields and paid the grain tax for over a decade, I wouldn't have been classified a landlord. Now cadres have seized some of the little land I have left as well as some of my oxen. Even Weiluan's mother has been classified as a landlord. Manfu, Manpo, don't think that we are naïve! Many people have told me in private that you have been labeled middle-class peasants."

"What the Communist Party confiscates is decided by the government," Weiluan replied. "I have nothing to do with it, and I certainly can't prevent it. None of this is because of anything we did."

Eventually, the two women ran out of steam and left, but Weiluan was still upset. "We work day and night and keep to ourselves. How can they say their landlord labels have anything to do with us? I want to ask them 'does our destitution have anything to do with them?'"

I also felt my sisters-in-law were unfairly blaming us for what was happening to them. No one had ever asked us to take part in any political meetings. In fact, everyone in the area went out of their way to avoid us.

We were discussing the upheaval around us one evening when we noticed Tian hobbling around the room with her arms outstretched. She was feeling her way around as though she were blind.

"Tian, don't play around like that," I scolded her.

"She's not playing around," Zi said. "Tian began to have difficulty seeing at night a few days ago."

"Why didn't either of you tell us right away?" I asked.

"You and father were both busy working."

"Tian, tell me how many fingers I am holding up," Weiluan said.

"Daddy, I don't know. I can't see."

My heart sank when I heard Tian's response.

"It's after dark now," Weiluan said. "I'll take you to a doctor in the morning. Don't worry. Everything will be okay."

That night after we went to bed, everyone else quickly fell asleep, but my mind raced. I prayed that Tian would be kept from harm and that her eyesight would be restored. The girls worked so hard with us in the fields. They didn't deserve this kind of childhood. I felt guilty and unworthy. I caressed each of my children's faces as they slept. They were sallow and emaciated, but they still radiated that innate, natural beauty that only children possess.

The next morning, I was awoken by Weiluan calling my name. The sun was bright, and he had already returned from buying medicine in Donghu. I felt guilty for sleeping in so long.

"I took Tian to see the doctor. He said she has night blindness but that it's not too serious. It's caused by nutritional deficiencies. He instructed me to give her some pig liver to eat along with some medicine. He said she should be cured soon. The salesman said, 'Manfu, I have never seen you buy any pork. Why not purchase some this time?' I declined, but he said, 'if you look at yourself in a mirror, you will see how pale and haggard you are. Do you really want to use the money to buy your coffin?' So I agreed to buy some meat."

Zi searched for our mirror when she heard this and handed it to her father. Weiluan looked into it and sighed. "I haven't seen my own face in a very long time. I barely recognize myself. Where has the handsome hero of the past gone?"

"Stop being so sentimental," I said. "Give Tian her medicine."

Weiluan prepared the medicine while I cooked the pork. I made an extra bowl for Weiluan's mother and suggested he take it next door.

"Mother is so aloof toward us these days. If she refuses it, what should I do?"

"If she refuses it, that's fine, but it's your responsibility as a son to offer her some. Whether she beats or scolds you is up to her."

Weiluan picked up the bowl and walked next door. I heard him enter her room through the partition.

"Mother, I'm bringing you this bowl of pork to eat."

"Ah? Have you struck a fortune? Has the Communist Party now given middle-class peasants pork to eat? Are you here to show off? Your mother has been labeled a landlord. Your brother and two sisters-in-law are all landlords. Everything has been taken from us. Only you, my unfilial son, have been deemed a middle-class farmer. This is all because of you! Get out!" She tossed the bowl of pork onto the floor.

Weiluan tried to explain, but Qisao pushed him out the door. He returned home dejected with tears in his eyes. I could tell it didn't go well.

"Where's the bowl?"

"She threw it on the floor and it shattered." My husband told me the whole story. I tried to comfort him.

"Don't be discouraged. You did nothing wrong. I read the report you wrote when Sisao hid her things in our home. It was honest and candid but has nothing to do with her or anyone else in your family being labeled a landlord. Why does everyone keep saying we have been classified middle-class peasants anyway? We have never been officially told that. We of all people should know our own classification."

"I don't know if it's true or not that we have been declared middle-class peasants. It doesn't make sense to me, either, for all of them to be considered landlords while we are considered middle-class. I'm really concerned about mother. She is old. If she is to be interrogated and punished as a landlord, she may not be able to withstand it."

"Father," Zi said, "the day before yesterday when Tian and I were outside, we saw some women tear grandma's gold earrings out of her ears. They called her a dirty landlord and slapped her across the face. Her mouth and ears were bleeding."

"No wonder she is so angry at me. I am very sad to hear this, but what can I do to help her? I am unable to protect even myself now. I cannot imagine what she will be put through. The treatment we endured at Hongli was frightening. Many people were beaten and tortured. Fortunately, because of my candor and connection to Director Cheng, I wasn't treated as brutally as others."

"I don't see why you had to be interrogated and re-educated in the first place," I said. "You left the KMT and defected to the Communist Party with Director Cheng."

"Yes, but the cadres said I left too late. They said my history is like an ink spot on a snow-white shirt. No matter how hard you wash it, the spot can never be fully removed. There will always be a trace. With just one glimpse, one can still see the spot. Mother and the rest of the family don't know what I endured at Hongli trying to erase that spot."

Donning a Hat

One cold winter morning after Chinese New Year in 1953, some Communist Party cadres and members of the Poor Peasants Association made a surprise visit to our home. I invited them into our tiny, cramped living room, which was only slightly wider than a hallway. Between them and the five of us, the room was packed.

"Mr. Han, we hope you had a good holiday," the cadre leader said.

"Yes, we did, thank you," Weiluan said.

"We have come here today to deliver this notice," he said and handed my husband a folded piece of paper.

"What's this about?" my husband asked.

"Mr. Han, the government has officially declared that you are a bad KMT element. From this point on, you are to 'wear a hat' of restriction." (In Chinese, the term 'wearing a hat (戴帽子)' is a metaphor that represents losing control over one's movements and actions, in the same way that an errant child donning a dunce cap in class loses his freedom.)

"What does that mean?" Weiluan asked.

"You will no longer enjoy any freedom of movement. Except for your home and your fields, you are not allowed to go anywhere else without first requesting permission from the Poor Peasants Association. Only if you receive approval are you permitted to go. Every evening you are required to give an account to the Poor Peasants Association about your time spent that day. You and your family are discouraged from communicating with anyone outside this area, and all of your correspondence will be monitored carefully. Every few days you will be put on display with other bad elements and subjected to public struggle sessions. You also will be forced to do mandatory hard labor whenever we request it. All of this is aimed at furthering the re-education that you began at Hongli and helping you turn over a new leaf. As for your economic status, you have been deemed a middle-class peasant because from the time you were young you studied out of town and never enjoyed any of your family's property and because you now have just a few small rooms, all completely bare. Your family is truly destitute. Because you are considered middle-class peasants, none of your possessions will be confiscated. Your wife and children will not be prevented from partaking in the benefits offered by the Communist Party, nor will they be forced to attend struggle sessions with you."

"Do you have any questions?"

My husband shook his head no, and the group quickly marched away. Weiluan stood in the living room motionless and silent for a long time.

"Weiluan, don't be discouraged. In the past, you said you would be willing to accept anything as long as you could be together with me and the children. All we do is go back and forth between our home and the fields anyway. Your donning a hat shouldn't impact us too much."

Weiluan looked at the piece of paper and angrily tossed it toward the stove. I hurriedly picked it up and placed it in a safe place. I hoped that one day the government would tear up this piece of paper and restore my husband's freedom and dignity.

The rest of the morning both of us were quiet. The more I reflected on what was happening, the more I felt personally guilty for Weiluan's suffering. If it weren't for me and the children, he never would have come back to Guangdong. He would have been able to stay in Changsha, go through training, and work under Director Cheng. He tried to cheer me up when he saw me getting upset.

"Fengxian, you're right. Since we have nowhere to go, donning a hat will not change my life. It's not a problem at all. I will not become discouraged. I will accept whatever comes my way as long as I can be with you and our children."

"Weiluan, I'm so happy you think this way. You are so resilient and tolerant. You are a true man."

The rest of my husband's family laughed with delight when they learned that he had been placed under restriction.

"Finally, your good life has come to an end!" Sisao said. "Look at yourself. Now you are under control like the rest of us. You no longer have the freedom to go to the pharmacy in Gaoshui. That is wonderful! You are a bad KMT element. You can no longer deny it!"

By then, the Communist Party had succeeded in vilifying the KMT so much that anyone called a bad KMT element felt extremely humiliated and ashamed. My sisters-in-law knew this and took every opportunity they had to remind us. As landlords, they had also been instructed to wear hats, so their movements were also restricted. Consequently, when all of us weren't in the fields, we were cooped up on the same grounds together. Tempers flared, and the bickering was nasty and endless.

Although my husband was hurt by the insults from his sisters-in-law, he was able to tolerate them in silence. I couldn't. After several days of criticism and taunting from my sisters-in-law, I finally hit my breaking point. One day I burst into the courtyard and screamed back at them.

"You are vampires who have sucked our blood and embezzled our properties! For over a decade, you ate the grains from our fields. You demolished our rooms in the mansion Weiluan's father built. You embezzled everything from us. We have never complained and always treated you politely. If you are going to treat us so poorly no matter how well we treat you, then it's time we stopped treating you so well. It's time for us to have it out!"

The sisters-in-law were taken aback and retreated. It felt good to lash out at them and even better to finally have some peace and quiet.

When the Communist Party cadres first informed us that Weiluan's movements would be placed under restriction, we both thought it would be a minor nuisance because we rarely went anywhere. But within a few days, we realized that his donning a hat carried several dire implications.

To begin, now that my husband had been officially declared a bad KMT element, he was put on display — along with landlords, rich peasants, and criminals — in public struggle sessions held every three to five days by the village government. During these meetings, which lasted for a few months, fellow villagers ridiculed, taunted, spat on, and beat my husband and the other bad elements. Fortunately, I never attended any of the sessions, but I saw the deep psychological impact they had on my husband. Every time Weiluan returned home from a session, he sat in a daze, dumbfounded. He frequently had nightmares and often awoke in the middle of the night with his pillow soaked in tears. Worst of all, the people attacking them were friends, neighbors, and relatives they had known their entire lives.

"I don't understand what I did wrong," Weiluan often said in the middle of the night after the sessions. "I fought for my country against the Japanese. I helped Director Cheng peacefully hand over Changsha to the Communist Party. When everyone else had evacuated Changsha, I stayed behind on my own and tried to prevent KMT planes from bombing the city so that no one would be needlessly killed. I would never have expected I would be treated this way."

In addition to having to attend struggle sessions, being officially labeled a bad element made it socially acceptable for anyone in the village to treat us as brutally as they wished. Often when my daughters were away from home, children of members of the Poor Peasants Association bullied and beat them. The girls returned home bruised and bleeding. Weiluan and I desperately wanted to intervene to protect them, but we had no power to do so. The girls were so terrified that they stayed at home as much as possible. The sad truth is that those young bullies I had encountered before were right: no one cared if any of us lived or died. As a bad element family in the new society, we lived a life hardly worthy of a dog.

The most important and tragic implication of Weiluan's restricted movement was the toll it took on our ability to work and put food on the table. The time my husband spent attending struggle sessions and doing mandatory hard labor meant less time doing field work. The size of our harvests shrank considerably. A vicious cycle ensued where less food to sustain the family turned into less energy to work, meaning even less food produced from our fields. In the past, Weiluan and I could collect and sell dung to smooth over gaps in our finances. But now that my husband's movements were restricted, he was no longer allowed to wander about and collect droppings during his downtime. That eliminated our final lifeline.

That summer, when the time came for the first grain tax payment, we fell short of our requirement. At that time, families were taxed based on a fixed percentage of the expected, not actual, harvest from fields under their ownership. This meant that if a family had a particularly bad harvest — as Weiluan and I often did due to our inexperience — little grain was left for themselves after paying their taxes. That year our first harvest was so poor that it didn't even cover the fraction in taxes we owed.

Weiluan begged the officials to allow us to finish paying the tax that fall after our second harvest. They had no choice but to agree, but the officials made it clear that paying the tax should take priority over everything else. The cadres considered our inability to pay the tax as irresponsible and shameful, so my husband was taken away for additional special struggle sessions. They even forced him to wear a tall dunce cap and paraded him through the streets of Donghu, criticizing him in front of everyone for falling into debt. Maintaining face is extremely important to Chinese people. Such a public spectacle was devastating to my husband's pride.

Weiluan's hat of restriction had pushed our family back to the brink of starvation. Clearly, the Communist Party's promise to be the savior of the poor didn't apply to all poor people. With my husband's movements under strict control and nothing to fall back on, we wondered if any of us would be able to survive starvation this time.

My Precious Children

By the summer of 1953, I was pregnant again. Thankfully, it was early enough in the pregnancy that I was still able to work in the fields. Weiluan had signed an IOU pledging that we would repay all of the back taxes we owed after the fall rice harvest. We had no idea how much grain, if any, would be left after paying the government, so we had to reap as much as possible from this second crop. The success of this harvest literally meant life or death for all of us.

Weiluan, the girls, and I spent day and night in the paddies preparing the soil for the rice seedlings. While we were in the fields, Hao remained at home alone with his tiny leg tied to the kitchen table. By then, he was two years old. He still couldn't walk, and his tiny body was emaciated and malnourished. We hated neglecting our son, but if we failed to make good on our IOU, the tax officials insisted my husband would face dire consequences.

Sometimes God gives people impossible choices to make, choices that we regret for the rest of our lives. Weiluan and I were forced to choose between neglecting Hao and giving our family a chance of survival, or remaining with our son and facing certain starvation and punishment. It is a choice that no parent should ever have to make. Our little Hao, the weakest of us all, bore the greatest sacrifice for our family.

By the time we returned home from the fields each night, our precious son would be fast asleep on the floor. Every night I picked him up, dusted him off, and cradled him in my arms as he slept.

"Little one, I know you're scared when we leave you alone. Please forgive us. It's not that we don't love you. My heart breaks to hear you cry and see you struggling, but I must bury this pain and bitterness deep in my heart. I must go to the fields to persevere for all of our survival. I hope one day you will understand."

With no one to look after him, whenever Hao became hungry, he ate anything in sight, no matter how filthy or unhealthy. Since the floor was made of dirt, he had ample opportunity to ingest things he shouldn't. Later that summer, Hao fell ill. He had intense diarrhea, which worried us greatly because of the potential for dehydration. Weiluan invited many doctors to examine our son. At first, the doctors thought Hao had dysentery; then they believed he had contracted roundworm. After a month of various treatments, our son remained extremely ill.

When all other avenues had been exhausted, I suggested that Weiluan take Hao to the pharmacy in Gaoshui to be examined by his brother, Sige, whose specialty was pediatrics. Weiluan asked the Poor Peasants Association for their approval to travel to Gaoshui, but the association said he would have to wait until the next day to go. In the meantime, one of the association members gossiped to Sisao about our intention to take Hao to be examined by her husband. Sisao rushed to our home to stop us when she heard the news.

"I told you before that you are forbidden from going to Gaoshui ever again to seek help from your brother!"

"Sisao, please be reasonable," Weiluan pleaded. "We are trying to save our son. I apologize for everything I have done in the past to offend you, but my son is innocent. Please don't hold this against him. Please help us save him."

"No! Absolutely not. Your son is your problem, not ours!"

No matter what we said, Sisao refused to help us. Later that evening, as we were deliberating how to proceed, Hao's condition worsened. I could tell we had very little time left to save him.

"Weiluan, you must take Hao to Gaoshui now," I said. "I don't know if he can make it until morning."

"What about Sisao and the Poor Peasants Association?"

"Don't worry about them right now. Our son could be dying. We must fight for him. We will deal with the consequences of breaking the rules later."

"You're right. He does look much worse."

As my husband was bending down to pick up Hao, he noticed that our son had stopped breathing.

"Hao! Hao!" Weiluan screamed.

Both of us panicked. We frantically searched for a pulse but could find none. We shook Hao's tiny body and repeatedly screamed his name, but there was no reaction. We waited and waited for our precious son to move or cry. Instead, his little body continued to lay there still and silent. After several wretched minutes, it began to sink in that our beautiful, innocent Hao was dead. All of us broke down. I picked up my baby boy, clutched him tightly to my chest, and completely fell to pieces.

Weiluan tried to comfort me, but I was inconsolable. "Fengxian, Hao has died. He can't come back to life. You have another baby in your womb to think about. Please don't get too upset or it may harm the baby in your womb."

"Maybe he's not dead!" I screamed "We don't know!"

Sisao, who had been standing there watching us since she heard our cries, smirked when she heard me say that.

"You stupid Hunan woman! How can you not know that your son has died? Why are you still holding him in your arms? It's useless. Put him down. Manfu, go and find someone to bury him."

After a while, Weiluan left. He returned with a fierce-looking man who showed me no sympathy.

"Woman, what are you crying about?" the man shouted when he entered our home. He walked up to me, grabbed Hao from my arms, and charged out the door before I could utter a word. That was the last time I ever saw or touched my beautiful baby boy. The man took Hao to a nearby mountain, where he laid him to rest with other children from the village who had died. At the time, it was customary in Donghu not to hold funerals for children, so no ceremony was held to say our final goodbyes.

Weiluan and I were overcome with guilt and grief. We had prioritized our promise to pay the grain tax above our responsibility as parents, and now our son was dead. Hao had died because of our neglect. For years, I had prayed for God to bless us with a son. In the end, we mistreated this gift, and now he was gone. To this day, Hao's death remains one of my greatest regrets.

Feeling bad about her earlier nastiness, Sisao tried to comfort me. "Perhaps the baby in your womb is also a boy."

"Hao can't be replaced!" I screamed at her. "Go away!" I was enraged that she had forbidden us to go to Gaoshui. If she really cared, she would have helped us when we still had time to save our son. Now it was too late.

I was so devastated that I soon became ill. Each day my body got thinner as I lay on our bed waiting for my own death. During the day, Weiluan went to work in the fields while Zi and Tian took the ox to graze. The girls were frequently attacked and beaten by other children who felt no sympathy about the loss of their brother. When my daughters returned home, they complained to me about the bullies, but I was too weak to respond.

I had no one to turn to. All I could do was place my life in God's hands. Life and death are predestined by fate, I told myself. If the time had come for me to die, I would accept it.

Weiluan was so exhausted and grief-stricken that he didn't have the wherewithal to look after me. Every night after returning from the fields, he collapsed onto our bed and immediately fell asleep. His last words before he closed his eyes were always the same: "I'm so sorry, Fengxian. I'm so sorry."

I knew Weiluan felt helpless. He barely had the energy to support himself, let alone me. Of course, he never intended any of this to happen. Even though everything was out of our control, we still felt profoundly guilty. Time passed like this for several weeks.

Eventually, I began to slowly regain my strength. I continued to stay home but was able to do some light work around the house. When the time for the fall harvest arrived, I joined my husband and daughters in the fields. The more I worked, the more I was able to get my mind off Hao's death. Slowly, the grief lessened. That fall we reaped a good harvest. We were able to fully pay our IOU to the government and still had a little bit of grain left for ourselves. We also reaped a bumper harvest of sweet potatoes, which we shared with our ox.

Work came to a standstill when winter arrived. With no distractions to preoccupy us, all of us sunk back into despair. Now that Weiluan's movements were restricted, he couldn't collect dung and firewood the way he used to during the down season. In order to avoid going stir crazy, he took it upon himself to build a new stone oven for our home. Until then, we had been using the small burner we inherited from Weiluan's mother when the family's possessions were divided. Every day my husband crafted bricks out of mud for the project. Little by little he built the stove.

The night before the final day of the 1953 lunar calendar, I awoke in the middle of the night in labor. I tried to wake my husband, but he was in a deep sleep. Eventually, Zi and Tian were able to wake their father. He went to the hospital to fetch a midwife.

When the midwife arrived at our home, she was shocked at how unprepared we were for the birth. Hao had died only a few months earlier. The grief was still so intense that it was all we could do to survive each moment. We couldn't muster the strength to make any preparations for the future, no matter how urgent or near.

"Where is your water?" the midwife asked us. "Without water, how can I wash the baby?"

"It's all my fault," Weiluan replied. "I don't have the ability to support this family. I am not a qualified father. I haven't prepared anything."

My husband went outside to fetch some water from the well, but the rope he used to attach to the barrel had become worn from carrying bricks for the stove. The rope broke. He returned empty-handed.

"If you don't have any water, then at least give me some toilet paper to wipe the baby clean," the midwife said.

"I'm sorry" Weiluan said. "We are too poor to spend money on toilet paper."

The midwife shook her head and took out some of her own paper to clean the baby. Around 3:30 a.m. of the second to last day of the lunar year, I gave birth to another sweet baby girl. We called her Meijiao, which means "beautiful," or Mei (Mā) for short.

Weiluan thanked the midwife and handed her some money. According to local traditions, it was customary to also give the midwife a bowl of eggs cooked in red wine, but we didn't have any eggs or wine to offer her. She looked at us with pity and shook her head.

"I often encounter poor people with no money, but that's not important. I have never seen anyone like the two of you, who haven't even prepared water for childbirth."

Weiluan and I felt ashamed. We were both so consumed by the loss of Hao that we could no longer cope with the simplest of tasks. Later that night, Weiluan cooked some of the rice and vegetables we had saved for our special Chinese New Year meal, so I would have sustenance to feed Mei. I knew Zi and Tian hadn't eaten any rice for a long time, so I shared some with them. I also gave some to Weiluan. He was exhausted and severely lacking nourishment. In the end, I was left with only a small bit of porridge.

On New Year's Eve, I rested while Weiluan worked to finish the stove. He completed the project that evening. Afterward, he cooked the little rice that remained, along with some soybeans, peanuts, sweet potatoes, and vegetables. Then the four of us sat down to have our special dinner to celebrate the beginning of 1954.

I watched Zi and Tian as Weiluan handed them their plates. The girls' faces were filled with disappointment and sadness. They could hear, smell, and see other families joyously welcoming the New Year with fish, pork, and beautiful new clothes. Instead, they were stuck with us eating the same pitiful dregs they did every day, dressed in rags. I felt so sorry for them and so angry at my and Weiluan's helplessness. If our daughters had had other parents, they wouldn't be suffering like this. Now we had brought another little girl into the world. Would we be able to prevent her from sharing an equally wretched fate?

I Will Not Let You Die

The year 1954 opened on a very bleak note. Soon after the New Year, we finished every morsel of food left from the fall harvest. Because I had nothing to fill my stomach, I became unable to breastfeed Mei. The baby and I both quickly shrank to a bag of bones. Seeing the two us lying on the bed emaciated, sallow, and without an ounce of energy, I was convinced that we were both destined to die.

"Where there is a will, there is a way," Weiluan said confidently. "I believe we can endure our way out of this adversity one day."

"I wish you were right, but I truly cannot endure any longer. I am going to die. Mei is probably going to die with me. Please take good care of Zi and Tian."

"Fengxian, don't say that. If that day really comes, let's all die together, so we can be together in the next life."

Weiluan looked at Mei and me and then broke down. I could see in his eyes that he feared I was right. We held each other and cried.

"I will not let you die," Weiluan murmured after a few minutes. "When I was sick in the past with malaria, you were desperate and decided to sell our belongings. In the end, I was saved. You are the mother of my children and have borne a lot of hardship. But now you are like an oil lamp without any oil, slowly fading and dying. What can I sell to save you? The only solution is to sell our ox."

"No! We shouldn't do that, no matter how difficult our situation. If you really want to sell it, sell it after I die."

We both lay on the bed crying, desperately thinking of what to do.

"There is one other option," I said. "You can sneak to the pharmacy in Gaoshui and ask to borrow some money from Sige. You are brothers after all. Perhaps he will have mercy on you. His old attitude may have changed."

"Sisao will throw a fit if she finds out, and I must get permission from the Poor Peasants Association. Besides, I don't know if Sige still has extra money to give away. He was classified a landlord like Sisao. I haven't been to the pharmacy in ages. I don't know what my brother's financial situation is."

"Well, we know the pharmacy is still open. Even if they did confiscate a lot of Sige's belongings, he still has that income. It's worth trying. Don't worry about getting in trouble. Tomorrow morning go to graze the ox before daybreak. Tie the ox to a tree on the mountain, then race to Gaoshui. You can get back by noon. If anyone comes looking for you, I will tell them that our ox disappeared last night and that you are looking for it now."

"What an intelligent woman you are! That's a great idea. Yes, let's do it."

The next morning Weiluan returned home before lunch with a big smile. I was curious to hear what happened, so the two of us went to our bedroom and shut the door. The partition between our living room and Qisao's was paper-thin. The last thing we needed was for her to eavesdrop on our good news.

"Sige has taken a mistress! When I arrived at the pharmacy, he took me to her home to have dinner. She sympathized deeply with our situation and gave me these salted fish to bring home. Sige is still earning money from the pharmacy. He gave me five yuan and told me if I ever need help in the future to go to the home of his new mistress. She works at the grain station in Gaoshui and receives a good salary. They have been together more than a year now."

"Does Sisao know Sige has another woman?"

"Of course, but what can she do about it?"

"Finally, we are saved!" I said with relief. We both headed to the kitchen to prepare the fish.

Zi and Tian jumped up and down when they saw their father carrying fresh fish. They weren't the only ones to notice the special food in his hands. Just as Weiluan opened the package, a cat belonging to Qisao lunged at him, snatched one of the fish, and then scurried away. When Qisao discovered the fish in her cat's mouth, she and Sisao immediately dashed to our home. Fortunately, I heard them coming and hid the rest of the fish in our new stove.

"Where did you get this fish from?" Sisao asked, dangling the half-eaten remains in my husband's face. "Did you go to Gaoshui and ask for money from my husband?"

"Weiluan bought it so I would have breast milk to feed our new baby."

"Where would you get enough money to buy fish?"

"We borrowed it from nephew Dong's wife, Li," I replied.

Sisao didn't believe us. She stormed to Li's home to corroborate our story. Thankfully, Li could see through what was happening and went along with our lie. If she hadn't done so, Weiluan could have gotten in serious trouble from the Poor Peasants Association.

Weiluan took some of the money Sige had given him and went to purchase some rice. That afternoon the four of us enjoyed the best meal we had eaten in months. The money Sige gave us was enough to put rice and sweet potatoes on the table for a few weeks. Occasionally, we splurged on some meat. With this new nourishment, my health gradually improved, and I was able to breastfeed Mei. Weiluan and I were both deeply grateful for Sige's kindness.

One afternoon a few weeks later, some members of the Poor Peasants Association visited our home. They instructed Weiluan to attend a special meeting that night but refused to explain what the meeting was about. I worried that someone had found out about Weiluan's unapproved visit to the pharmacy and that he was going to be punished.

"Did anyone see you go to Gaoshui?"

"No. I didn't come across anyone I recognized. Fengxian, don't worry. They probably just want me to do some volunteer work."

"I don't know. Usually when they want you to work, they just say so. They don't hold meetings about it."

Later that night, Weiluan returned from the meeting with a relaxed look on his face. "It turned out to be nothing serious," he said. "The land reform cadres have finally finished their work in Donghu and left. Their last instruction to the local Communist Party officials was to begin establishing work teams. The meeting tonight was about forming these teams."

"What's a work team?"

"A group of households joins together and works each family's fields together. After they complete the job of one household, they move on to the next. This way the burden of labor, tools, and animals can be shared among families. Each family's harvest remains its own, and each family is responsible for its own taxes. Because it's all about working together and helping one another, they are called 'mutual aid teams.' They said we can choose ourselves who we want to form teams with."

"I doubt any family is going to want to form a team with us," I said. "We have lots of fields, little labor, few tools, and only one ox. On top of that, we have a newborn baby that needs our care. We will not make the same mistake we did with Hao and neglect Mei. We would bring little benefit and a lot of headaches to any team."

"Who knows? Let's see what happens. Working on our own certainly gives us a lot more freedom. We can do what we want when we want, but it would also be nice to have some help during the busy season. It could be a good opportunity for us."

Regardless of what happened with the new teams, I was relieved to hear that Weiluan wasn't punished for his trip to Gaoshui. Everything else we would handle one day at a time.

Mutual Aid Teams

The introduction of mutual aid teams constituted phase one of the Communist Party's plan to collectivize agricultural production into vast communes. For millennia, Chinese farmers worked small parcels of land independently. With each new generation of male descendants, the parcels were carved into tinier and tinier plots. The result was an incoherent mix of thin, winding strips of farmland that the government believed were inefficient, hindered mechanization, and, by extension, kept families in poverty.

The new government sought to remove private ownership of land and tools, tear down the divisions between plots, and establish massive communes consisting of thousands of households. The belief was that greater collaboration would lead to larger yields, lower costs, and an overall improvement in farmers' lives. Families would work the land together, share communally in their harvests, and no longer be exploited by greedy landlords.

Shortly after the announcement about the introduction of mutual aid teams, we received a visit from nephew Dong's wife, Li, who was eager to see our new baby and to check on how I was doing.

"Little Mei is so adorable. Fengxian, how do you feel? You look pale. Do you have enough milk to feed your new baby?"

"My wife's health is very poor right now. She is suffering from severe malnutrition. To be honest, it's a miracle she has survived. She and Mei almost died."

Li shook her head in sympathy, took two yuan from her pocket, and handed it to me.

"Go and buy yourself some pork. You need sustenance if you are to feed your daughter."

"Thank you so much, Li. I really wish there was something we could do for you. We will surely repay you when our life gets better."

"Don't worry about repaying me. It's not a large sum of money. Anyway, there's another reason I came here today. I have some good news. Your family has been invited to be part of a mutual aid team."

Weiluan and I looked at each other in surprise. "Who wants to form a team with us?"

"My family does. Our families are both middle-class farmers. We are of the same economic class and, therefore, like members of the same family. My family and the families of some of my relatives want to form a team with you."

"Are you sure?" Weiluan asked. "We are extremely poor. We can't even afford to eat three times a day. We don't have a lot of manpower or energy to contribute labor. Plus we aren't skilled farmers, and we are weighed down by a new baby. Are you sure you've thought this through?"

"Don't think of it that way. Every household has its own difficulties. That's why it's called a mutual aid team. We should help each other to solve our problems."

Weiluan and I smiled and agreed to join.

The team's first order of business was electing a leader who would schedule our work and set the ground rules for the group. The man we elected to lead our team was the most experienced farmer in the group. After evaluating each family's land, he decided that the optimum way to proceed was to first begin cultivating the fields of Li's family, then move on to her brother-in-law's, and so on.

From that point on, all of us worked each family's fields together, and we shared our tools and oxen. Every day we talked and laughed. It felt good to be part of a community rather than constantly mired in our own difficulties. Our daughters played with the other children and were seldom bullied as before. On the whole, our lives improved after the introduction of mutual aid teams, though we remained as penniless as before and had less freedom to do what we wanted each day.

Out of courtesy, whichever household we were working for provided lunch or dinner for everyone. When the time came to work on our fields, Weiluan and I had nothing to offer our team members except a few vegetables. In order to avoid losing face, Weiluan decided to make another visit to Sige at his new mistress's home to see if he could borrow additional money from Sige or her.

"Why are you here again so soon?" Sige snapped as soon as he saw his brother. "I just gave you five yuan not that long ago. You shouldn't come to seek help from me so often. Weiluan, you need to solve your own problems."

"When one is thirsty, a drop of water can quench his thirst. But after a long drought, how can the problem be solved by just five yuan?" his mistress asked. "What's more, Weiluan's movements are controlled, and he has no freedom to do anything to rectify his situation. This time is important. He needs rice to cook dinner for his team."

Sige hastily handed my husband another five yuan.

"So little?" the mistress asked. "Even 10 yuan isn't enough this time."

"I thought you said 'when one is thirsty, a drop of water can quench his thirst.' Isn't this enough? You've got a job at the grain station. Give him your own money."

The mistress snatched another five yuan from Sige and handed it to Weiluan. Then she stood up and prepared another bag of salted fish for my husband.

"Take this with you."

Weiluan smiled, thanked them, and then rushed to the store to purchase some rice. By the time he arrived back, all of our team members had returned to their own homes for lunch.

"Since I see rice in your hands, I assume it went well," I said.

"Yes, Sige's mistress is so kind. Without her help, I don't think my brother would have given me a cent."

When the team returned to our fields that afternoon, we invited them to dinner. It was the first time so many people would be dining in our home. We had to borrow several stools, bowls, and chopsticks for the occasion.

That evening we shared a joyful meal with our team. We considered sending some food next door to Weiluan's mother, but we feared igniting a storm as we had the last time we invited guests to eat in our home. Qisao still managed to peep at us through the cracks in the living room partition. Throughout the dinner, she scolded us as bad KMT elements. Fortunately, everyone on the team was familiar with our family situation and ignored her.

One key benefit of being part of a mutual aid team was that it reduced our need to rely on our daughters' labor. With other adults to do the work, Zi and Tian were finally able to relax and enjoy their childhood. Weiluan was outside working one day when some female Communist Party comrades visited our home and asked if we were interested in sending the girls to school. School would never have been fathomable in the past because we relied on the girls to help us in the fields, but now things were different.

"Of course, we would love to send them to school," I said. "How much does it cost?"

"It's very inexpensive. Only two yuan per semester."

"We don't have a cent right now. Perhaps we can send them next year."

I told Weiluan about the invitation when he returned. Both of us had been blessed with parents who bent over backward to educate us. We wanted to do the same for our children.

"We must send the girls to school," Weiluan said.

"I know, but where are we going to get the money? We've spent everything Sige gave you."

"I don't know. Don't worry. The start of the school year is a long time away. I'm sure we'll find some way to get the money before then."

I wanted to believe my husband, but I was skeptical. Weiluan continued to spend a lot of time doing mandatory labor on top of working in the fields with the team. He was already overworked and had no freedom of movement. How would he find a way to earn such money?

Auspiciously, a couple of weeks later, all of the leaders of the area's mutual aid teams were summoned to a special meeting. The local government informed them that it was in desperate need of charcoal. The officials ordered them to allocate laborers from their teams to assist in collecting wood from the mountains and burning it into charcoal. Each worker would receive a salary of 0.1 yuan per day along with 500 grams of rice – or about three fistfuls when cooked. The team leader asked Weiluan if he was interested. My husband jumped at the opportunity.

For over a month, Weiluan trekked up and down the mountains every day gathering and burning firewood. After 40 days, he had earned 4 yuan and more than 20 kilograms of rice. We used the money to send Zi to school. Although Tian had also reached school age, we didn't have the ability to pay her tuition. We also needed Tian to help us look after Mei and assist with housework, so we delayed sending her to school for another year. Weiluan generously left all of the rice for the children and me to eat while he subsisted on sweet potatoes and vegetables.

A couple of weeks before the school year started, I decided to make Zi some new clothes out of our duvet, the last decent piece of cloth we possessed. For years, all of us had desperately needed new clothes, but I had avoided tearing apart the duvet because without it the cotton wadding of the quilt would become tattered. However, Zi could not go to school in rags. It was imperative that she have decent clothing. I made outfits for both Zi and Tian, as well as one pair of trousers each for Weiluan and me.

"Fengxian, you really are a genius seamstress," Weiluan said.

"My mother was a good teacher. I am happy to support this family in any way I can. I feel lucky to have married such a faithful husband. Besides, it is my duty as a mother."

A Box to Bury Tian

Between Weiluan's job making charcoal and the help we received in the fields from our team, our day-to-day pressure had eased considerably. Nonetheless, we remained penniless and continued to live from one meal to the next. Except for the brief period when we collected and sold dung, we were never able to accumulate any savings to carry us through difficult times. This inability to get ahead meant we remained vulnerable to even the smallest of challenges. Nowhere was this more evident than when one of us became ill.

One day in the fall of 1954, Tian came down with a serious illness. Her feet turned red, became swollen, and ached terribly. By the time she informed Weiluan and me, she could barely walk and had a high fever. My husband and I immediately suspected that our daughter had contracted an infection while walking barefoot. It was a common occurrence among poor peasant families like us who couldn't afford the luxury of wearing shoes and went everywhere barefoot.

Knowing that such a high fever could be fatal, and still scarred by the death of Hao, we knew that Tian needed to see a doctor straightaway. I instructed Weiluan to take Tian immediately to Gaoshui to be examined by his brother.

"Sisao is staying at the pharmacy right now with my brother," Weiluan said. "She will throw a fit when she sees me."

"I know. But I don't think your brother is such a cold-hearted man. He has helped us on a couple of occasions recently. Hao's death taught us an important lesson. We can't lose another child because of our timidity."

"You're right. I'll take her now."

Tian groaned in pain when Weiluan clutched her legs and lifted her onto his back.

"Be careful," I said anxiously. "Get there as fast as you can."

"I know. Don't worry, Fengxian. Everything will be okay."

Gaoshui was miles away. After a half hour of walking briskly, Weiluan's legs quivered from exhaustion. He stopped for a brief break at a small teahouse on the side of the road. He wanted to purchase a cup of tea for Tian but didn't have a cent in his pocket.

"Please just give us two cups of hot water," Weiluan told the owner.

"Is that your daughter?"

"Yes. She's very ill. I'm taking her to Gaoshui to be examined by my brother. He's a doctor."

Weiluan tried to give some water to Tian, but she was unresponsive. Her face had become extremely pale, and she appeared to have fallen into a light coma. "She looked just like Hao prior to his death," my husband later said. Seeing Tian's condition worsen, Weiluan panicked. He quickly hoisted Tian onto his shoulders and raced off.

When Weiluan arrived in Gaoshui, he laid Tian on the ground outside the pharmacy so he could go and look for his brother. Unfortunately, the moment he stood up, Sisao caught sight of him.

"Manfu, what are you doing carrying a dead body here? Are you trying to destroy the reputation of this shop by making it appear like your brother isn't a good enough doctor to cure a patient?"

"Of course not!" Weiluan said. "Sige! Sige! Sige, please come out! I need your help!"

Sige took his time but eventually came outside. He examined Tian and confirmed that she had contracted a serious foot infection.

"It's too late," Sige said coldly. "Tian's too far gone. She's going to die. Get her out of here." He flicked his hand as though he were brushing away specks of dirt.

Dismayed at his brother's callousness, Weiluan stood there silent.

"Servant," Sige said, "give my brother 0.5 yuan so he can buy a box to bury Tian. Weiluan, take her and get out of here!"

"Sige, please! Tian's not dead yet. Please, give me some medicine to treat my daughter. I cannot handle losing another child. I will not leave until you help me."

Annoyed, Sige went inside, fetched two bottles of liquid penicillin and then angrily tossed them at my husband.

"Don't stand here and cry in our pharmacy!" Sisao ordered. "Get out! Take away your bad luck."

Weiluan stuffed the bottles in his pocket, lifted Tian over his shoulder, and headed home. Tian's body was still and silent during the entire journey back. "Please God, don't allow another child to die in my arms," Weiluan said over and over again. He walked home as quickly as he could, hoping that if Tian was going to die, then at least Zi and I would get a chance to say goodbye.

By the time they returned, the sun was setting. Weiluan rushed into the house, laid Tian on the bed and frantically searched for a pulse. Eventually, Tian coughed and began to cry.

"Thank you, God!" Weiluan cried out in relief. "Thank you for not taking my daughter's life!"

After catching his breath, Weiluan relayed everything that had transpired at the pharmacy that afternoon.

"How can an uncle turn his back on his dying niece?" I asked in dismay. "How can a doctor turn a blind eye to a dying patient? I can't believe Sige made no attempt to treat Tian but instead gave you money to buy her a coffin when she wasn't dead!"

"I know. It's unbelievable, but we don't have time to talk about this right now. Sige gave me some penicillin. We need to take Tian to Donghu Hospital immediately, so they can give her the injections."

Knowing how exhausted Weiluan was, I picked up Tian and we raced to Donghu. Since it was nighttime, few staff were at the hospital, but Weiluan managed to track down one doctor. My husband explained our situation.

"Let me see the medicine," the doctor said. "I'm sorry, but I can't give her these injections. The bottles have expired and are no longer usable. Giving her this medicine could worsen her condition."

"Doctor, we have no other choice," Weiluan pleaded. "Please, please! We have no money for new medicine. We understand the risk. We won't blame you if they don't work."

The doctor looked at Tian. She was burning up, in a daze, and groaning loudly. "Okay, okay, I'll try it. By now, the infection may have already reached her heart. I hope she can be cured, but at this point it's really up to fate."

The doctor took out a syringe and gave Tian one of the injections.

"Tonight you will know if the medicine worked or not. You can take her home now. If the medicine worked, come back tomorrow, and I will give her the second dose. I won't charge you for the injections."

We thanked the doctor and then carried our precious daughter back home.

"I can't believe your brother gave us expired medicine!" I said in dismay on the journey back. "First, he refuses to treat his dying niece, then he only gives you money to buy her a coffin. When he finally does decide to provide some help, he gives us expired medicine that he knows could do her more harm. Weiluan, why does he treat you this way?"

"It's all Sisao's fault. When Sige is around his new mistress, he is completely different."

By the time we arrived home, Tian had begun to awaken. We could see the life slowly returning to her eyes. We breathed a sigh of relief when she asked for some water. The penicillin had worked.

The next morning, Weiluan carried Tian back to Donghu Hospital. The doctor was delighted at her dramatic turnaround. He gave her the second injection. Within a couple of days, the pain and swelling in Tian's feet completely disappeared. Soon our daughter was back to being a lively little girl. We had escaped the throes of death yet again.

Cooperativization

After the 1954 fall harvest, the Communist Party launched the second phase of its effort to collectivize agriculture, which involved the merging of mutual aid teams into cooperatives. The process took place in two stages over the course of 1954 to 1956.

In the first stage, groups of mutual aid teams with adjoining land merged into small cooperatives consisting of a few dozen households each. In addition to pooling our labor, tools, and oxen as before, now every family was required to hand over all of its land to the cooperative for shared cultivation, although the titles to the land remained in each family's name. The aim was to further increase efficiency by pooling more resources, tearing down the divisions between plots, and shortening the time people spent traveling to and from the fields by assigning them work closer to their homes.

Harvests were shared communally among all of the families in the cooperative after the government quota was fulfilled. How much food each family received was determined by the amount of land and labor they contributed. Because our family owned a large amount of dry land and wet rice paddies, we received a decent share of each harvest. Although not plentiful, the food we received was sufficient to keep the children and us from going hungry. On the whole, our lives improved during the early phase of cooperativization. We were grateful.

During this time, the government launched numerous water control projects aimed at redirecting the flow of river and flood waters. The projects required considerable manpower, and many men were co-opted into them during the down season. The men earned a salary of 0.1 yuan and 500 grams of rice per day. Weiluan frequently worked on the projects, and we used his earnings to pay the tuition for Zi and Tian.

One chilly spring afternoon, some project supervisors came to our home to inform Weiluan that they would be sending him to work on one of the new reservoirs for an entire week. That particular morning it had rained. When Weiluan returned home for lunch, he took off his only clothes to dry them in the sun. He was lying on our bed naked under the quilt when the supervisors knocked on our door.

"Manpo, we'd like to speak to your husband about a reservoir project."

"I'm sorry. He's resting right now. He caught a cold in the heavy rain this morning. I just fed him some ginger soup, and he fell asleep. I will make sure that he reports to work this afternoon."

"I was working right next to him this morning," one of the supervisors said. "I didn't catch a cold. Is your husband is trying to avoid work by faking illness?"

I tried to get the supervisors to leave, but they became more and more suspicious. I knew the only way they would leave was if Weiluan talked to them in person, so I rushed into the bedroom, took off my pants, and handed them to my husband.

"There are some supervisors here to see you. I tried to get them to leave, but they won't. Put on my pants. You must go out there and talk to them."

"I can't wear your pants! These are for women. They're too small. They will laugh at me."

"It doesn't matter. You must go out there and speak to them. If you don't, there could be serious consequences. It's not worth a few moments of humiliation."

"I can't believe I'm doing this," Weiluan said as he squeezed into my small black pants and waddled to the front door. They were tight around his waist and groin and just covered his knees. The team leaders burst out laughing when they saw him.

"Manfu, your wife said you caught a cold. It seems that isn't true. What have you been doing? Why are you wearing a woman's trousers?"

"I don't feel embarrassed or ashamed about wearing these pants because it's all I have right now. If you are kind-hearted, why not give me a pair of trousers as a gift?"

"Sure. I'll ask my wife to make a special pair of ladies' trousers just for you! Snug in all the right places and short enough to show off your pretty knees!" one of them joked. The supervisors laughed, informed him about the project, then left.

I was hysterical as I watched Weiluan shuffle back to the bedroom.

"I'm glad to see you're enjoying this, too!" he said.

"I've heard people say 'he is too poor to own a pair of trousers.' I never thought it was true. Now we are living in such circumstances," I said and chuckled.

"Of course it's true."

The episode makes me laugh to this day.

In 1956, the government launched the second stage of cooperativization. In this phase, small cooperatives were combined into larger cooperatives consisting of a couple hundred households each. The new cooperatives were massive, spanned multiple villages, and held vast tracts of land.

Because the previous system of allocating harvests based on a family's land and labor favored wealthy people with a lot of land — precisely the people the Communist Party despised — in the second phase of cooperativization, labor became the sole criterion determining what amount of rations a family received. Every day, supervisors of the cooperative's production teams monitored each person's work and assigned points based on his or her productivity and performance. Families combined their work points and used them to purchase food and other goods at the cooperative store.

This new system devastated families like ours with five mouths to feed and only two adults to earn points. Because Weiluan was frequently away working on reservoirs, attending struggle sessions, or doing mandatory hard labor, the main burden of earning points for the family fell on my shoulders. As a result, our rations dwindled considerably. We returned to barely being able to subsist each month.

Friends and team members who saw us struggling suggested we stop spending Weiluan's salary from the irrigation projects on the girls' tuition. However, both of us were adamant that our daughters attend school. Nothing compares with the power of education in opening doors for a young person's future. My and Weiluan's futures were sealed but our children's weren't. We were determined to give them every opportunity to succeed where we hadn't. Our one saving grace was that the reservoir project Weiluan had been assigned to was located in the woods, which gave him the opportunity to gather firewood on his way home from work each day. In this way, we were able to scrape by for several months.

The work Weiluan performed at the reservoir was backbreaking and took an extremely heavy toll on his body. As a bad element, he was assigned one of the most taxing jobs on the project: clearing large, heavy stones. For hours every day, he pounded large rocks until they loosened from the earth, then carried them uphill from the center of the new reservoir to the shore. The pounding left behind thousands of small, sharp pieces of stone that tore into his bare feet every time he trekked back and forth across the reservoir.

Each night Weiluan returned home with bloody, aching feet and collapsed on our bed in agony. I cleansed and put balm on the wounds, but it did little good. As a bad element, my husband was required to work 365 days a year. He wasn't allowed a single day of rest or sick leave, so his body never had time to recuperate. Every morning he had to muster the strength to drag himself out of bed and go through the entire routine again, no matter how much pain he was in. His life proceeded like this for months at a time until the project ended or the next planting or harvest season arrived.

Weiluan's perseverance and grit were inspiring, but both received a devastating blow after a member of the Poor Peasants Association came to our home one day to deliver a letter. As a bad element family, all of our communications with people outside the village were closely monitored. In six years, I hadn't received a single letter from my father in Hunan, although I know he must have tried to write to me. Weiluan and I were both very curious when we saw the long, wide envelope.

"Who's it from?" I asked.

"Director Cheng!" he responded with a big smile. Weiluan quickly tore open the envelope. After glancing at the letter a few seconds, his face turned crestfallen, and he fell backward onto our bed.

"What's wrong? Isn't it good news?"

My husband didn't respond, so I walked over to the bed, picked up the letter, and read it.

"To Weiluan, since you have returned home, do not come back to Hunan. The farm work you are doing is also part of our revolution. Director Cheng"

I shook my head and looked at my husband. He was devastated. His entire body trembled in frustration. I didn't know what to say to comfort him. Suddenly he stood up and grabbed the letter from my hands.

"I don't think it was written by Director Cheng. He wouldn't speak to me so callously. It must have been written by his assistant. He was always jealous because Director Cheng was good to me."

He tore the letter into tiny pieces and flung them onto the floor.

News of the letter's arrival soon spread throughout the village. Many neighbors and relatives came to inquire about it. We shared with them the bad news. Although they never said so, I know many people had wondered if Weiluan had ever really worked for someone as prestigious as Director Cheng. At least now they knew he was telling the truth.

It took my husband several weeks to get over Director Cheng's devastating reply. Over the years, I increasingly had my doubts that we would ever return to Hunan, but up to that point Weiluan truly believed that one day he would be requested to go back, and we would be saved from our nightmare. When everything else in our lives was falling apart — when it seemed like the future held nothing but more anguish — Weiluan clutched tightly to the hope that one day a letter would arrive in the mail from Director Cheng with good news. After six years, the letter had finally arrived. The news wasn't good, and now that hope had vanished.

Wild Winds Cause the Flame in a Broken Lantern to Flicker

From 1956 to early 1958, Weiluan worked almost year-round on two local reservoir projects. The work was extremely taxing and completely drained him physically and emotionally. Every inch of flesh on his feet became torn. Anyone who saw his feet winced. A relative of Li's took pity on my husband and gave him a pair of broken straw sandals to wear. The sandals helped for a short while, but the gravel was so sharp that soon those also became paper-thin.

Eventually, Weiluan became so desperate that, one night after work, he suggested taking the drastic measure of searing the wounds on his feet with a burning hot brick.

"I've heard it can make the wounded flesh melt into itself and heal. I think it's worth a try."

"Weiluan, are you crazy? You can't do that! It sounds like torture. You could get a bad infection. That could make it worse."

My husband didn't listen to me. That night after I went to bed, he heated a brick, and melted together the raw wounds on his feet. To my surprise, it actually worked. He did this every night until the wounds were healed.

The treatment helped Weiluan for several months, but by February 1958 his feet had again become raw, red, and swollen. This time searing the flesh didn't seem to do any good. My husband felt such intense pain that for the first time he asked his production team supervisor to grant him some sick leave. The supervisor showed him no mercy.

"You are a bad element," the supervisor said coldly. "You must go on working even if you work yourself to death."

Weiluan tried to soldier on, but each day it became more difficult for him to do so. During this time, I became pregnant again. I hoped that news of a new baby would lift my husband's spirits, but it didn't. Instead, day-by-day he became more discouraged. He abandoned his optimistic outlook and will to survive. He began to look to death as his only escape.

"Fengxian, if I don't return from the reservoir one evening, you will know that I have died. Please don't be sad for me. To die is human. To me, death means being free of all of this pain and worry. We can reunite and be husband and wife in our next life. Please take care of the children and the new baby in your womb."

"How can you say such a thing with no regard for the feelings of your wife and children? How can you talk about death repeatedly like this? Don't you know that if you die we will surely follow you? Do you think we can survive in this world without you? We can't! If you want to die, then let's all die together. Then all of us can be free of this nightmare."

"I didn't say it to hurt you. I just can't go on anymore ... I can't."

"I know. I understand. But if you have really reached that point, then stop going to the reservoir. At least then you can die at home."

"But if I do that I will be punished."

"Punishment is better than death. I will go and talk to your supervisor and make another request for sick leave."

I visited the leaders of my husband's production team and the public security bureau responsible for the supervision of bad elements. I pleaded with them to show some compassion toward my husband.

"Weiluan can't walk right now, let alone carry large, heavy stones. If he continues to work, he is bound to die. Please allow him to take some time off. My husband is the backbone of our family. We can't survive without him. Do you want to see our entire family perish?"

The head of the security bureau understood and said he would grant my husband one day off. However, the leader of the production team was merciless and wanted to make him continue working. In the end, they agreed to allow Weiluan to take one day of sick leave. They also gave me permission to stay at home with him.

I knew that one day wouldn't cure my husband's feet, but I thanked them anyway. It was extremely rare for bad elements to ever be given even one day off. I went to purchase some special ointment and returned home.

"One day?" Weiluan said when I got back. "That's it? It's of no use."

"One is better than none," I said as I spread the ointment on his wounds.

After a few minutes of silence, I delicately raised an issue we hadn't discussed in years.

"You know, if you had gone to Hong Kong in the past as we had discussed, we probably wouldn't be suffering like this right now."

At first Weiluan didn't respond. Then he replied quietly. "I could try again. Maybe God would show sympathy toward us and help me succeed."

"I would support you trying to sneak away to Hong Kong again. Now is a good time. Even though I'm pregnant, the cooperative has opened a new day care center for our production team. I wouldn't have to leave our newborn at home alone as we did with Hao. Plus I'm much more familiar with farm life and the customs here than before. You don't need to worry."

"Fengxian, you're right. Since not going means certain death, what is there to lose by trying again?"

That afternoon I visited the local Buddhist temple to see what God had to say about our idea.

Standing before a statue of Buddha, I lit some incense, bowed three times, and prayed for God's guidance. Then I placed the burning incense in the offering trough and went straight to the fortune-teller stand.

"Sister, what can I do for you?" the fortune teller asked.

"My family is faced with a problem. I'm here to seek God's guidance."

"Tell me what question you have."

"My husband and I want to know if it's a good idea for him to flee to Hong Kong."

"Take this," the fortune teller said, handing me a narrow, round container with a small opening on the top. "Inside this container are several thin sticks of wood with prophecies written on them. Shake the cup up and down until a stick pops out. Whichever stick emerges will provide you with your answer."

I followed his instructions. A few moments later a stick popped out and landed on the counter.

"Sister, I'm sorry to say that the prophecy you've drawn isn't a good one. It says, 'wild winds cause the flame in a broken lantern to flicker.' Although the lantern is broken, the flame remains bright at first. But when subjected to wild winds, it turns dim and almost burns out. Do not take rash action. Otherwise, you might regret encouraging your husband to go."

I shook my head and sighed.

"My five cents please," the fortune teller said. I handed over the money. I wanted to draw another lot, but didn't have any more money. I returned home deflated.

"What does God say?" Weiluan asked eagerly as soon as I entered the house. "Does he say I should go to Hong Kong?"

I showed him the stick.

"God says I shouldn't go?"

"I think we should give up the idea. It's too risky."

"If God really wants to help us, he will protect me from danger. God knows the misery and suffering we have endured. We are dying. I don't believe God will turn his back on us."

We discussed the issue some more. This time Weiluan was more determined than I was that he should go, but he wanted to wait a little bit longer before he left. His one day of sick leave passed in the blink of an eye. The next morning he returned to the reservoir.

A couple of days later, my husband's feet began to ache terribly again. That night he asked me to prepare some food for him to take on his journey to Hong Kong.

"I can't do this any longer. I must go now. I will leave tonight."

"Okay. What should I say when they come looking for you?"

"Tell them we are desperate and have no food at home, so I went to the woods to collect firewood."

"I'm afraid they'll track you down and find you."

"By the time they come searching for me, I will have been walking several hours. I'm sorry, Fengxian, to abandon you, the girls, and the new baby in your womb."

"Don't worry about us. We'll be all right. You have already sacrificed so much for this family."

"The journey to Hong Kong is very difficult and dangerous. The terrain is rough. It's possible that I could die during the journey. If I do die, and the baby is a boy, tell him to be like his father and fulfill the dreams that I haven't been able to. If the baby is a girl, tell her to be like her mother, who is virtuous and beautiful."

After the children went to sleep, Weiluan bandaged his wounds, took the snow peas and sweet potatoes I prepared, and set off for Hong Kong. The sky was dark and cloudy, and it was drizzling. We were both in tears.

The next morning, Zi and Tian went to school, leaving just Mei and me behind in the empty house. Later that morning the head of the production team knocked on our door to remind Weiluan that it was time to report to the reservoir.

"Tell him if he is late, he will be punished."

"He already left. He went to collect firewood near the reservoir, so we can get some money to buy food. He's probably already there waiting for you."

The team leader left. I knew that I wouldn't be able to hide my husband's absence for very long. All day I felt nervous. I could think of nothing else. That evening the production team leader returned to our home, this time in a much angrier mood.

"Where is your husband? I didn't see him the entire day!"

"What do you mean you didn't see him?" I asked, trying to act surprised. "Did he fall into a ravine and get injured? What do we do?"

"Did your husband run away?"

"No! Weiluan wouldn't abandon us. I'm pregnant again. He wouldn't leave me at such a time."

"Well, maybe he did fall into a ravine, in which case he is probably dead or at least crippled. I will go look for him."

As soon as the team leader left, the girls returned home from school. "Where's Dad? Why hasn't he come back from work yet? Should we go look for him?"

"No, don't worry about your father."

"Has he tried to escape to Hong Kong?" Zi asked.

"If Father wanted to escape, he would have left a long time ago," Tian said.

That night I barely slept. I envisioned every possible scenario of what might happen to my husband on his journey. Since he was a bad element, I knew that if he was discovered he would be shown no mercy and would be severely punished. I awoke exhausted.

The next morning as I was working in the fields, I overheard some co-workers gossiping about Weiluan. They said he had been arrested. "In the past, it was possible to sneak away to Hong Kong," one of them said. "But now it is illegal. Sometimes people who are caught are sentenced to death." I pretended not to hear, but inside I was terrified.

That evening Zi and Tian returned from school in tears. "People are saying that Dad is in prison. Is it true?"

"No, it's just a rumor," I said, although I was increasingly worried that it might be true.

Later that night the head of the production team made another visit to our home. He confirmed our worst fears.

"By now, you have probably heard that your husband has been arrested. Did you know about his intention to escape to Hong Kong? I think you conspired with him and lied to us!"

"No! No, I didn't know anything at all. If I knew my husband was going to abandon us, I surely wouldn't have let him go. How can I keep this family alive on my own?"

"You should be punished for what you have done!" the leader screamed at me as he left.

The girls and I looked at each other and began to cry. The rest of the night I beat myself up for encouraging Weiluan to go to Hong Kong in the first place. The fortune teller had told us not to take rash action, but we had done so anyway. I naively believed that where there is a will, there is always a way. I was so stupid to think that we could avoid such an outcome. Now Weiluan could possibly be executed.

That night I pleaded with God to keep my husband safe, to return him to us quickly, and to give this penniless, pregnant, single mother the strength to persevere. The entire family's survival now rested on my shoulders. I promised to follow Weiluan's inspiring example of putting one bloody, aching foot in front of the other every day until we reached the light.

PART SIX

Bitter and Sweet Days

A Successor

Weiluan's absence left a large void in our family. The sadness weighed heavily on all of us, particularly me. Every day I anxiously awaited news about my husband. There was none. After a while, I prepared myself for the worst: that he would be executed, that we would never see each other again, and that I would be left on my own to raise the girls and the new baby I carried. Weiluan's fate was out of my hands, but how to react in the face of such adversity was in my control. I vowed to do everything I could to raise our children to be worthy descendants of my husband.

As the fetus inside my womb grew, I displayed symptoms that I had never experienced in any of my previous pregnancies. The baby restlessly kicked day and night — was it angry at me for sending its father away? — and I felt an overwhelming urge to smoke tobacco. In the past, even the odor of smoke made me ill. Now multiple times a day I smoked whatever tobacco I could borrow. I interpreted the symptoms as a good omen that I was carrying a boy, which made me proud and ecstatic. When Hao died, Weiluan lost his sole successor. I desperately wanted to produce a male heir for my husband.

In my heart, I was determined to soldier on for our family, but the farther I got into the pregnancy the weaker my body became. Soon I no longer had the energy or strength to work in the fields. The production team supervisor re-assigned me to a new position where I was responsible for looking after and grazing oxen. I was thankful to be assigned lighter work, but I earned fewer points in the new position. We already struggled to get by without Weiluan's wages from his reservoir jobs. I wondered if we could survive without him.

One morning while grazing one of the oxen, the animal suddenly went berserk. The ox trampled many crops and even gored a couple of villagers. The production team supervisor became extremely upset when he learned what happened.

"Manpo, I blame you for this! If you had fulfilled your duty, the ox wouldn't have run away. I'm taking away all of your work points for today."

"How can I be blamed for the animal snapping? There was no way I could control it. Please don't deduct my points. I need them to feed my children."

"Either I deduct your points, or you compensate us for the crops that have been destroyed. No matter what you say, it's useless. I will not change my mind. I will not allow this to go unpunished."

I returned home that afternoon in tears. Fortunately, we had a small stash of food to draw on. It included a hodgepodge of vegetables and potatoes that I had found growing in the wild while grazing the oxen as well as one small chicken. It wasn't much, but it would be sufficient to carry us over a couple of days until I earned more work points.

When the spring planting season arrived, the oxen were taken to till the fields, and I was assigned light work in one of the cooperative's small gardens. One morning I encountered my old friend Liu in the garden. She sneaked over and whispered to me in a low voice.

"Fengxian, I'm so sorry we haven't been able to have any contact the past several years. My sons and I fear we will be criticized if we maintain relations with your family since Weiluan is a bad element. I feel awful about how you and your family have suffered. You are destitute, and your relatives don't lift a finger to help you. Now your husband is gone. I wish there was something I could do for you."

"Liu, we understand. We are of different classes now. The Communist Party despises bad element families like us. We know it would be detrimental for you to have any contact with us, which is why we haven't bothered you."

"Thank you, Fengxian. You've always been so understanding. Do you know the whereabouts of your husband?"

"No. I have no idea where he is or how he is doing. I haven't heard one word about him."

"I heard that he was sent to a re-education through a labor camp in Luozhou (Lwō-jō). Please don't let anyone know you heard it from me."

"Thank you, Liu. Of course, I will keep my mouth shut."

Hearing that Weiluan had been sent to a re-education camp was comforting. If the Communist Party intended to execute him, they probably
wouldn't go to the trouble of re-educating him. I rushed home, opened
one of Weiluan's maps of Guangdong, and searched for Luozhou. I
discovered it was located a few days' journey away.

My body became weaker as my due date neared, yet each day I
forced myself to get up and go to work. I had no choice but to continue
doing so if I wanted to earn enough points to feed my children. One
morning after the girls left for school, I was preparing to go to work
when I collapsed onto our bed. I was too weak to stand up, so I lay there
and allowed myself to fall back asleep. I awoke in great pain an hour
later. My water had broken, and my legs were wet. I knew I was about
to give birth. With no one to assist me, I panicked. I screamed for help
several times, but everyone was at work. No one heard me except little
Mei who could do nothing to help me.

"God," I said aloud, "if you can see me, please send someone to
rescue me. If you don't want to help me, then please let me die as soon
as possible. Then I can get rid of all of the pain and bitterness in my life."

The contractions were so intense that all I could do was curl up on
the bed and groan. Later that morning, Fang (Fǒng), the wife of one of
Weiluan's cousins, came to our home to borrow a fan. She discovered
me writhing in pain.

"Fengxian, are you okay? What's wrong? Are you giving birth?"

"Yes. Fang, please help me."

Fang helped me roll onto my back. As soon as I spread my legs, the
baby immediately slid out. It was 9 a.m. in late May of the lunar calendar.

"It's a boy! Fengxian, congratulations! Do you have any clothes for
me to wrap him in?"

"No. I've been too busy and weak to make any preparations."

"A cloth?"

"No."

Fang looked around, grabbed some of Zi's clothes, and covered the
baby. When the girls returned from school, Fang instructed them to find
a midwife to cut the umbilical cord.

While I rested, Fang slaughtered our small chicken and prepared a pot of soup for me.

"This will nourish your body. Eat it, so your baby will have milk to drink."

"Fang, I'm so grateful for your help. One day I will repay you."

"Don't talk about reciprocation. We are both women. We help each other when we can."

Over the next two days, Fang excitedly told everyone she encountered that I had given birth to a boy. When Weiluan's mother heard the news, she called to me through the partition separating our living rooms. Mother-in-Law hadn't spoken a word to me in ages. The moment I heard her voice, flashbacks of her past cruelty raced through my mind. I hesitated speaking with her, but she kept knocking on the wall.

"Manpo? Manpo, are you there?"

"Yes, Mother-in-Law, I'm here."

"Manpo, I want to apologize for how poorly I treated you in the past. I'm so sorry. It was not my own intention."

"I know, Mother. Weiluan and I know you are under Qisao's control."

"My good Daughter-in-Law, it's too late now to change the past. Tell me, was Manfu really arrested trying to sneak to Hong Kong? I don't know if it's true or a rumor."

"Yes, it's true. Weiluan is in a labor camp."

"This son's fate is very bad. I feel so sorry for him. I heard that you gave birth to a baby boy. Manfu now has an heir. I'm so happy to hear this. I would like to come see the little one, but I fear that Qisao will quarrel with me, so I dare not go. However, I have chosen a good name for my grandson. Please accept it. You have given birth to several girls. This is the only living boy. It's such a blessing. I think we should call him Duoxi (Dwō-shē) since it means 'much happiness.'"

"I think that's a great name. Thank you, Mother."

At that moment, Qisao returned and discovered Mother-in-Law conversing with me through the partition.

"Old woman, all you do every day is stay at home," she screamed at her. "Now I see you talking with that despicable woman from Hunan.

It's about time you did something useful and went to the fields to collect dung."

Qisao walked up to the partition and bullied me. "Manpo, is it really all that great that you gave birth to a boy? What a pity that he has no father from the moment he is born!"

"No matter where Weiluan is, he is living a more honorable life than a heartless woman like you!" I screamed back.

The production team allowed every woman to take one month off after giving birth to allow their bodies to heal. However, during this time, we accrued no work points. I tried to stretch out what little food we had, but it wasn't nearly enough for all of us. Every day after school the girls had to spend hours scavenging for food. Often I had little to no breast milk to feed Duoxi. When my breasts were empty, I fed him a mixture of rice flour and water. Both of us were malnourished and emaciated, but we couldn't afford to see a doctor. All I could do was lie on the bed and hold my son tightly to my chest to comfort him.

One month passed quickly. According to tradition in Donghu, no matter how poor a family was, a special ceremony would be held for a baby boy's one-month birthday. I asked Fang if she could help me purchase the items to host Duoxi's celebration. She was happy to help. We bought a chicken, some pork, a small salted fish, and some wine. I invited Mother-in-Law to join us the morning of the celebration.

"Manpo, thank you for inviting me. I would like to go, but I dare not do so. If Qisao were to find out, she would curse me to death."

"You don't have to come for the ceremony. Just come for lunch. Duoxi is your grandson."

"Manpo, now I know you are sincerely filial. That's enough to make me happy. Whether I eat lunch or not isn't important."

That morning, we hosted a joyous celebration marking Duoxi's one-month birthday. I proudly held my beautiful son on my lap as friends and neighbors congratulated me. The smell of the food attracted the attention of Qisao. She snickered at us repeatedly through the partition, but I was content no matter what she said. I had fulfilled my single-most important duty as a wife: I had given Weiluan a successor.

The Great Leap Forward

The morning after Duoxi's one-month birthday, I took him and Mei to the production team's day care center and returned to work. Because I had consumed so little food the previous month, my body had not fully recuperated from childbirth. I remained very weak. I mustered all of the energy I could to put in a full day of work, so I could begin earning points again. Without them, all of us would perish.

As the weeks passed, I slowly regained my strength. I was able to take in enough nourishment to breastfeed Duoxi, who was becoming bigger and livelier by the day. Life was by no means easy, but the children and I were managing without Weiluan.

In the fall, we learned that another wave of agricultural collectivization would soon be implemented. Most villagers' lives had improved after the introduction of cooperatives, so most people welcomed further reforms. Everyone shared the Communist Party's desire to build a new, modern China and reclaim our glorious past. More than a century of exploitation by foreign countries — who had divided and pillaged our major cities — was a source of disgrace. The Communist Party was intent on ensuring that our country would never again be so weak that it would fall prey to foreigners, and we supported them.

Impressed by the USSR's success, the Communist Party adopted the Soviet model of economic planning. The first plan, which ended in 1957, focused on the organization of family farms into cooperatives and establishing the foundation for industrialization. In 1958, an aggressive new plan was laid out that targeted large increases in grain and steel production, as well as the completion of the final stage of agricultural collectivization: the merging of cooperatives into communes. This ambitious program became known as the "Great Leap Forward," for it was hoped that, during this time, we would complete our transition to full-fledged communism and vault from a backward, rural economy into an industrial power.

Chairman Mao believed that we could achieve anything if we put our hearts into it. He challenged all of us to rise to the occasion and defeat the obstacles keeping our country poor and weak. Rural areas were quickly mobilized into two tasks: producing more food, and helping provide the inputs, predominantly steel, for industrialization.

In late 1958, our cooperative was merged with several others in the area into the new Donghu Commune. The commune spanned several villages and was nearly equivalent in size to an entire county. Similar communes were established across the countryside. For the first time in our country's history, all farming was now under state control. The government dictated what crops we could plant, when, where, and how, as well as what share of each commune's harvest had to be submitted to the state and what share the commune could keep.

During cooperativization, families had been allowed to retain small private plots, where we could grow whatever food we wanted for our own consumption or to sell in local markets. These personal gardens were a critical source of food and side income for everyone, including us. However, shortly after Donghu Commune's establishment, the leadership seized all private plots and closed many rural markets because both were considered bastions of capitalism. As a result, families became reliant on the commune for nearly everything.

The merging of so many cooperatives created a vast pool of labor that the government mobilized for large infrastructure projects that would have been impossible in the past. Numerous people were assigned to work on water conservation, while others gathered materials to make into steel. The government's target of a multifold increase in steel output sparked a national obsession. Every commune in the country set out to contribute as much as possible to this goal.

Donghu Commune, like many others, lacked the raw materials to cast into steel, so every family was ordered to contribute whatever iron, copper, and steel items they had in their possession. We owned one iron wok, one iron cooking pot, and one steel kitchen knife, all of which I dutifully submitted. This left us and other families with little to cook with. The commune promptly addressed this by opening several public canteens to feed everyone.

The old system of work points was abolished, which pleased me because families like ours with few point earners were at a severe disadvantage. A new system called "eating from the same big pot (吃大锅饭)" was introduced. Fish, pork, and rice — rare luxuries in the past — were now regularly distributed to everyone. For families like us who constantly lived on the brink of starvation, the new canteens were a major improvement in our lives.

Before each meal, everyone in the canteen recited in unison: "I will be faithful to Chairman Mao, the Chinese Communist Party, and the Chinese people forever." Then we denounced the "dark old days" and praised the "sweet new days." People secretly watched whether you made these statements, so one dared not forget to do this or else risk being perceived as unsupportive. Nevertheless, in my heart, I believed these words to be true. The Communist Party had done a lot for poor people.

After the commune finished smelting all of the metal items that we had submitted, we were tasked with searching for iron ore on the nearby mountain slopes. For weeks, we dug all over the mountains but discovered nothing. As a result, families were asked to dismantle their metal doors and window frames and sell them to the commune to be re-cast into steel. Everyone gladly obliged. Our window frames were thick and solid, so we earned a decent sum of money.

Around this time, the commune was in the midst of reorganizing its stockpiles of goods and animals and was in need of storage. They offered to purchase rooms from villagers' homes and barns. We owned one ox stable, which I sold for 20 yuan. With this money and the money from the sale of our door and window frames, suddenly I had dozens of yuan in my possession.

With food no longer a worry, I set some of the money aside to pay the tuition for Zi and Tian and purchased some cloth to make a new duvet cover and clothes for the children. I also made a pair of cloth shoes for each of us. None of us had worn shoes in ages.

Within the span of a few months, our lives dramatically improved. All that was lacking was my beloved Weiluan, who had accompanied us through the hardest and bitterest of days but was not with us to share in our newfound comfort and joy.

Sadly, this carefree life did not last long. Prior to opening the canteens, little thought had been given to whether there was actually enough food to be handing it out so generously. The resulting rise in consumption led to a rapid drawdown of food stockpiles. This decline was exacerbated by an increase in the amount of grain that had to be submitted to the central government as well as a reduction in harvests from bad weather and poor management.

At the time, many local officials were caught up in a revolutionary fervor and in a frenzy to outdo one another. Many were inexperienced at farming and didn't comprehend the gravity of the dwindling stockpiles. Many parts of the country suffered as officials blindly implemented any new idea that might increase production. When the initiatives failed, rather than tell their superiors the truth, they often submitted exaggerated figures on the size of harvests. These false numbers misled the government into believing that it could take more grain from communes like ours, when, in fact, harvests in many places had plummeted, and there was nothing extra to give.

The combination of increased grain consumption, falling grain output, and over-confiscation of grain by the central government triggered the start of what would eventually become one of our country's deadliest famines. Food shortages emerged everywhere. Within a few weeks of opening the canteens, fish, pork, and rice disappeared from the menu. Donghu Commune switched to feeding us thin rice porridge three times a day. When the rice ran out, we were given sweet potato porridge, and when that began to dwindle, we were given just a few small pieces of sweet potatoes at each meal. Everyone lost weight and energy.

The food shortage was worsened by a devastating flood that occurred in our area soon after the Dragon Boat Festival in 1959. Zi and Tian had gone to the pharmacy in Gaoshui to watch the races, and I was home with Duoxi and Mei. The day after the festival began with beautiful blue sky and bright sun. But by mid-afternoon, a vicious storm moved in that brought torrential rainfall. Everyone was instructed to stay away from the canteen, and a small number of gourds and sweet potatoes were distributed for people to eat at home. As the flood waters rose, I took

Duoxi and Mei, as well as our clothes and other important belongings into the attic.

That night we listened helplessly as many houses collapsed and people screamed for assistance. I was terrified because I didn't know how to swim and feared I wouldn't be able to save my children. The higher the water rose, the more convinced I became that the three of us were going to die.

I cradled the children all night and eventually fell asleep. When the sun rose the next morning, I saw nothing but devastation out the window. Parts of the ceiling and walls downstairs had collapsed. The water was two inches from the second floor where we had taken refuge. It was still raining lightly when I awoke. I could do nothing but sit there and wait for the storm to end and the waters to recede. Around dusk, I heard some villagers rowing a boat nearby. I screamed out to them, and they navigated over to our window.

"Manpo, are you okay?"

"Yes. I'm so glad you're here."

"How many people are in there with you?"

"Just me and my two youngest children."

"You must evacuate. It's not safe to stay here."

Because the frames on our windows had been dismantled, it was easy for the three of us to climb out. I handed my children to the men and then crawled into the boat.

"Where have you been taking everyone?" I asked.

"The old mansion that your husband's father built. It's located on a hill. It's large, and there is no flooding there. Last year it was turned into an agriculture university."

When we arrived at the mansion, I couldn't help but smile at the irony of everyone taking refuge there. Weiluan would have been proud to see his father's dream home being put to such good use. After getting settled, my attention immediately shifted to finding Zi and Tian. I asked everyone I encountered if they had seen my daughters. They managed to find me after several hours.

We stayed at the mansion for two days. During this time, most conversations revolved around the flood. Older villagers noted that a disaster of such magnitude hadn't occurred in more than a century. Others insisted that the flood wouldn't have been so severe if the embankment at one of the nearby reservoirs hadn't burst. Regardless of the causes, everyone agreed that it would devastate the crops. Our food shortage was about to get much, much worse.

Because our family had few possessions, we incurred minimal losses from the flood. One of our downstairs rooms was filled with silt. Rather than empty it, I decided to leave it that way so we could grow some vegetables. I knew that soon we would desperately need food.

The local government launched several irrigation and water control projects immediately after the flood to repair the damage done to existing structures and to prevent a similar disaster from re-occurring. Every adult in the commune was conscripted into the projects. Afterward, I worked on various odd jobs for the commune, including planting and harvesting crops and dredging rivers.

Workers usually were fed at the canteens, but occasionally during reservoir projects we were fed on-site. At those times, the only way I could share my 500 grams of rice per day allotment with my children was by having Tian temporarily stop school to bring Duoxi and Mei to the work site. Some co-workers complained about my bringing the children to the work site, but I didn't care. I was determined to see that my children were fed. Zi fortunately received some food at school, and I didn't need to provide for her.

When Chinese New Year arrived in 1960, it passed without fanfare. Food plays a central role in the Chinese New Year celebration. Villagers had little to rejoice about without it. All of us hoped that 1960 would bring more fortune. In reality, life became even more difficult. Although the soil in Donghu had recovered from the previous year's flood, a vicious draught in northern China and more flooding in coastal areas led to a worsening of harvests across the country.

The canteen remained open, but the rations we received dwindled considerably. Every villager was severely malnourished. Families with money could purchase extra food in the few markets that remained open, although the offerings were much scarcer than in the past. Poor families like us, who relied solely on the canteen for food, had no choice but to spend every spare minute scavenging for leaves, grass, bark, bugs, seedlings, and anything else that could be eaten. The children and I spent hours each day searching for food. If we didn't start early and keep at it, we would find nothing and go hungry.

Many villagers, including Weiluan's mother, suffered edema, which caused parts of their bodies to swell like balloons. The commune distributed special rations to these people of 600 grams of rice per day. However, Qisao and her children always ate the rice and left Mother-in-Law to eat the scraps from the canteen. Mother-in-Law was so desperate one day that she knocked on the partition and pleaded for help.

"Manpo, I'm so hungry. Please can you give me something to eat?"

I felt awful about her predicament, so I picked two eggplants from the new garden in our house and tossed them over the partition. Within minutes, Qisao caught Mother-in-Law with the eggplants, snatched them out of her hands, and tossed them into dirty sewage.

"Old woman, are you hungry? Why do you need these eggplants when all you do all day is stay at home? I have to work from daybreak to midnight and have to bear hunger, but I must carry on."

At that moment, it became clear that Qisao was deliberately starving Mother-in-Law to death. Many neighbors began to comment that Mother-in-Law had become as thin as a monkey. Everyone knew Qisao was starving her, but no one dared to stand up for Mother-in-Law because she had been labeled a landlord. If they did, they risked being accused of over-empathizing with bad elements and being labeled a bad element themselves. Nevertheless, many villagers stopped and exchanged kind words with her when they passed by the house.

"Qisao and her children killed a chicken today. Were you able to eat any of that?" I overheard someone ask Mother-in-Law one day.

"I couldn't see the feathers of the chicken, let alone eat it or drink its soup."

One day, Mother-in-Law found a small gourd outside and secretly cooked it. Just as she was about to eat the gourd, Qisao's daughter grabbed it from her hands, threw it away, then poured a bowl of water on Mother-in-Law's head. Zi and Tian fought with Qisao's daughter when they saw what happened. I had to drag the girls back home.

As long as I had known her, Qisao had always been a cruel woman, but as the famine intensified, she became even more vicious. One sad lesson I learned during those years is that nothing tests the limits of a person's kindness like starvation. "Only when the granaries are full does one know etiquette and ethics (仓廪实而知礼节)" is a common saying in China.

Although our situation in Donghu was dreadful, our location in the temperate south, where plants grow year-round, meant most villagers were able to hang on by scavenging. It wasn't until I met my American cousin, Charlene, decades later that I learned that other parts of rural China had fared much worse and that millions of my countrymen had died. By contrast, urban areas were barely scathed. Fearing that widespread starvation in cities might spark social unrest, the Communist Party ensured that urban areas received adequate rations.

To this day, many people refer to the time from 1959 to 1961 as "the three years of bitterness." What started as a campaign to catapult us into a modern industrial state ended in catastrophe. More people began to quietly question precisely where the Communist Party was leading us.

Emergency Dispatches

I received my first letter from Weiluan in the spring of 1960, during the middle of the Great Leap Forward famine. By then, he had been locked up two years. We hadn't had any contact since the day he left in 1958. He had spent the entire time in Luozhou Re-education through Labor Camp, which was situated on a sweet potato farm. He said he was participating sincerely and actively in the re-education and labor activities and hoped he would be released soon. He apologized for leaving me and the children on our own.

"The main reason I was arrested is that I didn't want to leave you. I feared that you couldn't live without me, and I hated the idea of leaving my pregnant wife alone. After walking for several hours, I decided to stop for the night and take shelter in a lime kiln. As I lay there, I worried about you and the children. I decided that I would return to you when daylight broke.

That morning when I emerged from the kiln, a woman discovered me. She immediately reported me to the authorities. They quickly captured me. I explained our situation to the officers, but to no avail. They sent me straightaway to Luozhou.

Do you recall how the fortune teller at the temple told us not to take rash action, and that 'wild winds cause the flame in a broken lantern to flicker?' It turns out the fortune teller was right. Please take care of everything at home and patiently await my return. Weiluan"

Hearing that my husband had been captured because he didn't have the courage to leave us frustrated me at first, but I quickly forgave him. Weiluan had tried time and again to flee to Hong Kong. For whatever reason, he just wasn't able to leave me and the children behind. This time his timidity had landed him in prison. I immediately wrote back.

"Weiluan, please return as soon as you can. Don't worry about me and the children. We are doing fine. You will be happy to know that I gave birth to a son. He is approaching two years old now. He is obedient and lively. Your mother gave him the name Duoxi. I believe you will love this name.

You must be surprised that your mother would even give our son a name, right? Mother told me that she deeply regrets what she has said and done in the past. She is older and thinner than before and doing poorly under the thumb of Qisao. Fengxian"

Weiluan's letter arrived at a time when the food shortage had become particularly acute, and I was weak physically and emotionally. Hearing from my husband after so long comforted me greatly. I knew that one day Weiluan would return, and this hope boosted my determination to soldier on.

Mother-in-Law knocked on the partition when she heard that Wei-luan had written me a letter.

"Manpo, is it true that Manfu wrote you a letter?" she whispered.

"Yes."

"Where is he? When can he come back home? I hope he returns soon so I can see him again. Otherwise, I'm afraid I will never be able to see my son again."

"Mother, don't worry. Weiluan is doing fine. I'm sure he'll come home as soon as he can."

Mother-in-Law's words worried me. I knew her health was deteriorating because of malnourishment. I wished that there was something I could do, but I was barely able to support myself and my four children. I simply didn't have the resources to look after her.

A few months later during the summer of 1960, I received a surprise one morning that I never would have expected in my wildest dreams. The busy season had not yet arrived, so I had some downtime. I was spending a leisurely morning at home with my children when I heard a loud knock on the door. I asked who it was, but there was no response. When I opened the door, I saw my younger brother Dian standing before me.

"My God, Brother, what are you doing here?"

"Of course, I came here to see you, Fengxian!"

Both of us immediately became teary-eyed. I invited him inside.

"Fengxian, it's so good to see you after so long."

"Please, sit down. Can I get you anything?"

"No, I'm fine."

"Girls, come here," I called out. "Zi, Tian, do you recall who this is?" They shook their heads no.

"It's your Uncle Dian! He came all the way from Hunan to visit us."

"The two of you have grown so much since I last saw you," Brother said, smiling and shaking his head. "And who are these two little ones?"

"I'm Mei, and this is my baby brother Duoxi."

"It's very nice to meet both of you."

Although Dian didn't say so, I could see the shock in his eyes at how emaciated and poor we were. I hadn't seen my brother since departing Rongxia a decade earlier. At that time, I was still wearing silk cheongsams with shoes and socks and had the aura of an affluent, educated woman. Now here I was, bone-thin, dressed in rags, and residing in a home a fraction of the size and grandeur of Rongxia. Perhaps most appallingly, I was barefoot. In all the years we had lived together, I don't know if Dian had ever seen my bare feet. It simply was unheard of for proper girls in Huaguo back then.

"Dian, please update me on everything that has transpired in your life since I last saw you."

"Well, not too long after you left Rongxia, I decided I wanted to attend college. I was accepted into Hunan Normal University in Changsha. Father was very supportive of the idea. In fact, he encouraged me to go. He was worried that the Communist Party might treat me badly since I had studied at the KMT military academy. Both of us thought it would be best for me to move to the capital, where I could live more anonymously. After I graduated, I got a job as a middle school math teacher in Changsha. I've been working at the school for more than five years now. Every summer I get several weeks off. This year I decided to spend part of my break visiting you."

Hearing my local Hunanese dialect after so long warmed my heart. "I'm glad to hear you've done so well."

"Where is Commander Han?" Dian asked eagerly.

The moment I heard his question, I choked up. "Weiluan was captured two years ago trying to abscond to Hong Kong. He's been in a re-education through labor camp ever since."

I explained to Dian all of the trials and tribulations our family had encountered over the past decade, including the tragic loss of our son Hao. He listened quietly and was very empathetic.

"I often think it's a miracle that we are even still alive," I said.

"Fengxian, life is full of ups and downs. Your children need you to sustain this family. Hold on and persevere. One day Weiluan will return. I believe it is God's arrangement for you to have bitter days first, then sweet days. Life will turn around for you one day."

By then, it was lunchtime. Luckily, I had a tiny bit of rice at home that I had received from one of my reservoir jobs, but I was embarrassed that I had nothing else to serve with it.

"Dian, I'm so sorry. All I have to serve you for lunch is this small amount of rice. The food shortage is getting worse each week. People with money can supplement their rations by purchasing food in the market, but I don't have a cent to buy anything."

"Fengxian, don't worry. I came here to see you, not feast. The situation in Hunan is also bad. I completely understand."

Dian chatted and joked with the children during lunch. That afternoon he asked me to take him shopping in Donghu. He bought me some cloth to make clothes for the children, as well as some fish, salt, oil, and cooking wares. He also gave me some money. It was a godsend, and I was extremely grateful.

As I prepared dinner that night, Dian meandered around our tiny home. A picture of Weiluan, me, and Zi in Hankou on New Year's Day in 1947 caught his attention. Weiluan was wearing a crisp, new military uniform along with a pair of shiny boots to illustrate his love of horse-riding. "This is our first photo since being married. I must pay attention to my appearance," my husband had said that morning. He looked handsome and valiant.

When Dian saw the photo, he lifted the frame from the wall, removed the picture, and tore out my husband's image. Then he placed the torn picture back in the frame and carried it to the kitchen to show me what he had just done.

"What happened?" I asked in surprise.

"Fengxian, I know this may anger you, but I did it for your own protection. You may not realize it, but hanging a picture like this on the middle of your wall is an extremely dangerous thing to do. Times have changed. The Communist Party is now in power. They are ruthless toward anyone they believe doesn't support them. Weiluan was a graduate of the Whampoa Military Academy. He worked as a KMT officer for several years. He fought *against* the Communist Party during the civil war. This is not something you want to display proudly in your home. I know you miss Weiluan very much, but keep in mind why he is in jail right now. Many people have tried to sneak to Hong Kong, but few were arrested when they got caught. Your husband was sent to prison because of his past connections to the KMT. I cut out Weiluan's image because I want to protect you and the children. I hope you won't be angry with me."

"Of course, Dian, I'm not angry," I replied, though part of me was heartbroken to see the photo destroyed. With Weiluan locked behind bars, that photo was all I had to remind me of his image. Still, I didn't want my brother to feel badly about what he had done. "I'm so ignorant, Dian. What you said never occurred to me. Thank you for your care."

After staying with us two days, Dian said he needed to return to Changsha, but first he wanted me to accompany him on a visit to the coast, which he had heard was beautiful. I hadn't been there myself in the decade I had lived in Guangdong. I requested a few days of vacation, and the next morning we set off.

The nearest coastal spot was located outside of Gaoshui, so we decided to go there first and stop at Weiluan's family's pharmacy. On the way, I explained the feud over the pharmacy, and warned Dian about Sige and Sisao. We picked up a few small gifts to smooth things over when we arrived. The couple treated us very hospitably to maintain appearances in front of my family. They invited us to dine with them and to spend the night at the pharmacy.

The next day Dian and I rode a small boat to the coast where an estuary of the Gaoshui River joins with the sea. It was the first time either of us had ever seen the ocean. The waves were powerful and loud. Dozens of boats packed with fish bobbed along the waterfront. The stench was overpowering. Around mid-afternoon, dark clouds gathered, and the wind picked up speed.

"It looks like the weather is starting to turn. Perhaps we should return to the pharmacy," I said, but Dian kept staring into the ocean as though he were mesmerized.

"Sister, how I wish I had a pair of wings so I could fly beyond this sea. In Hunan, I heard from many people that it's very easy to sneak into Hong Kong from Guangdong. Now that I see how far away it is, I know it's much more difficult. Now my dream is dashed. Perhaps I should follow in Weiluan's footsteps and still have a try."

This was the first indication I had that something was bothering my brother. "Dian, don't do anything foolish. You are young and will have a bright future. Cherish everything you have now."

"Fengxian, you don't understand my situation. These days it's very dangerous for intellectuals and anyone who graduated from university. The Communist Party believes that all educated people come from privileged backgrounds, lead sheltered lives, and therefore are out of sync with the masses. Our free thinking and open minds also are considered a threat because we don't blindly toe the party line as they want. A brutal campaign against intellectuals has been going on in the cities for a few years now. I've seen many people hauled away to re-education camps or subjected to violent struggle sessions. I'm afraid of what the future holds in store for me."

"I had no idea that kind of thing was going on in the cities. We get no news out here. Be careful and persevere, Dian. Do you have a girlfriend who you can share your difficulties with?"

"There's a doctor at the school that I'm interested in, but I haven't told her."

"Don't give up, Dian. Don't give up."

We took refuge from the weather at an oceanfront restaurant. Brother ordered some large crabs and other seafood. As we enjoyed a hearty, leisurely meal, he continued to update me on our family. He didn't know as much as I expected since he lived alone in Changsha. Still, any news was better than none.

"During land reform, the Communist Party split Rongxia into separate units and allowed several poor peasants to move into our home. Grandfather, Father, and their wives were kicked out and forced to live in tiny makeshift huts on the hill behind the garden. Everyone in the family was labeled a landlord. All of them have had a very rough time. They are frequently trotted out for criticism and abuse at struggle sessions. I'm sure you know how brutal those sessions can be."

"Yes, I do. Weiluan has attended his fair share of them. How has Father taken all of this?"

"You know him, the eternal optimist. He takes everything in stride."

"So much has changed for all of us since I left Rongxia," I said. "Sometimes I feel like my life there was just a distant dream."

Even though the news was sad, it felt comforting to finally hear about my family. Dian and I returned to the pharmacy after dinner. The next day, I escorted him to the train station. I wanted so much to hop aboard and join him. Now that Father had been labeled a landlord, I knew his life must be miserable. I wished I could be there to support him, but it was impossible.

I was preparing to go to work the next day when the post office delivered another letter from Weiluan. This one was accompanied by a money order for 15 yuan. I thought the money order must be a mistake since Weiluan was locked up. But in the note my husband explained that the camp had given him a new job as an unlicensed doctor. Each month he earned a salary of a few yuan. He didn't spend a cent and saved it all for us. He instructed me to use the money to purchase some nutritious food and to share it with his mother. I was dumbstruck.

Because my husband's entire family had been doctors and pharmacists, I knew Weiluan had learned a lot about medicine while growing up, but I never realized how much he knew. I surmised that the camp must have been confident in his ability or they wouldn't have given him such a job. The fact that they were paying him also suggested that they looked upon him quite favorably. I felt proud.

The villagers were flabbergasted when they heard that Weiluan had sent us money from prison. "I've never heard of anyone earning money in a labor camp ... The Communist Party is so kind ... It's all because your husband is so capable ... It's not surprising that he has become a doctor given the family's long tradition ... How fortunate you are, Fengxian ..."

I went to the post office, cashed in the money order, and set all of the proceeds aside. Dian had already given us a lot of financial assistance, so we didn't have any pressing needs. That night I wrote a letter to Weiluan thanking him for the money and encouraging him to continue to do a good job there. I told him about Dian's surprise visit and how hospitable Sige and Sisao were.

In the midst of the famine, when rations in the canteen had dwindled and we were forced to resort to scavenging, emergency help had been dispatched to our doorstep from Dian and Weiluan. To this day, I don't know if the children and I would have survived those three years of bitterness without it.

Sojourn in Luozhou Labor Camp

In late 1960, I received another money order and letter from Wei-luan. However, this letter contained devastating news. My husband explained that he had fallen seriously ill, was dying, and couldn't hold on much longer. Every sentence was sad and fatalistic. My heart sank to my stomach as I read the letter over and over again.

> "I don't know if I will be able to live much longer. If I die here, please send my body home to bury me. Then my spirit will be able to watch over you and the children. That is my last wish in this world.
>
> Fengxian, do you think you could come visit me so I could see you one last time? If so, I would die without any regrets in this life. If you can't come, that's okay. We can meet in the next life. To die is human. Don't cry for me. Weiluan"

The thought of losing my husband without having a chance to say goodbye was heart-wrenching, but getting approval to visit him wouldn't be easy. By then, millions of peasants had fled China's countryside and gone to the cities in search of food and work. In response, strict new policies had been put in place limiting peasants' ability to travel beyond their counties. Anyone wanting to travel further required approval from several layers of authorities and had to be given an official letter of introduction, which served as a form of identification. Without such a letter, one couldn't check into a hotel and could quickly be sent back home.

I took my husband's letter to the head of my production team and begged him to give me some time off to visit Weiluan.

"No, I will not approve this request," he replied coldly. "Fengxian, your husband is a prisoner. No one is allowed to see him."

"If that was the case, he wouldn't have asked me to come. Please let me see my husband one last time. He's dying."

"No."

"I believe Chairman Mao would have the compassion to allow me to see my husband."

"Then go and beg Chairman Mao!"

I left and went straight to the public security supervisor to see if he would grant me some time off. I needed at least one of them to approve this first phase of the application. The public security supervisor had more sympathy and agreed to give me two weeks off.

The next step was to visit the Communist Party secretary of my production team to request a seal of endorsement for the application. Lastly, I had to petition the commune leaders for their final consent. In the end, I received all of the necessary approvals to visit my husband, including a letter of introduction.

I wanted to leave as soon as possible because I didn't know how much longer my husband would be able to hang on. By then, Duoxi was a toddler. Weiluan had never seen his son. Knowing this might be his only opportunity, I decided to take Duoxi with me, even though it would complicate the journey. I arranged for Tian to take two weeks off from school to look after Mei.

Early the next morning Duoxi and I left. The trip was long and arduous and took three days by boat and bus. I felt nervous and restless the entire way. I tried to prepare myself for the possibility that I might arrive too late to see Weiluan alive, and that I might only be able to escort his body home. But one can never be truly prepared for something like that.

Around 1 p.m. on the third day of the journey, we arrived in a village close to Luozhou. I asked for directions to the camp. The terrain was unfamiliar, so every time I encountered someone I asked if we were going the right way. After walking for several hours, we came upon a building and farm surrounded by fences in a valley.

"Where is the sweet potato farm associated with Luozhou Labor Camp?" I called out to one of the workers.

"You're standing on it."

A guard came out of a nearby building and asked me who I was and what I was doing there.

"I'm here to see my husband, Han Weiluan," I said, handing him my papers.

"Doctor Han is here. Please come with me."

My legs shook and my heart raced as I followed the man onto the grounds. I didn't know what to expect when I saw Weiluan. How ill would he be? No matter how awful, you must face it and accept it, I told myself repeatedly.

The man led me and Duoxi into a room and asked us to sit down and wait. He returned with my husband a few minutes later. Weiluan was much thinner and had some grey hair, but otherwise he appeared healthy and energetic.

"Fengxian, I'm so glad to see you! Thank you for coming all the way here. I'm so sorry I made you anxious about me. If I hadn't written you such a desperate letter, I knew the commune leaders wouldn't allow you to visit me. I miss you so much. I wanted to see you. Please forgive me."

"It's okay," I said with relief. "I'm just glad to see that you're healthy and safe."

Weiluan looked proudly at Duoxi. "So this is my successor," he said with a smile. He picked him up and gave him a big hug and kiss.

After a few minutes, one of the guards announced that he had prepared a room for the three of us and instructed us to follow him. I thought we would be led to a cell. Instead, the man led us to his home on the grounds of the camp. He introduced us to his wife and showed us a room in his house where we could stay. They gave us some food, and we ate dinner in our room. I had never expected people in a labor camp to be so considerate.

"I want to hear everything about your life in the camp since you arrived," I said as we ate. "I hope it's not as bad as your experience at Hongli."

"Some things are similar to Hongli. For example, the group meetings in which we talk about our pasts and ways to reform ourselves. But Luozhou isn't nearly as brutal as Hongli was. When I first arrived, I was put through several lengthy interrogation sessions, but none of them was as intense as those at Hongli. During this time, the doctors treated my feet, and within a few weeks they healed. Afterward, I labored in the fields like everyone else. The work was exhausting but much easier to bear because I wasn't subjected to the psychological harassment I was in Donghu. Here we are all criminals. We are equals. No one has any basis to bully anyone else. After a couple of years, the leaders of the camp summoned me to their office one day. They asked me if I was interested in working as an unlicensed doctor. They thought I might be a good fit given my family's medical background. Of course, I jumped at the opportunity. I really like my job. I feel like I am making a difference in people's lives rather than just passing time in the fields."

"I couldn't believe it the first time you sent me a money order. The villagers were astounded. They couldn't stop talking about it for days. Everyone here seems so kind and hospitable. It's not at all what I envisioned."

"I know. That's because this is a re-education through labor camp. They are more humane than regular prisons. Most of the people here committed minor, nonviolent offenses."

"Perhaps, but I still think this place is exceptional. I doubt other re-education through labor camps are as civilized as this one."

After dinner, Weiluan left to check on some sick prisoners. He returned around 10 p.m. Later, in the middle of the night, he sneaked out and collected some vitamin injections, calcium, and glucose tablets for Duoxi and me. He saw that I had lost a lot of weight during the famine and was concerned about my health.

We spent what time we could together for the next several days. Both of us were elated to be reunited. After living so many years in desperation, having some relaxed, carefree time together as a couple provided a much-needed respite for both of us. Weiluan particularly treasured the time with Duoxi.

When my husband was working, I passed the time with the wife of the guard whose home we were staying in. She took me on a tour of the area. The camp was surrounded by lush, green hills, at the foot of which was this very fertile sweet potato farm. The prisoners were responsible for doing all of the farming. The main crop was sweet potatoes, but they also planted peanuts, beans, and vegetables. I had never seen such large sweet potatoes.

Even though Weiluan was locked behind bars, his life in Luozhou was much better than it was in Donghu at the time he left. There was more food to go around, his clothing was decent, and he had a job he enjoyed where he earned good money. Most importantly, he was treated respectfully, not like scum.

"I never would have guessed that your being imprisoned would turn out to be so fortuitous," I said one night.

"I know. I was so broken and desperate when I arrived. In fact, it has been very healing to be here. I just hate being away from you and the children."

Because the return journey would take three days, Duoxi and I had to depart after staying eight days in the camp. The night before we left, Weiluan gave me several things to take home.

"Fengxian, here are some vitamins and drugs in case you or the children become ill. I also want you to take this bed sheet and quilt because I know we only have one at home, and it's very old and tattered."

"But then you will be left with nothing to keep you warm at night."

"I'll be fine. Don't worry about me."

"I don't know if I should take the sheet and quilt. I feel like it's stealing. If this was discovered, it would be considered a very serious crime."

"Don't worry. If I thought it would be a problem, I wouldn't give them to you."

The next morning, I was so anxious about the stolen items I was carrying that I began to sweat every time we encountered someone. It was the first time in my life that I had ever stolen anything. I felt guilty and ashamed. If we hadn't been so desperate, I would have refused to take them.

I thanked the guard and his wife for their kindness and hospitality. Then Weiluan escorted Duoxi and me to the front gate where we said farewell. We had no idea when we would see each other again.

"Please tell my wonderful daughters that I am doing fine and that I miss them. I know the famine is severe right now, so it's imperative that you look after your own health as well as that of the children. Promise me you will take the vitamins I gave you."

"I promise. Don't worry about us. We will find a way to survive. Come home as soon as you can."

After another lengthy journey, Duoxi and I eventually arrived back in Donghu. My daughters bombarded me with questions as soon as I entered the house.

"How is father? … Is he okay? … Is he getting better? … How bad are the conditions there?"

"Your father is doing fine. He's very healthy. There is nothing to worry about."

The girls were ecstatic. They played with Duoxi as I unpacked. I took out the sheet, quilt, and vitamins Weiluan had given me and immediately instructed the girls to take some of the calcium pills.

When I returned to work the next day, everyone was eager to hear about what life was like in the camp. The villagers were stunned to learn how well the prisoners were treated. I'm sure other labor camps in China were more brutal, but fortunately Weiluan wasn't sent to any of them. To this day, I remain very thankful to the Communist Party leaders in Luozhou for fostering such a humane environment.

Devoured by Bedbugs

By the time I returned from my trip, winter had arrived. Everyone was busy wrapping up work in the fields. One evening after work, I noticed that Qisao was still out, so I knocked on the partition to speak with Mother-in-Law. I had yet to fill her in on my visit to Luozhou.

"Manpo, is that you?"

"Yes, Mother-in-Law."

"Did you see Manfu?"

"Yes. He's doing fine. He's very healthy. The living conditions at the labor camp are excellent. There is nothing for you to worry about."

"Thank God. I wish I could see him. I've been ill myself for several days, but no one here cares. Soon I will return to the place I came from."

"Mother, stay strong. Why don't you ask your son to come and see you? Since he's a doctor, maybe he can help you."

Mother-in-Law heeded my suggestion. The next day Sige came to check on her. By then, we were two years into the famine. Mother-in-Law was so malnourished and weak that Sige could tell immediately she wasn't going to survive. Word of Mother-in-Law's imminent death spread throughout the village. Many neighbors and relatives came to say a final goodbye. That afternoon I went to visit Mother-in-Law one last time. I sat beside her bed and held her hand.

"Manpo, thank you for everything. You are a good daughter-in-law. I am so sorry for wronging you in the past."

"It's okay. It's okay, Mother. Weiluan and I always knew it wasn't your intention."

Mother-in-Law wouldn't stop apologizing to me, which brought tears to my eyes.

"Manpo, can you please do me one last favor?"

"Of course. Please, tell me what you need."

"This bed is full of bugs. They have been feeding on me for weeks. They have almost gnawed me to death. Can you please get rid of them? They are driving me crazy. I don't have the strength."

I gently pulled away the blanket and discovered thousands of blood-filled bedbugs crawling everywhere on Mother-in-Law's body, the mattress, and the blanket. The bugs had stayed away from her face and hands, presumably because they were so emaciated. I was horrified and shrieked. Sige flew into a rage when he saw so many insects devouring his mother.

"Qisao, every month I give you money to look after my mother, and this is the kind of care you give her?"

"This is the first time I've seen any bedbugs," Qisao said, trying to defend herself. "Don't blame me. It must be that despicable woman, Fengxian, who brought the bugs here with her."

"That's ridiculous!" I replied. "It takes a very long time to accumulate this many bed bugs. This just goes to show how poorly you have been treating Mother-in-Law!"

Wanting to maintain the peace around Mother-in-Law's bedside, I quickly left. It broke my heart to think about how much Weiluan's mother was suffering. On top of being famished, ill, and weak, she had been enduring the bites of 10,000 bedbugs for who knows how long. It made my skin crawl. I knew she must have told Qisao, but Qisao ignored her. I couldn't believe it.

We were harvesting sugar cane in the fields a few days later when the leader of our production team announced that Mother-in-Law had died. The children and I immediately went to pay our respects to the body, which had already been placed in a coffin in the village's ancestral temple. The children and I knelt in front of the coffin for several minutes. I wept thinking about how much Mother-in-Law had suffered while living with Qisao and how Weiluan wouldn't be able to see his mother ever again. The next morning the entire family accompanied Mother-in-Law's body to her final resting place.

According to local tradition in Donghu, the family holds a feast after the burial to celebrate the life of their loved one. However, at the time I didn't have a cent to contribute to the meal because all of our money had been spent on my trip to Luozhou. As a result, neither I nor my children were invited to partake. The children couldn't sit still smelling the delicious food being served next door, so when I wasn't looking they ran outside and made a ruckus. When I went to drag them home, I encountered Sige, who had come out to investigate the noise.

"I apologize for the disturbance, Sige. My children are misbehaving because they are so famished. Please, can you give us some food?" Sige hated losing face, and I hoped that begging him for help in front of others would yield some food for the children.

"Go back home. I'll have some food sent to you later."

The children ran home and anxiously awaited the delivery. After an hour, Sisao finally brought us a bowl of turnip soup and a few slices of pork fat.

"This is all that's left. One small slice of pork fat for each of you. Nowadays, it's hard for anyone to get food. You should be very grateful for this. Weiluan is an unfilial son. He didn't contribute a cent to burying his mother. By rights, we don't need to give this food to you."

"I know," I said. "Thank you, Sisao."

The amount of food she brought was so miniscule that the children fought over the few turnip slices in the soup. I handed them some pieces of sugar cane to fill their stomachs, but they were still hungry. I recalled that the canteen was distributing sweet potato rations that day, so I rushed there before it closed.

"You're too late, Manpo," the cook said. "Nothing is left. Besides, you should have been eating to your heart's content today after the burial. You shouldn't be here asking for more food."

"The family wouldn't allow us to partake in the meal because we didn't contribute. Please, my children are so hungry that they won't stop crying and arguing."

The cook found a few small sweet potatoes and handed them to me.

That night after the children went to bed, I wrote Weiluan a letter notifying him about his mother's death. I didn't mention a word about the bedbugs because I knew it would break his heart.

"Your mother has passed away. I have done what is required to express our respects. You don't need to worry about her any-more. Now that she has died, it's useless to cry for her. There is one joy, and that is that Mother realized all of the hurtful things she had done to us and regretted them deeply. Now we know that blood is thicker than water and that the truth always emerges. Fengxian"

About a month later, I received a letter back from Weiluan inform-ing me that he had been approved to take a short leave of absence from the prison to pay his final respects to his mother. He would return soon for a brief visit. The children were overjoyed when they heard that their father would be back.

"When is he coming, Mother?"

"He didn't say. It's a long trip. We need to be patient. He's only coming back for a couple of days, then he must return to the camp."

A few days later around lunchtime, I heard some commotion on the path near our home. I went outside to investigate and saw Weiluan limping toward our house hauling two large bags over each shoulder. He grinned when he saw me. I waved at him to come sit down. The girls immediately raced to their father with a cup of tea.

Many villagers saw Weiluan on the road and followed him to our courtyard. The atmosphere was joyful and festive. The villagers bombarded him with questions about Luozhou.

"Manfu, if you hadn't tried to escape to Hong Kong, you surely would have died a long time ago," one of them said. "Only because you were arrested were you given the opportunity to work as a doctor. Now you have money and food. What a fortune in all the misfortunes!"

The villagers encouraged my husband to stay at the camp as long as possible. "Don't come back to Donghu. The famine here is very serious. You can see how emaciated all of us are. We are slowly starving to death. The canteen no longer has any food. The only things we have to eat are grass, leaves, and roots that we can find on the ground."

Weiluan could see how the villagers were suffering. He took pity on them. While everyone was present, he opened one of the large bags he had brought home. It was filled with dried slices of sweet potatoes. He distributed potato slices to everyone. All of them were grateful.

After the villagers left, Weiluan reached to the bottom of the bag and lifted out some rice. By that point, the famine was so severe that even people with money often weren't be able to eat rice because there was so little available. The children were so happy that they jumped up and down and clung to their father.

The next morning Weiluan purchased a 1.5 kg goose to pay tribute to his mother. He killed, cleaned, and cooked the goose. Then Weiluan and I took some of the goose's cooked liver to Mother-in-Law's tomb to nourish her spirit. Weiluan knelt in front of the tomb crying for a long time.

"Weiluan, mother knew you were a good, filial son. Now that you are here to see her, I know she must be happy. If you continue to be as sad as this, she will feel sad, too. Let's go home. The children are waiting for us."

Weiluan slowly stood up and dried his eyes. The children were eagerly waiting by the door when we arrived home. They were famished and couldn't wait to eat. That afternoon, we ate goose and rice to our heart's content.

The next morning Weiluan had to depart. We got up early, ate breakfast together, then I escorted him outside.

"You take care of yourself," I said.

"I'll be back for good next year, Fengxian. Look after yourself and the children."

Exodus

In 1961, the famine reached its apex in Donghu. The commune canteen closed down. Villagers were left to survive on what they could find scavenging, which was quickly diminishing. Weiluan had spent all of his salary and savings on his trip home, so I had no money to buy food. My children and I spent hours each day scouring the fields and mountains for knotgrass and other edible items. Knotgrass was brittle and pungent, but it was safe to eat. At that point, that's all that mattered. Whatever we found I brought home, cooked, and divided amongst the five of us to get us through another day.

Fortunately, we still had a few potato slices left from Weiluan's visit. I tried to stretch out the slices as long as possible, but after several weeks they turned moldy. I laid them out to dry on our roof. While we were away, some children stole the slices. When their parents found out, they came to our home to apologize.

"Manpo, our children just admitted to us that they stole some of your sweet potato slices. We're so sorry. We know we should compensate you, but we have nothing."

"That's okay. This is a difficult time for all of us. They are children. I understand."

Their children were even more emaciated than my own. I took pity on them and gave them a few more slices to take home.

By then, the only people in our area not reduced to skin and bones were those with connections to Communist Party officials, some of whom had access to the granaries and could secretly hoard food for their families, or people with relatives in Hong Kong who periodically sent money home. Only these two groups consistently had access to food, while the rest of us foraged the earth for anything we could find to survive.

Conditions across the country became so acute that the authorities moved millions of urban migrants back to rural areas to reduce the amount of food required to support the cities. Restrictions on emigration to Hong Kong also were eased. In the spring of 1962, the government opened several new border crossings into Hong Kong. Suddenly, droves of strangers appeared in Donghu. At first, we didn't know who these people were or where they were going. After speaking with a few of them, we learned that all of them were making their way to Hong Kong.

"If we stay here, we are destined to die," one of them muttered.

After three years of starvation, people were so distraught that they felt they had nothing to lose by trying to flee, even if it might land them in jail. Soon a mass exodus ensued. For weeks, hordes of people streamed south day and night toward Hong Kong. Many came from provinces in the north where conditions were much worse than in Donghu. How they mustered the physical wherewithal for such a long trek is a testament to human beings' will to survive.

The crowd consisted predominantly of young and middle-aged men interspersed with some women, children, and elderly people. Their bodies were emaciated, and their eyes were sunken, dark, and dazed. Many walked with nothing but the clothes on their backs.

Several villagers and members of our commune were inspired by these individuals and decided to join them. The most noteworthy person to leave Donghu was the leader of my production team. Conditions in our area had become so dire that even a politically well-connected person like himself saw escaping as the only source of hope for his family's future.

At the time, Zi was attending a nearby boarding school. She raced home one day afraid that we may abandon her.

"Some of my classmates have decided to flee to Hong Kong. They invited me to go with them. I don't want to leave all of you, and Father isn't back yet. I was afraid you might have left without me."

"Zi, don't worry. I would never leave you. All of us are awaiting your father's return later this year. No matter what happens, we won't leave. Don't worry."

I had no intention of going anywhere. In fact, I thought the more people exiting the country, the better, because it would leave more food for those of us who stayed behind.

The exodus caused so much upheaval in the southern part of the country and in Hong Kong that the government closed the border after a couple of months. Fleeing to Hong Kong again became illegal. The crowds of walkers thinned and eventually disappeared.

A few days before the 1962 summer Dragon Boat Festival, Weiluan appeared on our doorstep out of the blue dressed neatly and carrying a small bag. The children rushed to welcome him.

"Father, where are your big bags? Why didn't you bring us sweet potato slices this time? We're so hungry."

"The camp didn't have any sweet potato slices I could bring. However, there are a few pancakes and candies for you in here."

The children tore open his bag and divided what he brought home.

"I'm so glad you're back," I said. "Why didn't you write to notify me when you would be returning?"

"The date hadn't been set, and I didn't want to make you anxious. On my way here, I stopped in Gaoshui to see Sige. He's ill with typhoid fever. He told me that thousands of people had come through here in the spring trying to abscond to Hong Kong. Is that true?"

"Yes, for weeks there was a never-ending stream of people walking through here day and night. I've never seen anything like it. It truly was a mass exodus."

"Sige suggested I try to flee to Hong Kong again, but I told him I don't want to be away from you and the children any longer. It's not worth it."

We didn't have a morsel of proper food and Weiluan had spent all of his money on his trip, so we weren't able to hold a proper celebration for his return. Instead, I prepared a dish of knotgrass and other random items we had collected while scavenging. The next day Weiluan visited the commune leaders and explained that he had returned for good. They informed him that the old rules still applied and that his movements remained under restriction. He returned to work in the fields.

Later that year, Weiluan decided to make a go at working as an unlicensed doctor to supplement our income. One day, after finishing work in the fields, he sneaked away to Gaoshui to visit Sige at the pharmacy. He asked his brother to lend him some basic medical equipment and drugs. Sige was reluctant at first but eventually gave them to him.

From then on, during his spare time Weiluan sneaked from door-to-door treating villagers who had fallen ill. After a few people recovered, he earned a reputation as a good doctor whose prices were low and whose drugs were inexpensive. Weiluan only accepted money from people who could afford it. If they had no money, he treated them for free. The villagers admired this. Soon people came to our home seeking treatment.

Every night after we returned from the fields, he attended to patients while I made drug powders. Our financial situation finally began to improve. We were able to purchase rice when it was available. Occasionally, Weiluan gave us vitamin injections. After years of starvation, all of us remained severely malnourished. He even taught me how to give myself shots.

The more successful Weiluan's side business became, the more we wished he could get approval to pursue a formal doctor's license. However, because he had been declared a bad KMT element, we knew the government would never support him in such an endeavor. Although the Communist Party talked about "re-education" and "rehabilitation" for bad elements, in reality they were never permitted any true chance at redemption. Once a bad element, always a bad element. This absence of hope for a better future was another reason so many people risked their lives fleeing to Hong Kong.

The Four Cleanups

The famine created by the Great Leap Forward left the countryside in shambles. The inability of the communes to meet the basic needs of their members, along with widespread corruption among officials

— who often hoarded what limited food was available for their own families — eroded many villagers' belief that the government truly had their interests in mind. Most of the people who outlasted the famine endured because of their own grit and ingenuity. They survived in spite of the government, not because of it. Consequently, many villagers had less interest in contributing their energies to the commune.

One day some villagers were bullying a bad element when he responded with some comments that struck a chord with everyone.

"Ah yes, this Communist government is so wonderful! All of you speak as though you are better off than me, but look at yourselves. Your lives are just as bitter as mine. All of us are skin and bones. We are so malnourished that none of us can propagate any offspring. At night, families no longer have to lock their doors because no one possesses anything of value. Someday these officials will taste for themselves the bitterness they have created. That will be the biggest joke of all!"

His comments were so shrewd that the villagers were at a loss for words. "You know, he has a point," I overheard several people whisper afterward.

Recognizing that the Great Leap Forward had been a failure, the Communist Party changed course. New policies were rolled out to extricate our economy from the disastrous losses of the past few years. Communes were kept intact, but a small percentage of land was re-allocated to families as private plots. As before, we could use the plots to grow whatever we wanted for our own consumption. In addition, production teams within the communes were given more say over which crops could be planted, when, and where, rather than abiding by mandated plans and quotas. The canteens were closed permanently, and we switched back to a system where every family purchased food using work points. These reforms were largely successful, and soon harvests were on the rise.

While conditions were improving, some leaders were concerned that the Great Leap Forward famine could undermine faith in our country's socialist revolution. To address these concerns, a new campaign called the "Socialist Education Movement" was launched to reintroduce core socialist values such as the importance of the group over the individual, public property above private property, and the evils of capitalism.

Every week special study sessions were held to re-educate villagers about the core tenets of socialism. People were encouraged to "emulate Comrade Lei Feng," a humble farmer from my home province of Hunan whom the Communist Party upheld as a model citizen, and to "learn from Dazhai Commune" in Shanxi Province, which was held up as the epitome of agricultural collectivization. As a bad element family, we weren't invited to participate in the sessions. It was yet another example of how the government kept families like ours isolated and oppressed.

In tandem with the Socialist Education Movement, a campaign called the "Four Cleanups" was rolled out in the countryside to specifically address corruption among rural Communist Party cadres. Nothing threatened the reputation of the party more than the abuse of power by local officials. Corruption would have to be addressed head on if the Communist Party was to win back the hearts and minds of rural people. The Four Cleanups took aim at the principal areas of official malfeasance: the oversight of granaries, the management of accounts, the assignment of work points, and the accumulation of personal wealth.

The Four Cleanups never fully got off the ground in Donghu or many other areas because the officials responsible for implementing it either had close ties to the accused or were the accused themselves. Rather than subject themselves or their friends to harsh public criticism, local officials instead focused attention on the Socialist Education Movement. They quickly deflected the spotlight onto everyone in the past who had been identified as bad elements. People such as my husband.

The process of class struggle was resurrected. Multiple times a week, vicious struggle sessions were held, where villagers were encouraged to direct their years of frustration onto the bad elements. Soon a new wave of cruelty was unleashed against our family that was equal to, if not worse than, the decade before. Fortunately, the children and I were spared the nightmare of being put on display. However, neighbors, family, and friends frequently bullied and tormented us in public. We always accepted the criticism quietly and without argument. Bad element families who had survived the wrath of the 1950s had learned long ago that fighting back only instigated more fury.

During the Four Cleanups, landlords also encountered another wave of intense brutality. Qisao, in particular, was subjected to severe criticism and violence. Over the years, the villagers had watched Qisao's cruelty toward many people, particularly Weiluan's mother. Whenever she was put on display in struggle sessions, the villagers screamed at, spat on, and beat her. Qisao had endured similar struggle sessions during Land Reform, but the sessions held during the Four Cleanups were even more vehement.

Qisao finally broke under the pressure. One afternoon after a struggle session, she returned home and hanged herself from a rafter in her bedroom. When her son stumbled upon her body dangling from the ceiling, he raced to our home and pounded on the door. The loud noise made us jump.

"Uncle Manfu! Uncle Manfu! Please, help!"

"What's wrong, nephew?"

"Please help me. My mother hanged herself. Please help me take her down and revive her."

Weiluan ran next door with his nephew. The two of them loosened the noose and lowered Qisao's body to the ground. It was too late. I caught a glimpse of her body as they were covering it. I had never seen the corpse of someone who had been strangled. The sight was horrific. I felt bad about what happened, but part of me also felt that justice had finally been done. Good is rewarded with good and evil with evil.

Qisao's suicide did nothing to reduce the intensity of the movement. During one struggle session, the villagers viciously attacked Weiluan. Many people were envious of my husband's talents. The villagers accused Weiluan of being a "capitalist roader (走资派)" for running his own business. Being deemed a capitalist was a serious offence. The commune officials quickly took action and banned Weiluan from working as a doctor ever again.

Losing this side income pushed our family back into the abyss. Seeing to our daughters' education became increasingly difficult. We couldn't afford to continue to pay tuition for both Zi and Tian. Because Zi was older and closer to finishing school, we decided to continue to support her education. We sent Tian to a new school where she helped pay her own tuition by cutting grass and collecting firewood.

We had no choice but to live day-by-day and tackle each challenge as it arose. Both my husband and I clung to the belief that where there is life, there is hope. "As long as the hills are green, there will always be wood to burn (留得青山在, 不怕没柴烧)" is a common saying in China. We believed that one day we would emerge permanently from our difficulties. Nevertheless, it was hard not to get discouraged.

We were unwinding after work one evening when we received an unexpected visit from the son of a Communist Party army veteran.

"Please come in and sit down," Weiluan said. "What can we do for you?"

"Manfu, my father has become seriously ill. I'm here to ask you to treat him."

"I'm honored by your trust in my ability, but I've been banned from working as a doctor. I'm sorry, but I can't treat your father. I suggest you take him to a hospital."

"We've been to the hospital, but they were unable to help. Please, I beg you to help us. We have connections. I guarantee that you won't be punished."

"I'm sorry, but I can't. The Four Cleanups campaign is very intense right now. It's too risky."

The man shook his head and left in frustration.

"Is that the man from the family who turned their back on me when I collapsed in the field several years ago?" I asked. "I can't believe he would have the gall to come here and ask us for help."

"Yes, it is, but Fengxian you shouldn't dwell on the past. Just because others aren't good to us doesn't mean we shouldn't be good to them."

Weiluan was always much more forgiving than I was.

The man returned after a few hours. This time he sounded even more desperate. "Please, my father is getting worse. Now he's shivering all over. I beg you, please save him. I have money."

"It's not a matter of money. We are neighbors. I want to help, but I'm afraid of being punished."

"Weiluan, saving a person's life is a good deed," I said. "Don't worry about being punished."

"Thank you, Manpo," the man said.

"What are his symptoms, so I know what drugs to bring?"

"My father's hands and neck were bitten by rats. Now his lymph glands are bulging."

"Okay, you return home. I'll go on my own later so as not to attract attention."

A couple of hours later Weiluan returned from the man's house with a big grin and money in his hand.

"The man is a Communist Party cadre. He was sleeping in a haystack in front of the stove. His body was trembling violently, and he had a high fever. I gave him a shot of antibiotics to fight the toxins from the rats. I told his family not to worry and that he would get better soon. They thanked me, gave me some money, and promised not to tell anyone. Maybe it will be okay after all, and I won't get caught."

The next morning the son came to our home with a package of duck eggs.

"How is your father?" Weiluan asked. "You didn't need to spend money on these eggs. You already paid me last night."

"These eggs were laid by our own ducks. Please accept them. My father is doing much better now. He can sit and walk, and the swelling in his lymph glands has gone down. I think it would be good for him to get another injection. Will you come see him again?"

"Sure, I'll go later today."

"You really are a good, kind-hearted doctor. What a pity you aren't allowed to work full-time as a doctor. I appreciate your taking the risk to treat my father."

Weiluan returned home later that day with even more money in his hand than the night before. After that successful experience, my husband occasionally treated other people who came to our home seeking help as long as they promised to keep quiet.

Circle of Life

One day in the spring of 1964, Weiluan and I were relaxing in the family courtyard when Sisao rushed home from Gaoshui in a panic. She informed us that Sige had been diagnosed with throat cancer. She was more flustered than I had ever seen her. A diagnosis of cancer was considered a death sentence.

"I'll visit my brother tomorrow and see if I can be of any help," Weiluan said in shock.

"That's not necessary. My husband said he doesn't want anyone to see or touch him right now. All he wants is quiet and calm."

Sisao instructed one of her sons to fetch a shovel and dig up the ground in their living room.

"Perhaps she's digging for treasure!" Weiluan jokingly whispered to me. As soon as he finished his sentence, Sisao's son lifted two pouches out of the ground. One contained glittering gold jewelry, and the other was filled with silver dollars. Apparently, Sisao had succeeded in hiding some of her valuables from the land reform inspectors years earlier.

I shook my head when I saw the jewelry and coins. Weiluan and Sige had been born of the same parents, yet their lives couldn't have been more different. Even one silver dollar would have solved many of our problems. Sisao had an entire pouch full.

The next morning, Weiluan requested some time off to visit his brother. The team leader was accommodating. He was kinder and more understanding than our previous supervisor who had fled to Hong Kong. He allowed Weiluan to take an entire day off.

Sisao charged downstairs as soon as Weiluan arrived at the pharmacy.

"Manfu, I won't permit you to see your brother. I know you are only here to make matters worse. I know you covet this pharmacy. Don't think for a minute that my husband will leave the pharmacy to you when he dies. No way! Everything here belongs to me and my children. Leave here now and don't ever come back!"

"Sisao, I'm not here to ask for anything. I just want to see Sige and find out if there is any way I can be of help. Please let me see him one last time."

"Don't think for a minute that I believe that. I'm not stupid. Now get out!"

Weiluan returned home devastated. I was infuriated after he told me about their exchange.

"Doesn't she understand that if we were interested in the pharmacy we would have tried long ago to get our share? When a person is dying, it's important that he be given an opportunity to repent about his past wrongdoings. If he doesn't accomplish this, he won't be released from the sins he has committed. How can she not allow you to see your brother one last time?"

"I could tell from her attitude that she has no intention of allowing me to see Sige until he's dead."

"I don't think she will ever let you see him again, dead or alive. I doubt she will make any effort to even tell you when he dies."

Weiluan had difficulty accepting the fact that he was about to lose yet another family member without getting a chance to say goodbye. His father had committed suicide when he was just three years old, his beloved eighth sister had fled the country while he was in the army, and his mother died while he was imprisoned in Luozhou. Now he was on the verge of losing another immediate family member. He desperately wanted a chance to say goodbye, so a few days later he tried again to visit Sige.

"I'm really worried about him. Perhaps Sisao will let me see him if I beg her."

"She told you in no uncertain terms last time that you would never be allowed to see Sige."

"I know, but I must try one more time. Otherwise, I will regret it for the rest of my life."

My husband requested another half day off, which he was granted. His second visit to the pharmacy was no different than the first. The guard refused to allow him inside, and Sisao came to the door and cursed at him.

"You are an unfilial son!" Sisao said. "When your mother died, you didn't visit her, nor did you contribute any money to her funeral. Do you really think you have the ability to cure your brother's disease? Get out of here!" She slammed the door in my husband's face.

"Does he really have throat cancer?" Weiluan asked the guard.

"Yes. The doctors say it's incurable. He doesn't have many days left."

Weiluan shook his head and wept the entire way home. No matter how badly Sige had treated him in the past, he never let go of his love for his big brother. To this day, I have never met a more forgiving person than my husband.

Sige hung on a few more months but passed away that winter. Weiluan decided not to attend the funeral or the banquet afterward to avoid creating a scene with Sisao, who he knew wouldn't permit him to partake.

"Since your family treats you with such little regard, why do you care whether any of them live or die?" I asked. "In all of these years, what has anyone in your family done for you? Nothing. Not one thing! All they want is to see us in misery. How can you tolerate their bullying?"

"We are branches grown from the same root. Tolerance is the correct way for us to treat each other. Since we were born of the same mother, I hope our kinship will last forever. We must cherish kinship while we are still alive because the underworld is cold for everyone."

"I hope Sige is in the underworld," I said.

"Perhaps I was predestined to lose kinship with Sige. I can only accept what fate gives me. If something is set by fate, I can't change it. Alas, the deceased are deceased. Regardless of their previous transgressions, it's useless to mention them again. My brother is dead."

A few weeks after Sige passed away, we learned I was pregnant again. The news greatly boosted Weiluan's spirits. I had just turned 40, and we knew this was likely to be our final child. Weiluan and I embraced the idea of bringing a final life into the world, even though we remained penniless.

Several months later, we had just laid down to sleep after a tiring day when I went into labor. I shook my husband to wake him, but he was out cold. After a while, my daughters heard me groaning and managed to wake their father.

"Is the baby coming?" Weiluan asked in a daze.

"Yes. I need you to get a midwife."

"It's almost midnight. I doubt we'll be able to find anyone willing to come. Anyway, we don't have money to pay anyone. I will be the midwife."

"What? You can't be a midwife. Midwives are always women. How can a man be a midwife? Besides, you have never done this before."

"Who said that only women can be midwives? Human beings are the most omnipotent creatures in the world. As long as we have confidence, we can achieve anything. Have faith in me!"

My husband quickly boiled some water, sterilized his scissors, and carefully timed my contractions. After a couple of hours, I gave birth smoothly. It was early October of the lunar calendar. Weiluan cleaned and wrapped the baby, cut the umbilical cord, and tidied everything in an orderly manner.

"Is it a boy?" I asked after a few minutes. I suspected it wasn't, or he would have had a stronger reaction when the baby came out.

"Boys and girls are all human beings. Don't focus too much on this." I knew from his reply that it was a girl.

The next morning Weiluan was required to take the baby to the hospital to get a birth certificate, but before doing so, we had to name her.

"This little one is very mild, pure, and beautiful," he said. "Let's call her Aijiao."

"That's a great name," I said. Aijiao, or Ai (Ī) for short, means amiable and kind.

Weiluan took Ai to the hospital after I breastfed her. Many neighbors stopped him along the way to look at our new baby.

"Wow! She's so beautiful. She doesn't look like a baby born to such a destitute family. Manfu, you must have injected Fengxian with supplements, right?"

Weiluan nodded yes.

"Who was the midwife?" one person asked.

Weiluan smiled and remained silent, but they kept asking.

"We were too poor to invite a midwife, so I helped my wife deliver the baby."

"Wow! You are a capable man. You are absolutely qualified to do so."

When Weiluan arrived at the hospital, he explained to the staff that Ai had been born the night before and that we needed a birth certificate issued.

"Let me see the paper given to you by the midwife."

"As I said, there was no midwife. We don't have a paper."

"A baby can't be born without a midwife. Someone must have cut the umbilical cord. Who cut the cord?"

"It was the middle of the night. It was too late to invite a midwife. I did it myself. I used to work as a doctor."

"What? You did it yourself? Were the scissors sterilized? Quick, show us the baby's navel. I hope there's no infection. Otherwise, you will be punished."

The doctor carefully inspected Ai.

"You did an excellent job for someone who hasn't done this before. Still, we can't issue the birth certificate until you pay the fee that's usually included in the cost of the midwife."

"Why do we need to pay the fee if the baby has already been born?"

"No matter who the midwife is, the same fee must be paid. If everyone did the same as you had done, many babies might be harmed. This is a mandatory charge to ensure that people hire licensed midwives."

Weiluan had no choice but to use some of the little money we had to pay for the birth certificate.

After the villagers learned that my husband had helped deliver Ai, more people sneaked to our home to be treated by him. Weiluan would only treat people he was confident would keep it secret. With seven mouths to feed, these occasional visits gave us just enough money to continue scraping by.

Descent into Chaos

By 1965, the countryside had recovered much of the ground that had been lost during the Great Leap Forward famine. Food reserves had been replenished, and previously emaciated bodies swelled with new life. The policies that led to this turnaround represented a retreat from collectivization. The success of the reforms contrasted sharply with the disaster of the communes, reinforcing doubts among many people about our country's communist path.

In this climate, keeping socialist values alive became increasingly challenging. Alarmed at how rapidly socialist policies were being undone in other countries, Chairman Mao was determined to prevent a similar outcome in China. In order for our country to avoid becoming infected by capitalism, he believed that the leadership of the Communist Party needed to be cleansed, works of art and literature infused with a more powerful socialist message, and citizens and party members galvanized with new revolutionary fervor. Recognizing that party cadres and bureaucrats couldn't be relied upon to attack party leaders, Chairman Mao turned to the army, his wife, and students to undertake his offensive.

In 1966, the Great Proletarian Cultural Revolution was launched. University and high school students were urged to rise up, become the vanguard of a new revolution, and attack the "four olds" holding back our society — old customs, old habits, old culture, and old ideas. Millions of students responded fervently to the plea by donning red arm bands and calling themselves "Red Guards" of the revolution. Squads of these students terrorized cities and villages across our country. They demolished old temples, churches, and museums, and held massive bonfires of books and precious art work. Countless government officials, teachers, intellectuals, and bad elements were dragged by Red Guards into the streets where they were publicly assaulted and humiliated for their "counter-revolutionary" ways. These victims often were beaten and tortured, and many people died.

The Red Guards even attacked senior Communist Party leaders in Chairman Mao's inner circle after he called on students to "bombard the headquarters." Numerous senior officials, including our future leader Deng Xiaoping and Mao's then number two in command Liu Shaoqi, were stripped of their posts, incarcerated, and put on display at mass rallies on the grounds that they had betrayed the socialist revolution and "taken the capitalist road."

The Cultural Revolution sparked so much chaos everywhere that schools, businesses, and government offices were closed across the country. Some areas even plunged into semi-civil war as bands of Red Guards and other groups battled to fill the power vacuum.

The pandemonium reached our quiet village of Donghu in the fall of 1966. In order to earn money, Weiluan often took advantage of the downtime during our lunch breaks to sneak behind the backs of our supervisors and tend to sick villagers. One day during lunch he raced off with his medical kit but neglected to take any food with him.

"You forgot your lunch," I said, running after him. "These are our last sweet potatoes. Don't work too hard."

"Thank you, Fengxian. I won't be gone too long."

When I returned home, I was surprised to discover Zi home from school. She had recently passed the medical test to enter university and was preparing for the college entrance exam. She was hunched over in the corner crying.

"Zi, what are you doing home? Today is a school day. What's wrong?"

"All classes have been cancelled. The entire school has been shut down."

"What? Why?"

"The school received a notice from the government ordering it to close immediately. The Communist Party has launched a new campaign called the Cultural Revolution. All schools in the country have been shut so students can participate. The college entrance exam has been cancelled. I'm afraid my dream of attending university may remain just a dream."

"When did they say the school would re-open?"

"They said they had no idea. It's been closed indefinitely."

My heart sank. Weiluan and I had pinned so many dreams on Zi attending college. We hoped that after she graduated she would be able to get a good job, earn a stable salary, and help lift our family out of destitution. Had all of our hard work been for naught?

Zi relayed the bad news when Weiluan returned. My husband was so shocked that he collapsed onto the floor. The girls and I had to help him to bed. All of us felt disappointed and frustrated.

"God," I said, shaking my head in tears, "why do you continue to allow so much misfortune to fall upon our family? Will you ever bestow any good luck on us? We are slowly dying. Can't you see that? Do you even care?" No matter how hard Weiluan and I worked, we never seemed to be able to get ahead. Now our one bright hope for the future was at risk of being snatched away.

After half an hour, Weiluan regained his composure and came out to join us.

"Fengxian," he said, "you are a wonderful wife. Children, you are such good kids. All of your suffering is my fault. Don't worry. I will find a way to provide for us. Fengxian, go purchase some food for lunch." He handed me a few cents. The children's faces lit up when they heard that I was going to buy food. I rushed to the neighborhood tofu vendor.

"Manpo, haven't you eaten lunch yet?" she asked. "It's almost time to return to work."

I raced home, hurriedly prepared the tofu and rice, then all of us sat down and ate lunch together. It was a brief moment of happiness amidst the bitterness.

We returned to the fields when our lunch break was over. The moment the production team leader caught sight of my husband and me, he approached us.

"Manfu, you and the other bad elements have been ordered to do mandatory hard labor for the rest of the afternoon. As usual, you will receive no compensation or points for the work. Go join the others."

"Manpo," he said turning toward me, "we just received a notice from the government announcing that the Cultural Revolution has been launched across the country."

"What's the Cultural Revolution?" I asked innocently. I had never heard the term until Zi mentioned it earlier that day. He gave me no explanation.

"You stupid Hunan woman. You must have seen that Zi returned from school today."

"Yes, I saw her during lunch."

"Well," he said and laughed, "then you must know that all schools in the country have been shut down. It looks like all of your family's efforts to educate Zi have been in vain. We told you it was useless for a bad element family to send their daughters to school. All of your hard work and money have gone to waste."

I was annoyed but shrugged off the comments and began to walk away.

"Where do you think you're going?"

"I'm going to join my team."

"You don't work on this team anymore. You have been re-assigned to the bad element brigade. From now on, you will fetch and distribute dung with the family members of landlords and other bad elements."

Until then, the Communist Party had focused its attention on Wei-luan because he was the one who had been associated with the KMT. The children and I had been largely spared from official persecution, although the villagers often bullied and harassed us in private. Now suddenly everything had changed. At that moment, I knew that the Cultural Revolution was going to be unlike any previous campaign. I took a deep breath and went to join my new team.

When we arrived home from the fields that evening, Zi had some news to lift our spirits.

"While you were at work, I learned that several of the teachers and students from my high school are planning to travel to Beijing. Everyone is eager to respond to Chairman Mao's call to unite with other youths and show our support for the new Cultural Revolution. I really want to go with them. Is that okay? The teachers say that we can prepare for the college entrance exam when we return."

"Such a campaign is important for the development of our nation," Weiluan replied. "Of course, we will support your going. What do you need?"

"Chairman Mao has declared that all rail transportation for students will be free, so all I need is a little bit of travel money and some food."

"No problem," he said.

"No problem?" I asked. "We barely have a cent right now. Where are we going to get money and food for Zi to go on such a long trip?"

"I will take some of our recently harvested food to the commune and sell it."

"But we need that food from our private plot for ourselves, so we don't starve."

"Zi's education is more important. Don't you want to see your daughter get a higher education? For years, we have worked day and night to send our children to school. We can't squander this opportunity."

I also desperately wanted Zi to go to college, so I decided to stop arguing with him. A couple of days later, she left with her classmates. We expected her to be gone for a few months, but she surprised us by returning in just a few weeks. When the villagers saw that Zi was back, they flocked to our home to hear about her trip. It was extremely rare for anyone in Donghu to travel so far.

"Tiananmen Square is vast and grand," Zi said. "It was packed with people and red flags fluttering in the wind. Megaphones blared throughout the square. Teachers led students in chanting, 'Long Live the Communist Party.' It was so loud that we couldn't hear what people were talking about. The journey there was long and difficult. So many people were making their way to the capital that it took us forever to get there. We wound up staying only one day and one night in Beijing before heading home."

"Did you see Chairman Mao in Tiananmen Square?" Weiluan asked.

"Of course. Chairman Mao's wife, Jiang Qing, delivered a speech, but we couldn't hear a word she was saying because it was so crowded and noisy."

Weiluan inquired about college after the villagers left.

"Our teachers say there is still hope that we will be able to attend university. They instructed us to return to campus tomorrow, so we can prepare for the college entrance exams."

"That's wonderful. I have pinned all of my hopes on you, Zi," Weiluan said. "I really want to see you attend university."

"I know, Dad. I saw how you collapsed when you heard that my school was closed. You and Mom have spent a lot of energy and money on my education. I won't let you down. I will never forget what you have done for me."

The next day Zi returned to school. Weiluan and I remained hopeful that she would still have a bright future. Neither of us foresaw what was about to transpire. Our entire country was descending into what is referred to today as "the ten years of chaos." The turmoil would become so deep and protracted that it would bring all civic life to a standstill for a decade.

Shortly after Zi returned to school, the full intensity of the Cultural Revolution was unleashed in Donghu. One morning our production team leader called everyone together and made an announcement.

"A new band of Red Guards, consisting of youths from poor peasant families in several local villages, has been formed to promote the advancement of the Cultural Revolution in our area. To kick off their activities, a struggle session against counter-revolutionaries is going to be held later today. All bad elements and their adult family members are required to attend." He turned and looked at me. "That includes you, Manpo."

Over the years, Weiluan had attended numerous struggle sessions, but I had never been to any. The stories I had heard about them were horrific. I felt anxious.

"Why do you think they want me to attend?" I asked Weiluan later that morning. "I'm really scared."

"Fengxian, it's no use being afraid. You have no choice but to attend. Think of it as an opportunity to see what a struggle session is like."

The session was held on a large stretch of grass next to the fields, where most of the meetings of our production team were held. The lawn was packed when we arrived. Most of the spectators consisted of destitute farmers. All of the bad elements and their family members were huddled together at the far end of the field. My husband and I joined them. The session began with a few brief comments from the village leaders.

"Bad elements are detrimental to the Communist Party," said the last of the leaders to speak. "They are disrespectful of Chairman Mao. They are harmful to the Chinese people." Then he turned and looked straight at my husband. "Bring out Han Manfu, the counter-revolutionary, bad KMT element!"

Two Red Guards grabbed my husband and shoved him in front of the crowd. "Kneel!" the leader commanded him before stepping back and allowing the crowd to take over. Dozens of villagers scurried up to my husband and screamed at him. Their viciousness was like nothing I had ever witnessed.

"Manfu is a capitalist!" they yelled. "He has been working a long time as an unlicensed doctor … He charged exorbitant rates and exploited ill people … He struck a fortune by sucking the blood of the Chinese people … He is disobedient toward the Communist Party and an enemy of the people … Down with him!"

The Red Guards standing next to my husband punched his head and kicked his body. I could do nothing but stand there helplessly in silence. I watched as my husband gritted his teeth and struggled to hold himself upright. The beating went on and on until he collapsed on the ground.

Satisfied that they had "struggled" sufficiently against my husband, the Red Guards turned and looked for their next victim. "Drag out big landlord Wang!" the crowd yelled. "He is colluding with counter-revolutionaries to sabotage the Communist Party … He is a spy!"

The Red Guards beat the landlord even more severely than Weiluan. At one point, foam seeped from Wang's mouth, yet they continued to beat him. I could see how much pain he was in. Tears streamed from his eyes, but the Red Guards showed him no mercy. Instead, they intensified their attack.

"Have we wronged you?" they asked Wang sardonically.

"Continue to beat him!" the crowd screamed.

The session went on like this until several bad elements had been beaten half to death. As a finale, the Red Guards hung signs with disparaging remarks around the necks of the bad elements and instructed them to put on tall dunce caps. Then the bad elements were paraded through the village and ordered to say over and over: "I am a bad element, a counter-revolutionary, a ghost, and a monster." At the end of the spectacle, the Red Guards beat them again, after which everyone was finally allowed to leave.

Weiluan could barely say a word when he arrived home. He went straight to our bed to rest. He had been back only a few minutes when the Red Guards came to our home and pounded on the door. I nervously opened it.

"We are here to search for counter-revolutionary contraband," they announced.

I dared not say a word and quietly stood aside. They confiscated all of the medical equipment and drugs they could find. When they discovered a small prayer niche to our ancestors and Buddha in the attic, they knocked it over and stomped on the candles, incense, and ancestral tablets. The Communist Party was vehemently against all religion, which they considered "an opium of the people." They believed religion was a tool used by the rich, exploiting classes to keep the poor oppressed.

"We expected to find more contraband," one of the Red Guards said to me on his way out our door. "We didn't realize your family was so poor."

"Well, we are, believe it or not," I replied flatly.

I watched in dismay as the youngsters scurried out of our courtyard on an adrenaline high shouting slogan after slogan: "Down with intellectuals and rightists! Down with capitalist roaders!" When they encountered an elderly man on the road, they shoved him into the fields and shouted, "You old counter-revolutionary! Down with ghosts and monsters!" Later the Red Guards visited all of the local temples and smashed their contents to pieces.

For thousands of years, Chinese children had been raised to treat their elders and history with reverence. Now these youths were treating every adult and historical artifact they encountered with disdain and violence. They had no qualms about beating their elders or destroying our country's precious culture. Was this where "destroy the four olds" was leading us? Who gave these youngsters the authority to wreak so much havoc? The way in which the local officials stepped aside and ceded authority to the Red Guards unnerved me. What benefit could possibly come from making life so chaotic? If farm work was superseded by politics, we would surely have another famine. Everyone in the village was upset about what was happening and harbored such thoughts. But no one dared to utter a word.

The next day the Red Guards unleashed their reign of terror in the fields. Both Weiluan and I had been doing hard labor for years. For that reason, we thought life couldn't get much worse for us on that front. We were wrong. Although our tasks remained the same, we were subjected to constant psychological harassment that raised the emotional intensity of our work to an almost unbearable level. Every second someone stood watch over us, barking out commands and berating us whenever we made a mistake or did something that annoyed them. We didn't dare disobey a word they said. If they told us to jump, we jumped. If they told us to work faster, we worked faster. If we didn't obey, we were beaten and faced worse abuse. Submission was the only path of survival.

Although I was now lumped in with other bad elements, I continued to be treated much less harshly than Weiluan. The brutality inflicted upon my husband during this period was more intense than anything he had previously encountered. After doing back-breaking work and listening to disparaging remarks all day, at night he was forced to stay awake and write self-criticism essays and letters of repentance for his past association with the KMT. Sometimes the Red Guards came in the middle of the night and dragged him away for lengthy interrogation sessions. The stress drained what little life Weiluan had left after each day. Soon he became so exhausted and frail that he resembled a walking corpse.

Occasionally, my husband found shelter under the protection of the old Communist Party army veteran whom Weiluan had secretly treated while he was working as an unlicensed doctor. Whenever the veteran was present during one of Weiluan's beatings, he quickly intervened to end it. On occasions when the veteran was distributing food, he gave my husband a little bit more than the other bad elements. Both of us were grateful for his protection and care.

However, no one else in the village showed us any sympathy. The merciless treatment we received from the Red Guards was matched by the villagers. We were subjected to harassment 24 hours a day. Some people mocked us out of callousness, while others did so to make themselves look good in front of the Red Guards.

When the Red Guards weren't busy tormenting bad elements, they passed their time painting revolutionary slogans on the sides of buildings and homes across the area, such as "Smash Anything that Doesn't Conform with Mao Zedong Thought," "Never Forget Class Struggle," and "Sweep Away All Monsters and Demons."

One evening, after we arrived home from the fields, we were shocked to discover the characters "Counter-revolutionary Family" painted in large, black characters across our front door. I could accept the fact that Weiluan had been deemed a counter-revolutionary, but that our children now were also labeled that enraged me. We were a good family. I was so incensed that I stood frozen in the courtyard, unable to take my eyes off our door.

"Fengxian, stop staring at what they wrote," Weiluan said. "They are just words. Let them write what they want. What's the point of getting upset?"

After it turned dark, I sneaked outside and tried to scrub the characters off, but they had penetrated the wood too deeply. Weiluan came out to get me as soon as he heard me outside.

"Fengxian, you must stop this! If you succeed in removing these characters, the Red Guards will brutally beat you for it. I cannot bear the thought of you being assaulted. Do you think you can wash off the evil in their hearts? Be magnanimous. If you need to vent your anger, then spit. But don't do anything that will invite more trouble. We will have a better life in the future."

"Okay, don't worry. You're right. I won't do anything stupid like this again." I followed my husband inside and told myself to be patient. Still, every time I saw the characters I felt like a knife was cutting my heart.

As the weeks passed, we prayed that the Red Guards' fervor would mellow and life would return to normal, but it didn't. Schools remained closed, every temple in the area had been destroyed, and our peaceful days in the fields had been replaced with constant, raucous criticism and harassment. All villagers lived under constant fear that at any moment anything they said could be misconstrued as counter-revolutionary. Then, like us, they and their families would be condemned to a life of torment and abuse. The Cultural Revolution had taken Donghu and our entire country hostage. How much more terror and chaos could we withstand?

Selling a Daughter to Save a Father

The combination of malnutrition, hard labor, ferocious beatings, and incessant psychological abuse eventually became too much for Weiluan to handle. Day by day, he became more exhausted and weak. I could see that my husband was on a path toward death and didn't know what to do.

One morning the leader of our production team came to our home to inform Weiluan that he had been assigned to a new project involving hard labor. By then, my husband was so feeble that he could no longer get out of bed. I got on my knees and begged the team leader to show our family some mercy.

"My husband is sick. He can barely move, let alone do heavy work. You can see the desperate situation we are in. Please, please don't force Weiluan to work. Otherwise, he will die."

This supervisor was much more understanding than his predecessor. He agreed to allow my husband to stay home as long as necessary until he recovered. I thanked him profusely.

I naively believed that all Weiluan needed was some rest and he would feel better. But after several days, I could see that his condition was much more serious. He was severely malnourished. Without nutrition, no amount of rest would revive him.

One day Zi returned from school for a surprise visit. Although classes had yet to restart, most students continued to live at the dorm. She was shocked by her father's condition.

"Mom, why is Dad so unwell?" she asked.

Weiluan had repeatedly instructed me not to tell the children about the beatings he received during struggle sessions or the harassment he endured in the fields.

"Zi, your father has been doing very heavy labor. The small amount of food we have is barely sufficient to sustain him. Between no food and hard labor, even an iron man will fall. Tian has been collecting and selling firewood to earn some extra money, and Mei frequently goes scavenging for food. But we have many mouths to feed. It's simply not enough."

Later that day Zi and Tian were searching for food in the mountains when they auspiciously stumbled upon a dead calf that had fallen into a pit. A few weeks later the children were out scavenging for food again when they came across another discovery in the mountains. Hidden beneath some tall grass and twigs was a large bag full of bread, meat, fish, noodles, candy, a water bottle, and some men's clothes.

All of us were elated at the girls' discoveries, but the spoils didn't last long. When the cold weather arrived that winter, Weiluan's illness worsened. I worried that he wouldn't be able to survive. Everyone has a breaking point, and my husband was nearing his.

I was pondering a way out of our predicament when a woman from our production team named Zoupo (Zō-pō) came to our home and suggested a dreadful solution: that I sell one of my daughters to get the money to treat Weiluan. Throughout Chinese history, it had been common for poor families to sell their daughters when they encountered financial difficulty. But I never dreamed that one day I would face such a situation. (The difference between selling a daughter and a more traditional arranged marriage is that the latter typically involved the bride's parents paying a dowry to the groom and his family. The Communist Party banned both when it came to power, but they continued to be practiced in the countryside.)

"Your family is too poor and weak to go on like this," Zoupo said. "You must come up with a solution to save your husband."

"I know. Thank you for your concern," I said curtly, hoping that she would see through my abruptness and leave. I had no interest in selling one of my children.

"I sold my daughter to a family in nearby Keluo (Kǔ-lwō) County," she said. "It's a well-to-do area. They cultivate sugar cane there. The groom's family gave us a large amount of sugar as a betrothal gift." She reached into her bag. "Here, take this small slab. Give some to your husband. Maybe it will give him some energy. I can help you find a good family for your daughter. It's not like you'd be selling her to a brothel. Think about my offer."

"Thank you. We'll consider it," I said as she left.

Had our lives really come to this? The rest of the day my mind raced through scenario after scenario about what might happen if we sold one of our daughters. Would any man even be willing to marry the daughter of a counter-revolutionary, bad element? If such a man existed, surely he himself would have questionable character. I could be condemning my daughter to a life of torment. As a youngster, I fought intensely against my own parents' betrothal of me to Cong. Selling one of our daughters for financial gain arguably was even worse. Yet I had to do something to save Weiluan.

Zi was still away from home preparing for the college entrance exams. If we were to sell one of our daughters, it would have to be Tian, who had just turned 20. Tian had endured so much hardship with us. I cringed at the thought of forcing her into a possibly worse situation.

I informed Weiluan about the proposal, but he was too weak to give a response. In our hearts, both of us knew Zoupo was right. We hated treating Tian as a commodity to be traded, but selling her was our only option if we wanted to save Weiluan's life. Seeing how weak my husband was, I knew the decision rested on my shoulders. I would have to choose between condemning my daughter or rescuing my husband.

A few days later Zoupo returned to see if we had made a decision. "Tian is already of marriageable age. She will have to get married at some point. Why not now? Do you really want her to endure more starvation and wait here for death with you?"

"I know," I replied quietly. I closed my eyes and took a deep breath.

"Why not marry off one of your daughters to help relieve your burden?"

"Okay, okay!" I blurted out in frustration. "I don't want to talk about this anymore. Just tell me where she would be going if we agreed to sell her. What kind of family is it? What's the name of the husband-to-be?"

"No one has been selected yet. I will notify the matchmaker in Keluo who made the match for my daughter. Life there is much better than in Donghu. They eat three meals of rice a day and often eat fish and pork. Their clothes are also decent. It's very difficult to find such a place. I'm so happy with the arrangement of my first daughter that I intend to sell my second daughter to a family in the same county."

That evening I discussed our decision with Tian. I knew she would be upset and hurt. I just hoped she would capitulate.

"Your father and I are useless parents. We've been unable to give any of you a better life. All we've done is make you suffer poverty and condemnation with us. Now we are facing even worse anguish under the Cultural Revolution. Tian, if you want to change this miserable life of yours, you must recognize this fact and seize the opportunity to leave this wretched family. Look at the four bare walls in this house. We have nothing. Your father is bedridden and on the verge of death. Your mother faces constant abuse and harassment. The well-being of your siblings also is precarious. The only way to preserve this family is to sell you in exchange for some food and money. Believe me, I hate the idea of doing this, but we have no other choice."

"Why don't you sell Zi?" Tian asked in tears. "She's older than I am and better educated. Why are you always so partial toward her?"

"Your father and I aren't partial toward Zi. But she's away from home right now. She has a chance of attending college, getting a job, and helping your father and me pull the family out of poverty. We can't lose that. I'm sorry if we have hurt you in any way. One day we will also marry off Zi, as we are doing with you. Maybe you will both be able to marry into families in the same village. Then you can visit each other frequently and won't feel alone."

Tian was silent and stared at the floor.

"By marrying, you can escape this miserable life here with us. You won't have to endure starvation anymore. People often say that knowing how to adapt and make changes is more important than being born into a good family. Well, the time has come for you to make some changes."

Tian nodded silently in consent. The two of us sat there quietly for several minutes crying.

The next day I told Zoupo to contact the matchmaker in Keluo. "You must find a good family for her. Otherwise, I will not sell Tian even if the entire family starves to death."

"I know how you feel," she said. "The only reason I sold my own daughter was because of poverty. If selling Tian can help solve some of your family's problems, don't think too much about other things. Let her go."

A few weeks later Weiluan's condition worsened. We needed to purchase some medicine for him, but we had no money. I went to Zoupo's house to see if she could lend us one yuan. She gave me the money and informed me that her counterpart in Keluo had identified a possible match for Tian. The family, surnamed Zhao, were members of the poor peasant class and therefore received a lot of preferential treatment from the Communist Party. The young man in mind was their eldest child. He was already working as a Communist Party cadre in his production team.

"Weiluan has been officially classified a bad KMT element and counter-revolutionary," I said. "We dare not marry Tian to a Communist Party cadre."

"Don't worry, it's no big deal," she said. "Even though he's a cadre, he's still a farmer. Having a wife would be a blessing."

"Did you tell him everything about our family situation?"

"Of course, after hearing about your daughter and your family, his parents were very interested. They asked the matchmaker to bring you and your daughter to visit, so the family can decide whether they want to purchase Tian or not."

Tian and I requested a few days of leave from the production team. Before we left, I made a new set of clothes for her using the cotton lining of Duoxi's winter garments. I wanted her to be presentable when we met the Zhaos.

A few days later Zoupo escorted us to Keluo. After two lengthy boat rides, we finally reached the village. The land was flat and imparted a sense of openness and freedom.

As soon as we arrived at the Zhao home, we were swarmed by villagers and family members who had come to size up my daughter and me. Everyone in the family appeared healthy and strong. They were dressed in clothes similar to ours, which gave me peace of mind.

After exchanging greetings, the potential groom, Hong (Hōng), served Tian and me a cup of tea. He was a gentleman and handsome. He said a few words to Tian and then shyly walked away. I could tell he was nervous. On several occasions, I saw him sneaking glances at Tian. He seemed pleased.

We stayed with the Zhaos two nights. During this time, the family prepared several elaborate meals for us. They invited us to stay longer, but I was worried about Weiluan and my other children. Before we left, the Zhaos gave us several gifts, including fish, pork, sugar, and ration coupons as well as the money for the journey home. Hong carried the gifts to the dock and placed them on the ship.

When the villagers in Donghu saw the armfuls of items that Tian and I were carrying, they were curious and followed us home. As soon as I arrived, I checked on Weiluan. Then I went to the courtyard and updated the villagers on our trip. I offered each of them some sugar. Most of them had never tasted processed sugar and were very appreciative.

"Manpo, you and Manfu are very fortunate and capable. You have suffered a great deal for many years. Now your daughters have finally grown up. You are selling Tian for a good price. Plus you still have three other daughters to marry. Then you will get even more food and money, which you can use to help Duoxi get a good wife," they said.

"If it wasn't for your encouragement, we never would have agreed to sell Tian," I said. "Now we have received a lot of food to help us through our difficulties."

I sat by Weiluan's bedside after the villagers left. I gave him some sugar to eat and relayed every detail about the visit. The sugar gave him just enough of a boost to speak.

"For 20 years," Weiluan said with a weak voice, "with sweat and tears, I raised Tian. Now she must bear this burden for us. It's all my fault. We couldn't give her a good life. Instead, we had to make her suffer with us. Now we must sell her in order to save me. I feel so bad."

"It's a good family and a good match," I said, trying to comfort him. "We are selling her into a good situation. Now we have food to eat to our heart's content. Everything will work out in the end."

The root of Weiluan's illness was malnourishment. He began to regain his strength after a few days of hearty meals. About a week after our trip, Zoupo informed us that Hong wanted to visit us in Donghu. If the visit went well, he intended to take Tian with him to Keluo. Knowing that our daughter would soon be leaving us made me sad and depressed, but it was too late to back out. We had already accepted and eaten the Zhao's food. All I could do is pray that they would be a happy couple.

Several days later Hong and Zoupo arrived at our home. They brought with them additional food and sugar. Weiluan and Hong got along well. Many villagers came to pass inspection on the young man. Some of them pulled me aside and advised me not to allow Tian to marry him. "Tian can do better."

I responded with a slight nod to acknowledge their remarks and then looked away to avoid continuing the conversation. I thought Hong was a good fit for my daughter. His family was friendly, he treated Tian kindly, and he was a production team leader. He also accepted Weiluan's bad element status. When I looked up, I saw Hong gazing at me with a look of dejection. I knew immediately that he had overheard the remarks.

"Hong, don't worry," I assured him. "We won't listen to other people's gossip and go back on our word. Tian will be your wife. However, you must agree to some preconditions." As I spoke to him, I recalled the day after my own wedding more than 20 years earlier when my mother had asked Weiluan to promise to look after me. In the end, all of Mother's worst fears had come true, but Weiluan had tried his best.

"Of course. I'll agree to anything."

"First, you must be good to Tian. You must love and care for each other for the rest of your lives. Second, she is a stranger in your hometown. Please keep this in mind and be considerate toward her. Last, we are selling Tian for the sole reason that we are penniless and desperate. Families who want to save face often won't admit that they are selling their daughters for food. For us, I can tell you honestly that we are selling Tian for food. We hope that the money you give us will be enough to put food on the table, pay off our debts, and restore my husband's health. Will you meet these requirements?"

"Yes, your demands are reasonable and justified. I will meet all of them. And if you run into difficulties in the future, I will also do my utmost to help you. You don't need to worry."

I spoke to Tian a final time to see if she had any objections. She and Hong had hit it off from the start. She was no longer against the marriage, which eased my mind considerably. I informed Zoupo that we would proceed.

"It's done!" Zoupo announced to everyone. "Hong and Tian will marry. This union will be beneficial for both families. For the Han family, it will give you a means of survival. For Hong, he will receive a good wife and enjoy life-long happiness. It's truly perfect. Don't forget this matchmaker!"

That afternoon, we bade farewell to Tian in the courtyard. "Goodbye, my precious daughter," I told her with tear-filled eyes. "I'm going to miss you so much."

"Don't cry Mother. I'll be back to see you often."

"Don't worry," Hong said. "I will take good care of Tian."

Tian climbed onto the back rack of Hong's bicycle, and the two of them rode away. I was happy for them, but felt heart-broken that Tian would no longer be with us every day.

"Fengxian, don't be sad," Weiluan said. "Our daughter has married a good man. She will no longer have to starve every day with us."

"I know. I'm just going to miss her. That's all."

Shortly after Tian arrived in Keluo, Hong's parents held an official wedding for the couple at their home. Neither Weiluan nor I were able to get time off work to attend. Tian periodically wrote us letters updating us on how things were going. She sounded happy. In one letter, she informed us that they would return to Donghu in a few weeks' time to hold a wedding banquet.

The couple arrived in August with armfuls of food and a pocketful of money. Hong handed Weiluan two wads of cash. "This money is to pay for Tian's hand and to help you repay what you owe the production team. And this money here is for you to host a wedding feast for your relatives and friends."

"Thank you, Hong," I said. "You really are an honest man. You have kept your promise to me. I believe you are trustworthy and reliable. Tian is really fortunate to have you as her husband."

That night Weiluan and I discussed what to do with the banquet money. Both of us were inclined to save it rather than spend it on a lavish feast, but doing so could make Hong lose face. Fearing that his family would criticize Tian, we decided to go ahead with the banquet.

Despite how poorly we had been treated by our fellow villagers over the years, we graciously invited dozens of friends, neighbors, and relatives to the celebration. We anticipated about 20 people would come. Instead, we had more than twice that number. No one wanted to turn down a free meal or miss out on the excitement. The banquet was held in the village hall and was lively and festive.

The next day the matchmaker and I bought some household items for Tian's dowry. Then the two of us accompanied Tian and Hong back to their home. Keluo was more fertile and abundant than Donghu, so I was under the impression that villagers there didn't have to work as hard as us. However, on this trip, I noticed many women performing hard labor in the fields, which I hadn't seen previously. Many of the women appeared to be lugging heavy loads of unhusked rice in their baskets.

Hong saw me looking anxiously at the women. "Mother-in-Law, don't worry. I will take good care of Tian. I won't let her do any heavy farm work."

"He's right mother," Tian said. "Don't worry about me."

On the third day of my visit, I returned to Donghu. Tian and Hong escorted me to the dock. They sent me home with more food, sugar, and several pair of goslings. Keluo was famous for its goose breeding.

On the journey home, I looked at our abundant gifts. I felt so fortunate to have a daughter like Tian. Her marriage had been dictated entirely by her parents. Yet rather than defy being sold, she responded with obedience. She sacrificed so much to alleviate our family's suffering. To this day, I remain grateful.

Sugar-Coated Cannonballs

Zi returned home from school for good in the fall of 1967. She had spent more than a year on campus preparing for the college entrance exam. However, all schools remained closed, and the exams were never held. Zi's teachers and principal kept the campus operating as long as they could in the hope that the government would officially re-open it, but eventually they ran out of funds. Zi arrived home crestfallen. Weiluan took the news surprisingly in stride.

"It doesn't matter," he said. "If all of us have good health, that's enough. Where there is health, there is wealth. It's not the end of the world."

"It's the end of my world," Zi replied. "Why is my fate so bad? Why did the Cultural Revolution have to occur now? All of my classmates cried when we departed the campus. No one wanted to leave. Now I am without a reason to live in this world."

"Zi, the world is constantly changing," I said. "You may still have a bright future. As long as you have ability, there is no need to worry about your future."

Now that Zi was no longer a student, she had no choice but to join our production team. Initially, she was assigned a job as a kindergarten teacher. We were overjoyed when we heard that she would be spared the burden of physical labor. However, many villagers protested against the daughter of a counter-revolutionary being allowed to hold such a cushy job. Zi was quickly reassigned to work in the fields with the rest of us.

As a youngster, Zi had assisted us in various farming tasks, but she had never done a full day of true hard labor. Now suddenly she was forced to engage in back-breaking work from daybreak to darkness. In addition, she had to adapt to the constant psychological abuse that came with being a member of a counter-revolutionary family. I watched in pity as she hobbled forward hauling heavy baskets of mud. Sometimes she collapsed under the weight of the mud, prompting the Red Guards to scold her.

"Get up, you stinking old ninth!" they said, a term commonly used then to demean intellectuals who were considered one of society's "nine black categories" (landlords, rich farmers, counter-revolutionaries, bad elements, right wingers, traitors, spies, capitalist roaders, and intellectuals).

Every night my poor daughter secretly wept. I knew because the next morning I saw her eyes swollen, red, and sad. Weiluan and I felt so helpless and desperately tried to think of a solution. There was only one: to marry her off to a good family as we had done with Tian. But when I raised the idea, Zi was steadfastly against it.

"I would rather die than not be able to have the chance to attend college. Every word I have learned from my books reflects your hardship in educating me. You have paid such a high price raising me. I must repay you. I will persist and never give up until I see this bright future become a reality and until I can reciprocate your love."

Weiluan and I shared the same high hopes for Zi, so we didn't push the idea of marriage too hard. Fortunately, it wasn't long before her struggles began to ease. In the summer of 1968, the fervor of the Cultural Revolution finally began to dissipate after raging at a fever pitch for nearly two years. Alarmed at the disruption caused by the chaos, Chairman Mao ordered the army to re-establish order in the cities and to dispatch Red Guard units elsewhere. This initially led to several bloody clashes between the army and students. After several weeks, most Red Guard squads caved in and dispersed. Their departure marked the close of the intense, radical phase of the Cultural Revolution, although the movement wouldn't fully end until the mid-1970s.

During this time, the Red Guard unit in Donghu also disbanded and returned home. The moment the fanatics left, the tension in the village eased. Weiluan, Zi, and I were still required to engage in hard labor, but the intensity wasn't nearly as severe as in the past.

One day, after the Red Guards left, a former classmate of Zi came to Donghu for a surprise visit. She lived in Gaoshui, not far from their high school. The two girls spent lots of time catching up. It was good to see Zi reconnect with an old friend.

"After all the students left, our school was occupied by Red Guards," the girl said. "They locked up the teachers and forced them to attend struggle sessions every day. They paraded them through the streets of Gaoshui dressed in dunce caps and wearing wood signs around their necks with disparaging words. The people in the streets screamed at them, 'Down with intellectuals!' Many of the teachers were beaten. Some quite badly."

"I am so sad to hear that," Zi said. "Thank you for coming to tell me."

"It was very sad to watch," her classmate said, "but that's not the main reason I came here today. Actually, I came to seek your solace."

"My solace?" Zi said with surprise. "For what?"

"The government just issued a new decree that all urban high school students be sent to live in rural areas to be re-educated by destitute farmers."

"Re-educated? By farmers? Why?"

"I don't know. I guess it has to do with teaching us about hard work and humility. We are considered pampered, naïve intellectuals. You're so lucky that you're already from the countryside."

"How long will you be gone?"

"I have no idea. My life is over. My parents wept for an entire day and night when they heard."

"Is it just for students from Gaoshui?" asked Zi.

"No, I think it's province-wide. Perhaps countrywide."

"Don't worry. You'll be okay. But you must take good care of yourself. Life in the countryside isn't easy. You'll be alone. If you fall ill, there will be no one to look after you."

I purchased some rice and tofu and treated Zi's classmate to lunch. After a hearty meal, the girl departed.

The fact that urban students were being sent to rural areas to be re-educated was a bad sign. It suggested that the educational system wouldn't be returning to normal any time soon, if ever. At that moment, Weiluan and I realized that our dreams of sending our daughter to university were over. We were heartbroken.

By then, Zi's health had deteriorated considerably. Several times she fainted from exhaustion. We knew she couldn't go on like this much longer. I wrote Tian a letter asking her to return home to discuss an important matter. I hoped that she and Hong might be able to find Zi a husband.

"When Zi marries into a good family like me," Tian said, "everything will be better. Don't worry, Mother. We are a bad element family. In this politically charged environment, even if the universities open tomorrow, it's unlikely that Zi would ever be given a chance to attend college. As a woman, her final destination is marrying a good man, isn't it? Well, then, she might as well marry a good man now."

Two weeks later Hong came to our home and announced that he and Tian had found a match for Zi. He invited Zi and me to accompany him back to Keluo to visit the family. I jumped at the opportunity.

The young man's name was Yang (Yŏng). He had just completed service in the navy, and his parents were eager for him to get married. When they saw that Zi was attractive and well-educated, they were very pleased with the match. Yang's family owned an organ and a violin. Zi knew how to play both, which impressed them. The two youngsters fell in love at first sight. Zi quickly changed her attitude toward the idea of betrothal. After some discussion, both sides agreed to the nuptials.

We stayed one night at Yang's home. The next day we returned to Donghu with armfuls of oil, food, and sugar. The villagers shook their heads in astonishment when they saw how much we were carrying home. For years, they had criticized our determination to see to our daughters' education. Now that they saw it paying off, they were envious.

With so much sugar in our possession, numerous people came to our house to borrow some. Our relationship with many villagers had improved after the Red Guards left, but some people still continued to harass us. They accused us of trying to buy popularity with "sugar-coated cannonballs (糖衣炮弹)," a common term used during the Cultural Revolution to describe how capitalists won over people.

A few weeks later Yang made a surprise visit to our home. Someone had informed him that Weiluan was a bad element and had warned him against marrying Zi. He decided to evaluate the situation for himself. He arrived in Donghu in his navy uniform and looked extremely handsome. Those villagers who were still nasty toward us immediately became jealous and tried to break up the couple. They encouraged people to stay away from our home and to avoid greeting Yang. They also made a public spectacle criticizing Weiluan as a bad element. Between these incidents, and the fact that "counter-revolutionary family" was painted in large black characters on our door, Yang quickly realized that the warnings about Weiluan were true. He stayed only one night in our home. The next day he asked Zi to escort him to the train station.

When Yang told his family about our situation, they backed out of the engagement and prohibited him from marrying Zi. She was heart-broken. Weiluan felt tremendously guilty. "I have ruined my daughter's future," he often said, shaking his head in anger. Sometimes he screamed in the middle of the night, "I am not a reactionary! I helped hand over Changsha peacefully to the Communists!"

Weiluan's guilt became so intense that it frightened me and Zi. "Father, it's not your fault," she said to comfort him. "Even though you've been labeled a bad element, we are still middle-class peasants, and that is more important. I believe I will find a good husband one day. You and Mother are the best parents in the world. I feel very fortunate, not unfortunate."

"There are plenty of fish in the sea," I said to my husband. "We must take things as they come and not tie our hopes to wishful thinking."

In 1969, Hong returned to our home and informed us that he and Tian had found another match for Zi. The man's name was Shen (Shǔn), and he was a tractor driver for the Keluo commune. Everyone in his family was a member of the Communist Party, and his elder brother was the party secretary of the production team.

"It's impossible for a family that politically well-connected to be satisfied marrying a girl whose father is a bad element and counter-revolutionary," I said. "Their class status is much higher than ours."

"Mother-in-Law, I told them the entire situation of your family, including Father-in-Law's history with the KMT. I left nothing out. They said it wasn't a problem and asked me to bring you and Zi to visit them."

I still had my doubts, but I figured it was worth a try. Zi and I accompanied him back to Keluo. The young man came to Hong and Tian's home to be introduced to us. His physique was strong and sturdy, and he was of suitable height. Zi didn't say a word the entire time, so it was difficult to tell if she liked him or not.

Shen invited Zi to dine at his family's home for lunch. She was reluctant to go but finally agreed after I persuaded her. Shen took Zi to his home by bicycle. After lunch, she insisted on returning. Halfway through the ride back, she jumped off his bicycle and said she would walk the rest of the way alone.

"What happened?" I asked, surprised to see her back so soon. "Why do you look so unhappy?"

Even though Zi had been treated very well by Shen's family, she lied to me and said the family was cruel to her. She begged me not to betroth her to him. I had no reason to doubt what she said, so I turned down the proposal. Shen was devastated. He had fallen for Zi the moment he saw her. But Zi couldn't forget Yang. She wasn't interested in anyone else.

A few weeks later, Hong returned to our home to persuade Weiluan and me to agree to the marriage. "I spent a lot of time and energy searching for someone as suitable as Shen. His family is very good. They don't mind that you are a bad element family. You should feel lucky to have found such a man. Be pragmatic. Otherwise, you will miss this excellent opportunity. Don't pin high hopes on impossible dreams. If Zi misses this chance, I'm afraid that she won't have another opportunity like this."

"Is Shen still interested?" I asked.

"He has come to my home several times to ask me to persuade you to betroth Zi to him. Tian also believes this is a reliable family, so she asked me to come here again."

"Fengxian, go back with Hong and meet the family," Weiluan said. "What Hong has said is very reasonable. Zi is 24 and getting older every day. She should have been married a long time ago. We can't allow her to wait any longer. Otherwise, she will be too old to marry."

I accompanied Hong to Keluo. Shen's family gave me a warm welcome. Shen's elder brother was kind and unpretentious, despite being the party secretary of the production team. He promised me that he would allow Zi to teach kindergarten rather than work in the fields. "I assure you that they will be a happy couple. I hope you will reconsider."

"You are all very kind. We are a poor family with nothing. We are very fortunate to have a production team leader like you treat us so well. I agree that your brother and my daughter would make a good match. I consent to the marriage."

When I left the next day, the family lavished me with food, sugar, ration coupons, and a handful of young ducklings. Weiluan smiled when he saw everything I was carrying.

"So I take it this means that Zi will be marrying Shen."

"They are a very good family," I said. "They are kind and hospitable. They really want their son to marry Zi. I agreed to the betrothal."

As we were talking, Zi returned from the fields covered in mud and sweat. "Mother, you're back."

"Yes. Shen's family was very hospitable. They have an abundant life. More importantly, they are good people. Zi, why did you speak badly about them? I know you don't want to marry Shen, but you are wrong. You should accept this marriage happily. I know that you want to further your studies in college and have a bright future. This is understandable, but you must acknowledge your situation. Look up and see the indelible label on our door given to us by the Communist Party: 'Counter-Revolutionary Family.' Yang was frightened off by this label. Do you really think you have a chance to further your studies in college? Such daydreaming is in vain. Face reality and accept that your fate is to be a rural housewife. Do you understand what I'm saying?"

"I know," Zi said in tears. "I will no longer daydream. I will learn to take whatever my fate brings me." I was happy to see Zi finally acquiesce, but it broke my heart to watch her hopes dashed. I knew myself how discouraging it was to have to abandon one's dreams.

Although Zi had resigned herself to her fate, it still took her several weeks to agree to leave us. The decision was hastened when she fainted at work one day while on a reservoir project. The team leader sent her to the hospital, and the doctors informed us that she was anemic. When we brought her home, I pleaded with her to get married.

"Zi, you can't wait any longer. You have no other choice. Please make the decision to marry Shen now. Otherwise, your health will be in danger. Where there is life, there is hope. Perhaps you will still have your day after this marriage."

Zi finally acquiesced. In the winter of 1970, the two youngsters got married. Shen's family showered us with even more food, money, and gifts than we had received during Tian's betrothal. For the first time in decades, we were financially secure. In the end, our daughters had brought us as much, if not more, fortune than if they had been sons. "The days in the future will be better," Weiluan said confidently. I knew my husband was right, but as a mother, I still felt saddened to see Zi leave. The house seemed so empty without her and Tian. Both of them loved to sing. When they left, so did their music.

A Long-Awaited Refurbishment

Shortly after Zi was betrothed, Weiluan received a letter from Sisao informing him that she was suffering from acute diabetes. She asked him to come examine her. Weiluan visited her twice. Sisao apologized repeatedly for the way she had treated us.

"I hope my death can rid me of all my sins. People are so selfish. Now I know that nothing can be taken to my coffin when I die. I see that physical possessions are empty. Manfu, now your children are grown and your life is improving. You are so fortunate. You are blessed to have such a good wife. I never expected Fengxian to have such perseverance. I admire her."

Sisao passed away toward the end of 1970. Weiluan and I were now the only members of our generation left in his family. After all of the torment we had been put through, we, the persecuted, had triumphed, not our tormentors. The victory was bittersweet.

With the Red Guards gone, the family bullies dead, and our financial situation strengthening, our day-to-day lives became more relaxed. As Chinese New Year in 1971 approached, I began making preparations for a large celebration. For decades, we had suffered through the holidays watching and listening to other families' joy. It was time we held such a celebration. At the time, we were raising a number of hens and geese that Zi and Tian had given us. I decided to slaughter some of the animals and exchange them for fish and pork.

On New Year's Eve, Weiluan, Duoxi, Mei, Ai, and I enjoyed a hearty meal full of happiness and laughter. On the fifth day of the New Year, Zi and Shen came to visit us from Keluo. Tian was unable to accompany them, as she was scheduled to give birth. Zi and Shen arrived with armfuls of cakes and sugar. I could tell they were a happy couple. I was thankful to see Zi content with her choice to marry.

After the New Year, Mei began working in the fields with the production team. With three people in the family now earning work points, we finally had the wherewithal to consistently provide two meals of rice porridge a day for everyone in the family. I also was able to purchase cloth to make each of us new clothes.

As our finances improved, Weiluan set his sights on refurbishing our small, dilapidated house, which was so old and poorly constructed that the walls shook whenever there were strong winds. Such an ambitious task required money and materials. By then, Tian was raising two children, so we turned to Zi for assistance. She sent us some money and instructed us to purchase a piglet, which she said we could exchange for a much larger amount of money when it grew up. She also encouraged us to raise more geese.

At the time, Weiluan, Mei, and I were working on a local reservoir project. After work each day, we and other villagers used our shoulder poles to carry home leftover stones that had been unearthed that day. Eventually, we accumulated enough large rocks to use as the foundation for our refurbished home.

Next, we moved on to the task of acquiring bricks to construct the walls. Bricks were far too expensive to purchase, so Weiluan decided that we would make them ourselves. Every day we hauled home heaps of mud from the banks of the reservoir. We mixed the mud with lime and molded it into bricks. The work was draining and arduous. When other families needed to make bricks, they were able to use the production team's oxen to help pound the mud into hard blocks. But because

Weiluan was a bad element, he was rarely able to use the oxen for help. Instead, he had to pound the mud himself.

"Why do you look so exhausted?" I asked him one evening after he returned home. "I thought you were permitted to use the ox today."

"I could only use the ox for a short while. I look exhausted because I worked as the ox."

"Weiluan, this undertaking is too much for us to do on our own. How about we give it up for now? When we save enough money, we can buy the bricks or hire some help. Besides, are you sure the authorities won't give us any trouble for doing this? We are a counter-revolutionary family after all."

"Fengxian, where is your perseverance and determination now? Do you think you can enjoy a comfortable life and be lazy at the same time? If this isn't the right time to prepare for refurbishing the house, when do you suggest we do it? We are getting older. One day we will become too old and weak to do this. We must build a new house for Duoxi. In a few years, he will be ready to marry. He and his wife will live in this house. Who will marry our son if they have to live in this dilapidated place? The cadres aren't nearly as harsh as they were in the past. I don't think they'll give us any trouble."

"The thought of building a new house for Duoxi to get married never crossed my mind. You are such a good father, thinking so far ahead for your son. Okay, we will pound the mud together."

From then on, whenever we had free time, we spent it making bricks. Little by little, we scraped together enough for the project.

"Why are you always carrying stones and mud?" a young man in the village asked Mei one afternoon.

"We're gathering materials to build a new house."

"Build a new house? That's ridiculous! If it was as easy as gathering rocks and mud, everyone would have a new house."

"We've also been raising a pig, which we intend to sell once it gets fat. All of the money will be used to refurbish our house."

"Do you think that selling a pig can give you enough money to build a new house? You're daydreaming!"

That afternoon Mei relayed the young man's words to Weiluan and me.

"It's not surprising that other people don't believe we can build a new house." I said. "To be honest, even I don't have full confidence that we can do it when all I see are a pile of stones and bricks."

"Where there is a will, there is a way," Weiluan said confidently. "We will give it our utmost effort."

By the winter of 1974, we finally accumulated enough stones, bricks, and money to begin the project. Altogether, we had spent three years gathering the materials for the refurbishment. Weiluan and I decided that the best way to proceed would be to remove the wooden partition separating our living room from Qisao's, replace it with a solid brick wall, and use the wood as beams in the new kitchen and living room.

Weiluan asked a cousin, who was a builder, to oversee the project. The man, his son, and Duoxi, who by then was a teenager, worked together on the refurbishment, while Weiluan, Mei, and I worked in the fields each day. At one point, we even hired members of our production team to help us during their spare time. We paid them with three hearty meals a day. The local officials gave us no trouble.

The refurbishment was finally completed toward the end of March in 1975. The new home was tall and spacious and had excellent ventilation. Our old entryway was demolished, and the door containing the characters "counter-revolutionary family" was replaced. It was a relief to finally be rid of that eyesore. Many neighbors came to see the finished project. They admired our foresight and perseverance, including the young man who had been so skeptical a year earlier.

"You have a magnificent new home. It's amazing!" the young man said. "What's even more formidable is that you never revealed to anyone the plan and vision you had in mind."

"Silence is golden," I said. "If we had divulged our intentions, it's possible that we would have been hindered and might never have completed the project. Success rests not only on hard work and perseverance but also one's ability to keep obstructive forces at bay."

By the time the project was completed, we had depleted our savings. I sought help from Zi and Tian, who generously gave us food, ration coupons, and cash. Both daughters were very filial and always more than willing to help.

When Duoxi turned 18 in 1976, he began working for the production team. With four people now earning work points, plus our continuing efforts to raise pigs and geese, we were able to quickly re-accumulate the savings we had spent refurbishing the house. Weiluan decided to sell some of the animals to purchase a sewing machine for me.

"Fengxian, for years you have worked so hard for this family, not only in the fields but also making our clothes stitch by stitch. I want to buy you a sewing machine to make your life easier. You deserve it."

I was so grateful and excited that I spent every free moment I had learning to use the machine. Later that year, we purchased a Flying Pigeon bicycle. Every family in China dreamed of owning a Flying Pigeon at the time. The fact that we now possessed one demonstrated how dramatically our circumstances had changed in just a few years. Zi's husband assembled the bicycle for us. Mei practiced riding it every day after work.

In the evenings, our new home buzzed with the sound of my sewing machine and Mei's giggles as she struggled to balance the Flying Pigeon on the path outside. Sometimes I watched her from the courtyard and recalled my beloved maternal uncle gliding by Rongxia on his magic bicycle. So much had changed in the two and a half decades since I had last seen my family. Would I ever be able to recover that part of myself that had been left behind?

Frogs in a Well Emerge into Daylight

Although our lives had become more comfortable, we continued to face difficulties as a bad element, counter-revolutionary family. By 1976, the Cultural Revolution was entering its tenth year. The movement was much less fanatical and impassioned than in the past, but it continued to cast a dark shadow over our family, particularly our children Duoxi and Mei. Both were in that phase of early adulthood when charting one's own course and establishing an identity separate from one's parents is paramount. Yet neither of them could escape their father's labels.

Duoxi's supervisor was fond of him. One day he suggested that our son apply to join the Communist Youth League, which might pave the way to a bright future. Duoxi was excited and eagerly submitted an application. Every day he rushed home after work to see if there was a reply. When there was none, he enthusiastically sent follow-up inquiries. For months, our son remained persistent and hopeful. In the end, his application was denied because of his unreliable origin as the offspring of a bad element, counter-revolutionary father.

Mei encountered similar difficulties when it came time for her to marry. Unlike her sisters, Mei wanted to marry someone in Donghu in order to stay near Weiluan and me. From the time she was a little girl, she had always felt protective of us. However, because our family had no standing whatsoever in the village, we weren't able to betroth her to nearly as high caliber a family as Tian or Zi.

A match was eventually arranged with a young man in the village whose family only begrudgingly agreed to the betrothal. They were tough and unwelcoming and gave Weiluan and me no gifts except for some money. However, we dared not say a word lest they take it out on our daughter.

Throughout the Cultural Revolution, it was not uncommon for children of counter-revolutionary families to ridicule and denounce their parents in public. Some children even cut off relations with their parents altogether. "The sky is vast and the earth is vast, but the kindness of the Communist Party is the greatest. Mother is close, Father is close, but Chairman Mao is the closest" was a song the young Red Guards frequently sang. Weiluan and I were fortunate to have children who always supported us. None of our children ever complained about their circumstances despite the tremendous hardship they endured. Still, Weiluan felt very guilty about how his status negatively impacted the children.

From the time my husband was officially labeled a bad element, our family had suffered endless discrimination. Tainted families like ours were considered "enemies of the people (人民的公敌)," which gave the people free license to treat us as savagely as they wished. No matter how diligently we worked, how much we overextended ourselves to help our neighbors, or how much we struggled to give our children a path to a better future, we could not break free of the shackles of my husband's labels. The best we could hope for was to have sufficient food to eat and clothes to wear. Anything more seemed like an unattainable dream.

Then one day in 1976, the walls that had imprisoned us for so long began to crumble. It was early September, and Weiluan and I had just finished an exhausting day in the fields. We were slowly making our way home when one of our neighbors shouted out to us, "Did you hear? Chairman Mao is dead!" Tired and hungry, the news, while startling, didn't immediately resonate.

Occasionally in life, events occur that carry great significance for us that we are oblivious to when they transpire. This was one of those occasions. For decades, our family had subsisted on the margins of society, banned from participating in village meetings or socialist study sessions and cut off from all sources of news. We lived, as Chinese people aptly say, like "frogs in a well (井底之蛙)," whose interaction with and knowledge of the world is constrained to the narrow circle of light above them.

For several days, grand ceremonies were held in Chairman Mao's remembrance across the country. However, in Donghu counter-revolutionary families like us weren't invited. While everyone else was memorializing and grieving, we and other bad element families continued laboring in the fields.

"Who will hold up the sky now?" was a common question people asked after Chairman Mao passed away. By then, he was revered as a demi-god. Nearly every home in the country contained a large poster of him, including ours. For years, many families had been bowing religiously in front of his portrait three times every morning and evening, asking his spirit for protection.

Soon after Chairman Mao's death, a power struggle ensued within the leadership of the Communist Party. Those advocating an end to the unruliness of the Cultural Revolution seized the opportunity to arrest Mao's wife and cohorts. This "Gang of Four," as they were later called, had been responsible for much of the movement's excesses and until then had been sheltered by the chairman. Once these figures were behind bars, the momentum of the Cultural Revolution quickly fizzled. At long last, the 10 years of chaos was brought to a close.

People in cities across the country took to the streets to celebrate. The reaction in the countryside was more subdued because the arrest occurred around the fall harvest. Weiluan and I were elated to hear that the Cultural Revolution was finally over. Yet deep down, we also knew that our country faced a long, difficult road to recovery. Some priceless items had been lost forever. An entire generation of youths, including Zi, had lost the opportunity for higher education; millions of precious works of Chinese art, literature, and architecture had been destroyed; and the bonds between youths and their elders had been forever altered.

The greatest tragedy of all was the countless innocent lives destroyed. People who had been beaten, committed suicide, or had their families and careers ruined because their words or actions had been arbitrarily deemed counter-revolutionary. Despite all of the agony our family experienced during the Cultural Revolution, we escaped the decade relatively unscathed. For that, we were thankful.

In the ensuing years, the normal rhythms of work, family, and village life resumed. Temples re-opened, harassment of counter-revolutionaries quieted, and a new dialogue of hope — centered on the future — replaced a previous dialogue dominated by ideology and fanaticism. During this time, Weiluan, Duoxi, and I continued to work in the fields while Ai attended school. Mei married the young man in our village and moved in with his family. Regrettably, Mei's marriage did not turn out as well as Zi's or Tian's. From the start, she was physically and verbally abused by her new husband and his parents who thought they could treat her as poorly as they wished since she came from counter-revolutionary roots.

When Chinese New Year in 1978 arrived, I prepared another large feast. The two-week holiday passed quickly. Early that spring our production team leader made an unexpected visit to our home. He had a big smile on his face.

"I have some great news for both of you!" he said as he entered our home. "Manfu, congratulations! I have a certificate from the local authorities declaring that all limitations on your movements have been lifted. You may remove your hat of restriction. You're free! I'm so happy for you."

Weiluan stood in the living room dumbstruck and silent. The news had taken him totally by surprise just as it had in 1953 when he was first informed that his movements were being placed under restriction.

"Thank you so much, team leader," I said and took the paper from his hands. "This is wonderful news. I appreciate your taking the effort to come here to tell us. May I ask what prompted this decision?"

"Your husband spent 25 years under restriction. The officials believe that is enough punishment. The new government also is encouraging a more open-minded view toward these cases. Congratulations to both of you," he said as he left.

I turned and looked at my husband. "Weiluan, you haven't said a word. Don't you feel happy and relieved?"

"For me, the sun is setting. What use is it to have these restrictions lifted now? After so many years, it can't restore my reputation. What hope is there for me at this late stage?"

"No, you are wrong! This isn't just about you. It's about our entire family. Can't you see the bitter circumstances your wife and children have had to endure because of these restrictions and your labels? Hao died because you weren't able to take him to Gaoshui to be examined by your brother. Duoxi couldn't join the Communist Party Youth League, and Mei couldn't marry into a good family. Why? Because of your political labels and these restrictions!"

"You're right, Fengxian. I'm sorry. I'm thinking about this too selfishly. I should be thankful for this gift from the Communist Party. Maybe this new government will bring a better future for us. Perhaps one day the reversal of verdicts I've been dreaming of will also come true, and I will be able to officially shed my bad element and counter-revolutionary labels."

We held a special dinner that evening to celebrate Weiluan's freedom. The next day, my husband went to town and bought a newspaper, something he had been forbidden from doing for 25 years. When Zi and Tian learned that their father's movements were no longer under control, they invited him to visit Keluo. Weiluan had never had the opportunity to see their new homes and families. My husband requested two weeks of vacation from the production team. He was quickly granted permission for the trip, which would have been unthinkable in the past. In late February 1978, he travelled to Keluo to visit the girls.

Shortly after Weiluan left for Keluo, an issue arose concerning Duoxi. Our son was 20 years old and becoming more independent. Like all young men, he was eager to explore the world. He often stayed out with his friends until midnight. The favorite topic of discussion amongst the boys was sneaking to Hong Kong. Some older boys in the group had tried to flee to Hong Kong but had been caught and briefly sent to jail. When they returned to Donghu, they relayed their experiences to their captivated friends. The boys stayed up for hours talking about what they envisioned life to be like in Hong Kong and possible ways to get there.

One afternoon a distant cousin the same age as Duoxi came to our home to visit him. The two boys talked energetically outside for hours. I could tell something was going on, but I wasn't sure what.

"You seem different lately," I said to him that night. "Is there something you're hiding from me?"

"Yes, but now is not the right time to tell you."

I gave him a concerned look but didn't reply.

"Okay, since you asked, I'll tell you. I'm planning to escape to Hong Kong with my cousin."

"What? Duoxi, are you crazy? You can't do that! The border was re-closed after the exodus in 1962. It's illegal to flee to Hong Kong. Your father tried to go when you were in my womb. It landed him in jail for four years. I don't want to see the same thing happen to you. Plus, you're still a boy. How can you handle such a long and treacherous journey? Many people have died while scaling the mountains or from starvation and dehydration. Other people drowned trying to swim there. Even if you were lucky enough to make it there, you don't have any relatives in Hong Kong to look after you. I won't let you do this."

"Mother, I'm going. No matter what you say, I'm determined to go. I'm not as young and naïve as you think. I'm not a boy. I'm an adult. Even though I haven't traveled anywhere, I've heard a lot about the outside world. I can't stay caged in this small, hopeless place forever. If one seeks fortune, he must be willing to take risks to achieve it. I must grasp this opportunity. Otherwise, I will regret it for the rest of my life. I understand why you don't want me to go, but I must. Please forgive me."

"I don't want you to carry any regrets in life. If it's that important, then I'll leave it to you to decide. If you do manage to get there, who will look after you?"

"You've forgotten that cousin has a relative in Hong Kong. He will help us out initially. Mother, you must promise not to tell anyone."

"I promise. Just be careful."

I decided not to relay the information to Weiluan since he was enjoying his first vacation in decades. However, I did inform Mei and Ai so we could pool our funds and give the boys some money for the journey. We were able to scrape together 8.8 yuan. Eight is considered a lucky number in China because it is pronounced similar to the words to prosper and fortune in some dialects.

The day before the boys left, they visited the home of a Taoist spiritual leader to get a blessing for the journey. She gave them each a small piece of paper imprinted with a hierogram.

"Crumple this up and swallow it before you set off to ensure a successful journey," she instructed them.

The next morning Duoxi and I got up at the crack of dawn. Before he left, he went to the attic to pray before the Buddha niche we had rebuilt after Mao died. I followed him. Tears streamed from my eyes as I watched him. When he finished, he crumpled the hierogram into a ball, placed it in his mouth, then gulped it down with water. It took him a while to swallow it.

"Mother, don't worry about me. I'll be okay."

"Be careful. Notify me as soon as you get there. I'll be praying for you."

Duoxi inhaled deeply and then quickly crawled down the ladder and rushed out the door. I followed him downstairs but stayed inside because I didn't want to make anyone suspicious. From the window, I watched him steadfastly walk away. He never looked back.

I felt so sad and anxious that I couldn't stop crying. I wiped away the tears and forced myself to smile when the time came to report to work. That evening after work, I rushed home and immediately went to pray. As dusk approached, dark clouds moved in, and it began to rain heavily. The lightning and thunder frightened me. I couldn't sleep and spent the entire night worrying about my son.

"Duoxi, where are you?" I whispered to him. "I shouldn't have let you go. It's pitch dark outside. How can you find your way forward?"

The next day one of the boys' friends delivered our bicycle. The boys had bicycled from Donghu to the foot of the mountain.

"Manpo, now we know they made it safely to the pass. Don't worry."

I was comforted to hear that they had made it that far, but traversing the mountain was the most treacherous part of the journey. I remained anxious.

After the boys had been gone a few days, everyone surmised that they had left for Hong Kong. Some villagers tried to comfort me, while others criticized me for allowing Duoxi to place his life in jeopardy. I ignored them. My greatest challenge was battling my own pessimistic thoughts. What if Duoxi gets injured on the mountain? What if he gets caught? Will they put him in jail? Will he be able to survive jail?

Duoxi's friends also were eager to escape to Hong Kong, so they paid close attention to the situation. They frequently came to inquire if I had received any word. If the boys arrived safely, their friends intended to follow.

One week after Duoxi left, Weiluan returned from Keluo. As he was walking home from the dock, villagers bombarded him with questions about Duoxi. By the time he arrived home, he was extremely confused.

"You're back," I smiled when I saw him.

"Fengxian, what's this I hear about Duoxi sneaking to Hong Kong? Is it true?"

"Yes, it's true. He went with his distant cousin. I tried to talk him out of it, but he wouldn't listen. I didn't want to ruin your vacation, so I didn't inform you."

"When did they leave? Have we received any information?"

"They left a week ago. We haven't heard a word."

As we were talking, a neighbor knocked on the door and informed us that Duoxi's cousin's family wanted to see us. We immediately rushed over.

"I just received a letter from my son," his mother said with a big smile. "Both boys made it to Hong Kong! They're doing fine." She handed us the letter.

Weiluan and I quickly scanned it. We were ecstatic.

"I am so proud of Duoxi," Weiluan said, shaking his head with a wide grin. "He managed to accomplish what I had always dreamed of but was never able to. His life will never be the same."

After decades of living like frogs in a well, our family was finally emerging into the daylight. I recalled the words of encouragement my brother Dian had said to me more than a decade earlier during his visit to Donghu: "Fengxian, I believe it is God's arrangement for you to have bitter days first, then sweet days. Life will turn around for you one day." It seemed as though anything was possible now.

PART SEVEN

Picking Up the Pieces

Return to Rongxia

One of the first changes under the new government was the loosening of restrictions on travel and communication. Since the 1950s, the authorities had strictly limited interaction between people from different parts of the country. This was intended to restrict the migration of poor farmers to more affluent cities as well as to limit people's access to information about happenings outside their communities. During the Cultural Revolution, any communication with people abroad, including family, was frowned upon. One could be punished just for possessing a letter from a relative overseas. Such behavior was considered "worshipping foreign objects" and hence potentially counter-revolutionary and subversive.

Bad element families like ours were prohibited from almost all communication. The only letters we received were from our daughters. Communication with anyone else was prohibited. As a result, I had lost all contact with my relatives in Hunan, who, as bad element landlords themselves, also were banned from writing to me.

The lifting of restrictions on communication immediately led to a barrage of letters between people searching for long lost relatives and friends. In the summer of 1978, we received a letter from Weiluan's eighth sister, his favorite sibling, who had managed to escape from China prior to the Communist Party's takeover in 1949. She was now living in the U.S.

We passed Eighth Sister's contact information to Duoxi in Hong Kong and instructed him to get in touch with her. We hoped that she would take pity on him and send him some money for living expenses. She was very generous and sent money to both Duoxi and us, which helped further ease our financial strain.

Weiluan and I were comforted to know that Duoxi now had some money to live on, but we remained anxious about our son. He was in Hong Kong alone without any support system. Weiluan tried to contact some of his relatives who had emigrated to Hong Kong in the 1950s but was unsuccessful. I had only one relative who fled to Hong Kong, my father's brother Uncle Jusheng and his wife and daughter. The last time

I heard from Uncle Jusheng was in 1953 when Weiluan had stayed with him briefly while looking for work in Hong Kong. I had no idea where Uncle Jusheng was, or how to contact him.

"Maybe your father has heard from Uncle Jusheng," Weiluan said one afternoon.

"It's possible, but I haven't had any contact with my family except for Dian's short visit in the 1960s. My brother never mentioned Uncle Jusheng."

"Well, Fengxian, perhaps it's time for you to return to Rongxia. With Eighth Sister's help, we have the money for you to make the trip. The government is less strict than before about permitting people to travel to visit relatives."

For 28 years, I had intentionally not allowed myself to give more than a fleeting thought to returning to Hunan in order to prevent being overwhelmed by the sadness of all I had left behind. Now, after so long, I had both the means and the opportunity to make the journey. The thought of returning gave me butterflies.

"It's been so long," I said in hesitation. "With everything that has changed in this country, I don't know if anyone is even still living there."

"The only way to find out is to go and see for yourself. It's because of me that you weren't able to return home all these years. I'm so sorry, Fengxian. Now the time has come for you to go back."

The next day I requested two weeks of vacation from the production team leader and got permission to make the trip. Since it was summer, Ai was out of school, so I decided to take her with me. Mei's husband and in-laws refused to let her accompany us. Weiluan stayed behind to work and look after the house.

The next morning, Ai and I took a ferry to Keluo to see if Zi and Tian were interested in joining us. At that time, phones remained a rarity in the countryside. Tian was nursing a three-month-old baby boy and couldn't make the trip. Zi jumped at the opportunity and requested two weeks of leave.

We departed that afternoon for Guangzhou and stayed the night at a nephew's home. The next morning, we went to the train station and purchased the cheapest tickets available to Huaguo. The train departed at 6 p.m. that evening and was scheduled to arrive in Huaguo around 4 p.m. the next day.

The sun set and the sky turned dark shortly after the train took off, leaving us with no scenery to gaze at. From then on, the girls and I dozed off and on until daybreak.

Early the next morning, we passed a sign announcing that we had entered Hunan. I was so nervous about seeing my family after such a long time that my heart raced. So much had happened in the three decades I had been gone. When I left Huaguo in 1950, I never would have dreamed that my life would take the twists and turns it had.

"Mom, you look anxious," Zi said. "Are you afraid we won't be able to find your family?"

"No, I'm just excited, and I guess a little nervous. I have so many memories."

"Look at those people in the fields," Ai said, pointing at some farmers holding hoes in one hand and paper parasols in the other as they worked the land. They appeared so natural and peaceful in the orange morning glow.

The train ran parallel to the Xiang River, so throughout the day I gazed at my dear river and reminisced. I recalled the lively annual dragon boat races and the dozens of boat trips I had taken back and forth between Huaguo and Fengmen. When I closed my eyes and allowed my memories to take over, I felt as though I had never left.

Late that afternoon, we passed a sign announcing that Fengmen Railway Station was approaching. I took a deep breath, then helped the girls gather our belongings, which had been strewn everywhere during the journey.

When we stepped out of the car and onto the cement platform, across from us stood the railway station I recalled so vividly from my childhood. The building was much smaller and quieter than I remembered. There wasn't a single soul anywhere, not even youngsters hawking goods, which after 1949 would have been scorned as capitalist behavior. I looked around to get my bearings, but everything seemed so different.

"I don't know which way to go," I said to my daughters.

"The sun is beginning to set," Ai said anxiously. "Soon it will be dark. What do we do if we can't find grandpa's house?"

I caught sight of a middle-aged man diverting water from a stream to his fields. I rushed over to ask directions. When I reached him, I realized I no longer remembered my Hunanese dialect, so I asked him how to get to Huaguo in Cantonese. He didn't understand a word I said and walked away. Moments later, I recalled a few Hunanese words and yelled out to him.

"Follow that path, and you will eventually reach Huaguo," he yelled back, pointing to a narrow trail.

"Thank you," I said. We smiled and waved.

"I walked along this path every day to attend primary school when I was young," I said and shook my head. "Why can't I recognize it now? It's been so long. Time changes everything. Time eventually erases the memory of everything."

The girls were getting increasingly nervous about being in the middle of nowhere in the dark, so the darker it got, the faster we walked. Eventually we arrived at an area that looked familiar.

"Grandpa's house shouldn't be far from here," I said. "Don't worry."

When we arrived at a sharp turn in the path, I expected to see the large banyan tree outside Rongxia, but there were no large trees anywhere. I paused and looked around.

"What's wrong?" Ai said. "Are we going the wrong way?"

"I don't know. It all just looks so different. Let's keep walking. I see some people ahead. We can ask them for directions."

As we got closer, we could see a building with a few lit windows. Several people were sitting outside on short wooden stools enjoying the cool night air. I approached one of them.

"We are looking for Rongxia," I said. "Is this the right way to go?" No one responded. "I am looking for the Chu family."

A man walked up to us out of the darkness and carefully inspected each of us. "Who are you?"

"My name is Fengxian. I am looking for my father and brothers."

"Ah, Fengxian! I'm your brother Liang! I can't believe you're standing here before me after so long!"

"Liang, I didn't recognize you in the dark."

Brother put his arm around me, then turned and shouted toward the house. "Everyone, it's Fengxian! Fengxian is back!" The entire group stood up and rushed to the path to greet us. Overwhelmed by the warm welcome, my eyes welled up with tears.

"Please, come sit down," Liang said as he eagerly led us into the house. "Who are these two young ladies?"

"These are my daughters, Zi and Ai. You haven't seen Zi since she was a child. Ai is our youngest."

"I see the family resemblance in both of them."

"Where is father?" I asked excitedly. "It's been so long since I've seen him."

The excitement quieted. Liang's face turned serious. "Fengxian, Father died last year."

My heart sank when I heard those words. I started to cry. If I could have seen only one person on the trip, it would have been Father. "Last year? If only I had come back earlier. I am such an unfilial daughter." Everyone tried to comfort me, but I was devastated.

Liang asked his wife and some other women to bring us some tea and to prepare food and beds for us. After dinner, the girls and everyone else went to sleep, while Liang and I caught up on family news. He informed me that, in addition to my dear father, our three siblings also had died. Liang and I were the only people in our immediate family still living.

"During land reform, Father was branded a landlord. His share of the house, his land, and all of his possessions were seized and distributed to poor farmers. He was banished from Rongxia and eventually moved into a shack in the outskirts of the village. Like all of the other landlords in this area, he was given minimal food and clothing. Our stepmother couldn't handle such a life, so she abandoned Father. During the periods of Class Struggle, the Four Cleanups, and the Cultural Revolution, Father and other landlords were often trotted out for public criticism. Father was frequently beaten by fellow villagers at the struggle sessions. Whenever he was being attacked, Father always responded proudly, 'I have never done anything to hurt the Chinese people or the nation. I have a clear conscience. Regardless of whether I am tortured or not, I will not plead guilty. I will take things as they come.' Last year he died a natural death peacefully without any illness or pain."

"Father was always so easy-going," I said with a sad smile. "He had such a kind heart. He was always so good to me. I just wish I could have been here to help him."

"Fengxian, don't be too hard on yourself. Father understood your circumstances."

"What about our siblings? What happened to them? Part of me suspected that Father may no longer be alive, but I never expected that all of our siblings would also be dead."

"After you left in 1950, Dian set his sights on attending college. He took the entrance exam and was admitted to Hunan Normal University in Changsha. Father couldn't afford to pay the tuition, so he and Dian decided to disassemble and sell all of the beautifully painted windows and engraved wooden doors in Rongxia. After Dian graduated, he got a job teaching math at a high school in Changsha. He never married and lived alone in the dorm. During the Cultural Revolution, he and many other teachers and intellectuals were branded counter-revolutionaries and enemies of the people. They became targets of the Red Guards. They were paraded through the streets wearing tall dunce caps and disparaging wood signs around their necks. They were forced to denounce themselves in front of large crowds, saying things like, 'I, Chu Dian am an evil man...I am a monster and a bad element...' Each night when Dian returned to the dorm, he was greeted by large posters plastered across his doorway vilifying him. Other counter-revolutionaries had been beaten and tortured after tearing down the posters, so every night Dian carefully crawled on the floor under the posters to enter his room. The room had been stripped of everything, including a light, so each night he returned to total darkness. One reason the Red Guards emptied his room was to prevent him from committing suicide. They didn't want to give him an easy exit from the pain. After living like that for a few months, Dian could no longer stand it. One night, he tore apart his clothes and crafted a noose out of the material. He tied the noose to the left and right bedposts above his bed, twisted the cloth around his neck, and then strangled himself. In the end, Dian was able to leave this world on his terms, not the Red Guards'." Liang chuckled.

"I could tell something was bothering Dian when he visited me in Donghu," I said. "He wouldn't go into detail about what was wrong. He was too young to have suffered and died like that. What happened to my dear sister Boya?"

"The Tang family that sister married into were branded 'big land-lords,' the worst of all class designations. She and the Tangs underwent unspeakable persecution and torture. Boya gave birth to several children. Even when she was pregnant, she was forced to attend struggle sessions and endure vicious beatings. Over time, Boya became severely malnour-ished and ill from the abuse. She died during the Cultural Revolution while giving birth."

The bad news seemed endless. My shirt became soaked from tears. "When we were young, Boya and I were inseparable, like two joyful birds residing in the same woods. The last time I saw her was when she came to visit mother on her deathbed. Now I've returned to our childhood playground, but my dear Boya has flown away." I sobbed.

"Fengxian, take it easy. There is no reason we have to discuss all of this now."

"Just tell me about Rong; then we can go to bed."

"Because of his illness, Rong was never able to marry. The poor farmers who moved into our home feared that Rong's illness was con-tagious. None of them wanted to live or work with him. As a result, the production team expelled him from Rongxia and wouldn't allow him to work. He became homeless. Rong lived a lonely life of starvation and misery scavenging in the hills. One day during the Great Leap Forward, he was so famished that he stole some sweet potatoes from someone's fields. When he was discovered, he was beaten severely. He died shortly after from his injuries and malnourishment."

"I always felt bad for Rong. Because of his illness, he wasn't able to enjoy playing as much as the rest of us when we were children. When Mother died, he lost his primary caretaker. He suffered his entire life."

"Fengxian, only you and I made it through the last three decades alive. We should be thankful for that. It's the one fortune in all the misfortunes."

"To be honest, Liang, it's amazing I'm still here. On several occasions in the past, I was within an inch of death."

"I guess it wasn't your time."

"No, no, it wasn't my time."

"We can share our stories tomorrow, Sister. Now it's time for you to rest."

Liang stood up and led me to a room where Zi and Ai were already fast asleep. It had been so long since I had stayed at Rongxia that I couldn't place where we were in the house. I couldn't recognize anything.

As I lay there trying to fall asleep, images of Liang's stories raced through my mind. Knowing how cruelly Weiluan and the landlords in Donghu had been treated, I wasn't surprised to hear that my family had faced similar trials. Still, it was crushing to hear how each of them suffered.

I closed my eyes and listened for familiar sounds in the house and the woods. I couldn't recognize any. In the time I was away, Rongxia had turned quiet and cold. Everything seemed so different. Everyone was gone.

My Beloved Uncle

The next morning before breakfast, I strolled around the grounds in search of old memories. I could find none. During land reform, the local production team had taken over Rongxia and made several changes to the structure. New rooms had been built over my beloved garden. Other rooms had been demolished, including the patio that housed our precious gold-coin turtles and my and Boya's boudoir, where we had spent countless hours as young girls. Father's study was nowhere to be found. The large banyan tree outside the house, from which Rongxia derived its name, had been cut down and its roots dug out. The complex felt empty without the tree, but in a way I was glad it was gone. Such a beautiful tree didn't belong on what had turned into a pigpen of the local production team.

We enjoyed a leisurely family breakfast. For the first time, I saw Liang's face in daylight. My little brother had aged so much. Because of his connections to Father and Grandfather, Liang initially had a hard time after the Communist Party seized power. However, as time went on, he became respected for his hard work and ethics and for always diligently following the Communist Party's instructions. As a result, he was selected to work as a teacher at the local elementary school. Later he was promoted to be the school's principal. Liang had two sons and three daughters. The sons continued to live at Rongxia, while the daughters had married into families nearby. We joked about old memories and caught up on news of other family members.

"One of the reasons I came back to see all of you," I said, "is because my son Duoxi fled to Hong Kong a few months ago. Weiluan and I are worried about him. We want to put him in touch with family members that are there. I know Uncle Jusheng fled to Hong Kong in 1949, but I no longer have his contact information. Do you have it, Liang?"

"Uncle Jusheng's daughter is still living in Hong Kong. She married and has three children. I can give you her address. Uncle Jusheng's wife died in the 1950s. He immigrated to the U.S. by himself more than a decade ago."

"The U.S.? It must be difficult for him to be in a foreign country on his own."

"He's not alone anymore. He married an American woman and has a young daughter."

"That's great. I'm so happy for him. Last night you didn't mention Grandfather and Qie. What happened to them?"

"Like Father, Grandfather was labeled a landlord. He and Qie were kicked out of Rongxia and forced to move into a shack in the hills. During the Great Leap Forward, they both starved to death. Grandfather died first, and then Qie died two weeks later. We didn't have any money for a coffin for Grandfather, so we dismantled the grand red door at the entrance of Rongxia and crafted it into a coffin. Now that beautiful door is accompanying him in the afterlife."

"I was wondering what happened to that door. This morning I noticed it was gone. What happened to their children?"

"One daughter died in the early 1950s before getting a chance to marry. The other daughter married a man in Fengmen. We rarely see her. One of their sons fled to Taiwan in 1949 with the KMT. Another son starved to death during the Great Leap Forward. Only one son is alive and still living here. We'll see him later today."

"It sounds like the Great Leap Forward was devastating here. Life in Donghu was dreadful at that time, but we didn't suffer nearly the same death rate."

"Yes, it was a nightmare. No family was spared. You could argue that our brother Rong also starved to death. It was the desperation caused by being so famished that prompted him to steal food from one of the villager's fields."

"What about my beloved maternal uncle?"

"Uncle is still alive. Somehow, he managed to survive the past three decades. He has had a very difficult life."

"You must take me to see him."

"Okay, I'll take you after lunch. First, we must visit the tombs of Father and our ancestors to express our appreciation for all they have bestowed upon us."

Father had been buried on one of the hills overlooking Rongxia. The mound of earth covering his body was still fresh. I knelt in front of his tomb and wept. We looked everywhere for Mother's tomb but couldn't locate it. At the time she died, we couldn't afford a gravestone. I whispered some words to her as we stood on the hill.

"Mother, three decades ago I visited your tomb before leaving with Weiluan to Guangdong. Now I have finally returned. So many years have passed. What an unfilial daughter I am. I can't begin to express all of the difficulties I went through since I left. I just hope that you can understand and not hold it against me."

Liang had no idea where the tombs of our siblings were, so we stood on the hill, and I said a prayer for them. "Boya, Dian, Rong, we don't know where each of you is buried. Please allow us to pray for you here by bowing to the sky. We hope that you can rest in peace forever."

After lunch, Liang, my daughters, and I left to visit my maternal uncle. Liang led us on a narrow path into the woods that I didn't recognize.

"I don't recall taking this route to our grandparents' home," I said.

"We aren't going to our grandparents' old home. Uncle lives in the mountains now. During land reform, our grandparents' home was seized and given to poor farmers. They were banished to living in a shack like Father. Uncle was in even more dire straits. In addition to being the son of a landlord, he had previously worked as an administrator for the KMT. People with two counts against them typically were executed. One day Communist Party soldiers came and led Uncle to the execution ground. They tied his hands behind his back and instructed him to kneel on the ground. One of the soldiers took out his pistol, cocked it, and stretched out his arm to shoot Uncle in the head. At that moment, a Communist Party cadre appeared out of nowhere and shouted at the soldier to stop. The cadre ran to the soldier and informed him that Chairman Mao had just issued a new directive that all arbitrary killings be stopped. Uncle's life was spared."

"That's amazing. That story gives me goose bumps. Uncle just narrowly escaped. He was so lucky."

"He was fortunate on that occasion, but he still had to bear vicious abuse and harassment as the son of a landlord and a former KMT staff. For years, he was forced to work like a slave on dangerous, back-breaking projects. One of them was located on the edge of a cliff. An iota of carelessness would have led to him plummeting to his death. In the end, Uncle managed to survive. The manual labor strengthened his body, and he was able to outlast his decades of hard labor. Now he no longer works. He lives alone in a shack in the mountains."

After walking and talking a long time, Liang came to a stop in the woods.

"Do you see that thatched hut ahead?"

"Yes."

"That's where Uncle lives."

"It's so remote out here. Isn't he afraid of wild animals?"

"He has no other choice."

Seeing the hut brought tears to my eyes. From the time I was a little girl, I had always looked up to my uncle. He cared for me and supported me wholeheartedly when I wanted to marry Weiluan. Without him, I couldn't imagine what kind of life I would be living. I thought about his Chinese New Year visits, which the entire family used to look forward to, as well as his beautiful Chinese calligraphy. I had wanted so much to be like him.

"The magic man on a magic bicycle," I murmured. "How things have changed."

"I had forgotten about that," Liang chuckled. "All of you stay here. I will go ahead on my own. I want to surprise him."

The girls and I sat on the grass. A few minutes later Liang returned.

"He's not in. We can wait here for him."

"What happened to his children?" I asked.

"His daughters got the opportunity to move to another province. Later, they took their younger brother with them."

"Uncle allowed all of them to go that far away?"

"He's the one who encouraged them to leave. He didn't want his children to stay here suffering with him. He wanted them to build a new future. Now his children send him some money every month. It was a wise choice."

"Perhaps, but now he's out here all alone."

About an hour later, an old man approached us carrying a shoulder pole filled with firewood. His back was so hunched over that his head was almost beneath his knees.

"That's him," Liang said.

The four of us rushed over to help. Uncle stopped walking and set down the pole.

"Liang, it's so good to see you! It's been a while. Who are these women you have here with you?"

I stepped toward him. "My beloved uncle," I said with a big smile. Then I turned to my daughters, "This is your great uncle."

Uncle scanned my face with a quizzical look. "You…you are…"

"I am Fengxian!"

Uncle's jaw dropped and his eyes filled with tears. He was speechless.

"What a great fortune that all of us can be reunited after so long," Liang said. "Let's go to your home."

Uncle's one-room hut was tiny and austere. It contained only a bed, a table, a few stools, and some kitchen wares.

"Fengxian, I never expected that you would come back like this. I must cook something for you. It's already late afternoon. I'm sorry I don't have any good dishes to serve you."

We hurriedly took out the pork and other items we brought for him.

"You didn't have to be so polite. You all have families. You need the money. I will go pick some fresh vegetables and peppers to add to this."

Liang prepared the food while Uncle and I caught up on each other's lives.

"Where is Commander Han?" he asked. "Why didn't he come with you?"

"He's at home looking after the house and working."

"Did Liang tell you my story?"

"Yes, he did. You are so fortunate to be alive."

"You and Weiluan must also have had a difficult time these years given his previous ties to the KMT."

"Yes, decades ago Weiluan was branded a bad element and a counter-revolutionary. We experienced a lot of persecution and hardship. Our family was classified as middle-class peasants, but in reality we lived in deep poverty. On several occasions, we almost died of starvation. One of our sons effectively starved to death. He was just three years old and died of an illness he contracted from putting unclean things in his mouth. He was so hungry that he was willing to eat anything. Fortunately, blessed by God's providence, I have been able to return to Hunan today."

We talked all afternoon. When the sun began to descend, we started our journey back to Rongxia. Uncle insisted on accompanying us part of the way. As we walked side by side, I looked at his white hair and the large hump on his back. Uncle had turned into an old man. About half way home, we said farewell.

"Fengxian, I have missed you so much since your departure. I always held out hope that I would see you again one day. Thank you so much for coming to see me. Your visit has brought me so much joy."

"Uncle, seeing you has been the highlight of my trip. I'm so glad to see that you are alive and doing well."

"Fengxian, stay here as long as you can. You don't know when or if you will be able to return."

"Okay, Uncle, I will."

When we arrived at Rongxia, Liang's wife had already prepared a large dinner. Many guests were present, most of whom I didn't know. They asked me all sorts of questions about what life was like in Guangdong and about Cantonese customs. It had been a long day. I was exhausted and retired early.

We spent the next several days visiting each of Liang's children. All of them greeted us with smiles and treated us hospitably. On the walks between my nieces and nephews' homes, the girls and I took in the beautiful scenery. At meals, we enjoyed the delicious food. Zi and Ai didn't grow up eating spicy food, but they quickly adapted to Hunanese cuisine. By the end of the visit, they were asking for hot peppers at every meal.

A couple of days before we were scheduled to leave, we paid a visit to my mother's sister, Auntie as we called her, who had provided us shelter at the cave during the war against Japan. Auntie's son, who had rescued my father from the throes of death, had passed away several years earlier, leaving her with a sole daughter. In the past, Auntie was destitute, but after the Communist Party took over, her family was classified as poor peasants. As a result, they benefited greatly from the preferential policies of the new government. Auntie was now living in a house rather than a hut at the cave. Her daughter had married the Communist Party secretary of a nearby town. I was happy to see how much her life had improved. Auntie and Liang were the only people in our family who survived the last three decades relatively unscathed.

As our trip was drawing to an end, I thought about trying to visit Changsha. Weiluan had asked me to visit the army base that he had worked at to see how it had changed. However, we didn't have the money or the time to make the trip, and I didn't want to impose further on my brother. I decided not to bring it up.

On the final day of our visit, many relatives and friends came to say farewell. The time had passed so quickly.

"Fengxian, please stay longer," Liang pleaded. "This is such a rare opportunity. It won't be easy for us to reunite again."

"I know, but I must get back. I wasn't given permission to stay any longer. At least now we can write letters. You can also come to see me in Guangdong. Perhaps one day I will have another opportunity to return to Rongxia."

More than a dozen relatives and friends escorted us to the train. When we arrived at Fengmen Station, I was stunned to see my beloved uncle waiting for us on the platform. His face was red and drenched in sweat, and he was carrying a basket. I hated to think that he overexerted himself just to see me off.

"Fengxian, I have nothing good to send home with you. Please take this basket of eggs. You and your daughters can eat them on board."

I was too choked up to say very much. "Uncle, thank you. Take good care of yourself. We will meet again one day."

"You also take care, Fengxian, and look after these wonderful grandnieces of mine."

We boarded the train. As the girls organized our luggage in the racks, I rushed to a window to wave goodbye to everyone. I couldn't keep myself from crying.

"Mother," Ai said, "we'll come back again someday to see our uncle, auntie, and other relatives. Don't be sad. Father misses us and is waiting for us at home."

"I know," I said, wiping the tears from my eyes. "I'm just worried about my uncle. I don't know when I'll be able to return. I'm afraid we'll never see each other again."

On the ride home, I reflected on the trip and all of the stories Liang, Uncle, and Auntie had shared with me. Two weeks earlier I had felt butterflies riding the same train. Now all of the questions I had been pondering for so many years had been answered, and I was left to grapple with all that I had learned.

Even Ferocious Tigers Do Not Eat Their Cubs

The day after we returned to Donghu, Weiluan wrote a letter to Duoxi passing on the contact information for Uncle Jusheng's daughter Ming in Hong Kong. Two weeks later, Duoxi wrote back informing us that Ming's family had taken him in.

"They are taking good care of me," he wrote. "You don't need to worry about me anymore." We were relieved to hear that our son was no longer struggling on his own.

As 1978 came to a close, we heard that the government was preparing to launch a new campaign called "reform and opening" to promote economic development and give citizens more freedom. No one was sure what the campaign would entail in practice, but the direction and spirit of reform struck a chord with many people. The architect of the new policy was Deng Xiaoping, who by then had emerged as the victor in the power struggle after Chairman Mao's death. Seeing Deng at the helm gave many people hope that the new government would follow through on its promises of change. Deng had been purged twice during the Cultural Revolution and had suffered greatly. No one understood the misguided policies of the previous decades better than he did.

As we eagerly awaited the reforms, Weiluan and I were confronted with a new dilemma concerning our third daughter Mei. Mei's in-laws and husband were extremely cruel and abusive toward her. After laboring all day in the fields, at night the family forced her to work like a slave at home. Every day they swore at and beat her. They frequently withheld food from Mei and wouldn't permit her to see a doctor when she was ill. Her husband did nothing to reduce her suffering. On the contrary, in order to remain a filial son, he helped his parents beat and mistreat his wife.

For three years, Mei had been unable to get pregnant. I suspected that this might be the root of her problem, so one day I walked several hours with her to visit the county gynecologist. Shortly after, she got pregnant. I thought this would make her in-laws more accepting of her. In fact, their treatment of her worsened.

Since our home was close, whenever Mei was hungry — which was quite frequent after she got pregnant — she sneaked to our home to get something to eat. Inevitably, she would be beaten and cursed when she returned. Each time Weiluan and I pleaded with her in-laws to treat her better. They never listened to a word we said. Instead, their response was always the same: "Your family is a counter-revolutionary family! Your daughter is beneath our son, and we will treat her as such."

There was nothing Weiluan or I could do. While Chinese society was modernizing, in the countryside most families continued to abide by ancient family traditions. According to these customs, when a woman married into a family, she became, in essence, the property of her husband's family. They could treat her as they pleased. Even if her husband died, she still belonged to her in-laws and couldn't leave. Weiluan and I shed many tears over Mei's predicament. We regretted the decision to allow her to marry someone within the village. We should have known better given how cruelly the villagers treated Weiluan. In the end, we had no grounds to fight against what was happening to our daughter.

About seven months into her pregnancy, Mei fled to our home one evening. She hadn't been feeling well that day and had stayed home from work. Her in-laws were so enraged by her nurturing herself that they chased her around the house with a knife. Fortunately, Mei managed to escape. She ran to our home and relayed her frightening story. Weiluan and I wanted to keep her safe with us, yet we had no choice but to return her. I asked a Communist Party cadre in the village to accompany us when we escorted Mei home. I hoped that his presence would keep her husband's family in line in the future. However, her in-laws were furious that she had acted so brazenly and fled. They threatened again to kill her.

Later that same night, Mei sneaked back to our home around midnight. "I can't bear my in-laws' torture anymore. Please, please can I stay here with you?"

We told her that she could stay the night, but that she must return in the morning. At daybreak, she begged us not to send her back.

"If you make me return, I will be killed with my precious baby in my womb," she said in tears.

We felt so sorry for her that we finally agreed to let her stay. However, if her in-laws put up a fight, we knew we would have to hand her over. To our surprise, neither her husband nor her in-laws came to inquire about her. They completely abandoned Mei. I felt so sorry for her. We decided to allow Mei to remain with us until she gave birth, after which we would decide what to do next.

Two months later in June 1980, Mei woke us late one evening and said she didn't feel well. I asked about her symptoms. I knew immediately that she had gone into labor. I woke Ai, and the three of us helped Mei walk to the hospital. We arrived just after 1 a.m. It took a while, but eventually we were able to track down a doctor.

The moment we placed Mei on the birthing table, a violent storm broke out. Lightning flashed in every direction, thunder roared, and rain poured. The electricity went out, and the hospital turned pitch dark. The doctor felt his way around and was able to find an oil lamp. Weiluan, Ai, and I rounded up some newspaper to shield the lamp from the wind.

Mei groaned and pushed for hours. Around 4 a.m., she gave birth to a beautiful baby boy. The storm had quieted by then, and the baby's first cry lingered in the damp air. The doctor washed and wrapped the infant, then handed Mei her new son.

"I've brought a lot of babies into this world, but I've never seen a baby born in the midst of such a violent storm. This boy will surely bring good luck and fortune to your family!"

Mei and her son returned to our home after staying in the hospital five days. She gave him the name Yubao, which means jade treasure. He was a joy. Weiluan and I paid all of the expenses for Yubao's birth. Her husband and in-laws didn't offer to pay one cent, which astonished us since he was a boy. When Yubao turned one-month old, we held a special birthday celebration for him. That day, Mei's husband finally came to see his son, but his parents didn't accompany him. He brought one egg and a bottle of rice wine. He smiled widely when he saw Yubao. I was glad to see my son-in-law so pleased with his child. Weiluan and I talked to him about taking back Mei and Yubao.

"Manfu, Manpo, there is no need for you to worry about Mei's future anymore. I am living separately from my parents now. We are in the process of dividing our house the same way your family did a few decades ago. When Yubao turns 40 days old, both of them can come live with me."

All of us were relieved. Ten days later, Mei and the baby returned to her husband's home.

Mei's in-laws were so angered to see her back that they punished their son for his defiance by immediately seizing his food rations. They left the young couple only two pairs of chopsticks and a few kilograms of rice. Mei didn't complain, but her husband was enraged when he saw what his parents had done. With Yubao in hand, he stormed to his parents' side of the house.

"Are you trying to starve me to death?" he screamed. "I've always been obedient to you! I didn't blame you when my wife left. What on earth do you want from me? Am I not permitted to live with my own wife?"

"What an unfilial son you are!" his mother shouted. "Now that you've brought your wife home, you no longer want your mother anymore."

The fighting was so loud and vicious that it attracted the attention of all of the neighbors, who flocked to the house. Weiluan and I happened to be in the fields at the time.

"There is no reason to be so hard on your son," the neighbors said, trying to reason with her. "It's natural that he wants to live with his wife."

The mother wouldn't listen. My son-in-law became so furious when his mother wouldn't back down that he set Yubao down in a haystack and charged toward her. "I know what you want. You want me to die! Well, now you will get what you want!"

"Every day you talk about dying. Why are you still here? Go! Go and die! Make good on your words!"

Mei was in tears. She dared not utter a word and quietly picked up Yubao. My son-in-law ran to his side of the house and latched the door shut.

The neighbors were worried and followed him. "Open the door! Don't do anything stupid, young man. Open the door!"

His mother was still fuming. "You damned son, how dare you threaten me!"

"You are his mother," one of the neighbors said. "Don't be so cruel. Otherwise, he really may kill himself."

"Young man, open the door!" one of them said. "Otherwise we will break in."

After a few seconds of no response, the neighbors broke down the door. They discovered my son-in-law lying motionlessly on his bed with an empty bottle of pesticide next to him. The neighbors carried him to the hospital, but it was too late. He had died.

Mei's in-laws didn't show an iota of regret or shed one tear for their son. "We have three sons. If one unfilial son dies, we still have two filial sons," they said heartlessly. I was dumbfounded to see parents act so callously. There is a saying in Chinese, "even ferocious tigers do not eat their cubs (虎毒不食子)." That day I learned for myself how humans can sometimes be fiercer than tigers.

Mei was crushed about her husband's sudden suicide. When she heard that he was living separately from his parents, she had gotten her hopes up that they actually might be able to have a normal family. She had only been there a short while before her in-laws had pushed her husband over the edge.

Given everything that had transpired, Mei couldn't bring herself to continue living with her in-laws, regardless of what Chinese tradition dictated. She came to us after her husband's burial and begged us to let her and Yubao move in. "My in-laws disowned their son, and they will disown Yubao. We will not survive there." We felt so sorry for her and welcomed them with open arms. For weeks, Mei was distraught. Every day she cried and was consumed by grief.

Despite the fact that so many neighbors had witnessed with their own eyes what had happened, they were still scandalized that Mei had the gall to abandon her in-laws and move back in with us. In their eyes, Mei was the property of her in-laws, plain and simple.

The villagers accused our daughter of being cursed for fleeing so many times from her in-laws. They blamed her for her husband's death. Over the years, Weiluan and I had put up with so much bullying and criticism that we were able to ignore it. But Mei was much more sensitive. She was devastated to hear the disparaging remarks people were saying about her and took it all to heart. The events of that fateful day left a stain on Mei's soul from which she never fully recovered.

Rebirth

1980 was an eventful year. In addition to losing our son-in-law and taking in Mei and Yubao, villages across the country started to undergo sweeping agricultural reforms. Communes were gradually dismantled, and rights to use the land were re-allocated to member families. Each family was required to meet a certain grain quota, but beyond that we could sell any excess grain in local markets or consume it ourselves. We also were given more freedom to do whatever we wanted to earn money on the side.

Since seizing power, the Communist Party had touted collective agriculture as our country's only path forward. For decades, all sideline economic activity, no matter how small, had been scorned as exploitative, capitalist behavior. Now suddenly the leadership was reversing course.

Decades of living under the commune had stifled people's initiative and entrepreneurship. Now villagers were energized. Families discussed what they could do to produce more grain and what other work they might engage in to earn additional income. We weren't as ambitious as other families and decided to stick with farming our plots and raising a few animals.

The reforms weren't limited just to the economic realm. In the fall of 1980, Weiluan read in the newspaper that the Communist Party was permitting citizens who believed that they had been wrongly accused as bad elements and counter-revolutionaries to apply to the government for a reversal of verdicts. By then, numerous former Communist Party leaders who had been unfairly attacked and stripped of their posts during the Cultural Revolution had been rehabilitated.

Weiluan was exhilarated at the news. Although the restrictions on his movements had been lifted, he continued to be branded a bad element and counter-revolutionary. For decades, he had dreamed of clearing his name.

"Deng Xiaoping himself was unjustly accused of being a counter-revolutionary during the Cultural Revolution. He understands our suffering. Now he is giving people like me a chance at redemption."

My husband immediately grabbed a pen and paper and wrote a petition to the Pingyang County government. I hadn't seen him so enthusiastic in a long time. I felt happy for him.

When my husband finished writing, he asked me to review the petition and give him suggestions. The letter was several pages long and very moving. It explained the many hardships our family had encountered since 1949 and how Weiluan believed he had been unjustly branded a bad KMT element, when in fact he had defected to the Communist Party with Director Cheng when they handed over Changsha. He requested that the government acknowledge his participation in Director Cheng's defection, reverse his verdicts, and give him the same reward that other high-level defectors received: a job in the Communist Party government.

"I think it's excellent," I said. "I don't have any suggestions."

"Okay, then I'll send it immediately to the government in Pingyang. I'll send it by registered mail so we can be sure it's received."

Weiluan eagerly awaited a response. Every day he scoured the newspaper for information on how the process was proceeding. Rather than get discouraged when there was no reply, he simply wrote another petition. When he came across the name of the man in charge of vindications for the entire province in the newspaper, he wrote him a letter. Still, there was no response. After countless letters, my husband became agitated.

I tried to get his mind off his concerns by turning his attention to the several letters we were receiving each week from old friends and relatives. I enjoyed re-connecting with everyone and hearing about their lives since 1949. However, even this created anxiety for Weiluan.

"In this big pile of letters, not one is from any of the people I used to work with. It's so strange. Have they all fallen?"

"They were KMT officers just like you. I'm sure they also faced intense persecution after 1949. You don't know where they are, so it's possible that they don't know where you are and therefore can't write you any letters."

"Fengxian, the only reason I survived all of those years was because of you, my good wife. You always have excellent insight on issues. Please give me advice about how I can achieve a reversal of verdicts."

"I don't know. You're the one who used to work for the government. You know these things better than I do."

"But I have run out of ideas."

"Well, perhaps you should write a letter to the same department in Beijing. It's possible that these lower levels of government can't make such an important decision on their own. It's worth a try. You have nothing to lose."

"That's a great idea! With perseverance, one can grind an iron stick into a needle (只要功夫深, 铁杵磨成针)!"

Weiluan combed through the newspaper for information about the relevant department in Beijing. When he found the name of the man in charge, he immediately wrote him a letter. Knowing that his petition was going all the way to the top gave my husband hope.

Around this time, Weiluan's eighth sister generously sent us more money. My husband was very appreciative but reluctant to spend even one cent. Decades of destitution had made him extremely tight. He refused to deposit any cash at banks out of fear that it might be seized by the Communist Party and always kept our money hidden in a secret place. The only time he went to the bank was when we needed to convert Eighth Sister's U.S. dollars into local currency. I encouraged him to spend some of the money to purchase nutritious food so he would have energy to work in the fields, but he laughed off my suggestion.

"Weiluan, you're in your 60s now. You are no longer a young man. If you continue like this, your body won't be strong enough to farm. If you're lucky enough to receive a reversal of verdicts and a job from the government as compensation, by then you may be too weak to work."

"Don't worry so much, Fengxian! I'm fine."

"You are not fine! You are extremely thin, and I am worried about you. In the past, we almost starved to death. We didn't eat well because we didn't have the means. Now that we finally have some money, we

should use it to improve our health. We must carry on. Without sufficient nutrition, we will get weaker even as our lives are getting better.
It's not worth it."

After reflecting on what I said, Weiluan bought some fish. "We
must not forget those days of poverty," he said that night at dinner. "We
should remember our suffering of the past. In times of plenty, when
we have food, we should prepare ourselves for the times without food.
Don't squander money! This is a good lesson I learned from the past."

A s our burdens eased, I felt increasingly energized and alive.
Although working in the fields was difficult — I was approaching 60 years old — I felt a new zest for life that I hadn't experienced in
decades. In 1983, I applied for a permit to travel to Hong Kong to visit
Duoxi and my cousin Ming, Uncle Jusheng's daughter. At the time, it was
extremely difficult for any Chinese citizen to leave the country, even for
somewhere as near as Hong Kong. To our surprise, that May the Chinese
government approved my application. The entire family was overjoyed.
Zi and Tian made a special trip to Donghu just to congratulate me.

On the day of my departure, Ai and Weiluan escorted me to Shenzhen, a small but blossoming city on the border with Hong Kong. There,
Ming, her husband, and Duoxi planned to pick me up in their car and
take me to their home. Knowing how poor we were, the minute Ming
saw me she handed me two bags of clothes to send home with Weiluan
and Ai.

Ming lived on the 18th floor of a skyscraper with an elevator. I had
never been in a skyscraper before. I felt scared when I looked down from
the window. Ming's home was filled with electrical appliances, and her
husband owned a car. For decades, I had heard about how life in Hong
Kong was so much better than in the mainland. Now I was seeing it with
my own eyes. To me, Ming was leading a rich, luxurious life. That she
had welcomed Duoxi into her home was so generous. I was very grateful.

The greatest part of my trip was getting to spend time with my son,
whom I hadn't seen in five years. During the day, Duoxi worked odd
jobs, and at night he took English classes. He was diligent and hardworking. I was very proud of him. When Duoxi had free time, he took me to

large fancy restaurants and local amusement parks. At one park, we rode a gondola. The entire time I fretted that we were going to crash into the sea. When Duoxi was busy, I visited Weiluan's relatives and friends in Hong Kong. Everyone I spoke with admired our family's perseverance. The more conversations I had about our past hardship and suffering, the further away those days felt. When it came time to return home, I had a new outlook on life.

On the day of my return, Ming and her children gave me several gifts to take home. My favorite was the color TV that they generously purchased for our family. I had never watched TV until I visited Ming. I quickly became addicted. Duoxi arranged for a car to pick me up in Shenzhen and take me back to Donghu. When I arrived home, all of our neighbors and friends came to hear about my trip and to see what I had brought back. I passed on many of the clothes Ming had given us and handed out sweets to everyone.

"Manfu, Manpo, you used to be the most destitute family in Donghu," one neighbor said. "We never would have expected you to have such prosperity today."

Spending time in a bustling city with tall buildings, neon signs, and millions of cars was invigorating. For me, the trip served as a clear demarcation between the past and the present. The past was finally over, and the present was promising.

By contrast, Weiluan remained rooted in our old life in Donghu. He became increasingly fixated on attaining a reversal of his verdicts. He eventually received a reply from the county government. They explained that, in order to complete the process, they needed to speak with some of Weiluan's former KMT colleagues to confirm his participation in Director Cheng's defection. They asked my husband to send references.

Weiluan was relieved to have finally received a reply. But he was anxious that he wouldn't be able to continue the process because he had no information about his old co-workers. After several days of wondering what to do, my husband decided to send a list of former colleagues to the Public Security Bureau in Changsha and ask them to track down the people. Meanwhile, he continued combing through the newspaper for any useful information. One day he discovered that Director Cheng's son, a close friend of Weiluan's when we were living in Hankou, was serving as a deputy commander of a military district in eastern China. Weiluan wrote him a letter explaining his predicament and asking him to vouch for his participation in the handover of Changsha to the Communist Party.

Despite having made some progress on his petition, Weiluan remained agitated and restless. Every day that he didn't receive word he became more upset.

"I don't know what to do next," he said to me one afternoon. "I feel unhappy every day."

"Weiluan, lately why do you only see the negative side of everything? Listen, the magpies in the trees are chirping. Be optimistic! Now that we have food to eat and clothes to wear, it shouldn't make a difference if your verdicts are reversed or not. Why not let it go and start enjoying life? How about visiting Hong Kong? You could see your son and friends and experience the prosperity there. Or you could apply for a visa to visit your sister in the U.S. It would be good for you to have a change rather than being haunted by this issue every day."

"Are you crazy, Fengxian? Attaining a reversal of verdicts is the most important thing in my life! It's about the happiness of our children and our children's children. How can I give up halfway? You should be encouraging me, not discouraging me! I have spent years writing petition letters. Do you want all of my efforts to be in vain? I have never thought once about visiting Hong Kong or the United States. I couldn't care less about going to those places. Right now all I care about is the day I can hold in my hands the certificate that exonerates me and affirms my participation in the peaceful handover of Changsha. Then, I will smile."

Seeing my husband get so upset worried me. I wondered how he would take it if the government denied his petition. I felt badly for belittling the issue. I would never be able to understand the suffering he experienced as a bad element and counter-revolutionary or the overpowering guilt he must have felt about how his labels impacted me and the children. It was easy for me to tell him to move on, but I didn't suffer the abuse and cruelty he did. Some wounds are so deep they never heal. They become part of our identity. The challenge is how to keep them from breaking our spirit and continue living. Weiluan struggled painfully with how to do this. As is often the case, it came down to this one simple question: was he to blame? If nothing else, a reversal of verdicts would give him the permission to exonerate himself.

An Old Pine Tree Falls

Chinese New Year in 1984 was joyous. That year, Duoxi became a permanent resident of Hong Kong and was finally able to return to Donghu for the holiday. For the first time in several years, the entire family was reunited.

Duoxi brought with him delicious seafood and several New Year's gifts for everyone. He also gave Weiluan and me a generous amount of money. Our son was not wealthy by Hong Kong standards, but the money he managed to save went a long way on the mainland at the time. We deeply savored the time we had with all of our children because it was such a rare occurrence.

After the holiday, Weiluan's melancholy returned. Watching my husband become increasingly gaunt was worrying. I insisted that he stop neglecting his health, but he continued to argue with me about spending money on nutritious food.

"Fengxian, do you really expect to eat fish and pork at every dinner? That is frivolous! How about we separate the money? You keep the money given to us by Duoxi, and I will keep the money sent to us by my eighth sister. When you use up all of your money buying expensive food, don't come asking me for more!"

By then, Weiluan had become so obsessed and irritated about his vindication that he frequently lost his temper. He was increasingly difficult to be around. When the warm weather and spring planting season arrived, he was able to take out more of his frustration through farming. Seeing how hard my husband labored in the fields every day to put food on our table reminded me how fortunate I was to be his wife. I regretted not sympathizing more with his anxiety over the reversal of his verdicts.

I was in the fields one day watching and admiring my husband's grit when I recalled out of the blue the old fortune book that Weiluan's parents had purchased for him when he was a toddler. The booklet had predicted that my husband would die at the age of 65, which was that year.

> "Looking backward, I can only see the clouded Qinling Mountains, but not my home beyond those hills. Looking forward, I can only see the snow-capped Blue Sky Pass, but whether to step forward, my horse hesitates. Around my ears, the crying of my wife and children still echoes."

I believe strongly in pre-destination and fate, and I worried about my husband's future. In the past, I had heard an old wives' tale that shifting the position of dishes of food on the table before meals could ward off death. I knew it sounded crazy, but the girls and I began to move the dishes at every meal just in case.

"What are you doing?" Weiluan asked one evening as he watched us shifting the food.

"Do you remember that fortune book given to you by your mother? It said that you won't live beyond the age of 65. Well, you're 65 now. We're doing this as a precaution to ward off your death."

"If moving dishes around a table could save a person's life, then no one would ever die. Fortune tellers aren't infallible. They can make mistakes. There's no need to move the dishes like this."

Weiluan initially brushed off the foreboding words in his fortune, but later that night his view had completely changed. Now he was convinced that the prediction would come true.

"Fengxian, if I am to die before receiving vindication, please continue my efforts so that we can achieve success. You would be the heroine of the Han family. Thank you for the long, hard road you have traveled with me. Be strong and don't be sad for me. In the future, I will have to depend on this Vermilion Impatiens to carry on for me."

"Weiluan, are you suffering from a mental disorder? Why would you talk like this? You are like an old pine tree, always standing tall.

Don't worry. One day you will hold your certificate of vindication in your own hands. Never talk like this again! You will live forever, and I will accompany you until the last moment of your life."

"I believe in fate and pre-destination. What the fortune book stated so clearly will become reality. Just remember what I have said."

After the spring planting season ended, many villagers flocked to our home. Most were interested in watching our color TV. Others sought Weiluan's help writing letters to long lost relatives, who they hoped would take pity on them and send money. My husband was one of the few literate people in the village. Most people he helped eventually received money and other goods from their relatives, which quickly motivated others to reach out to their families. Soon Weiluan had a long list of correspondence to complete. It was extremely taxing, and the stress was taking a toll on him.

"Weiluan, you are drained. You need to protect your health. These people don't know how much energy goes into writing a letter. Tell them you can't help them right now. Take a break."

"Fengxian, we shouldn't refuse when others ask for assistance. In the future, we may need their help. We are neighbors. If we can do something for them, we shouldn't turn them down."

"I know, but you have written so many letters for them. Over the years, you've also written many eulogies for them. What did you get from it? Nothing. It has only added psychological stress and damaged your health. Why do you insist on continuing?"

Weiluan was so compassionate that he simply couldn't turn away anyone asking for his assistance. Rather than turn down our neighbors, my husband began giving himself glucose and vitamin injections to maintain his energy. At night, he watched television to relax and often wouldn't go to bed until after midnight. I couldn't stay up so late, so I always went to bed first.

One night shortly after lying down, Weiluan woke me and said that he didn't feel well. He was in pain and very pale. His voice was extremely weak. I woke Mei and instructed her to run and get help. By the time neighbors arrived, Weiluan was groaning in pain. The villagers helped me carry my husband to the hospital while Mei stayed behind with Yubao.

The doctor spent nearly an hour with Weiluan before coming out to speak with me.

"Your husband suffered a massive heart attack. We tried several different treatments, but none of them was successful. It was too late. There was nothing we could do. Your husband has died." It was late March 1984.

"Died? That can't be...Weiluan!" I screamed. I started to run toward his body, but the villagers grabbed me and pulled me back. I fell to the floor crying.

"Your husband has passed away," the doctor said. "He will not come back to life. There is no reason for you to stay here at the hospital. Go home and prepare for his funeral."

"Let me say goodbye to him one last time!" I cried and stood up. But neither the doctor nor the villagers would allow me near his body. They dragged me away.

On the walk home, I screamed out to my husband. "Weiluan, you can't have died! You survived barrages of bullets and bombs in the battle-field. How can you die so suddenly now? How can you abandon your wife and children? Your precious reversal of verdicts is still unfinished. Please come home with me!"

When Mei saw me return alone and in tears, she knew immediately that her father had died. The two of us cried nonstop until daybreak. In the morning, many neighbors and friends came to offer their condolences and help. They notified Zi, Tian, Duoxi, and Ai and instructed them to return home immediately.

All of us were in shock. My children tried to comfort me, but they were also devastated and distraught. All of us felt as though we had been struck by lightning. Gradually, we shifted our energies onto the funeral, which was becoming increasingly contentious.

Outside our home, an argument broke out amongst the villagers about the appropriate funeral procedure for my husband. Some of the villagers believed that because Weiluan had died in the hospital and not in the village, his body was not eligible to undergo the traditional village ceremony. Instead, they believed his body should go straight from the hospital to be buried. I was adamant that Weiluan receive a traditional funeral and went outside to express my views.

"Today my family experienced a terrible tragedy. My beloved husband died of a heart attack in the hospital. Now we are in a new age under the rule of the Communist Party. New medicine and science are saving lives. Who doesn't want to go to the hospital if he or she is ill? In the future, more and more people will die in the hospital, just like Weiluan. Should all of them be denied the traditional funeral ritual? My husband spent more of his life here in his ancestral village than anywhere else. Why can't his body be brought back here to undergo a traditional funeral? If you don't believe the ceremony should be conducted in the ancestral temple, then please bring his body to our home. We will hold the ceremony in our house, so that my husband can rest in peace, and I can fulfill my last responsibility to him."

After the villagers heard my plea, they agreed to bring my husband's body back to Donghu and give him the traditional funeral he deserved.

That evening Weiluan was laid out in the ancestral temple. For nearly an hour, the children and I knelt before his body weeping. Afterward, a vigil was held that lasted the entire night. At one point, I became so overcome with sadness that I began sobbing uncontrollably. I didn't have the wherewithal to stay any longer, so I left. Several people helped me home. The children stayed the entire night.

The ritual ended at 7 a.m., when Weiluan's body was carried to the cemetery and buried. Many friends and relatives came to pay their final respects. Later that day, I wrote letters to Weiluan's eighth sister and my brother Liang notifying them of his passing.

"Weiluan has gone to the immortal world, leaving me alone beating my chest and shedding tears of blood. This was his fate. Do not be as sad as I was. Fengxian"

In China, the formal mourning period when a family member dies is 49 days or seven weeks. The children stayed with me as long as they could during this period. It gave me great solace to be surrounded by the offspring that Weiluan was so proud of and would carry on his legacy.

As we prepared to commemorate the one-week anniversary of my husband's death, the mailman delivered a letter from the public security bureau in Changsha. The bureau's staff had looked up all of Weiluan's old KMT colleagues. Some had died, others had retired. The letter contained the addresses for all of them. Weiluan had agonized for months over the possibility that he may find no colleagues to testify on his behalf. Now we had the contact information for all of them, but it was too late for him to experience this joy. I placed the letter in front of his funeral placard, so he could read it in the next world.

"Weiluan, I wish so much that you were here to receive this notice. You asked me to be brave and continue your efforts for vindication if you died. I thought you were speaking nonsense. I didn't realize that those would be your last serious words to me. Do you see how much pain I am in? I am just a weak woman. Where will I get the strength to shoulder such a heavy burden? Please bless me so that I can succeed in achieving your final request. I promise that I will give everything I have to continue your fight. Please rest in peace."

I had lost the love of my life, my closest friend, the core of our family. Weiluan's death left a gaping hole in my heart and in my life that I feared was so large it would never close. How would I survive without him? I had no idea how to answer that question. All I knew was that I had promised my husband I would continue his quest for vindication. I wouldn't let him down.

Standing Up with Courage

I spent most of the next six weeks inside the house grieving. I lost my appetite and soon became as thin as Weiluan. When I slept, I had nightmares about the day my husband died. The children became very worried. Mei also suffered deeply. The villagers continued to call her a cursed woman and accused her of being the cause of Weiluan's death. Those poisonous words added enormous guilt to her already overwhelming grief.

As the official mourning period came to a close, my physical and mental condition slowly improved. I began eating more and giving myself injections of vitamins and ginseng, just as Weiluan had taught me. I wrote a poem about my husband's achievements, which helped release some of the pain. After the poem was completed, I mustered the wherewithal to pick up a pen and continue where my husband left off in his request for a reversal of verdicts. I wrote a long letter to the county government.

"Distinguished director of the United Front Department of the Communist Party of China, my name is Chu Fengxian, and I reside in Pingyang County, Guangdong. I began attending school at a young age and am well-versed in propriety, justice, and patriotism. I am writing on behalf of my late husband, Han Weiluan, who was born in 1919 and graduated from high school in Pingyang. When Japanese soldiers invaded China in 1937, they burned and looted houses, raped women, and caused numerous other tragedies. To help save our nation, my husband joined the army. In 1937, he graduated from the Whampoa Military Academy. Later he served as a platoon leader, company commander, and battalion commander. He fought vigorously on the battlefield in Hunan and Guangdong, including in the Battle of Changsha. He sacrificed a lot and was willing to die for our country. He had no regrets. After the war with Japan, my husband was transferred to Hankou and then to Changsha, where he served under Director Cheng Qian, who was a National Military Council member and later the governor of Hunan.

In 1949, my husband helped Director Cheng surrender to the Communist Party forces and peacefully hand over Changsha. Afterward, Director Cheng arranged for my husband to attend Communist Party training in Changsha. However, burdened by myself and our two children (with a third in my womb), my husband had no choice but to take us to his hometown in Guangdong while we waited for his class to start. In the end, he never received word from the school, and he was forced to become a farmer. He toiled in the fields for more than three decades. He was hardworking and law-abiding. Nevertheless, due to his past ties to the KMT, he was branded a bad KMT element. For this reason, he suffered greatly during the Cultural Revolution.

The Communist Party is a wonderful party, whose light shines in each and every corner of the world. You care about veterans and look after officers who participated in the Communist Party's rise to power. My husband wrote numerous letters to different levels of the government seeking vindication and the removal of his labels. He was instructed to find former colleagues who could serve as references, but he had lost touch with everyone. Eventually, he managed to track down Director Cheng's son, who worked alongside my husband, and wrote him a letter requesting his assistance. Just recently, I received the addresses of many of my husband's former colleagues. My husband fought for vindication for six years, during which he was constantly under stress. Even though he was becoming old and weak, he never gave up hope. The harder he tried, the stronger and braver he became. He believed that one day the Communist Party would come to know his situation, reverse his verdicts, and treat him as a member of its uprising against the KMT.

Sadly, this year my beloved husband died suddenly of a heart attack. It felt like I had been struck by lightning. Just as the sky is filled with wind and storms, there are fortunes and misfortunes in every person's life. Before his death, my husband urged me to carry on his effort. I know of no other way to help him than to write this petition, kneel down before you, and beg you to investigate his case. Only this way can my husband smile in the next world and I can fulfill my duties as his wife. I pray that you can help me. My children, my children's children, and I will never forget your kindness. Best regards, Chu Fengxian"

I wrote several copies of the letter and mailed them to all of the departments Weiluan had communicated with. I hoped that at least one of them would sympathize with me and continue the process.

The ensuing weeks were difficult. There were times when the grief was so overpowering that I couldn't get out of bed for days at a time. I frequently thought about all of the hardship and suffering Weiluan had endured for me and the children. Now our lives were finally improving, but he was not here to share this happiness. It wasn't fair. At one point, Mei became so concerned about me that she asked Duoxi to return, hoping that a visit from my son would enliven me. During Duoxi's visit, I raised an idea that had been on my mind for weeks.

"Duoxi, your father never received any recognition or thanks for all of his hard work and the countless ways in which he helped people. I think we should build him a special tomb as a way of honoring him for all he did for us."

"That's an excellent idea, Mother. Since I live in Hong Kong, you will have to make most of the arrangements. Whatever it costs, I will pay for it."

The tomb gave me a new task to focus on as I awaited word about Weiluan's vindication. I was evaluating how to proceed with the project when my brother Liang unexpectedly showed up on our doorstep one afternoon.

"Brother, what a pleasant surprise! What are you doing here?"

"I received your letter about Weiluan's death. I wanted to pay my final respects and check on you. How are you doing, Fengxian?"

"It's hard, but each day gets a little easier. Still, I feel lost. Right now I'm focusing my energy on building Weiluan a special tomb. Duoxi generously agreed to pay for one."

Liang stayed with us for a few days. After catching up on family news, he helped me search for a location for the tomb. Chinese people consider the ideal resting place to be on a mountain overlooking a river, so the two of us spent hours scouring the local mountains for the perfect spot. We eventually settled on a site in a nearby valley. At the time, villagers were permitted to freely choose where to bury their loved ones, as long as the site wasn't for government use. No special permits were required.

After we chose a site, Liang returned to Hunan. "Fengxian, I apologize for leaving so soon, but I must get back."

"I understand, brother. Thank you so much for making the effort to come and see me. Your visit has been a great comfort and distraction from the grief. We will reunite again someday."

After Liang left, I searched for a feng shui expert to select the precise spot on the mountain to build the tomb and an auspicious day to begin construction. I learned of a famous 90-year-old feng shui master in the area. I walked several miles to his home and asked him to assist me. The two of us visited the site that Liang and I had chosen.

"You made an excellent selection," he said.

He inspected every aspect of the location, then he walked to the general area where he believed the tomb should be constructed and handed me a hoe.

"Take this and throw it in the direction that I am pointing. No matter where the hoe falls, it will be the correct place to build the tomb."

I asked God to bless my throw and tossed it as the master had instructed. He marked the spot where the hoe landed with a small sign. He declared August 28 at noon as the optimal time to begin the project.

Before starting construction, I took Duoxi to inspect the location. He agreed that it was a lovely site and gave me the money to hire laborers and purchase materials. I chose cousins and nephews of Weiluan to do the work. Over the years, my husband had helped all of them a great deal, so I knew they would do their best for him.

According to tradition, tomb builders were to be treated especially well and receive high wages and good food for their labor. Otherwise, it was considered a sign of disrespect to the deceased and could lead to ghosts haunting the family and their descendants. Duoxi spent a lot of money on the tomb ensuring it would be perfect.

On August 28, 1984, we held an official groundbreaking ceremony at the site. The monk in charge prepared three offerings — a cow head, a sheep head, and a pig head — for the God of Land and the God of Mountains. He instructed Duoxi to present the offerings to the gods by placing the heads in specific locations on the site. Incense was lit, and Duoxi and I knelt down to pray. Construction of the tomb began immediately after the ceremony.

One week after breaking ground on the tomb, we received a letter from the Communist Party Committee of Pingyang County. The committee had confirmed Weiluan's participation in the peaceful handover of Changsha and had decided to officially reverse my husband's bad element status. Mei and I clapped our hands and rejoiced. We shouted our thanks to the Communist Party, Deng Xiaoping, and Director Cheng's son. I placed the letter in front of Weiluan's funeral placard, lit some incense, and bowed three times.

"My dear husband, do you know what we just received? The precious paper from the Communist Party that you had been dreaming of for so long! It confirms your participation in the handover of Changsha. I have put this glorious letter here for you to read in the next world. I believe it was you who helped me to complete this task. As you instructed, I stood up bravely for the entire family. Now you have been proven innocent. You can rest in peace with a smile."

The construction of Weiluan's tomb was completed a few weeks later. However, tradition dictated that we wait until the eight-year anniversary of his death to transfer his remains.

With the tomb completed and Weiluan's bad element verdict reversed, I became listless. Both projects had kept me going in the months after my husband's death. Now I had nothing to occupy me. Grief quickly filled the space. I spent more time in bed and soon fell ill. I gave myself vitamin and ginseng injections, but this time nothing seemed to help.

After several weeks, my mind drifted back toward Weiluan's vindication. I wondered why the government hadn't offered us any compensation when it exonerated my husband. Weiluan had specified in each of his petitions that he was not only seeking a reversal of verdicts but also the compensation that other defectors received: a government job. It dawned on me that the government wouldn't just freely hand out compensation. If we wanted it, we would have to fight for it. *I* would have to fight for it. That gave me the spark I needed to pull myself out of bed.

I opened our trunk and took out the letter we received from the county Communist Party Committee. I decided to take it to the township government the next day and make a formal request for compensation. First, I wanted them to remove my husband's counter-revolutionary label. Even though they had reversed his bad element status, his counter-revolutionary label remained unchanged. Second, I decided to continue pushing for the government job Weiluan had wanted, but that instead it be given to our youngest daughter Ai. Third, I wanted permission and assistance for Mei, Ai, Yubao, and me to move from Donghu into a city. Without a man to plow the fields, Mei and I were unable to yield much from our land. I also desperately needed a change.

The next day I went to the town hall and spoke to the person in charge.

"Mrs. Chu, I'm sorry, but we haven't heard anything about your husband's situation. We haven't received any instructions from the county that we need to do anything."

I laid out my requests. The man jotted them down and said he would transfer the issue up the chain.

A few weeks later, I received a letter from the county explaining that it was dealing with many cases like Weiluan's and hadn't decided how to proceed. In the meantime, they agreed to pay me a very small monthly allowance.

As the days passed and I awaited an answer, I became increasingly frustrated at the slow process. I understood why my husband had become so agitated and obsessed. "Why did you leave me to deal with this issue on my own?" I frequently mumbled to Weiluan. I felt stuck and powerless. All I could do was wait and hope that the Communist Party would be kind and generous.

A Fresh Start

As winter settled in, I eagerly looked forward to the New Year. I hoped 1985 would bring us better luck and a new beginning. I became increasingly fixated on the idea of starting a new life in a city. The farm in Donghu carried too many painful memories. Everything there made me feel angry, sad, and sick. That place had deprived me of my beloved son and poor husband. I simply couldn't stay there any longer.

However, because of China's strict system of residence permits, none of us could move without the government agreeing to transfer our residency. At the time, such transfers were extremely rare, particularly for rural villagers looking to move to a city. Given our special circumstances, I hoped that the government would be willing to make an exception and help us resettle. Any city was fine. I just wanted out of Donghu.

For weeks, I continued writing petitions and visiting government officials, pressuring them to make a decision. I eventually received a letter from someone at the county government summoning me to his office.

"Mrs. Chu, were you with your husband when he was in the army?" the man asked.

"Yes."

"Okay," the man said and left. Before long, some other county officials came to speak with me.

"Mrs. Chu, we will do our best to arrange a job for your youngest daughter, and we will help your family resettle in a city. But we can't do either of these right now. We hope you can understand and be patient."

"Okay. How long do you think it will be?"

"We don't know. There are so many cases like your husband's. We're swamped."

I went into the meeting with high hopes that the process would be completed, so I left extremely discouraged.

"Why are you always playing tricks on me?" I screamed at God when I got outside. "Just when I think something good is about to happen, it's snatched away. You've given me an entire life of misfortune! I endured them one by one. Are you ever going to bestow anything good on me?"

We still had received no word from the government when the spring planting season arrived. Since Mei and I were unable to plow our land on our own, I subcontracted our fields to other farmers so they wouldn't go to waste. We still had to meet the government's grain quota and couldn't afford to let the fields lie fallow.

With no farm work to occupy me, I had an overabundance of time to ruminate. I dreamed about leaving Donghu day and night, but I couldn't think of a way to make it happen. Without a proper permit, no one would allow us to rent or buy an apartment in a city. There was no way to sneak away because the government had eyes everywhere. During its more than three decades in power, the Communist Party had established an elaborate network of neighborhood watch groups in every rural and urban community in the country. These "neighborhood grandmas (居委会大妈)," as we called them, kept close tabs on everyone. There was no way to sneak past them.

After several frustrating weeks, a solution finally emerged one day during a visit from Tian. She informed me that her eldest son was going to work in Shenzhen, an up-and-coming city nestled between Donghu and Hong Kong. In 1980, Shenzhen had been selected by the government to serve as a special economic zone, where international trade and foreign investment would be less restricted. I had been to Shenzhen on my way to and from Hong Kong and liked it. That was all the prompting I needed to spring into action.

I called Duoxi and asked him to return to Donghu as soon as possible to discuss an important family matter. The moment he arrived, I sat him down.

"Son, your mother needs your help. I can't stay in Donghu any longer. The memories this place evokes are too sad and painful. The local government said it would help us resettle us in a city, but that we had to be patient. I can't wait any longer. Tian's son is moving to Shenzhen. I would like Mei, Ai, Yubao, and me to move there also. If we take the first step and tell the authorities precisely where we want to go, then all the government has to do is give its approval. That may be quicker than waiting for them to identify a location on their own. The problem is I need money for the move. I have some savings but not enough. Can you help us?"

"I understand, Mother. Your life here has been very difficult. You and Father suffered a lot in this village. I will give you whatever money you need to move."

"Thank you so much, Duoxi. You've always been so filial. I'm very proud of you, and so was your father."

The next day I visited the county government and presented my plan. The officials weren't against the idea but said it would still take a long time to officially transfer our residence permits. In the meantime, they agreed to give us the temporary paperwork to allow us to arrange a place to live in Shenzhen.

The money Duoxi gave me, along with our savings, was enough for us to buy a modest apartment. Prior to Deng Xiaoping's reform and opening, purchases of private property were unheard of and remained rare outside special economic zones. Mei and I made several visits to the city looking for a new home. We eventually settled on a three-bedroom apartment on the top floor of a five-story building in the western outskirts of the city.

In the summer of 1985, we packed our few belongings into a moving truck and left to start a new life. The day of our departure was bittersweet. Although I desperately wanted a change, I still felt deep emotional ties to Donghu. Most of my children had been born and raised there; the majority of my time spent with my beloved husband was in Donghu. I had lived more of my life in that village than anywhere else.

"Farewell, old house," I whispered as I closed the padlock on the front door of our home for the last time. "Farewell, old village. You will always hold a very special place in my heart."

Life in Shenzhen was a welcome change. Only a few years earlier, the city had been a small, quiet hamlet on the sea. But after being designated a special economic zone, the area was bustling with activity. City life was energizing but also required some adjustment. Rather than spending our days outside with nature, we spent most of our time indoors in our new apartment. The exercise we used to get from farming was replaced by daily treks up and down five flights of stairs. Our neighbors kept to themselves, and apartment doors stayed shut. It was refreshing not to hear people constantly gossiping about one another.

Settling into our new home took longer than I had anticipated. All we brought with us was kitchenware, clothing, a few pieces of furniture, and our TV. We had to spend a lot of time and money acquiring additional furniture and household items. Duoxi and Weiluan's eighth sister generously helped us with these additional expenses.

In the fall, Yubao started kindergarten at a school in the neighborhood, and Ai began attending university in Shenzhen, where she boarded. I felt so proud to finally see one of my children attend college. To earn some money, Mei and I decided to have a go at making and selling our own tea. Every week Mei visited nearby mountains and scavenged for tea and herbs growing in the wild. Afterward, the two of us dried the ingredients and processed them into a special mixture. Once we made enough to sell, we opened a small stand on the street outside our building. The revenues weren't much, but they were sufficient to get us by each month. Sometimes I grinned thinking about how — despite all of the twists and turns my life had taken since leaving Hunan — I was now making a living in the same business as my ancestors. Perhaps tea was in the Chu genes.

The next couple of years were uneventful in the way that routine city life is, which is exactly what I wanted. I frequently travelled back and forth to Donghu to deal with matters related to Weiluan's reversal of verdicts and the transfer of our residence permits. The government insisted that we hand over our fields before they would transfer our residency. However, they allowed us to retain ownership of the house because it had been in Weiluan's family for generations.

Every time I returned to the village I visited my husband's tomb and wept. I missed Weiluan greatly. He had sacrificed so much for me and the children. Often during my visits, villagers who previously had mistreated us would seek me out to apologize for their past behavior. Despite all of the terrible things that had happened between us, the conversations were always full of gentle words and smiles. In my heart, I carried no hatred or resentment.

"I forgave you a long time ago," I said. "Let bygones be bygones. Those days have disappeared like the wind and the clouds."

"Fengxian, you really are a learned woman. Thank you for your kindness and magnanimity."

In 1988, all of the red tape associated with Weiluan's vindication and the transfer of our residency permits was finally completed. We became official citizens of Shenzhen. The government removed my husband's counter-revolutionary label and issued an official certificate documenting his participation in the peaceful handover of Changsha to the Communist Party. The government also arranged a job for Ai in the county government when she graduated from college and gave me a one-time payment of CNY100 (USD27 at the time). They were under the impression that I was well off because I owned an apartment, but in reality that wasn't the case. I was disappointed that I didn't receive a larger sum, but I decided not to push for more. In total, it had taken a decade for Weiluan and me to complete his reversal of verdicts and acquire the compensation he deserved.

With these administrative matters complete, I was able to spend more time exploring Shenzhen. One day while out walking, I encountered some people hawking books on the sidewalk. I stopped to leisurely glance through the titles. A book about the Cultural Revolution immediately caught my attention. I picked it up and scanned the back. My eyes were instantly drawn to one phrase: "Down with Liu Deng Tao!" I recalled the frequent tirades of the Red Guards in Donghu. They often denounced someone named Liu Deng Tao. I had always wondered who Liu Deng Tao was and what he possibly could have done to incur such wrath. I always assumed he was a counter-revolutionary in our commune. But if that was the case, he would be too inconsequential to be mentioned in a book. I immediately purchased it.

I spent the next few days glued to the book. For years, I had had so many questions about the Cultural Revolution. Most people living in the countryside during that period had no idea what the movement was really about or why it occurred. All we knew was that one day the youths in the commune began talking passionately about a new socialist revolution and ideological purity. "To rebel is justified," the Communist Party told them, so that is precisely what the youngsters did.

The book discussed the important historical events leading up to the Cultural Revolution and detailed several key moments during those 10 years of chaos. Blame for the excesses of the movement was placed on Mao's wife and cohorts, which to this day is what I and most Chinese people have been taught to believe, although my relatives abroad insist that Chairman Mao was at the helm. I finally learned who Liu Deng Tao was. He wasn't a man in our commune. Liu, Deng, and Tao were three of China's previous top leaders: Liu Shaoqi, who had been Chairman Mao's number two in command since the 1940s; Deng Xiaoping, our current leader; and Tao Zhu, the former governor of our province. All of them had been purged by Mao during the Cultural Revolution and suffered greatly. The more I read about how our leaders and countrymen were persecuted during those 10 years, the angrier I became. It all seemed so senseless and absurd. When I finished reading the book, I was so furious that I tore it to shreds and threw it away.

Our country and family had come a long way since the Cultural Revolution, but I and many other people were still haunted by painful memories from that and previous eras. Often I had difficulty sleeping. During one long, restless night in 1989, I decided to get out of bed and begin documenting my experiences. Writing had always been a means through which I purged my sorrow. I also felt compelled to explain to my children why their childhood had been fraught with so much hardship. That was the genesis of these memoirs.

For the next three years, my life revolved around working at our tea stand, caring for Yubao and Mei, and writing. During this time, Duoxi and Ai got married, and Mei remarried. Mei had decided that Yubao needed a father figure and began looking for another husband. Someone introduced her to an older man from Hong Kong whose wife had recently died. He had an apartment in Shenzhen, and Mei and Yubao moved in with him after they wed.

In early 1992, we began making preparations to exhume Weiluan's remains and transfer them to his new tomb. Duoxi searched for a master mason to craft a tombstone, while I wrote a long epitaph. The inscription highlighted all of Weiluan's achievements, including his participation in the war against Japan, his involvement in the peaceful handover of Changsha to the Communist Party, and his role as an upstanding husband and father.

"What a good man your husband was!" the mason said when he read the epitaph. "What a pity there is no grandson's name to engrave on the tombstone."

Despite the fact that Zi, Tian, and Mei all had sons, according to Chinese tradition none of these grandsons were considered a continuation of Weiluan's ancestral line because they had been borne by his daughters. I also felt it was a pity not to have a grandson's name on the tombstone. If Hao hadn't died as a toddler, he surely would have been married and had a son by then. I thought about how much Weiluan loved Yubao, and how he was like a father to him. Then I was struck with an idea. Why not symbolically bestow Yubao to Hao? That way my husband would have a grandson. Such symbolic transfers of parentage were quite common in China as a way around ancient customs.

I discussed my idea with Mei. She had always felt grateful for her father's suffering and sacrifice. She agreed to bestow Yubao to Hao. The next day I visited the mason and instructed him to engrave Yubao's name on the tombstone. "That's perfect!" he replied. From that day on, Yubao called me nainai, which is the Chinese word for paternal grandmother, rather than waipo, which means maternal grandmother.

On the eight-year anniversary of Weiluan's death, we transferred his remains and placed him at rest. Dozens of family, friends, and villagers attended the ceremony. The scene was grand and moving. I knew Weiluan would have been humbled and honored.

Shortly after moving my husband's remains to his final resting place, I finished writing these memoirs. The completion of both gave me a much-needed sense of closure and peace. After much deliberation, I decided against sharing the manuscript with my children. They were wrapped up with their own young families, and I didn't know how they would react to my revealing so many intimate details. Instead, I decided to lock the manuscript in a safe deposit box at my bank and bequeath it to them as a surprise gift upon my death.

In the end, I managed to achieve Weiluan's precious vindication and pioneer a new path for my family. I was proud to see myself triumph. One important lesson I have learned is that happiness does not fall from the sky; it is earned through painstaking effort.

The Day the Earth Shattered, the Sky Exploded, and the Sun and Moon Stopped Shining

The joy and closure I felt from laying Weiluan to rest and completing my memoirs was short-lived and quickly overshadowed by a new, heart-wrenching predicament with Mei. For years, Mei had been a workaholic. Day after day she labored nonstop making and selling tea and raising Yubao. She kept herself as busy as a spinning top and was constantly exhausted. Mei's second marriage also had many problems. Her second husband was vicious and often beat her. Early in the marriage, the beatings were sporadic, but over time the frequency increased. The combination of overwork and abuse slowly pushed Mei into a state of severe depression.

"Mei, you always seem so down," I said to her on many occasions. "What's wrong? You know you can talk to me."

However, Mei never shared the pain in her heart with me or anyone else. As a result, her toxic feelings intensified. She began to lose her sanity. She became increasingly withdrawn and hid herself for lengthy periods of time in her bedroom. Occasionally, she giggled uncontrollably. At other times, she roared with a horrible ferocity in her eyes. Her thoughts became paranoid. Eventually she was no longer able to work. I had no choice but to close our tea business.

Ai and her husband took Mei to be examined by a doctor. He diagnosed her with mental illness and prescribed some medicine. The drugs helped a little but only for a brief period.

As Mei's condition worsened, her husband no longer wanted to have anything to do with her. They separated, and he rented a second apartment for her and Yubao. I frequently checked on them to make sure they were managing. Day by day I could see my daughter becoming more demented.

Mei's condition got to the point where I no longer felt comfortable allowing her to live alone with Yubao, so I brought both of them home to live with me. One day Mei was cooking in the kitchen when she started a fire that destroyed our entire apartment. Fortunately, because we were located on the top floor, the fire didn't spread to any other apartments, and no one was hurt. At that point, I had no choice but to admit my daughter to a mental hospital. Yubao and I moved into the apartment Mei's husband had rented for them. In the meantime, Duoxi arranged and paid for my apartment to be renovated.

After one year, the doctors declared that Mei had recovered and released her from the hospital. I escorted her home and helped her settle back into her apartment. Despite what the doctors had said, I could tell that Mei was still very ill. She spent hours every day wandering back and forth across her apartment in a daze. She frequently talked aloud to herself. Fearing that she might start another fire or get into some other trouble, I made sure that I visited her every day. I cooked nearly all of her meals for her.

Mei was in no shape to look after Yubao, so I continued to keep my grandson with me. One morning I decided to bring Yubao with me to see his mother. By then, he was 14 and becoming a young man. I hoped his visit would inject some life into his mother. However, she had no reaction whatsoever when she saw her son.

A couple of weeks later, Mei seemed to be doing well during one of my visits, so I decided to take her outside for a walk. The entire time she was nervous and fidgety. She didn't say one word. I began to wonder if my daughter would ever recover.

Toward the end of the 1994 lunar year, I brought Mei to my home for a few days, so we could celebrate her 41st birthday and welcome Chinese New Year 1995. We held a small birthday celebration that went smoothly. But on New Year's Eve, Mei's demeanor changed. Her behavior became confused and anxious. She walked aimlessly through the apartment and periodically murmured to herself. Later that day, my precious Mei leapt off our fifth-floor balcony and departed this world forever.

Our plans to celebrate the New Year were discarded. Instead, we spent the holiday in grief. Yubao and I were crushed and inconsolable. I spent most of my time in bed weeping. I lost my appetite and quickly became thin and weak. The agony was so overpowering that I thought I might follow my daughter into death.

No funeral ceremony was held for Mei because at that time in Shenzhen any death before the age of 60 was deemed to be premature and didn't qualify for a funeral. Yubao and some cousins attended her cremation, and my children, Yubao, and I held our own small gathering, where each of us lit a candle and said some final words to her. Her ashes were placed under the care of the crematorium, where we can still visit them.

In the ensuing days, memories of Mei flooded my mind. Her life had been filled with suffering from the moment she was conceived. Hao passed away when I was pregnant with Mei, so she experienced profound grief while she was still in my womb. The first few years of her life were a particularly desperate period for our family. Often, we had little or no food to eat. Consequently, Mei never received proper nourishment while she was in my womb – nor after she was born. As a toddler, she contracted a bout of meningitis, which left her with a small amount of brain damage. Later, she grew into an aggressive, stubborn young girl, who couldn't bear any bullying or humiliation and never listened to what Weiluan or I said. Whenever anyone attacked her, she vehemently fought back. I kept her near my side as much as possible to minimize these occurrences.

Mei mellowed when she became an adult. But shortly after Yubao was born, she watched with her own eyes as her husband's parents bullied him into suicide. Afterward, she had to bear the disparaging remarks of the villagers who were scandalized that she would abandon her in-laws. Mei suffered another heart-breaking loss when Weiluan died. Years later, she risked another chance at love and re-married. But her second husband also brutalized her.

No woman could survive so many tragedies unscathed. Yet I asked myself over and over why Mei couldn't share her troubles with me. Would it have helped? Were her problems emotional or a result of childhood brain damage? We will never know. For me, Mei's demise comes down to her bad fate. If Mei had good fate, she would have been born into a wealthy family, where she would have enjoyed a comfortable life. But her fate was not good, so she was born into our poor, pathetic family, which wasn't capable of nurturing a healthy, happy child.

For the first couple of weeks after Mei died, I was completely immobilized by grief. The totality of the sadness was like nothing I had experienced before. It was as though the earth had shattered, the sky had exploded, and the sun and moon had stopped shining. The light in the world had gone dim.

Fortunately, grief, like everything else in life, is transitory. As the days passed, the tears and agony gradually lessened. Eventually, I was able to drag myself out of bed and eat. The fact that Yubao had no other caretaker but me also helped me to pick myself up and carry on. I felt so sorry for my grandson, who now had lost both of his parents to suicide. Mei had died during the holiday, so Yubao had extra time off from school to grieve. When classes re-started, both of us returned to our routines, but we were still in shock and just going through the motions.

Residing day after day in the same home where Mei committed suicide was difficult for both Yubao and me. That fall both of us left. Yubao started boarding school, and I went to Hong Kong to stay with Duoxi and his wife as they awaited their first child. I spent much of the next six years going back and forth to Hong Kong.

I didn't return to Shenzhen permanently until 2001 when I became ill and returned to recuperate. In 2003, I fell ill again. Yubao had just graduated from college, so he moved back in to our apartment to nurse me back to health. As an elderly woman, I was glad to have someone young around to help me. Yubao also was happy to save on rent.

The two of us fell into a new, comfortable routine. While Yubao was at work, I would spend my days reading health and medical books and strolling through the park. I acquired an interest in raising plants, feng shui, and fortune-telling, and I read several books about each.

I was content with my life, but our finances remained tight. As Weiluan's wife, I qualified for financial assistance due to my husband's role in the Communist Party's rise to power, but I never requested any because I wanted to do my best to be self-sufficient. Fortunately, in 2007 the government began giving all senior citizens a monthly living allowance of CNY200 (USD26 at the time). For the first time in my life, I had my own permanent source of income from the government. I began purchasing two lottery tickets a week, which I continue to do to this day. Perhaps someday God will bestow some luck on me.

Around this time, Uncle Jusheng's young daughter from America, Charlene, tracked down our family in Rongxia. When I heard about her surprise visit, I welled up with tears. It had been so long since I had had any contact with family members from my father's generation. We made arrangements for her to visit me in Shenzhen.

Charlene arrived on my doorstep with a giant smile. The moment I saw her, my heart grinned. Our eyes filled with tears as we hugged each other. We spoke about our families for the entire day. My unique mix of Cantonese and Hunanese and her rudimentary Mandarin made it difficult for us to understand each other, so Yubao acted as a translator for us.

Charlene was overflowing with questions about people and events I hadn't thought about in decades and gave me several pictures that belonged to her father. She visited me several times. I was deeply moved by how eager she was to learn about her father's life in China. Because we had a difficult time communicating, I thought this memoir could shed more light on our family history. During one of Charlene's visits, I gave her the manuscript to read. Afterward, she offered to help me publish it abroad. I was overjoyed.

These days I spend most of my time staying in touch with my children and grandchildren, keeping healthy, and working on this book. Charlene has asked me to fill in several gaps in my stories. But, as an old woman, my memory is fading. Please forgive me for any inaccuracies.

I still feel tremendous sadness and regret about Mei as well as Weiluan and Hao. All three entered this world in pain and departed in sorrow. Sadness haunted them their entire lives. Yet I take comfort in knowing that, in time, we will be reunited. No pain is greater than the loss of a loved one, but it is imperative that we, the living, move on. Just as a candle's tears do not cease until it burns itself to ash, so too does the agony of our losses stay with us until our death. We simply learn to live with it.

Vermilion Impatiens at Sunset

A year consists of four seasons. Last night the bitter north winds arrived in Shenzhen. Yubao placed a hot water bottle in my bed to warm it for me. The thick duvet was so cozy that I quickly fell asleep in its warm embrace. When I awoke this morning, the sun was glistening into my bedroom, illuminating everything in an orange glow. Yet the room still felt frigid. In winter, even bright sun cannot avert the freezing cold.

Lazy mornings are a privilege of being old. Unwilling to abandon the warmth of my bed, I stayed snuggled in my duvet. The apartment was still and quiet, which meant that Yubao had already left for work. When my stomach began to rumble, I picked up the watch near my pillow. *It's nine o'clock!* Mortified at having stayed in bed so late, I rushed to the kitchen.

After a leisurely breakfast, I was returning to my room when an old photo atop my television caught my eye. It was the one of Weiluan, Zi, and me taken on New Year's Day in 1947 that my brother Dian disfigured. I picked up the photo and gazed at it. Ever since Weiluan's image had been torn out, the picture has felt unnatural and incomplete. Just as my life still feels empty without his presence.

In the past, the photo evoked deep emotions in me. Sometimes I smiled at it, sometimes I wept at it, sometimes I spoke many words to it. Now, in my old age, I am becoming numb. Today I had nothing to say to it. Still, I treasure this precious photo because it is one of the few keepsakes I have from the past. The photo puts me in a reflective mood. I decide that today I will write.

Although my family was wealthy, for some reason they rarely had themselves photographed. As a result, today I have no photos of my parents, my siblings, or myself when I was growing up. As a girl, I recall only one picture in our home — a photo of my parents during the early years of their marriage, which hung on their bedroom wall. I remember the image vividly. Mother was wearing a white mandarin jacket with broad sleeves and a long, black skirt, tucked beneath which were her small, bound feet. Her hair was tied in a bun, and her face was round and white. Father was dressed in a long, brown Chinese gown, black leather shoes, and a round, silk cap. They looked refined and elegant. When I first moved away from home, I wanted to bring the photo with me, but it was the only image my father had of my mother after she died. I couldn't bear to take it away from him.

A few years ago, Charlene gave me pictures of her father, our grandfather, and our great grandmother. They were the first images I had seen of any older family members in decades. When I looked at them, I felt as though they were transported before me. Today families can document every moment of their loved ones' lives from the time they are in the womb. In this way, one's relatives and the past are always accessible. But for me, I lack such photos. My images of loved ones and the past are slowly fading away. All I am left with are memories, so many memories.

I am now in my 90s and in the final season of my life. At this age, one cannot help but spend much time reflecting on the past. Often I am reminded of my father and mother, who I haven't seen in so long, yet still feel so close to my heart. I am so thankful to have had such nurturing parents who brought me up with abundant care and love. Although I was born in China's old, feudal society, I was blessed with a father who understood the importance of teaching his daughters how to read and write. Only because of my father's education was I able to use my writing to defy an arranged marriage. In this way, I broke out of the dark, old society and marched forward into brightness and freedom. For this, I am forever indebted to my father. Although my mother was strict with me, it was always out of love and a yearning for what was best for me. As a mother myself, I understand this deeply now. One of my greatest regrets is that I never had the chance to reciprocate my parents' care. I wasn't even aware of my father's death when it occurred. I only hope they can understand.

I also feel deep gratitude for having been Weiluan's wife. Although our lives seemed to be a never-ending struggle, at every step of the way we were filled with love for each other and our children. One cannot ask for a greater gift in life than that. The most splendid period of our marriage was the time we lived in Hankou, but the good times didn't last long. Sometimes misfortune strikes unexpectedly, like a sudden, swift storm. When the Communist Party seized power, Weiluan was branded a bad element, and I became the wife of a bad element. Our lives were never the same.

As a young girl growing up in Rongxia, I never imagined I would encounter the trials and tribulations I did. I had grand dreams of a future as a modern, educated working woman. I never imagined that I would lose a son to the effects of starvation, that I myself would teeter on the brink of death several times from malnutrition, or that I would be so desperate and destitute that I would have to sell a daughter to save my husband.

How and why did these things happen? How do I make sense of them? Why am I still here when others have long gone? I ask myself these questions frequently. Age gives us wisdom, but it doesn't always give us answers. Instead, over time we learn to accept the questions as an integral part of life itself.

Many people in China encountered similar, often far worse, suffering than I experienced. For some, the experiences sank them. Even my dear Weiluan couldn't completely extricate himself from his past torment after it was over. How is it that I survived? My parents' instruction and nurturing are the main reasons. A good upbringing cannot preempt suffering, but it does prepare us for how to deal with it. My parents instilled in me the important principles of tolerance, magnanimity, forgiveness, and perseverance. Then, as a grown woman, I was fortunate to have married a man who exemplified these ideals in everything he did. Weiluan was the most principled, forgiving person I ever met. At times, it drove me crazy, but it was also one of the traits I loved most about him. A father sets the tone for a household. Just as my father's optimism rubbed off on my mother, my siblings, and me, Weiluan's tolerance and forgiveness meant that neither the children nor I harbored any resentment for the way we were mistreated. Nothing is more poisonous for the spirit than resentment.

Occasionally I am asked how I feel about the people who abused us for so many years. I am still saddened and hurt by what occurred. I hope that one day they will be brought to justice. But justice is for God to impose – not man. Vengeance and hatred are most destructive for the person who harbors the feelings rather than the target of them. By contrast, magnanimity and acceptance calm the soul. Without a calm soul, one cannot let go of the past and move forward.

Only God knows the full context of the misdeeds perpetrated against us. Everyone has his own pains. Perhaps there was something pressuring the villagers to do what they did. They weren't bad by nature. They just couldn't clearly discern what was right and what was wrong in an environment in which morality had become so politicized.

I can rationalize our friends' and neighbors' actions, but what continues to pain and baffle me is the cruelty of Weiluan's family. I cannot understand how or why my husband's siblings and mother treated us so cruelly. Chinese people are raised to revere family. Why his relatives disowned us is a mystery I will carry to my grave. But these are the nightmares of the past, and they should be left in the past.

Some people harbor resentment toward the Communist Party for their suffering. They say that the Communist Party is ruthless. But I don't share that view. I believe the Communist Party has done a lot for our country, particularly for women, and I am grateful. Since taking power in 1949, the Communist Party has abolished foot binding, childhood marriages, and polygamy. Today Chinese women work side-by-side with men and are free to leave their husbands and re-marry. A woman's fate is now in her own hands – not in her father's, husband's, or son's. Chairman Mao famously said, "Women hold up half the sky." I appreciate everything the Communist Party has done to build this new, woman-friendly world.

Today what I feel most in my heart is gratitude, for my parents for giving me life and nurturing me, for my husband for his love and companionship, and for my precious children. I also thank God for his arrangement of my life. Despite all I have been through, I can't imagine having lived any other life.

I have learned to find contentment, forgiveness, and gratitude, but there is still one area in which I struggle: enjoying life. I entered the world in an era when there was no gender equality, and a woman had no value or identity beyond her husband or son. Girls were locked in their rooms until marriage, and women were kept from straying too far from their

husbands by their bound feet. My father's open-mindedness helped me
to experience some of the outside world, but the old mentality was still
pervasive in society as I was growing up, including in my mother. After
I married and had children, all of my time was dedicated to taking care
of my family and home. When we moved to Guangdong, working in
the fields consumed every ounce of my energy and time.

The result is that, at this late age, I still have never experienced the
warm enjoyment of life. Since the time I was a little girl, I have felt as
though I were living a cold existence. When Weiluan died, the grief was
so overwhelming that the only way I could endure it was by becoming
frozen and numb. Mei's death pushed me deeper into this abyss. To this
day, I have not broken out of this icy world.

It has been more than 30 years since I moved to Shenzhen, yet during
this time I have rarely visited well-known tourist attractions. I spend
most of my time holed up in my apartment, just as I did in my boudoir
as a little girl. I have returned to Rongxia only twice. My excuse has
always been that I must work and save money for my children, and that
when they are better off I will have the opportunity to do these things.
Yet here I am now with these desires still unfulfilled.

Now, in the final season of my life, I see that each of us is given only
one chance at life. We must take advantage of every opportunity that life
presents. For when we do not truly live, life loses its meaning.

The Shenzhen government recently began issuing retirees discount
cards that allow them to enjoy free public transportation and cheap
admission to tourist attractions. Zi and her husband are also retired
and have the cards. One day last week the three of us rode the subway
to Window of the World and Splendid China Folk Culture Village. The
next day we visited the Shenzhen airport. That night I was so energized
that I couldn't fall asleep, so I got out of bed and wrote down the exciting
things I had seen, just as, two decades earlier, I had gotten out of bed to
write the stories in this volume.

There is a saying in Chinese that "only those who have endured the
deepest suffering can enjoy a life superior to others (吃得苦中苦, 方为人
上人)." I have endured a lot. Now the bitter days have gone, and only
sweet days await me. It is time for me to enjoy this life I have been given

while I still have the health to do so. When it is time for me to depart this world, I will leave with a smile for my struggle will finally be over. But in the meantime, I will live.

Life can be a song or a whine. I prefer to sing.

Vermilion Impatiens at Sunset

The Vermilion Impatiens at sunset
Is the flower at its best,
Moistened by dews in twilight,
The evening breeze spreads its scent

The Vermilion Impatiens at sunset
Is bright and alluring,
Adorned in lush, fragrant foliage,
She stands leisurely and composed

The Vermilion Impatiens at sunset,
Full of contentment, smiles
But night is quickly approaching
Sun, must you descend?

When darkness falls, God listens to
The sorrowful sounds of the heart,
Sadness is replaced with sprinkles of joy
The Vermilion Impatiens is refreshed

How I wish human happiness were eternal
Like flowers that bloom every year

– Fengxian Chu

Dedication

My Dear Children,

In these final years of my life, I find myself thinking of you often. You have been my greatest achievement in this world. I am so proud of each of you. Time passes so quickly. I miss the days when we were all living under one roof. Now each of you has your own family, and I have become old and feeble. Soon it will be time for me to depart this world. What legacy will I leave with you?

Above all else, I hope that the one gift you take away from your time with your father and me is love. The universe is filled with many different kinds of love, all of which contribute to the warmth of the world, but the most fundamental of them all is that between parents and children. For all of us, this is our first love, and the source from which all other love emanates. Your poor mother has no gold, silver, or other luxuries to bequeath to you, but I bestow upon you all the love I have from the bottom of my heart. For only with love can one live and die happily.

I have always felt guilty about how much suffering you endured as children due to our family's poverty and political persecution. It was never the intent of your father and me to put you through such agony. We had wonderful dreams for each of you, but fate and the forces of history were against us. You have always been so understanding and never complained about the deprivation and pain we know you felt. I'm sorry that we weren't able to give you the carefree childhood you deserved, that we exposed you so early to life's harsh realities, that we couldn't shelter you from oppression and hard labor, and that we couldn't lift you out of hardship even after you grew into adults. The guilt we feel is beyond expression. As parents yourselves now, I hope you can understand.

Your poor mother is now in her 90s. My heart has been shattered, my tears have run dry, and I have one foot in the grave. Soon I will be reunited with your father in the next world. At that time, everything in this world — rights, wrongs, tears, sorrows — will end with my death.

As I think of leaving you, I am saddened that your father and I were unable to accumulate any savings or property to pass on. I feel we have failed you in this regard. Yet I also know that wealth can be harmful and divisive, so perhaps it is fortunate that we spare you that trouble.

It is my own belief that one of the most priceless possessions one has in this world is his or her story. Each life is a drama. Some scenes are sweet and joyful, others tragic and sad. But what is most important is one's performance, his acceptance of the circumstances and setting presented to him, his reaction in the face of adversity, and, most of all, his willingness to participate. A person's story cannot be bought with money. It is full of love, care, disappointment, agony, regret, sorrow, joy. Life is a drama, and each drama a life.

I have deep love and admiration for your father. He endured so much for us, and I ask that you never forget his sacrifice. When your father left us so suddenly, the pain was more than I could bear. He died without our being able to say goodbye, without leaving a final word to any of us. During this time of profound sorrow, I picked up a pen and began to write out my heartaches of the previous decades. Even today, the memories are still raw and bring tears to my eyes.

I spent three years writing my story. I never intended it to be any-thing more than a commemoration of your father and a memoir to help you understand the greater context of your own lives. But life is full of surprises. Today, with the help of my American cousin, Charlene, this book is being published abroad.

My children, this book, my story, is my lasting gift to you, your most precious inheritance. It is written in love, honesty, and humility. Life is full of laughter and tears, ups and downs, happiness and sorrow, departures and reunions. One must experience all of these to know the true meaning of life. I hope this book will teach you that life itself is a priceless gift and to treasure it.

My final wish for each of you is that you will find the courage to shake off your inhibition and timidity, which are so common to all of us, so that you can move forward bravely and participate more fully in your own dramas. If you try and have faith, you surely will emerge from any difficulty.

I hope you will read this book often and never forget your parents. I hope that the image of your father and me will live in your hearts forever, as you do in ours.

- Your humble mother

Afterword

Now 92, Fengxian remains the same wise, tenacious woman as in these stories. She continues to reside in the same apartment in Shenzhen that she moved to after Weiluan passed away. Multiple times a week she walks up and down five flights of stairs to fetch provisions and run errands. She has never celebrated a birthday out of fear of tempting fate. "But if I make it to 100, I intend to hold a giant bash!" she says with a big smile. She has an excellent chance of making it.

The family that Fengxian and Weiluan gave birth to has grown to include 14 grandchildren and 16 great grandchildren. Every Chinese New Year the entire clan converges on Fengxian's apartment to pay their respects. Several boisterous games of mahjong are played. Fengxian almost always walks away with the most cash. As someone who has played against her, I can attest that this is not because her opponents are throwing the game. Even at her late age, she is still one of the sharpest players in the room.

That *Song of Praise for a Flower* was written by Fengxian herself may seem inconsequential, yet it is one of the book's most distinctive features. Most women born in 1920s' rural China never attended school and are illiterate. Few are capable of writing a book, and those who are often see little value in their own stories. Hence, most books about the lives of Chinese women from Fengxian's era have been written by later-generation descendants or historians. The stories are often imaginary, in some cases biographical, but very rarely autobiographical.

A common question from readers of drafts of the manuscript was whose voice do we hear in the narrator: Fengxian's or yours? The answer is about equal parts of both. The original manuscript was written more than 25 years ago by hand for an audience of immediate family. It was the first time Fengxian put pen to paper about all of her heartache and hardship; inevitably, at times the text was more journal- than book-like. In her 80s when we began this undertaking, Fengxian was not up to completing heavy rewrites of the manuscript on her own, nor was she in a position to do so given her lack of knowledge about the political forces behind what befell her and her family.

While the English book here was written solely by myself, Fengxian's original manuscript forms the core of the work. From the outset, she established a clear voice and style that I was able to carry throughout, including those places where extensive editing was required. The two areas where my narration supplants Fengxian's are: (1) the Preface, final vignette, and Dedication, which are compilations of selections from several of Fengxian's later writings, most of which were drawn out reflections on life that were too much for the start or end of what is already a lengthy work; and (2) those places in the book that discuss the historical and political backdrop in China at the time.

Adding this latter information in a way that wasn't disruptive and flowed seamlessly in and out of Fengxian's daily experiences was a challenge. After trying numerous approaches, I decided that keeping Fengxian as the narrator in these parts created the least disruption and provided the best continuity and union between macro-level history and her micro-level experiences. It also made the telling of this history much more vivid and forceful than bland insertions of academic explanations about each political campaign. However, at times this inevitably meant my putting words into Fengxian's mouth that weren't her own and portraying Chinese history through my own Western lens rather than hers. While certainly not ideal, the lack of knowledge among Western readers about Chinese history meant that presenting these events through the lens of Fengxian — whose own very limited knowledge has been shaped entirely by the Communist Party's version of events — was even more problematic.

In these areas, I drew as much as I could on material from my own father's experiences in China during these periods and the explanations he gave me of historical events, so as to keep the story as authentically Chinese and near to Fengxian as possible. Any perceived biases, predispositions, or inaccuracies in these parts — which comprise less than three percent of the book — are my own and should not be perceived in any way as the views of Fengxian. Outside of the historical insertions noted above, only one scene in Fengxian's life was partly fabricated by me: the dialogue between her and Weiluan when he returned home from the re-education camp in Hongli (Part 5, "An Ink Spot on a Snow-White Shirt"). I felt readers would naturally want to know what Weiluan's experience was like, yet Fengxian wrote little about it in her original manuscript, and it was too distant for her to recall in detail. Hence, I created a dialogue between the two of them based on my own father's account to me of his experience in a Communist Party re-education camp in the 1940s. Everything else about Fengxian's experiences is as she presented it in her original manuscript, later additions and/or in conversations with me.

While the writing of this book has been a collaborative effort, only one person lived this story and that is Fengxian. The experiences, reflections, and emotions herein are hers alone. I cannot think of a more poignant closing chapter for Fengxian's extraordinary and colorful life than to see her story in print. Both of us are grateful for your participation as readers. It has been a privilege to take part in documenting Fengxian's life and an even greater honor to know her.

- Charlene Chu

We would like to extend special thanks to Ms. Sophie Zhang for translating the original stories into English.

Made in the USA
Columbia, SC
20 January 2020